NEW
TESTAMENT
CONVERSATIONS

Suzanne Watts Henderson

NEW TESTAMENT CONVERSATIONS

A Literary, Historical, and Pluralistic Introduction

Abingdon Press™

Nashville

NEW TESTAMENT CONVERSATIONS:
A Literary, Historical, and Pluralistic Introduction

Copyright © 2019 by Abingdon Press

Library of Congress Cataloging-in-Publication Data has been requested.
ISBN 978-1-5018-5492-7

19 20 21 22 23 24 25 26 27 28—10 9 8 7 6 5 4 3 2 1
MANUFACTURED IN THE UNITED STATES OF AMERICA

Contents

Contents

Foreword:
An Invitation to the Table

I remember the first time I was invited to a conversation about the New Testament. A pastor friend was recounting to me the good Samaritan story, and he paused on the part about the identity of the Samaritan. Here is what he said:

> Most Christians correctly emphasize that the Samaritan was the other, but what they do not fully reckon with is that the Samaritan was the religious other, in fact the despised religious other. Jesus was telling his community to follow the example of an individual who did not pray or believe as they did, but who was ethically impeccable. The best analogy for our times would be a Christian leader telling his church to follow the example of a righteous Muslim rather than a callow pastor.

My friend fixed me with a warm, direct gaze, and I felt a shiver go down my spine. As a Muslim, I had long admired the Bible (considered a holy book in Islam) and Jesus (considered a prophet in Islam), but this is the first time that I had felt invited "to the table."

Suzanne Watts Henderson, in the terrific text you hold in your hands, is issuing a similar invitation to you. She presents the various books of the New Testament as "conversational documents," introduces you to a variety of interpreters of these books, and, as my pastor friend did, invites you to the table.

For me, "coming to the table" is the ultimate metaphor in a diverse democracy. When we come to the table, we bring our own contribution, and we engage with the contributions of others. Who are those others? They include people from every end of the earth, such as people who worship God in remarkably different ways and also those who do not worship God at all. They are your neighbors, your friends, your classmates, your coworkers. They are the descendants of those who stepped off the *Mayflower* and those who were dragged in chains. They are recent arrivals from Asia, Africa, Latin America, and Europe.

In this book, Suzanne asks you to listen to all of them and to join the conversation. It is the perfect way to celebrate the holiness of the New Testament and the symphonic multitude that is America's diverse democracy.

—Eboo Patel
Founder and President, Interfaith Youth Core

Introduction:
A Place in the World

Increasing globalization. Technological progress. Rampant immigration—some forced, some at will. Religious and philosophical diversity. Patriotism aligned with glorified military power. A degree of social mobility, but growing polarities between groups: the "haves" and the "have-nots"; urban and rural populations; the educated elite and the "regular people."

Sound familiar? It was in this world—this first-century CE Mediterranean world—that a small, countercultural movement sprung to life. It coalesced around devotion to someone called the "Christ," and its adherents soon became known as "Christians." Like its founding figure, the movement emerged not from the halls of power in Rome but from the empire's outskirts: a region called Palestine, conquered by Pompey in 63 BCE and occupied by the Roman army. There, an obscure Jewish prophet named Jesus had provoked officials during a Passover celebration and found himself, like so many before and after, hanging on a Roman cross.

But something happened to convince some of Jesus's allies that his death wasn't the end of the story. They'd seen their "risen Lord" with their own eyes, or they believed those who said they had. Even Rome had met its match, they thought; the Jewish God had somehow snatched life from the jaws of death, securing a decisive defeat of evil by forces that give life. In the story of this crucified and risen "Christ" named Jesus, a small but committed band of believers found reason to cast their allegiance with a different kind of kingdom—Jesus called it the "kingdom of God"—that ruled not by conventional force but by liberating, life-giving love.

The twenty-seven writings that make up the New Testament capture an unfolding conversation among a handful of early adopters in this movement.

Their authors share the view that, *in Jesus the Christ, the kingdom of God had established a foothold on earth.* They may differ in some details and literary style, but each text reflects on the meaning of Jesus's messianic mission for the world he left behind. Each NT book makes a case for its readers' place in that world.

This textbook serves as a "reader's guide" for those who want to listen to that first-century CE conversation. So we'll ask questions that are typical of books that introduce the NT in an academic setting:

- What do the texts actually *say*? (Spoiler alert: It's not always what we think they say.)

- How do the NT writers interpret Jesus's significance for their *first hearers*? (Caution: These books weren't originally written with us in mind.)

- How do they pitch their messages about a crucified and risen Christ in relation to the *wider social, religious, and cultural context* of the first-century CE Mediterranean world? (Reminder: Most people found that message strange, irrelevant, or otherwise preposterous.)

Together these *literary* and *historical* questions help us read the NT as a dynamic exchange about Jesus's impact on some of the earliest groups that called him "Lord."

More so than in other introductory textbooks, though, the discussion found here brings the NT conversation to life—for Christians and non-Christians alike. Our approach takes seriously the NT's *pluralistic* encounter with other Christian and non-Christian thinkers across time. To orient you to the pages that follow, let's consider the NT's conversation partners, its diverse conversation styles, and the promise this study might offer our own place in the world.

CONVERSATION PARTNERS

By their very nature, all the books that compose the NT are conversational documents. In both explicit and implicit ways, they negotiate the meaning of Jesus's messianic mission by interacting with other religious and philosophical worldviews. Over time, these texts have led to animated discussion among believers and nonbelievers alike. Let's take a look.

Within These Walls: Conversation among Diverse Christian Voices

Students of the NT are sometimes surprised to learn how varied the NT views are on such important matters as women's leadership in the early church, the relationship between Jewish and non-Jewish (Gentile) believers, and even the saving power of Jesus's death. The NT writings sometimes disagree with one another on historical matters (e.g., the day Jesus died), questions about religious practice (e.g., what believers can eat), and even topics of ultimate concern (e.g., who'll be "saved" in the end). Our study, then, will pause along the way to trace this *diversity of thought and practice within the pages of the NT itself.*

In other cases, we can detect *early Christian conversation partners whose viewpoints we know only indirectly*—that is, through what the NT writers say about them. Paul's letter to the Galatians features one side of a vigorous dispute between the apostle and a group of Christian teachers who've insisted that Gentile Christians must comply with Jewish law. The writer of Revelation disputes the Nicolaitans' teaching (see Rev 2:6, 15) without explaining their views. Both instances remind us that the NT's contents are only part—albeit an ultimately important part—of a wider conversation about what it means to call Jesus "Lord." That's why we'll do our best to give those voices some airtime of their own.

We'll also note intra-Christian conversations beyond those featured directly or indirectly in the NT itself. For instance, we'll pay attention to *"noncanonical" early Christian writings* that somehow engage the views found in the NT. Composed mostly in the first few hundred years after Jesus, these texts remind us of the ongoing reflection on his significance. Some traditions, such as the Gospel of Thomas, emphasize the special knowledge he imparted through his teachings. Others, such as the Infancy Gospel of Thomas, fill in narrative gaps about Jesus's childhood that the NT Gospels leave out of the story line. Though they're not included in the NT, these writings remind us that Jesus's legacy was up for interpretation and debate among believers from the start.

Other Christian conversation partners have both accepted the NT's authority as sacred text and explained its meaning in changing time and place. But just because they agree that the NT offers a reliable witness for Christian faith doesn't mean they agree on what that witness entails. Our study of NT conversations, then, will feature the *diverse ways Christian believers have interpreted its contents*—sometimes in direct competition with one another. After all, both slaveholders and abolitionists used the same NT texts to justify their views. We'll note those who've used Jesus's teachings as sanction for "just war" theory and those who think they preclude military service among Christians.

Finally, we'll devote special attention in this book to Christian interpreters whom scholars call *subaltern voices*. Like many early Christians, they read the NT from the "bottom side" of conventional power. Marginalized on the basis of gender, sociopolitical location, sexual orientation, skin color, and ethnicity, these conversation partners have been mostly neglected in public—and published—discourse, at least until lately. Since the "mainstream" approach of this textbook mostly reflects a white, privileged, and Western conversation, the subaltern Christian readings featured here will help honor NT conversations in greater breadth and depth.

"With Those Outside": Conversation with Other Religious and Philosophical Traditions

Hopefully, it's already clear that the NT wasn't written in a vacuum. Besides engaging diverse Christian viewpoints, its writers reflect on Christ's meaning for their world in conversation with other traditions as well—from Second Temple Judaism to Stoic philosophy, from the emperor cult to nascent rabbinical Judaism. True, the NT was written mostly for insiders. But its texts' first hearers inhabited a richly diverse religious and philosophical landscape. Something of a "cafeteria plan" offered options that mostly weren't mutually exclusive. You could perform your civic duty by worshipping Caesar, cultivate a Stoic mind-set, and join a tight-knit gathering devoted to the god Asclepius. In most cases, you could "have your cake and eat it too."

The book of Acts captures what the NT writers were up to as they interpreted the story of Jesus and its significance within the first-century CE world. There, an apostle named Paul brings word about Jesus's resurrection to the Athenian marketplace of ideas. Rather than starting with Jesus's story, though, he points to an altar devoted to an "unknown God" and cites two famous Greek poets to try to convince the audience that there's only one God who holds sway over all people—the Jewish God who has raised "a man" from the dead (see Acts 17:22-34). The NT writers share this impulse, often forging their claims about Jesus the Christ in both explicit and implicit conversation with other worldviews.

Of course, the most natural conversation partner for emerging Christian writers was *Judaism*. It's hard to say when the lines between "Christian" and "Jew" became clear. Many followers of Jesus—probably even Paul himself—remained Jewish, as Jesus did! But already in these early writings, the fault lines between Jews who thought the Messiah had come and those who didn't were becoming evident. As we'll see, the NT's conversations with Judaism can be heated and, over time, sowed seeds of anti-Semitism that still haunt our world. But have you ever noticed that family disputes are often the most animated? It's probably best to see the NT conversations with Judaism as squabbles among those who share more than divides them—especially their devotion to the same God.

Besides Judaism, the NT engages *other ancient religious and philosophical worldviews* as well. Some writers quote popular philosophy to prove their point, as when Paul invokes the Stoic value of self-discipline. Other texts show that early Christian practices—such as the Greco-Roman memorial meal that became the "Lord's Supper"—co-opt other religious forms, reinterpreting their meaning. At times, the NT writers can be downright provocative, calling Jesus "Savior" and "Lord" as a subtle challenge to a world in which many thought that Caesar was both. Throughout our study, we'll highlight places where NT authors engage other worldviews and patterns to help convey Jesus's messianic mission for their place and time.

Indeed, the NT's conversation with its own pluralistic world helps us read it in conversation with our pluralistic world as well. This leads to the feature of this textbook that sets it apart from others. In the chapters that follow, we'll note the NT's place in our world by noting *points of contact with other sacred traditions and worldviews*. Where Luke features Jesus's mother, Mary, for instance, a passage from the Qur'an will show Muslim reverence for her. When Jesus says he's "the way" in John, an excerpt from the *Daodejing* will convey a different take on the same concept. Like that of the NT writers, our aim is to foster conversation rather than diminish differences among traditions and worldviews. It's also to show that religious and philosophical traditions often consider the same questions and arrive at answers that can be either oh-so-close or miles apart.

CONVERSATION STYLES

If it's not clear by now, it will be by the end of the study: the NT doesn't speak with one voice. That's true not just about specific details, beliefs, and practices but also about the conversation style its writers adopt as they engage different perspectives. Let's briefly note the three main approaches they take.

Accommodation

Sometimes, NT writers adopt prevailing cultural practices and assumptions wholesale. Paul frequently includes stock "vice lists" when he's showing how the power of evil shows up in the human condition (e.g., Rom 1:29-31; Gal 5:19-23; cf. 1 Pet 4:3). These lists aren't explicitly Christian, but he thinks they retain value within a Christian worldview. Some of the stranger NT teachings probably reflect their writers' accommodation to existing worldviews as well. For instance, the notion that women would be "saved" through childbirth (see 1 Tim 2:15) doesn't fit well with the rest of the NT's teachings of salvation and probably derives from cultural views on gender.

Appropriation

In other cases, the NT seems to adapt settled views or social structures in light of its writers' views about Jesus and his saving significance. The authors of Colossians and Ephesians, for instance, provide guidelines for household relationships that both mirror and revise wider cultural assumptions (see Eph 5:21–6:9; Col 3:18–4:1). On the one hand, they preserve a hierarchical structure, promoting submission on the part of wives, children, and slaves; on the other hand, they encourage (male) heads of household to show their authority through sacrificial concern rather than coercion. Likewise, when NT writers cite Jewish scripture to confirm Jesus's messianic position, they often use freewheeling interpretation to allegorize, spiritualize, or christologize sacred tradition (e.g., Heb 1:5-14). In all these ways, the NT writers appropriate their conversation partners' claims or assumptions to serve their own aims.

Demarcation

In some cases, NT writers engage others' views in ways that mark off clear lines of distinction from them. Paul insists that those who say non-Jewish Christians must be circumcised are flat wrong; worse than that, he even wishes they'd castrate themselves (Gal 5:12)! In these passages, the writers "take off their gloves" when it comes to different worldviews because they think the stakes are especially high. Rather than meeting in the middle, they think it's time to take a stand. Yet even this conversational style—much more strident in tone—is still conversation; it still makes meaning by engaging different worldviews.

This range of conversation styles will be both evident and easier to grasp as we consider the settings the authors are addressing. Generally speaking, when they write from a position of strength or security, the NT writers employ a style that's measured and thoughtful. When under siege, their tenor grows more forceful, strident, and even testy. As we examine their contexts, we'll come to terms with the NT's vastly different ways of engaging the religious and philosophical "other."

ENTERING THE CONVERSATION: THE PROMISE OF A PLURALISTIC APPROACH

If you're reading this book, it's because either you or your instructor sees value in reading the NT as *more of a conversation starter than a set of beliefs to be embraced*. Sure, its writings *do* share the view that, *in Jesus, the messianic age has begun*; this is its unifying claim, from start to finish. But to consider the NT's lively conversation in its own place and time better equips us to read it in ours. After all, the NT is a *pluralistic collection* of documents written in a *pluralistic world*. As a result, it's left behind a legacy of *pluralistic interpretation* that can help us—believers and nonbelievers alike—read this sacred tradition in conversation with our *pluralistic communities* today.

Why is this important? Let's be honest. Christianity ruled the Western roost for millennia. That afforded the Christian Bible, and especially the NT, a privileged place not just in the church but in wider society as well. But a seismic shift is taking place. Everywhere we turn, we see reminders of religious diversity—from a hijabi working the airport security line to a Buddhist community making a home in a Baptist church. And even in the Bible Belt, where I live, many in our community find Sunday mornings to be the perfect time for brunch or a walk in the park or sleeping in. Some call themselves "spiritual but not religious" (the "SNRs"); others think religion is neither necessary nor beneficial (the "nones"). The evidence is clear: we're more diverse, in terms of both religious and nonreligious identities, than we've ever been.

Another, related shift has taken place as well. This landscape of religious diversity has led to rampant syncretism (the blending of traditions). Christians chant "ohms" in yoga class; Jews gather for Buddhist meditation; and Muslims celebrate Christmas. In America, most show equal—if not deeper— loyalty to nation or political party or sports team or economic system than they do to their religious tradition. Some see this syncretism as dangerous; some see it as healthy; some don't see it at all! Our pluralistic approach helps us both to see and to understand the distinctive claims of the NT forged in conversation with both competing and complementary claims that hovered in the first-century Mediterranean air. It helps us consider hard but great questions, such as the one my daughter recently asked: Can you be a Christian and a capitalist in today's world?

For believing readers (I count myself among this group), this book's pluralistic approach just might leave you with a clearer, sharper understanding of why you call yourself "Christian" and how that identity shapes the contours of your life. I hope you'll grapple anew with the—let's admit it—strange notion that God's power showed up two thousand years ago when a prophet named Jesus got the Roman death penalty and somehow appeared again, alive. I hope you'll see, too, that the NT can still guide readers on how to live together with one another and in relation to the wider world. By seeing, from the beginning, the NT writers' take on their place in the world, believers today can read their sacred tradition in conversation with—rather than isolation from—those whose views differ from their own.

But this isn't just a book for believers. After all, even where Christianity has lost some of its social and political power, the NT still crops up in the news, in public policy, on social media, and even around family meals. Often, though, our views of what the NT says are skewed and uninformed. Our "sound bite" culture means we often neglect context and nuance. At a minimum, then, nonbelieving students will be equipped for responsible conversation with believers and unbelievers alike. If you're not Christian, learning about the texts, their original contexts, and the pluralistic conversation that they reflect and generate will make you a more thoughtful critic; you'll be better able to articulate your own worldview because of your deep, and deeply pluralistic, understanding of the NT.

As many have noted, pluralism goes beyond mere diversity (a fact) to include deliberate engagement (a strategy) across religious and philosophical difference. That means noticing some similarities, yes, but also naming and claiming our worldview with its distinctive features. It means valuing conversation without resolving tension, contradiction, or even heated disagreement. It means listening well and being willing to "unlearn" what we've always known to be true—especially about others. Never has the time been riper for a pluralistic study of the NT. Never has our world needed resources for sharing conversation about ultimate concerns more desperately than we do today.

After all, we find ourselves in an uncanny moment of déjà vu. We, too, live in an era of increasing globalization, technological progress, and people on the move by choice and by calamity. We, too, live and work alongside those whose religious and nonreligious worldviews are markedly different from our own, and we mix and match our values and beliefs in a "cafeteria plan" of options. It was in a setting much like ours that the NT emerged as a conversation about what it means for Jesus's followers to live together, forging their place in the world. Whether or not you believe some or all of the claims these ancient texts make, the questions they explore are as timely as they've ever been. Will you join the conversation?

A final word of credit to my students: I was asked to write this textbook during a semester when I had two students taking my Bible class alongside my Global Religions class. The connections they detected between the two courses brought them to deeper, clearer understanding of both the biblical tradition and the other texts and worldviews we were exploring. As Christians, they no longer felt threatened by or afraid of religious difference; instead, they both described the semester as one in which they'd grown both in their own faith journey and in their capacity to share the human journey with those who see things differently than they do. Thanks to their insights, I realized it's time to read the NT not just in its pluralistic context but in ours as well. I hope this book helps us do just that. So thanks, Anna and Lexi. As happens so often in this line of work, my students have pointed the way once again.

What Is the New Testament?
Building Blocks

CONVERSATION STARTERS

- What writings are included in Christian scripture?

- Why might we call the NT a "collection of collections"?

- What kinds of literature (genres) appear in the NT?

- What makes determining the original version of the NT writings so difficult?

- How do scholars make educated guesses about the text of the NT?

- What factors shaped the formation of the NT canon?

- What factors shape the NT translations across time and place?

As part of the Christian Bible, the New Testament belongs to the world's best-selling book. Scan the religion collection at any bookstore, library, or online, and you'll find an almost endless array of options. Choosing a Bible in English is a daunting task! But despite the Bible's popularity, relatively few people today—believers or nonbelievers—know what it contains, how it was written and compiled, and why it appears in so many forms.

Our study of the New Testament begins at square one, with these very basic questions. In this chapter, we'll get our bearings for our study by listening in on the conversations that lie behind the NT's contents. Whether your interest in

1

the NT is academic, personal, or some combination of the two, you'll learn in this chapter about its origins and development across time. You'll gain a deeper grasp of the complex process that's shaped the NT we read today.

On the one hand, if you've read the NT in a faith-based setting, you may be surprised to find that none of its books was *written* as scripture. In fact, the NT as we know it didn't exist for almost four hundred years after Jesus's earthly career ended on a Roman cross. On the other hand, if you're familiar with *The DaVinci Code* or other "conspiracy theory" explanations, you'll likely be just as surprised by the fact that both Paul's letters and the four NT Gospels circulated among Christian communities long before the Emperor Constantine sanctioned and underwrote the collection of Christian scripture.

As we turn to our basic questions, I invite you to set aside what you already "know" about the NT and its origins—at least as best you can. Notice where new information fits or challenges your prior understanding. Take your time to reflect on the material we discuss. How does it deepen, complicate, or illuminate these ancient writings that remain sacred for billions of people around the world today?

WHAT'S THE NT'S BACKSTORY?
CHRISTIAN SCRIPTURE'S STARTING POINT

Pick up any Christian Bible, and you'll find the NT comes only *after* what Christians call the "Old Testament." Together, the thirty-nine books that precede the NT are called the **Hebrew Bible** or **Tanakh**, which is an acronym for its three main parts: **Torah** (law), **Nevi'im** (prophets), and **Kethuvim** (writings). (See Figure 1.1.) As we'll see, Jewish sacred traditions lie behind every NT book and serve as their main religious conversation partner. That makes good sense, since Jesus was a Palestinian Jew whose worldview and mission grew out of Jewish scripture. Even Jesus's earliest followers thought of "scripture" as *Jewish* scripture (see 2 Tim 3:16; 2 Pet 1:20), not the Bible as we know it today. After all, the NT's contents came later and gained authority only gradually. Believers from both Jewish and non-Jewish (Gentile) backgrounds looked to Jewish sacred tradition to make sense of Jesus's life, death, and resurrection.

In the first-century Greco-Roman world, the most influential version of that tradition was the **Septuagint**. According to the **Letter of Aristeas**, a group of seventy scholars gathered in Egypt in the third century BCE to translate the Torah and other Jewish writings from their original Hebrew (and patches of Aramaic) into Greek. Scholars think the translation happened

FIGURE 1.1: COMPARING JEWISH SCRIPTURE WITH THE CHRISTIAN OLD TESTAMENT

Most people assume the Bible contains a well-established, consensus list of books. But even the Bible's table of contents is open to pluralistic conversation. Here's a comparison of the Jewish Bible, or the Tanakh (sometimes called the Hebrew Bible), with Protestant, Catholic, and Eastern Orthodox Christian Old Testaments. Notice where all traditions agree, as well as their differences in contents and order.

Hebrew Bible (Tanakh) (24 books)	Protestant Old Testament (39 books)	Catholic Old Testament (46 books)	Eastern Orthodox Old Testament (50 books)	Original language
Torah	*Pentateuch or the Five Books of Moses*			
Bereishit	Genesis	Genesis	Genesis	Hebrew
Shemot	Exodus	Exodus	Exodus	Hebrew
Vayikra	Leviticus	Leviticus	Leviticus	Hebrew
Bamidbar	Numbers	Numbers	Numbers	Hebrew
Devarim	Deuteronomy	Deuteronomy	Deuteronomy	Hebrew
Nevi'im (Prophets)	*Historical books*			
Yehoshua	Joshua	Joshua (Josue)	Joshua (Iesous)	Hebrew
Shofetim	Judges	Judges	Judges	Hebrew
Rut (Ruth)	Ruth	Ruth	Ruth	Hebrew
Shemuel	1 Samuel	1 Samuel (1 Kings)	1 Samuel (1 Kingdoms)	Hebrew
	2 Samuel	2 Samuel (2 Kings)	2 Samuel (2 Kingdoms)	Hebrew
Melakhim	1 Kings	1 Kings (3 Kings)	1 Kings (3 Kingdoms)	Hebrew
	2 Kings	2 Kings (4 Kings)	2 Kings (4 Kingdoms)	Hebrew
Divrei Hayamim (Chronicles)	1 Chronicles	1 Chronicles (1 Paralipomenon)	1 Chronicles (1 Paralipomenon)	Hebrew
	2 Chronicles	2 Chronicles (2 Paraleipomenon)	2 Chronicles (2 Paraleipomenon)	Hebrew
			1 Esdras	Hebrew
Ezra–Nehemiah	Ezra	Ezra (1 Esdras)	Ezra (2 Esdras)	Hebrew and Aramaic
	Nehemiah	Nehemiah (2 Esdras)	Nehemiah (2 Esdras)	Hebrew

			Tobit (Tobias)	Tobit	Aramaic (and Hebrew?)
			Judith	Judith	Hebrew
Esther	Esther		Esther	Esther	Hebrew
			1 Maccabees (1 Machabees)	1 Maccabees	Hebrew
			2 Maccabees (2 Machabees)	2 Maccabees	Greek
				3 Maccabees	Greek
				3 Esdras	Greek?
				4 Maccabees	Greek
Ketuvim (Writings)			*Wisdom books*		
Iyov (Job)	Job		Job	Job	Hebrew
Tehillim (Psalms)	Psalms		Psalms	Psalms	Hebrew
				Prayer of Manasseh	Greek
Mishlei (Proverbs)	Proverbs		Proverbs	Proverbs	Hebrew
Qoheleth (Ecclesiastes)	Ecclesiastes		Ecclesiastes	Ecclesiastes	Hebrew
Shir Hashirim (Song of Songs)	Song of Solomon		Song of Songs (Canticle of Canticles)	Song of Songs (Aisma Aismaton)	Hebrew
			Wisdom	Wisdom	Greek
			Sirach (Ecclesiasticus)	Sirach	Hebrew
Nevi'im (Latter Prophets)			*Major prophets*		
Yeshayahu	Isaiah		Isaiah (Isaias)	Isaiah	Hebrew
Yirmeyahu	Jeremiah		Jeremiah (Jeremias)	Jeremiah	Hebrew
Eikhah (Lamentations)	Lamentations		Lamentations	Lamentations	Hebrew
				Baruch	Hebrew[7]
			Baruch	Letter of Jeremiah	Greek (majority view)
Yekhezqel	Ezekiel		Ezekiel (Ezechiel)	Ezekiel	Hebrew
Daniel	Daniel		Daniel	Daniel	Hebrew and Aramaic

		Twelve Minor Prophets		
The Twelve or Trei Asar	Hosea	Hosea (Osee)	Hosea	Hebrew
	Joel	Joel	Joel	Hebrew
	Amos	Amos	Amos	Hebrew
	Obadiah	Obadiah (Abdias)	Obadiah	Hebrew
	Jonah	Jonah (Jonas)	Jonah	Hebrew
	Micah	Micah (Michaeas)	Micah	Hebrew
	Nahum	Nahum	Nahum	Hebrew
	Habakkuk	Habakkuk (Habacuc)	Habakkuk	Hebrew
	Zephaniah	Zephaniah (Sophonias)	Zephaniah	Hebrew
	Haggai	Haggai (Aggaeus)	Haggai	Hebrew
	Zechariah	Zechariah (Zacharias)	Zechariah	Hebrew
	Malachi	Malachi (Malachias)	Malachi	Hebrew

For a helpful discussion about the differences, check out this article:

Amy-Jill Levine, "What Is the Difference between the Old Testament, the Tanakh, and the Hebrew Bible?" Bibleodyssey.org, 2019.

> **YOUR TURN:** What similarities and differences do you notice between the Old Testament, the Tanakh, and the Hebrew Bible? Do they matter? Why or why not?

more gradually than this letter suggests, but by Jesus's day, Jews throughout the Mediterranean world had access to their own sacred writings in the "common tongue" of their region: Greek. (More often than not, when NT writers cite Jewish scripture, they refer to the Greek, not the Hebrew, text.)

Across the centuries, the terms *Old Testament* and *New Testament* came to designate for Christians the superiority for what was "new" in Jesus, as if it replaced, superseded, or otherwise diminished the "old." Many Christians today perpetuate this view of the OT's secondary status. Some contrast its "harsh God" with the NT's "merciful God." (As we'll see, there's plenty of harshness to the NT God as well; there's also plenty of mercy in the OT's portrait of God, though we leave that discussion to OT textbooks!) Others **christologize** the OT by reading its texts as if they mainly point to Jesus Christ. We should note that both these approaches have, over the millennia, fueled intense Christian persecution of Jews—a shameful legacy indeed.

But this was not the impulse of most NT writers, who located Jesus squarely *within* the framework of God's covenant with the Jewish people, not

FIGURE 1.2: JEWISH AND CHRISTIAN TRADITION IN ISLAM

Much as early Christian writers thought Jesus's career invited fresh reflection on Jewish scripture, the seventh-century CE revelation to the Prophet Mohammed, known as the **Qur'an,** both affirms earlier sacred traditions and reframes them:

> We sent Jesus, son of Mary, in their footsteps, to confirm the Torah that had been sent before him: We gave him the Gospel with guidance, light, and confirmation of the Torah already revealed—a guide and lesson for those who take heed of God. . . . We sent to [Muhammad] the Scripture with the truth, confirming the Scriptures that came before it, and with final authority over them: so judge between them according to what God has sent down. . . . We have assigned a law and a path to each of you. If God had so willed, He would have made you one community, but He wanted to test you through that which He has given you, so race to do good: you will all return to God and He will make clear to you the matters you differed about. (Sura 5:46, 48, *The Qur'an*, M. A. S. Abdel Haleem, trans., *Oxford's World Classics* [Oxford: Oxford University Press, 2005], 72)

YOUR TURN: What view of scripture do you detect in this excerpt? What's the relationship among Jewish, Christian, and Muslim sacred traditions, according to the Qur'an?

---

in opposition to it. In this book, we'll consistently note Jewish sacred tradition that undergirds the NT story—from the Gospels to Acts to the letters to Revelation. Though the NT writers sometimes invoke Jewish scripture as proof texts to support their claims about Jesus, they generally assume the validity of the sacred story that frames Jesus's messiahship. To take the NT on its own terms requires us to read its contents in dynamic conversation with, rather than repudiation of, its scriptural forerunner. (See Figure 1.2.)

WHAT'S "IN"? THE CONTENTS OF THE NEW TESTAMENT

Twenty-seven writings make up the NT. Written over the span of several decades, these texts all take Jesus to be the Jewish Messiah whose life, death, and resurrection have established a foothold for God's reign on earth. They also share an interest in equipping believers to participate in that reign and perpetuate Jesus's witness to God's power. They capture vibrant conversations about the impact of Jesus's messianic career for those who live, as one writer puts it, as "immigrants and strangers" (1 Pet 2:11) within their own setting. Through story, poetry, and sometimes vigorous (if one-sided) debate, they proclaim Jesus's allegiance to God and God's kingdom as the basis of the faith that carries his legacy forward. Put simply, the NT's a collection of *internal memos that translate Jesus's messianic message and vision* for a diverse coalition of Jews and non-Jews united in their devotion to a God whose power and wisdom have been disclosed by Jesus of Nazareth.

As the chart in Figure 1.3 shows, the NT is made up of several collections of documents, with a couple of outlier writings included along the way. Early Christian writers named the four Gospels as an authoritative group late in the second century CE, and they've played a prominent role in teaching and worship ever since. In some Christian communities to this day, the congregation stands for a Gospel reading. Likewise, the Pauline Letters circulated as a group in the second century CE. However, it took hundreds of years before Revelation was widely accepted as part of the NT, and many believers today avoid its bizarre (and frightening) images at all cost.

WHAT DIFFERENCE DOES "GENRE" MAKE? LITERARY CONTEXT CLUES

Despite their common interest in Jesus the Christ, the NT writings feature a variety of literary forms, called **genres**. As readers, we follow genre clues without even thinking about it. When a story begins with the phrase "once upon a time," we know we're about to enter the world of fairy tale. An article that leads with the phrase "AP-Washington" can be trusted as a journalistic source. And though some readers are easily spoofed, most know that a post from *The Onion* is satire.

The NT includes neither journalism nor satire nor fairy tale, at least in the purest sense. But its contents do generally fit genres that were common in the ancient world. Let's consider the main forms that appear in the NT, as well as how those forms convey meaning to their audiences.

Narratives

Matthew, **Mark**, **Luke**, and **John** each tells the story of Jesus's life, death, and resurrection in narrative form. That means they're mostly stories with detectable characters, settings, plots, and ironic twists. As we'll explore more fully later, scholars sometimes detect special kinds of narrative in play: ancient

FIGURE 1.3: THE NEW TESTAMENT: A COLLECTION OF COLLECTIONS

The New Testament's contents fall mostly into the sub-groups of "gospels," or narratives about Jesus's life, death, and resurrection, and "letters," written by early followers of the risen Lord. Three other writings, the Acts of the Apostles, Hebrews, and the book of Revelation, fall outside these collections.

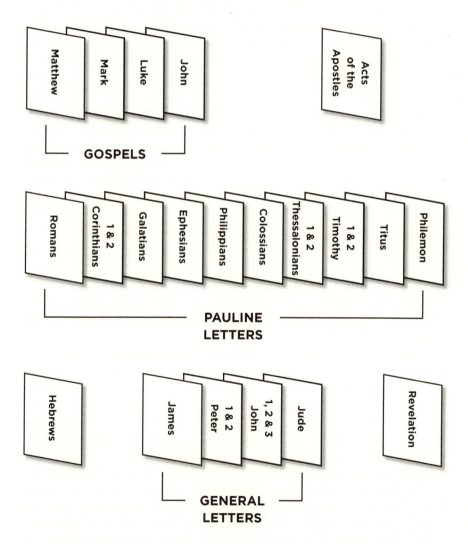

GOSPELS: Matthew, Mark, Luke, John

Acts of the Apostles

PAULINE LETTERS: Romans, 1 & 2 Corinthians, Galatians, Ephesians, Philippians, Colossians, 1 & 2 Thessalonians, 1 & 2 Timothy, Titus, Philemon

Hebrews

GENERAL LETTERS: James, 1 & 2 Peter, 1, 2 & 3 John, Jude

Revelation

YOUR TURN: Why do you think gospels and letters make up most of Christian scripture?

biography, ancient history, or even the creation of "gospel" as a new genre. After all, these stories exhibit both similarities to and differences from other ancient accounts such as Plutarch's *Lives* and Philostratus's *Life of Apollonius*. Broadly speaking, the Gospels' narrative form leads us to read them for *meaning more than fact*, for the *story they tell more than historic or scientific accuracy*.

Remember, too, that the NT authors wrote their stories not just to *inform* but also to *transform* their hearers. And "hearers" they (mostly) were; the literacy rate in the ancient Mediterranean world was probably well below 20 percent. Rather than poring over separate passages (separation by chapter and verse came much later), early Christians gathered to *listen* to the Gospel stories, an affective experience that those who attend live performances today can best appreciate.

Besides the Gospels, the **Acts of the Apostles** also fits the broad genre of narrative. Written as a sequel to Luke, Acts tells the story of the early church from the days just after Jesus's resurrection until the end of Paul's life. Like its Gospel companion, Acts uses some literary tools found in ancient history-writing, such as reconstructed speeches and name-dropping of key political figures. Both help the audience to experience the story as if they were there. But as we'll see, ancient history doesn't attempt the same degree of objective accuracy that historians seek today. Its narrative strategy fits more closely with today's historical novel.

Letters

Most of the remaining NT books are written as private communication from one or more individuals to groups or to specific people. As with letters, e-mail, or even text messages we send today, each of these letters arises out of its own context, which is hard to piece together in great detail. Consider this: if you read a letter I wrote my dad while I was in college, it would probably leave you with more questions than answers. Who's Elizabeth? And is there more than one (short answer: yes)? What did I spend that money on anyway (I don't say much about beer)? What was my major (I barely mention my classes)? What's "rush" anyway? (Okay, maybe you know the answer to that last one.) To read the NT letters, one of the first things we'll do is remind ourselves that we're outsiders to a conversation that didn't originally involve us.

Among this subset, thirteen letters belong to what scholars call the **Pauline corpus**—the body of writings attributed to the Apostle Paul. As we'll see, several of those letters were probably written after Paul died by those who wanted to preserve his legacy for a new generation. (The book of **Hebrews** isn't a letter—it reads more like a sermon—but it follows the Pauline corpus because it sometimes circulated as part of this collection.) The remaining letters are called the **"catholic" (or general) epistles**, a catch-all designation of other letters eventually included in the NT. This set includes letters attributed to Jesus's earliest followers such as **James** (Jesus's brother), the apostles **Peter** and **John**, and **Jude**, though scholars generally doubt their authorship, for reasons we'll discuss later.

Apocalypse

The NT ends with a bang rather than a whimper. The book of **Revelation** is so named because its title in the original Greek is *apocalypsis*, which means "unveiling" or "revelation." For many believers across time and place, this book is the NT's most troubling text, mostly because of its vivid and often gory imagery, its portrait of Jesus as a divine warrior, and its disturbing portents that point to the end of the world as we know it. Others have drawn loosely from its visions to insist that we're living in those "end times" (see Hal Lindsey's *The Late, Great Planet Earth* [Zondervan, 1970] and Tim LaHaye's Left Behind series [Tyndale, 2011], as well as television evangelists such as John Hagee). Their interpretations have even shaped American environmental and foreign policy based on the planet's imminent demise and the particular steps that will lead to it.

But as strange as Revelation might sound to readers today, the genre of apocalypse was quite well-known in the ancient world. Typically, both Jewish and Christian apocalypses brought *messages of hope to those suffering persecution*. How? Their surreal imagery offered an alternative vision of a divine kingdom that would defeat the forces of evil once and for all. For those struggling under the present world order—we can assume this describes Revelation's original audience—it's good news, not bad, that the world as we know it will soon be brought to its knees. Thus Revelation promises that justice is "coming soon" and that its hearers' perseverance in faith will find its reward.

This brief discussion of the NT's contents reminds us that taking the Bible on its own terms means that, though we'll take the NT *seriously*, we simply can't take it *literally*. After all, the literary forms that they deploy show little interest in objectivity or literal truth. What they do share is a devotion to *a Palestinian Jew named Jesus, specially designated by God to institute the messianic age of God's kingdom on earth and to inspire others to cast their allegiance with that kingdom.* Together, these writers see Jesus's life, death, and resurrection as part of the larger story of God's redemption of the whole world from the power of evil, wherever it appears.

WHERE DID THE NT COME FROM? THE ORIGINS OF CHRISTIAN CANON

Where did the NT come from? Some believers might provide a simple one-word answer to this straightforward question: God! But already, we've noted the complexity that lies behind the NT as we read it today. Of course, the discussion that follows doesn't preclude the possibility of a divine hand at work in the production and transmission of the NT. But our academic approach to these texts neither assumes nor requires it. Instead, we'll explore the NT's origins from the human side of the equation. How did those texts, written mostly in the second half of the first century CE, become the NT? We'll answer this question in two stages. The first has to do with the process of producing and preserving the manuscripts that form the *text* of the NT. The second concerns the official designation of the NT as a *canon* of authorized writings. As we'll see, various sociopolitical, religious, and cultural factors lie behind the emergence of both text and canon.

The Text of the New Testament

Imagine that it's late in the first century CE, and you've been given an important task. Back in the 50s, before you were born, your parents joined a group of believers who cast their allegiance with the Jewish Messiah named Jesus. They'd heard about Jesus from another Jew, a certain Paul from Syria. In between visits to your town, Paul wrote letters to instruct your parents and their "brothers and sisters" (the movement used familial language) about their common loyalty to this Christ. But Paul's now long gone—eliminated as a threat by Roman officials—and your parents' generation is dying out. You're better educated than most in the community, so some respected elders have named you archivist and asked you to compile and copy Paul's letters for safe keeping.

Your assignment brings with it several challenges. For one thing, Paul didn't date the letters he wrote. What's more, they were written on fragile **papyrus**, an ancient version of "paper" made out of plant stems or reeds, and they've broken apart in places. Both factors make it hard to piece the letters together in any kind of order. But you give it your best shot. Once you sit down to make a new copy, you face other obstacles as well. Sometimes, you struggle to read the original handwriting; you wonder whether or not you should correct spelling errors you occasionally encounter. If you're honest, you realize you, too, can get sloppy, especially at the end of the day. Your eye skips from the end of one letter, word, or line to another, and there's no easy way to undo your error. In the end, what you have is a very faithful effort to get things right, with a few best guesses and human flaws thrown in the mix.

This thought experiment highlights several differences between ancient and modern writing. The NT authors didn't benefit from spell check, Autosave, Grammarly, or the Cloud. They also didn't write—or dictate—their messages with any sense their texts would endure for thousands of years. Once they grew in popularity, the texts' preservation depended on faulty, inconsistent humans rather than (more reliable) computers. The scribes' abilities were spotty because the scribes were human.

That leads us to several basic observations about the text of the NT:

- No original copies of the NT—or its books, chapters, or even verses—exist today. (The earliest manuscript discovered so far dates to the early second century CE. This fragment known as P^{52} contains a brief excerpt from John's Gospel. See Figure 1.4.)

- Over 5,400 ancient manuscripts survive. They range from tiny fragments to copies of entire Bibles, and they span centuries. The earliest full-length manuscript is **Codex Sinaiticus**, which dates to the fourth century CE. (See Figure 1.5.)

- Among these manuscripts, scholars have counted more than 200,000 textual variants, or instances where the texts differ from one another.

- Differences among the manuscripts range from the insignificant (misspellings and copyists' errors) to the meaningful (additions, deletions, or revisions that somehow alter the meaning of the text).

These observations highlight just how hard it is to know what the NT writings originally said. The NT we study today is a reconstruction based on painstaking analysis of each manuscript. Scholars weigh the evidence at hand to see which variant is more likely to be closer to the original. This

FIGURE 1.4: THE EARLIEST FRAGMENT (P⁵²)

Ancient fragments of the Gospel of John
John Rylands Library, public domain

This fragment, known as the Rylands Library Papyrus, is generally thought to be the oldest remaining fragment of a New Testament text. It contains a small portion of verses from John 18. The fact that it is two-sided shows that it's from a **codex,** or book, rather than a scroll. Scholars think the fragment dates to the early second century CE, based mainly on the handwriting style. (Wikimedia Commons)

YOUR TURN: Reflect on the significance of this earliest evidence of the New Testament text. What does it show? What questions does it raise?

process, known as **text criticism**, operates according to a set of guidelines that help determine which "witnesses" are more reliable. Much like attorneys in a courtroom, scholars interrogate the manuscript evidence, using these criteria:

1. *Number of witnesses*: In general, more frequent agreement across manuscripts supports the case for authenticity. This criterion can be misleading, though, since errors or changes introduced early in the transmission process often take root in the tradition, especially when they improve style (e.g., better spelling or smoother syntax) or provide more appealing content (e.g., a more divine view of Jesus).

FIGURE 1.5: CODEX SINAITICUS

This **codex** (ancient form of book) was produced in the fourth century CE, perhaps as part of Constantine's support for standardizing the biblical canon. Discovered at St. Catherine's Monastery in the Sinai desert in the 19th c., it's the oldest remains of a full Bible. Scholars think it included the entire Old Testament, along with the New Testament, the deuterocanonical writings, and two non-canonical books: *Shepherd of Hermas* and the *Epistle of Barnabas*. This page includes Matthew 9:23b–10:17. (Wikimedia Commons)

2. *Age of witnesses*: Earlier manuscripts are favored over later ones. This criterion counts heavily especially when a witness that's earlier also features the more difficult reading (see below).

3. *Quality of witnesses*: Inevitably, some scribes were more meticulous than others. Those manuscripts that have repeated spelling mistakes and copyists' oversights are considered less likely to preserve authoritative readings.

4. *Tendencies of witnesses*: This criterion evaluates variants as they relate to the manuscripts' other features. For instance, manuscripts filled with scribal emendations (e.g., additions, revisions, explanations) seem less reliable overall.

5. *"More difficult" witnesses*: This rule of thumb grows out of the view that scribes are more likely to improve a text than to introduce a problematic reading. Text critics thus take the "more difficult" reading to be earlier.

Let's consider two examples to illustrate how these criteria work together in the task of text criticism. One important variant appears early in the Gospel of Mark, when a leper begs Jesus to "make me clean" (Mark 1:40). Though some Bibles today say Jesus was "moved with pity" (Mark 1:41 NRSV; cf. KJV), other ancient manuscripts explain his motivation differently: he was "incensed" (CEB). Both the *number* and the *age* of the witnesses would support the first reading: it shows up in more manuscripts and many earlier ones. But scholars think it's "more difficult" to imagine a change from compassion to anger than the other way around. In this way, many scholars think the last criterion overrides the first two, so that the more authentic reading reports Jesus's angry response.

A second case involves a familiar passage about a woman caught in adultery, found today in the Gospel of John (John 7:53–8:11). Most of the best ancient witnesses lack the entire story in which Jesus says, "Whoever hasn't sinned should throw the first stone" (John 8:7). Those manuscripts that do include the episode sometimes feature it in different places. Both observations lead most text critics to think the story was added to this Gospel later in the transmission process. (Many Bibles include the story but place it in square brackets to indicate the likelihood it's a later insertion.)

An honest appraisal of the evidence leads us to this conclusion: there's simply no way to recover an original version of the NT with any degree of certainty. After all, those who copied its contents freely altered them, for a variety of reasons. Sometimes, they "improved" the writings by correcting errors; other times, they clarified confusing material or made it fit better with emerging church teachings. The scribes themselves were, in essence, in conversation with the tradition for centuries. Thus the text of the NT reflects this complex and unfolding conversation.

The Canon of the New Testament

We turn now to the question about the NT's origins as an authoritative collection, or **canon**, of sacred writings. Who decided what would be included? When and how did they decide? And why were some books left out? Like the process that lies behind the NT text, the process called **canonization** is more prolonged and complex than most people realize.

In Greek, the word *kanōn* ("canon") designates a ruling stick or measuring rod. As a literary term, it refers to a formal or informal set of texts that "measure up" to standards of authority and value. In biblical studies, *canon* denotes an official list of books that have become part of our Bibles. (Some traditions include writings designated as "deuterocanonical," or a "second" level of canonical status. See Figure 1.6.)

Several historical factors led to the formation of the Christian canon, which includes the Old and New Testaments. The first has to do with *timing*. The early Christian writings eventually included in the NT took shape, not entirely coincidentally, at the same time that written sacred tradition grew more prominent in Judaism. With Jerusalem's destruction by the Roman army in 70 CE, the **temple** lay in ruins and with it a vital part of what it meant to be Jewish. As a result, Judaism reoriented around the **Torah** in ways that made a canon of official Jewish texts more important than ever. As the Tanakh gained authority in Judaism, it provided prototype for the Christian canon that would follow.

A second factor concerns *ideology*, or what we call **orthodoxy** (literally, "right mind-set"). Partly, the Christian canon coalesced around efforts to draw a "line in the sand" separating acceptable from unacceptable teachings. In other words, the canon emerged partly as a counterpoint to views deemed problematic by church officials. One such view came from a second-century CE writer named **Marcion**, who endorsed only those Christian writings—the letters of Paul and the Gospel of Luke—that he could interpret in contrast to Jewish tradition, which he associated with an evil God. Another approach church leaders rejected came from a Christian named **Tatian**, who created a harmonized version of the Gospels called the **Diatesseron** (ca. 170 CE) that eliminated their contradictions. Finally, as time passed, more and more gospels appeared throughout the Mediterranean—many of which were part of the **Nag Hammadi** collection unearthed in Egypt less than one hundred years ago. They

FIGURE 1.6: DEUTEROCANONICAL WRITINGS

As you can see in Figure 1.1, the list of writings considered "scripture" differs even within Christian traditions. Roman Catholicism, for instance, counts these books as canonical, since they're found in the Septuagint (LXX), the Greek translation of the Hebrew Bible:

Canonical by the Catholic Church and the Orthodox Church

Tobit

Judith

1 Maccabees

2 Maccabees

Wisdom of Solomon

Wisdom of Sirach (also called Ecclesiasticus)

Baruch including the Letter of Jeremiah

Additions to Esther

Additions to Daniel:
    Prayer of Azariah and Song of the Three Holy Children (Septuagint Daniel 3:24–90)

    Susanna (Septuagint prologue, Vulgate Daniel 13)

    Bel and the Dragon (Septuagint epilogue, Vulgate Daniel 14)

In addition, the Eastern Orthodox church considers these books sacred as well:

The Prayer of Manasseh

1 Esdras

3 Maccabees

Psalm 151

YOUR TURN: Why might church leaders have included different writings as "sacred scripture"? How do these differences affect your understanding of Christian scripture or the Christian tradition as a whole?

FIGURE 1.7: THE NAG HAMMADI LIBRARY

Discovered in the sands of Egypt in the 1940s, this collection of ancient Christian writings has provided a helpful window into the proliferation of gospels across time and place. You can read them for yourself at www.earlychristianwritings.com. Together, these texts offer a glimpse of gnostic Christianity, since they share the view of the salvation Jesus brings as a matter of securing secret "knowledge" (Greek: *gnosis*). Among the most well-known of the Nag Hammadi texts is the Gospel of Thomas, a collection of sayings attributed to Jesus that lines up closely at times with the NT Gospels. Other texts attributed to Jesus's closest companions include the Gospel of Judas, the Gospel of Mary, and the *Apocryphon of James*. The collection also features texts attributed to Seth and Melchizedek, legendary figures from Jewish scriptures, some with generic titles such as Gospel of Truth and Dialogue of the Savior. We'll encounter many of these texts as they relate to our study of the NT books along the way.

YOUR TURN: Go to www.earlychristianwritings.com and read a portion of one of the Nag Hammadi writings mentioned. What is striking about the text to you? Why? What does it reveal to you about early Christian diversity?

portray Jesus in ways that diverge quite significantly from the canonical Gospel stories. (See Figure 1.7.) All of these trends elicited a response from church leaders that laid a foundation for the NT. By 200 CE, **Irenaeus**, bishop of Lyons, authorized the four-Gospel set that's part of the NT today. Around the same time, a scholar named **Origen** coined the term "New Testament," though it didn't yet refer to the twenty-seven books eventually included in the canon.

Third, the Christian canon emerged for a more positive reason: *church unity*. Evangelistic efforts by Paul and others meant that Christian communities cropped up throughout the Mediterranean world and beyond. A shared canon offered just the kind of common ground this culturally diverse movement needed. In the mid-second century, **Justin Martyr** claimed the "memoirs of the apostles" were a regular feature of Sunday worship at Rome (*1 Apology* 67:3). In a strategic move, Christians adopted a new technology called the **codex** (an ancient book), which was much easier to transport than the traditional scroll. Thus the canon emerged organically as the "glue" that held together parts of the movement located in disparate places.

For these reasons and others, this "collection of collections" took shape over time. First came the Gospels, favored with highest authority since they anchor the movement in Jesus's story. Paul's letters also circulated as a group (though with varying contents) and played an important role in church teaching. The remainder of the NT gained widespread acceptance more slowly and sporadically. The Catholic Epistles, Acts, and Revelation eventually joined the list, while other writings (e.g., *Didache, Shepherd of Hermas, Epistle of Barnabas*) enjoyed canonical status in some collections but didn't ultimately make the cut.

On what basis did leaders assess a text's fitness for scriptural status? Several criteria influenced the outcome:

1. *Age of the writing*: Texts linked to the historical careers of Jesus and his first followers counted as more reliable. That's why the gospels written in the first few centuries after Jesus didn't gain canonical status. They were simply too far removed, in place and time, from the movement's origins with a Palestinian Jew.

2. *Apostolic ties*: As we'll see, historians doubt that Jesus's disciples wrote any of the NT's contents. But church leaders identified the four canonical Gospels either directly or indirectly with recognized apostles. They thought two of the original twelve—Matthew and John—wrote their own Gospels. Some claimed Mark wrote as Peter's interpreter or translator, and others attributed Luke to one of Paul's companions. These views, which appear in the writings of a second-century CE bishop named **Papias**, strengthened the case for these four Gospels' legitimacy.

3. *Traditional use*: This criterion is more descriptive than prescriptive. It just means that, the more widespread a writing's readership, the more likely it was to show up in the NT. Texts that diverse Christian communities saw as instructive for their life together rose in prominence throughout the Mediterranean world.

4. *Acceptable content*: Some texts passed the first three criteria but fell short because they sound, well, a bit strange. The Gospel of Peter is one such example. A bishop named **Serapion** at first gave it a thumbs up based on its ties to Jesus's closest disciple, but he reversed his position when he actually read it. Apparently, the story's walking, talking cross, along with its insistence that Jesus didn't suffer, constituted "questionable content" and so disqualified its use. (This Gospel fits a group of early Christians called **Docetists**, who insisted that Jesus only *seemed* human.)

Stories like this one remind us that the NT canon took shape not at one moment but over time. Several canonical lists that appeared in the third and fourth centuries CE illustrate just how fluid the process remained. One such list known as the **Muratorian Fragment**, which probably dates to around

200 CE, captures an early conversation about what Christians considered scripture. As its name suggests, it's a fragment, not a complete document, but the books it does mention all appear in our NT today.

The oldest existing full manuscript of the NT was produced in the fourth century CE, when Christianity became a state-sanctioned religion. The **Codex Sinaiticus** mentioned above combines Jewish scripture, the deutero-canonical works, and the NT writings, in addition to *Epistle of Barnabas* and the *Shepherd of Hermas*. This codex's contents remind us that the biblical canon—including the NT—was emerging, but not yet fixed, even three hundred years after Jesus died.

The earliest complete list of writings included in today's NT appears in **Athanasius's** Easter list, which dates to 367 CE. Three decades later, the Council of Carthage was the first meeting of church leaders to affirm the canon as we know it. Still, Christian writers continued to debate the place of Revelation, as well as the *Epistle of Barnabas* and the *Didache*, for centuries.

As an aside, notice that questions of biblical inspiration didn't play an important role in conversations about the emerging canon. No doctrine of biblical inerrancy even existed until modern times. Indeed, ancient Christians knew full well that the Gospels disagreed with one another on matters ranging from Jesus's named disciples, to the length of his ministry, to his itinerary, to the day on which he died. For them, these detailed differences didn't undermine the texts' legitimacy. Their value as scripture came instead from their reliable witness to the mission of Jesus Christ and its significant for living together within believing communities. (See Figure 1.8.)

Review and Reflect

- Name and explain two criteria used to decide the authenticity of textual witnesses and two criteria used to determine canonical status.

- Reflect on how you'd answer the question, "Where did the NT come from?" What factors seem most significant in its formation?

WHY DOES TRANSLATION MATTER? THE QUESTION OF ACCESSIBILITY

So far, we've discussed the NT's relationship to Jewish scripture, its content, and its origins. Along the way, we've detected a complex story behind the NT as we read it today. We'll conclude with one more dimension of that

FIGURE 1.8: DIFFERING VOICES ON SCRIPTURE, INTERPRETATION, AND AUTHORITY

Consider these different ways of understanding scripture across time and place:

From Origen (about 225 CE): "For our contention with regard to the whole of divine scripture is that it all has a spiritual meaning, but not all a bodily [or literal] meaning; for the bodily meaning is often proved to be an impossibility."

From John Calvin (1536): "Since no daily responses are given from heaven, and the Scriptures are the only record in which God has been pleased to consign His truth to perpetual remembrance, the full authority which they ought to possess with the faithful is not recognized unless they are believed to have come from heaven as directly as if God had been heard giving utterance to them."

From Chicago Statement on Biblical Inerrancy (1978): "Being wholly and verbally God-given, Scripture is without error or fault in all its teaching, no less in what it states about God's acts in creation, about the events of world history, and about its own literary origins under God, than in its witness to God's saving grace in individual lives." (See http://defendinginerrancy.com/chicago-statements/)

"Progressive Christians" (patheos.com, 2014): "We don't think that God wrote the Bible. We think it was written by fallible human beings who were inspired by (not dictated to by) the Holy Spirit. Hence, we don't consider it to be infallible or inerrant." (See http://www.patheos.com/blogs/rogerwolsey/2014/01/16-ways-progressive-christians-interpret-the-bible/)

YOUR TURN: What do these approaches to biblical interpretation share? How do they differ? What's at stake?

complexity: the fact that most people today read the NT in translation. From the outset, the Christian tradition has prioritized translating the NT into language that's accessible. True, some have attached sacred significance to certain translations—the Latin Vulgate or the King James Version, for instance. But over time, the impulse to render the NT message in the "common tongue" of the people has persisted.

We begin with a simple but often overlooked observation. Even if we had the original NT Gospels, they'd already be translations, since Jesus and his followers spoke Aramaic while the Gospels themselves were written in **koine Greek**. All NT authors used this simplest version of the language to communicate their message as broadly as possible throughout the Greco-Roman world.

But if Jesus and his first followers lived within the Roman Empire, why are the texts written in Greek? We can pin that on **Alexander the Great**, an ambitious and successful Macedonian conqueror, whose brief fourth-century

BCE rule had established Greek as the dominant language throughout the Mediterranean. The Roman Empire largely adopted the widespread use of Greek as an effective tool for communicating throughout the empire's conquered nations. Just as Chinese and Mexicans may speak to one another in English today, so, too, did koine Greek facilitate conversation across different cultures in the ancient world.

Over time, Latin replaced Greek as the region's common tongue, a shift that roughly coincided with Christianity's growing acceptance as a state-sanctioned religion. In a defining move, a church leader named **Jerome** translated both the Old and New Testaments into a Latin version known as the **Vulgate** (from the word *vulgar*, or common). Notably, Jerome's NT included the same documents found on Athanasius's list and omitted such widely read works as the *Epistle of Barnabas* (which had appeared in the Codex Sinaiticus) and the *Apocalypse of Peter*. While Greek versions of the Christian Bible continued to circulate in the East, the West quickly adopted the Latin Vulgate, which remained the church's authoritative text for almost a millennium after the collapse of the Roman Empire.

During that time, translations of the Bible into emerging European languages occasionally appeared, but church leaders consistently rejected this impulse toward the vernacular. After all, the church's power throughout the Middle Ages depended on the religious authority of the clergy, who alone were permitted to read and interpret scripture. Then, in 1517, a Catholic monk named **Martin Luther** publicly protested ninety-five church practices, many of which had to do with the abuse of ecclesial power and, in his view, the corruption of the gospel. Though Luther didn't set out to start a whole new branch of Christianity, historians see this act as the beginning of the Protestant Reformation.

Luther's core commitments to the "priesthood of all believers" and "scripture alone" led him to translate the Bible into German, working not from the Vulgate but from the original Hebrew and Greek texts. (See Figure 1.9.) Likewise, **William Tyndale** translated the original NT documents into English, though he was executed for heresy before he finished his translation of the OT. Other versions appeared soon thereafter: the Coverdale Bible, the Bishop's Bible, and the Geneva Bible. Since the printing press had been invented in the previous century, the Reformers rode the wave of mass production to translate and publish the Bible more widely than ever before.

The most popular English translation to date came on the heels of these earlier efforts. The **King James Version** was commissioned by the English monarch James I as a revision of the Bishop's Bible. The scholars who undertook this project worked carefully for almost a decade, poring over the latest

FIGURE 1.9: LUTHER'S BIBLE

Martin Luther's translation of the Bible into German was groundbreaking. Though not the first German translation from the original Hebrew and Greek texts, Luther's intent was to capture the everyday language of German people, many of whom were illiterate. His aim was to make scripture accessible to commoners, and the recent invention of the printing press (mid-fifteenth century CE) meant that more than 100,000 copies were produced in the early years. Not only did Luther's Bible help to standardize the German language, but it also promoted unprecedented growth in literacy.

YOUR TURN: Reflect on the impulse of Luther and other reformers to make the Bible broadly accessible to people. What's the significance of such a shift? Can you learn more about its impact on education more broadly?

discoveries of ancient texts to determine the earliest available readings. Many today continue to revere the eloquent prose found in this translation; some even consider it to be the only acceptable translation of the Bible. (See Figure 1.10.) Notice the irony, though: when it appeared, the KJV was the most contemporary, trendy Bible available in English.

In recent decades, Bible translations have proliferated at an astonishing rate. Two factors have contributed to this phenomenon. First, a desire for *accuracy* means that text critics have incorporated recently discovered manuscripts in a persistent quest to secure the most authentic version of the text possible. Second, a desire for *accessibility* has led scholars to ensure their translations remain true to their languages' current meaning.

In this spirit, several recent translations of the Bible are more aptly called *paraphrases* than translations. Traditional translations render the original text as closely as possible, using a principle called **formal equivalence** (e.g., NRSV, ASV). This can create awkward and difficult-to-understand translations because the structure (or form) of the original language is brought into the target language. Modern paraphrases, by contrast, seek a **dynamic equivalence** that translates the meaning of the original text into the natural structure and usage of the target language. In many cases, these dynamic equivalence translations also use colloquial language that's familiar in the contemporary world (e.g., The Message). Some translations attempt a middle ground between these two approaches (e.g., CEB, NIV).

Those shopping for a Bible today can also choose from a wide range of study Bibles. These Bibles include not just a specific translation or paraphrase but also material used to explain, interpret, and sometimes apply the biblical text for readers' benefit. Those features include introductory essays,

FIGURE 1.10: THE KING JAMES VERSION
AND ITS SUPPORTERS

The "King James Only" movement insists that this version alone is authoritative for Christians. Its proponents see *text criticism*, which has developed the criteria discussed in this chapter, as corrupted by subjective opinion. Here's what the Baptist Bible Translators Institute website has to say:

When there are many biblical authorities the result is that there is no authority at all. When we select which version of the Bible is authoritative for us, the Bible loses its independent authority. The only authority remaining resides in the selector and his personal basis for selecting this version or that version. By so doing we undermine all biblical authority and we ourselves become the authority instead.

Because of the confusion caused by so many translations in English, the King James Version stands out more than ever as the one authoritative Bible in the English language. We do not accept the King James Version because of some sentimental connection to it nor because of its old-fashioned Elizabethan English, nor because it is the oldest translation in use today. We accept it because it is the most accurate and reliable translation in the English language today. There are some tried and true reasons for accepting the King James Version as the standard for English speaking people.

First, the King James Version, New Testament, is a translation of the Textus Receptus Greek text. This leaves the King James Version as the only translation of the New Testament that is based entirely on the Textus Receptus [used by Erasmus in the early sixteenth century CE]. All other English language translations since 1881 have followed modern "scholarship" and based their translations on texts other than the Textus Receptus Greek text. There are good reasons why the Textus Receptus, and the King James Version which is a translation of it, is the only valid text of the New Testament that should be translated into other languages. (See the full discussion at https://baptisttranslators.com/why-the-kjv/)

YOUR TURN: Can you identify several working assumptions that lie behind this view? (You may need to learn a bit more about the Textus Receptus.) Write a response from a text critic's perspective.

verse-by-verse footnotes, and often topical discussions appearing in sidebar boxes. These additional resources guide readers in their biblical understanding and span a wide range of perspectives, from academic (e.g., New Oxford Annotated Bible, HarperCollins Study Bible, The New Interpreter's Study Bible), to church-based (e.g., CEB Study Bible), to a more focused concern (e.g., various options for women, men, and teens; Green Bible, an ecological reading).

In all these ways, Bibles today carry forward the impulse that guided the writing of NT texts in koine Greek in the first place. Though readers often prefer one style or translation over another, most options attempt to balance accuracy with accessibility. As has been true since the first century, the NT documents continue to be read, translated, and interpreted with each new generation.

SUMMARY

In this chapter, we launched our study of the NT with a historical review of what lies behind this collection that plays such an important role in Christian scripture. We've addressed basic questions about what the NT is and how it came to be. Along the way, we've turned attention to the fluid, still-unfolding conversation that lies behind the NT. Those who have copied, collected, translated, and packaged the NT canon have played an active part in determining which texts are sacred, what they mean, and how they're read in changing times. To take the NT on its own terms is to honor this animated conversation and its implications for how we read and understand its contents in our place and time.

Review and Reflect

- Name three historical turning points in the translation of the NT.

- How might you determine the "best" translation for your own study? What factors shape your decision?

GO DEEPER

Ehrman, Bart D. *Lost Christianities: The Battles for Scripture and the Faiths We Never Knew.* New York: Oxford University Press, 2003.

Ehrman, Bart D., and Michael W. Holmes. *The Text of the New Testament in Contemporary Research: Essays on the* Status Quaestionis. 2nd ed. Leiden, Netherlands: Brill, 2013.

Gamble, Harry. *The New Testament Canon: Its Making and Meaning.* Philadelphia: Fortress, 1985.

Lewis, Nicola Denzy. *Introduction to "Gnosticism": Ancient Voices, Christian Worlds.* New York: Oxford University Press, 2013.

Tabor, James D. "Older Is Not Always Better: Remembering Westcott and Hort." Bible and Interpretation, 2009: http://www.bibleinterp.com/opeds/tabor_357913.shtml.

Chapter Two

How Will We Study the New Testament? Critical Methods

CONVERSATION STARTERS

- What's the difference between biblical studies and Bible study?

- What kinds of questions will we ask about the NT's backstory?

- How do scholars investigate the composition of NT texts?

- What approaches study the NT's interpretation across time and place?

- How does pluralism fit into our conversation?

In the first chapter, we explored basic questions about the NT's contents, production, and translation. Along the way, we noted the conversations that have shaped this set of ancient texts as we read them today—conversations about what their original versions might have said, what belongs in this canon, and how best to make the NT accessible for readers in changing times. By now, you've encountered some complex human factors that lie behind this collection that many call scripture.

This chapter takes on the question of method: What critical tools will we use to investigate the NT? After all, there are many ways to study these texts. Some probe them devotionally, in the quiet of a dorm room perhaps, or in a hammock strung up in the quad. Others go to church to hear a priest, pastor, or preacher interpret the NT's meaning for a congregation's life together. Still others absorb some of their teachings without even realizing it. Perhaps you've

26

heard sayings such as "the love of money is the root of all evil" or your parents taught you about the Golden Rule ("love your neighbor as yourself"), and you carry a vague sense that these are Bible verses. And you would be right.

But have you ever stopped to think about *how* you read (or absorb) the NT—what assumptions you bring, what questions you formulate, and who decides how you answer them? In this chapter, we'll explain the field of "biblical studies" as an academic approach to the NT. We'll lay out various methods used in this approach, as scholars explore the NT texts in conversation with their own context as well as ours.

If you're a Christian who's familiar with the NT, you may find some of the critical lenses we use to be unfamiliar, and perhaps unsettling. If you're a NT newcomer, you may be surprised to learn that we'll apply rigorous academic investigation to religious literature. In either case, the conversation we'll engage in throughout this book will hone your ability to think "critically"—that is, carefully and deliberately—about the NT's meaning from the first century to the present day.

If there's one phrase that best captures the academic study of scripture, it's this: we'll read the "text in contexts." Context, as we'll see, makes all the difference in how we read any text. But most of us are too busy or distracted to notice how our own cultural setting affects how we make meaning of messages we encounter in everyday life. We're so immersed in our own world that it's hard to step back and examine our assumptions about meaning and where they come from.

Let's consider a nonbiblical example. Take the case of a phrase whose meaning has changed dramatically in recent decades: Twin Towers. Chances are, these two words take you almost instantly to September 11, 2001, when hijacked passenger planes crashed into the two tallest office buildings at the World Trade Center in Lower Manhattan, and also into the Pentagon outside Washington, DC, and a field in Pennsylvania. Those who are old enough likely have vivid memories of just where they were when they first heard the news. They may recall, decades later, graphic images of the fiery towers, the cloud of dust, or the faces of those who made it out alive.

Now think about how the phrase's meaning has changed. My grandmother, who died in 1997, could have located the Twin Towers in New York City, even though she lived in Chicago. For her, though, these words carried no tragic overtones. However, those who lost loved ones at the Pentagon or in a Pennsylvania field on 9/11 may wonder if the prominence of the term Twin Towers has diminished public recognition of their own part of the tragic day.

Let's take things a step further. Since 9/11, the meaning associated with Twin Towers has justified many shifts in American culture and policy. We've learned about Al-Qaeda and militant Islam. We've lived through US wars in Iraq and Afghanistan, stories of torture at Abu Ghraib, and the rise of ISIS. If we fly somewhere, we take off our shoes in the TSA line. Even NFL games are different in the wake of 9/11: field-sized American flags, veteran recognition, and jet flyovers all elevate patriotism and equate it increasingly with military symbols—an association forged more closely in the aftermath of 9/11.

The loaded meaning now associated with Twin Towers isn't unusual, but it is an unusually vivid example of the fact that *context matters*. The meaning of any text—from a Tweet to a text message to a news article to a poem— depends not just on its *words* but on the *world* to which it belongs. That's why we devote so much attention to context in this study of the NT. After all, these books *first* addressed people far removed from our own place and time. Our study takes us back, across time and place, to the first-century world to which they belong. Only after situating the NT in its original context will we explore its meaning and influence in the world across time.

Here's what you'll find in this chapter. First, we'll learn about the field of biblical studies as an academic discipline. Next, we'll introduce the kinds of questions—or the "critical tools"—scholars use to explore these ancient texts. Then, we'll explain this book's most distinctive feature, that is, the pluralistic conversation it engages. Finally, we'll lay out the "both/and" approach we'll take as we use this array of critical tools to probe the NT texts in their contexts.

BIBLICAL STUDIES AND BIBLE STUDY

These terms, *biblical studies* and *Bible study*, sound almost identical, don't they? They both have to do with the Bible, and they both involve its active and thoughtful exploration. But for our purposes, it's important to distinguish them from the outset. What's the relationship between *biblical studies* as an academic discipline, and *Bible study* as a faith-based approach to these sacred texts? It turns out that this relationship, too, has a lot to do with context.

Students and readers open a book like this one from different starting points. You may walk into your NT classroom with your guard up or with outright eagerness. You may come with lots of questions or lots of answers. Perhaps without thinking about it, you bring expectations about your instructor and what you'll learn in this course. Have you thought about those assumptions?

Some Christian students have well-meaning pastors, friends, or family members who warn them about taking an academic course on the Bible.

Perhaps they know that a study such as this one highlights the *human* dynamics that shape scripture and its interpretation. They may think this approach undermines core convictions about *divine* inspiration and biblical authority. It's the same concern they'd likely register about a science class that teaches evolution or the big bang theory. They think biblical studies *opposes* Bible study, and they may caution students to "learn just enough to pass the class" but not to believe a word.

Others sign up for a NT course because they see biblical studies as an advanced, intensive version of Bible study. They're eager to go deeper than Sunday school or small group in their grasp of Christian scripture. They may think this course will strengthen their beliefs or help their evangelism. They assume that biblical studies *equates with* Bible study, at least in its aim of growing students' faith.

A third (and growing) group of students don't identify with Christianity at all. These readers—who may be Jewish or secular or Sikh—probably think they're starting behind since they haven't been raised on the NT stories. If they're guarded, it's because they wonder if the course intends to convert them (though it doesn't); if they're eager, it's because they don't have as many cherished beliefs about the NT to defend.

Whatever your starting point, know that you have much to gain from this course—both academically and, I'd suggest, personally. Regardless of your faith tradition or worldview, you live in a world that's shaped, in both explicit and subtle ways, by the NT and its interpretation. The more we know about these texts and their interpretation—whether we "believe in" them or not—the more responsible global citizens we become.

Now that you've thought about your starting point, it's only fair to be transparent about the assumptions that underlie this study. Let's take a moment to explain what this book will and will not address and why students of any faith tradition—including those who claim "none"—can find its content both intellectually challenging and personally rewarding. Consider these points of distinction between biblical studies and Bible study:

1. Biblical studies mainly *describes* the NT texts, along with the religious and sociopolitical factors that shaped, preserved, and promoted their interpretation over time. Bible study mainly *interprets* the texts' meaning for "us here today" (see Deut 6:4).

2. Biblical studies fronts the NT's *original setting and composition*, situating the texts in a place and time far removed from our own. Bible study assumes the NT's *timeless relevance* for faithful

readers, effectively collapsing the historical gap between the NT world and ours.

3. Biblical studies sees the NT texts—and the collection itself—as the product of *human writers and their communities*. It treats the writings as literary windows into the earliest generations of Christian gatherings. Bible study emphasizes *divine revelation* conveyed in the texts, with less attention to the human factors in play.

4. Biblical studies remains neutral, even uninterested, on questions of *scriptural authority* or *doctrinal conformity*. Bible study assumes a coherent set of *beliefs and moral practices* that the NT texts confirm.

5. Biblical studies probes the *truth claims* of the ancient texts, without weighing in on their legitimacy. Bible study sees the NT as both *true and indispensable* for believers' lives.

In this book, we'll explore what the NT texts say, how their content relates to their ancient setting, and how they've been read and interpreted across time. If you're a Christian, you'll learn some new information that will likely revise your views about Jesus and his legacy. That information may challenge or grow your faith—hopefully, both! If the NT isn't your sacred scripture, you'll have the chance to deepen your grasp on these texts that appear in our wider culture mostly in soundbites and on signs at football games.

What does this mean for our study? For one thing, Christian and non-Christian readers are on equal terms. This book neither presumes nor requires religious beliefs about the NT or its contents. Instead, we'll seek to understand the NT writers' views about what it means to call Jesus the Messiah. But we won't stay in the first century. Instead, we'll pay attention to how others have read the NT in changing contexts, including our own. Ultimately, our own pluralistic context means we're well-positioned to appreciate the NT conversation that's evolved from shortly after Jesus's death to this very day.

One more thing before we get started: pay attention along the way. Notice when what you're learning here challenges, surprises, or unsettles your views about the NT and Christianity as a whole. Take time to reflect not just on content but on the questions it raises and the new landscape it opens up for you. My deepest hope is that this academic study will equip you to read this sacred tradition more carefully, thoughtfully, and purposefully than ever before.

BIBLICAL STUDIES: A MODERN INQUIRY

As an academic discipline, biblical studies arises from a context of its own. With the Enlightenment came a form of scientific inquiry that brought questions of "truth" and "fact" under closer scrutiny. After all, premodern readers mostly didn't pose scientific questions about Jesus's healings, exorcisms, or nature miracles. Sure, they noticed differences—even contradictions—among the Gospels. But as a rule, they were less interested in historical accuracy than they were in the NT's meaning.

Biblical studies mirrors the kind of historical and scientific inquiry that's developed in recent centuries across other fields of study. Thomas Jefferson was no biblical scholar, but his **Jefferson Bible** reflects the modern impulse to separate scientifically unprovable Gospel material from Jesus's more palatable teachings. (See Figure 2.1.) The approaches we'll discuss below employ a range of critical lenses to analyze NT texts in light of modern questions.

Not everyone has embraced this modern approach, especially its emphasis on the human aspects of scripture. One significant backlash arose in the 1800s at Princeton Seminary, where Charles Hodge led the charge to anchor biblical authority in claims about its divine inspiration and infallibility. Today, some conservative churches and leaders carry this view forward, insisting that scripture is reliable both for its religious truth and as an "inerrant" (without error) source of historical and scientific facts.

Still, most biblical scholars—many Christians among them—continue to study the NT, its authors, and their communities in light of the contexts that shape all three. To do so, they probe questions about the texts' composition, their transmission, and their interpretation. At every step along the way, critical tools yield important insights about the NT writers' message—both as crafted by their authors and editors, and as interpreted by their audiences across time and place. As Figure 2.2 illustrates, different critical tools focus deliberately on different stages of the NT's production and interpretation.

FIGURE 2.1: "THE LIFE AND TEACHINGS OF JESUS OF NAZARETH," KNOWN AS THE JEFFERSON BIBLE (1819)

While president, Thomas Jefferson made his first attempt at compiling an authoritative account of Jesus's story, using scissors to remove Gospel episodes deemed unbelievable to modern minds and arranging material from the four accounts into a harmonized narrative. Though the initial effort was lost to posterity, his second version was preserved by family members for decades and published by the Library of Congress in 1904. Here's an example of how Jefferson tells the story of Jesus's birth:

Luke 2:6-7: And so it was, that, while they were there, the days were accomplished that she should be delivered. And she brought forth her firstborn son, and wrapped him in swaddling clothes, and laid him in a manger; because there was no room for them in the inn.

[Omits Luke 2:8-20, which narrates the story of the angel Gabriel announcing Jesus's birth to shepherds and their visit to the stable]

Luke 2:21: And when eight days were accomplished for the circumcising of the child, his name was called Jesus.

[Omits Luke 2:22-38, which tells the story of Simeon and Anna in Jerusalem, who recognize the infant Jesus as Messiah due to a revelation of the Holy Spirit]

YOUR TURN: Learn a bit more about the Jefferson Bible and its contents. How do you respond to Jefferson's handling of the NT text? Why?

Stage One: Backdrop

As we noted in chapter 1, all NT books share a common interest in Jesus of Nazareth, a Jew who lived in first-century CE Roman-occupied Palestine. Some NT texts (the Gospels) focus squarely on his story, while others (such as James) mention him only in passing. Still, they all see Jesus as the long-awaited Jewish Messiah, anointed by God to implement God's reign on earth. Though Jesus died on a Roman cross, they agree, God raised him to new life, and believers can look forward to the day when he returns to establish God's just rule for all to see.

But where did they get such a shared "take" on Jesus's story? The first set of critical lenses we'll employ situates these claims in the first-century CE Mediterranean world in which they emerged. Broadly speaking, we call this approach **historical criticism**. For starters, historical critics reach behind the

FIGURE 2.2: TIMELINE AND CRITICAL METHODS

Critical approaches to scripture explore different stages in the texts' composition, transmission, and interpretation. That means that each approach poses complementary rather than competing questions as they explore meaning at three basic levels:

1. **Backdrop: Historical Criticism**

    • What lies behind the text?

    • What was the world and worldview in which it took shape?

2. **Composition: Source, Form, Redaction Criticism**

    • What appears within the text?

    • What sources and earlier oral forms does it include?

    • What editorial input did the author(s) offer?

3. **Interpretation: Textual, Canonical, Reader-Response, History of Interpretation, Deconstructionist, and Post-Colonial Criticism**

    • How has the text been read and interpreted over time?

    • How did ancient scribes preserve or alter the text in its earliest forms?

    • How does the text relate to other canonical writings?

    • How have people found meaning in the texts in different historical and social circumstances?

    YOUR TURN: Which of these questions seems most important or significant to you, and why? How do readers today benefit from the wide range of critical approaches?

texts to examine the social, political, and religious forces that shaped Jesus's life as a Palestinian Jew living under Roman occupation.

The study of the **historical Jesus** is one form of historical criticism. Have you ever noticed how family stories change over time, depending on who's telling the story to whom? Now consider the decades that elapsed between Jesus's own career and the written accounts of it. This branch of NT scholarship sifts the Gospel evidence in order to determine what Jesus really said and did. Not surprisingly, their findings don't always agree, but a strong historical consensus does emerge on several points. Historians widely agree that Jesus had a lot to say about *God's coming kingdom*, that he earned a reputation as a *teacher and miracle worker*, and that he was *crucified by Roman officials* in Jerusalem during Passover. They even agree that *some of his followers soon believed he'd been raised from the dead.*

Other kinds of historical criticism explore both Jesus's world and the wider Mediterranean world where the NT texts emerged. Such critical tools equip us to read and understand these ancient texts on their own terms. But what kind of evidence comes into play? **Archaeology** is one tool that supports historical criticism by excavating items from the material culture of the first century. Findings at **Sepphoris**, a Roman town four miles from Nazareth, point to a thriving cultural center in close proximity to Jesus's hometown, while Roman coins minted by the emperor **Tiberius** confirm Rome's presence in Jesus's native region of Galilee. (See Figure 2.3.) Likewise, excavations at Corinth highlight the city's socioeconomic and religious features addressed in Paul's letters to Christians there.

Besides evidence from material culture, ancient texts unearthed in the Judean and Egyptian deserts help us understand the NT texts in conversation with their pluralistic landscape. Scholars think the **Dead Sea Scrolls**, found in caves in the Judean wilderness outside of Jerusalem, belonged to a sectarian Jewish community that was alive and well during Jesus's lifetime. The scrolls share Jesus's **apocalyptic** worldview but develop it differently. Together, they emerge as a vital conversation partner for the NT texts. Likewise, early Christian writings found at **Nag Hammadi** in Egypt help us understand early Christian **Gnosticism**, a variety of beliefs that some parts of the NT seem to anticipate.

Historical criticism also deploys tools from the **social sciences** to explore first-century culture. Sociologists and anthropologists examine Roman imperial policies (e.g., taxation, forced labor), social roles assigned to genders and ethnic groups, and the trauma of military occupation and its justice system for those living under it. These angles of inquiry highlight, for instance, the complex power relations between Roman and Jewish officials, as well as the function of terms such as *honor* and *purity* throughout the ancient world.

Jesus's religious tradition, **Second Temple Judaism**, constitutes a major part of the NT's historical background. Every NT writer explains Jesus's significance against the backdrop of Jewish tradition, from the **law** (Torah) and the **prophets**, to the Psalms and other **writings**, and even to nonbiblical writings found in the **Apocrypha** and **Pseudepigrapha**. Besides those cited in the NT, other Jewish texts inform our study as well. For instance, the writings of first-century CE Jewish historian **Flavius Josephus** such as *The Antiquities of the Jews* and *The Jewish War* provide a window into life under Roman occupation and so shed invaluable light on Jesus's own context. Though it was compiled later (ca. 200 CE), the **Mishnah**'s collection of rabbinical conversations about Jewish law situates Jesus's disputes about its interpretation within, not outside of, his own Jewish tradition.

FIGURE 2.3: ARCHAEOLOGY FROM GALILEE

Excavation site of a street in the Galilean town of Sepphoris, where Jesus and his family likely took part in commercial trade. The coin is a *denarius*, or "tribute penny," that was excavated from the site and features the image of the Roman Emperor Tiberius, who ruled the region from 14 to 37 CE. (Wikimedia Commons)

YOUR TURN: How does archeology and its findings affect your reading of biblical texts? What difference does this kind of historical criticism make, and why?

To summarize, our study of the NT's backdrop explores the contexts of both *Jesus's career* and the *early Christian movement* that spread throughout the Mediterranean world soon after his death. These critical tools position us to understand Jesus in relation to his own religious tradition, as well as life in Roman-occupied Palestine. They also situate the NT writings in conversation with prevailing social, political, and religious features of the ancient Mediterranean world in which they emerged.

Stage Two: Composition

A second stage of biblical scholarship concerns the composition history of the texts. Who wrote them? When? For what purpose? And in what settings? Like the tools that probe the NT's backdrop, these questions belong mostly to the field of historical criticism. Rather than delving into the world *behind* the text, though, this approach prioritizes the writings themselves.

In the modern era, questions about the composition of the NT grew out of noticing similarities and discrepancies among the four Gospels. In fact, the high degree of overlap among three of them—Matthew, Mark, and Luke—points to the likelihood that one or more Gospels was used as a source for the others. But which one(s)? And what about the material they don't share? These kinds of questions belong to the field known as **source criticism**. Outside the Gospels, source critics detect literary seams that suggest two or more texts have been combined into the NT book we have today. Second Corinthians, for instance, probably weaves together parts of at least two separate letters.

The findings of source criticism lead in turn to an approach called **form criticism**. To see the composite nature of the NT texts draws attention to the "forms" their pre-existing sources took. Form critics ask questions about how oral traditions are passed along. They also detect pre-existing hymns and creeds that have been borrowed from early Christian worship and incorporated in the NT. (See Figure 2.4.)

Attention to underlying sources and their use raises a third set of questions that constitute **redaction criticism**. A "redactor" is an active editor, one who freely rewrites, alters, and incorporates pre-existing material. All of the evangelists were redactors, since they all employ some literary license in what they include and how they tell Jesus's story. Redaction critics detect the editorial imprint of each story, noting telltale signs of authorial bias that characterize each one. Mark's urgent tone reveals the evangelist's sense that the end is coming soon, while Matthew's insistence that Jesus fulfills Jewish law indicates an originally Jewish audience.

FIGURE 2.4: A PRE-PAULINE HYMN

Paul's letter to the Philippian church includes several verses that form critics think were part of an early Christian hymn. Not only does Paul's writing style shift from prose to poetry, but the language and rhythm of these verses also suggest that he's citing a well-known song. Notice both Paul's introduction and the hymn itself:

> Therefore, if there is any encouragement in Christ, any comfort in love, any sharing in the Spirit, any sympathy, complete my joy by thinking the same way, having the same love, being united, and agreeing with each other. Don't do anything for selfish purposes, but with humility think of others as better than yourselves. Instead of each person watching out for their own good, watch out for what is better for others. Adopt the attitude that was in Christ Jesus:

> Though he was in the form of God,
>   he did not consider being equal with God something to exploit.
> But he emptied himself
>   by taking the form of a slave
>   and by becoming like human beings.
> When he found himself in the form of a human,
>   he humbled himself by becoming obedient to the point of death,
>   even death on a cross.
> Therefore, God highly honored him
>   and gave him a name above all names,
>   so that at the name of Jesus everyone
>   in heaven, on earth, and under the earth might bow
>   and every tongue confess
>   that Jesus Christ is Lord, to the glory of God the Father. (Phil 2:1-11)

YOUR TURN: What sounds "hymn-like" about the second part of this passage? How does Paul use the hymn to illustrate his teaching?

A final approach that has to do with composition is called **narrative criticism**. Narrative critics shift attention away from historical context to examine the literary features of a given text. What themes emerge across a NT book? What's its literary structure or rhetorical flow? What about plot, characterization, literary devices, and other details from the story? Narrative criticism explores meaning mostly in the text as we read it today.

Stage Three: Interpretation

Besides exploring the NT's backdrop and its composition, biblical scholars also study the texts' interpretation over time. Remember, the NT is part of a chart-topping best seller. As a result, its impact on the church and the wider world is hard to overstate. Biblical studies takes seriously not just the NT texts but also their use over the last two millennia—for good or for ill.

Critical questions about NT interpretation begin with the text itself. As we saw in chapter 1, **text criticism** deals with the dynamic and fluid nature of the textual tradition. Hundreds of thousands of differences in the earliest manuscripts remind us that we have no original text, but that doesn't mean scholars can't try to reconstruct one! That's the business of text critics, who assess those discrepancies to determine the version that's likely to be more authentic. Already, text critics notice the interpretive impulses that lie behind many scribal changes.

A second interpretive approach called **canonical criticism** explores the NT texts in relation to the wider canon of sacred scripture. For instance, canonical critics might read one Gospel in light of the others, or in conversation with Paul's letters and Revelation. They also go beyond early Christian writings to consider the Old Testament as interpretive guide. Most canonical critics assume deep value in sacred scripture and think its separate messages illuminate one another even where they differ.

Other critical approaches interested in "meaning making" focus less on text and more on audience—both original hearers and readers in a wide range of times and places. **Reader-response criticism** acknowledges that the meaning of any text depends mostly on how its message registers with those who receive it. (Just think back to an e-mail or text message you've sent that's been "heard" very differently from how you intended it.) Since NT audiences were mostly illiterate until modern times, **performance criticism** imagines how the NT texts would have been presented and experienced when delivered orally. Both critical lenses study the rhetorical impact of the texts' language and structure.

History of interpretation criticism tracks Christian readings of NT over time. Key figures from Origen to Augustine to Catherine of Siena to Martin Luther have written sermons, poems, treatises, and letters that find wide-ranging meanings in biblical texts. Scholars today sometimes value these premodern voices as conversation partners whose fresh insights have been lost over time. Like canonical critics, scholars who take this approach often operate from within a Christian worldview.

Other critical methods arise from a more oppositional, or suspicious, interpretive location. Taken together, inquiry linked to **deconstructionist criticism** comes from our postmodern setting. This approach destabilizes conventional notions of power and authority. Deconstructionist critics note that scripture—including the NT—has long been aligned with and deployed by the few in charge whose privilege usually comes at the expense of the many. As a group, these scholars tease out the sociopolitical impact of scripture and its interpretation.

Within deconstructionism, **post-colonial criticism** (also called **empire criticism**) examines the NT in light of imperial power—both the imperial context in which its contents appeared and the empires or colonial powers that have used its texts as means of control to this day. Some post-colonial critics reclaim the NT's subversive, anti-imperial messages found especially in the Gospels, Paul's letters, and the book of Revelation. Others highlight the ways in which some NT texts accommodate imperial strategies of oppression (see e.g., 1 Tim 2:8-15). Post-colonial critics sometimes privilege **subaltern** readings that interpret the NT from the bottom side of the power structure.

Those readings characterize other deconstructionist approaches as well. **Feminist critics** study the question of gender in the NT and its interpretation. Some concentrate on the biblical characterization of women, while others examine the NT's interpretive impact on women in different contexts. **Womanist criticism** reads the NT from the intersectional perspective of women of color. **Queer criticism** explores both text and interpretive tradition through the lens of sexual identity and often from within the LGBTQI community. **Environmental criticism** (called **creation criticism**) scrutinizes the ways in which the NT and its readers have shaped environmental policy, especially in light of the consistent message that the world as we know it is passing away.

Scholars deploy each of these critical approaches to join in conversations about the NT's meaning and impact over the last two thousand years. Each arises out of its own set of assumptions and biases—some sympathetic, some highly critical—about the NT as sacred scripture. Along the way, each brings important insights to bear on these ancient writings that continue to impact our world. That's why our study will draw widely and deeply from these diverse critical tools in our unfolding conversation about a man named Jesus and the NT writings that reflect on his identity and mission.

Review and Reflect

- For each of the three stages (backstory, composition, interpretation), name and explain two critical tools used by scholars.

- Which of the critical tools addresses questions you're most interested in? Why?

A PLURALISTIC CONVERSATION

You'll find the critical tools discussed so far in most introductory NT textbooks. But this study deploys yet another kind of inquiry that grows out of our religiously diverse landscape. The reasons for this have a lot to do with our own context. Sure, Christianity still dominates much of the globe, both numerically and culturally. But demographic trends show that we're more likely than ever to live, work, and play among those who subscribe to a wide range of religious and philosophical views.

We've already noted that religious diversity alone doesn't automatically engender goodwill across these differences. In fact, our default mode takes us in the opposite direction: the more *diverse* our society grows, the more *segmented* and *fractious* it becomes. By default, we run to our corners and hang out in echo chambers that reinforce our own ways of making meaning. Only those who *deliberately and respectfully engage across difference* strengthen what social scientists call "social cohesion"—the glue that binds us as humans rather than the walls of hostility and enmity that keep us apart.

Since this is a book about the NT, our primary aim here is to understand its writings and their worldviews—not the broad array of early Christian writings, the history of Christian thought, or Islam or Mormonism. But there's a paradox in play here. *We can better grasp the NT texts on their own terms by hearing their voices in conversation with the voices of others—both Christian and non-Christian, both within the NT canon and outside of it, both ancient and contemporary.* The pluralistic dimension of our study, then, is all about that conversation.

We'll note, for instance, the pluralistic framework of the NT itself. As a canon that includes not one but four Gospels, this collection features diverse voices even within its unified witness to Jesus the Christ. Particular stances on women's church leadership, on the meaning of Christ's death and resurrection for believers, and on the relationship between church and society often diverge from one another. Sometimes they even argue outright. By noticing these differences, we honor the pluralistic impulse of those who compiled the NT canon in the first place.

Our pluralistic lens also keeps in view the pluralistic landscape of the NT world. As we'll discuss in chapter 3, the Greco-Roman setting that was home to both Jesus and his earliest followers was something of a lab experiment in "coexistence." But lines between worldviews were never hard and fast. Even Jesus's own Palestinian Judaism had been shaped, to some degree, by such disparate traditions as Persian Zoroastrianism and Hellenistic philosophy.

Within Judaism itself, diverse perspectives flourished alongside each other through the lively conversation embedded in the rabbinical tradition. In many ways, the NT writers raise a voice in the wider world's conversation, weighing in about Jesus the Christ in ways that both adopted and adapted their competitors' views.

But there's another, more contemporary reason for introducing a pluralistic lens into our NT study. For millennia, the NT and its advocates have offered religious sanction to those in positions of sociopolitical power. Thus Christian leaders have relied on the NT to justify the Crusades, the Inquisition, slavery, and pogroms—all of which deployed coercive force against those they deemed "outsiders." More recently, many Christians in the West have taken up the mantle of scripture to justify persecution of, or outright violence against, Muslims, Sikhs, and others.

The time is ripe to recover the NT's own pluralistic conversation and to recalibrate it for our place and time. In this way, our literary, historical, and pluralistic study challenges the legacy of Christian supremacy from inside Christian scripture. Our conversation will feature the NT's lively and sometimes boisterous voices as they reflect on Jesus's meaning as the Christ. May this study open for you a wider world that starts important conversations in your classroom and beyond. (See Figure 2.5.)

FIGURE 2.5: HARVARD'S PLURALISM PROJECT

Consider this piece describing the origins of Harvard's Pluralism Project:

In 1991, Diana Eck first offered a course at Harvard University on "World Religions in New England." The subject matter came organically from her growing interest in the changing religious landscape of America, a trend that could be seen in the changing face of the student body at Harvard. Twenty-five students joined Professor Eck in the inaugural course. . . . Based on their findings in Boston, researchers set out to investigate the changing religious landscape of other American cities. From the beginning, it was clear that diversity alone does not constitute pluralism. Pluralism requires a degree of engagement with our diversity and the knowledge—both of others and of ourselves—that such engagement brings. And so, in 1991, the Pluralism Project was born. (pluralism.org/about/our-work/history.)

YOUR TURN: How do you understand pluralism? Reflect on a time when your own "engagement" with diversity brought knowledge about others and yourself.

SUMMARY

There are many different ways to read any book, and the NT is no exception. In this chapter, we've described the field of biblical studies in some detail. We've also explained many critical approaches biblical scholars employ as they study the ancient texts. Finally, we've returned to the question of pluralism and its relevance for our conversation.

Perhaps it's clear by now that this textbook will use a "both/and" strategy to examine the NT through a wide range of critical lenses. Here are some of the approaches we'll combine in the pages that follow:

- *Both appreciative inquiry and critical examination.* This textbook takes the NT texts on their own terms by investigating their claims in a critical light.

- *Both text and context.* We'll consider the writings themselves ("text") in conversation with their original settings as well as with the settings where they've been read and honored across time and place ("context").

- *Both history and theology.* History plays a key role in exploring those contexts, but part of that history has to do with the theological claims that make meaning out of concrete human existence.

- *Both unity and diversity.* The NT texts consistently interpret Jesus's life, death, and resurrection for believing communities that lived in widely different settings. Our study thus tracks their shared claims alongside their tensions and animated disputes.

- *Both dominant and subaltern readings.* Consensus findings from the field of biblical studies anchor our discussion, but we'll also attend to voices that read the NT from the underside of conventional power.

- *Both alignment with and distinction from other worldviews.* Sometimes, we'll note conceptual points of contact between the NT and other religious and philosophical texts. In other cases, we'll trace key differences to sharpen our view of the NT.

Now that you have a better sense of the assumptions and questions that lie behind this study, I invite you to settle in for the journey. I hope you'll find it as rewarding as it is challenging. If the conversation's sometimes jarring, if the material here sometimes seems lofty or foreign or unsettling, I hope you'll also reach the end of the book with a baseline competence as a beginning biblical scholar. Let's go!

Review and Reflect

- Explain one way that a pluralistic approach fits either the NT itself or our contemporary setting.

- What have you learned about biblical studies that seems relevant to our world today?

GO DEEPER

Brown, Jeannine K. *Scripture as Communication: Introducing Biblical Hermeneutics.* Grand Rapids, MI: Baker Academic, 2007.

Dietrich, Walter. *The Bible in a World Context: An Experiment in Contextual Hermeneutics.* Grand Rapids, MI: Eerdmans, 2002.

Dunn, James D. G. *Unity and Diversity in the New Testament: An Inquiry into the Character of Earliest Christianity.* 2nd ed. London: SCM Press, 1990.

Green, Joel B., ed. *Hearing the New Testament: Strategies for Interpretation.* rev. ed. Grand Rapids, MI: Eerdmans, 2008.

Penner, Todd, and Davina Lopez. *De-Introducing the New Testament: Texts, Worlds, Methods, Stories.* West Sussex, UK: Wiley-Blackwell, 2015.

Chapter Three

What Was the NT World Like? An Ancient "Pluralism Project"

CONVERSATION STARTERS

- How do the NT's contents relate to their wider world?

- What is "Second Temple Judaism," and why is it important for studying the NT?

- What is the "Greco-Roman" world?

- How did the Roman Empire treat religious and philosophical diversity?

- What religious and philosophical worldviews characterized the first-century CE Mediterranean world?

- How does learning about the NT's setting help us read its contents more responsibly?

By now, you understand we can't take the NT on its own terms without setting aside, at least for the moment, some beliefs and assumptions we may have brought to this study. Already, we've shed light on human inputs that lie behind the NT as we read it today. From the scribes to the people who determined what's in the canon to the translators responsible for making the Bible accessible to us, the human dimension is undeniable, regardless of your views about divine inspiration. In other words, the Bible—in our case, the

NT—didn't drop from the sky; it emerged over time, and in conversation with its wider world.

In this chapter, we'll lay out some features of the setting in which the NT texts first took shape: the first-century CE Mediterranean world. After all, the NT authors incorporate the worldviews and experiences of their audiences as they relay the good news of an executed Jewish messiah named Jesus. The Jerusalem temple shows up in the NT. So does the **Areopagus** in Athens. The writers borrow familiar religious and philosophical terms from their wider world, often imbuing them with fresh meaning. John's Gospel says the abstract philosophical term *logos* (or "word") has taken on human flesh. Matthew and Paul both transform the sociopolitical gathering called an "ecclesia" into a group of Christ-followers (our Bibles translate this word as "church"). Thus, the NT writers use language and concepts from popular culture to communicate what was, in many respects, a countercultural message.

That brings us to an important paradox. To read the NT responsibly in *our* setting, we begin in a setting that's "long ago and far away." Two interrelated aspects of the ancient world are especially relevant as we sketch the NT's backdrop. The first comes from Jesus's own setting. Not only was Jesus a Palestinian Jew from Galilee, but also his movement grew out of Jewish hopes for the world. (See Figure 3.1.) We'll begin with a broad summary of the defining features of **Second Temple Judaism**, the term scholars use to describe Jewish tradition during Jesus's lifetime.

But both Jesus and the NT writers also belonged to the wider **Greco-Roman world**—that is, a world shaped both by Greek (or Hellenistic) culture and Roman imperial power. The NT texts themselves originated mostly outside Jesus's Palestinian landscape. They also translate Jesus's mission and its meaning for both Jews and non-Jews (**Gentiles**) who'd been deeply shaped by Greco-Roman culture.

Diverse NT voices offer their own responses to basic human questions that were as common in the ancient world as they are today. What is human life all about? How do I find meaning in the midst of suffering? What happens when I die? What does an ideal human society look like? And what's my place in this world? The NT texts forge their answers in dynamic conversation with religious and philosophical views that dominated their ancient landscape. We turn now to sketch out some basic parts of those worldviews.

SECOND TEMPLE JUDAISM

If you take the NT at face value, it's easy to come away with an understanding of Jesus's own religious tradition—Second Temple Judaism—that's

FIGURE 3.1: MAP OF ANCIENT PALESTINE

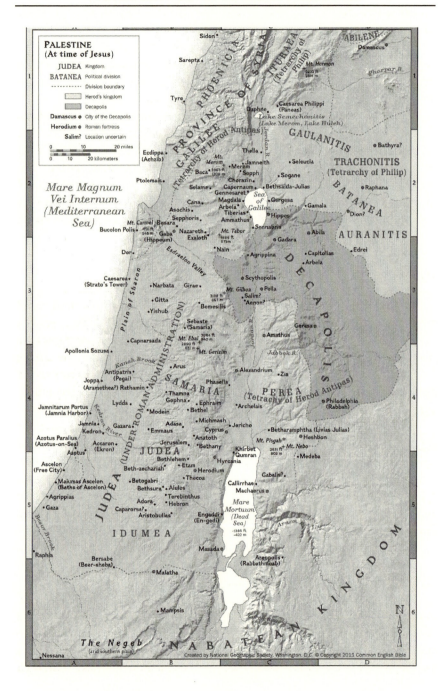

neither favorable nor historically accurate. In the Gospels, Jesus calls Jewish leaders "hypocrites" (e.g., Matt 23:13) and claims his Jewish opponents are children "from your father . . . the devil" (John 8:44). The book of Hebrews implies that Jesus's sacrifice has replaced God's covenant with Moses (e.g., Heb 8:6), rendering it null and void. Over time, Christians have used such texts to sanction oppression and violence against Jews—violence that culminated in the last century with Hitler's Final Solution.

But the fact is that Jesus and his earliest followers weren't Christians; they were Jews. Jesus didn't come to start a new religion but to call his own people back to the roots of their own tradition. True enough, the NT texts cast his Jewish conversation partners in an unflattering light, to say the least. But though Jesus surely debated his contemporaries on matters of biblical interpretation, he did so from *within* Judaism, not as an outsider. That means we simply can't understand Jesus's mission without exploring core elements of the Jewish practice and belief that framed it.

One God: Monotheism

Throughout the ancient world, Judaism set itself apart in its unusual devotion to one God, known by the unspeakable name "YHWH." Jews in Jesus's day regularly cited the **Shema**, a term meaning "hear!" that signals the opening line of Jewish law: "Hear, O Israel: The Lord is our God, the Lord is one" (Deut 6:4, author's translation). In fact, God's "oneness" remains such a central part of Judaism to this day that this line is counted as the first among the Ten Commandments. (See Figure 3.2.)

For Second Temple Jews, this strict monotheism didn't mean there weren't other divine beings, just that worship was reserved for this particular God. Six-winged creatures called "seraphs" appear in visions of God's heavenly throne room (Isa 6:2), and a quasi-divine "Human One" sometimes represents humanity before God's court (Dan 7:13). Even humans—from biblical characters to first-century rabbis—sometimes wield divine power. But faithful Jews worshipped none of these as God.

Chosen People: Israel

The distinctive devotion to one and only one God served as the "glue" that united Jews throughout the ancient world. Together, they saw themselves first and foremost as part of a spiritual "people" called **Israel**. For most Second Temple Jews, this term designated neither a political nation-state nor a geographical location; the borders that defined Israel came instead from their

FIGURE 3.2: A MONOTHEISTIC SIBLING

Of all global religious traditions, **Islam** most closely resembles Judaism's strict **monotheism**. Indeed, the First Pillar of Islam, known as the *Shahadah*, is the daily recitation of these words: "There is no God but Allah, and Mohammed is his messenger." In Islam, these are the first words uttered in the ears of newborn babies, and they constitute the creedal core of the tradition.

On this point, Islam and Judaism are closer, theologically speaking, than either tradition is to Christianity. Though both traditions honor Jesus as a prophet (Islam) and as a rabbi (Judaism), claims about his divine origins and nature challenge the view that there's one and only one God. Christian theologians explain that the Trinity—Father, Son, and Holy Spirit—are all part of the same Godhead and so insist Christianity is monotheistic as well. But Jews and Muslims generally find this doctrinal "work around" unsatisfactory.

> **YOUR TURN:** "Christianity is a monotheistic religion." From what you know about the Christian tradition, argue both for and against this statement.

identity as a people chosen by the one God to bear God's blessing to the whole world. (See Figure 3.3.)

What made Israel God's chosen people? According to biblical tradition, God conferred a special blessing on a legendary nomad named Abram (who later became Abraham). Through Abram and his descendants, the story goes, that blessing would in turn extend to "all the families of the earth" (Gen 12:3). (Abram's grandson, Jacob, was renamed "Israel," which means in Hebrew, "he struggles with God.")

These ancient stories gained special importance during the **Babylonian exile** (587–539 BCE), when many Judeans (who soon became known as "Jews") were forcibly removed from their homeland. During this crisis, community leaders reminded these migrants that they belonged to Israel, a chosen people whose mission it was to bear God's "light to the nations" (Isa 42:6; 49:6). Many Jews returned to Jerusalem after the exile, but others remained scattered, or in **diaspora**, throughout the ancient world. In Jesus's day, Jews everywhere held fast to that strong sense of blessing and shared identity as God's people.

Covenant Relationship: Torah

This chosen status carried with it the responsibility to reflect God's righteous ways to one another and to the wider world. A third indispensable part of Second Temple Judaism was the blueprint for human community found

FIGURE 3.3: ISRAEL AS A SPIRITUAL COMMUNITY

Many people today think of "Israel" mostly in terms of the nation-state established by the United Nations in 1947 in part of the former Ottoman Empire known geographically as "Palestine." But the Bible most often uses the term *Israel* to designate a spiritual people who live in covenant relationship with a God called YHWH. (According to Jewish scriptures, "Israel" existed as a political state around 1000–597 BCE.)

When the NT was written, Israel referred to God's people, living both in Palestine under Roman authority and throughout Europe and Asia. As recently as the nineteenth century CE, a founding document of Reform Judaism (one of modern Judaism's three main branches) featured this statement: "We consider ourselves no longer a nation, but a religious community, and therefore expect neither a return to Palestine, nor a sacrificial worship under the sons of Aaron, nor the restoration of any of the laws concerning the Jewish state." For more information on the 1885 Pittsburgh Platform, see https://www.jewishvirtuallibrary.org/the-pittsburgh-platform.

Today, the term ***Palestine*** is an ambiguous one, and faithful Jews disagree about whether or not the "return to Palestine" (which most Jews today call **Israel**) is an important part of Jewish identity. In the wake of the Holocaust, some think the establishment of a Jewish state in the Middle East is vital to the people's survival. Others separate their Jewish identity, based in ethnicity, ritual, and ethics, from the nation-state of Israel today. In this book, we will follow the impulse of the NT to identify Israel as God's people, regardless of geography. (See e.g., Gal 6:16.)

YOUR TURN: In your view, what's the difference between Israel as a people and Israel as a political state? Does the distinction matter? Why or why not?

in **Torah**. Also called the "law of Moses," this collection contains the first five books of Jewish and Christian Bibles today (Genesis through Deuteronomy). Though traditionally associated with Moses, the Torah as we know it was likely compiled around the time of the exile. These books establish the terms of God's relationship with the people. As a covenant, Torah cultivates reciprocity between God and God's people. It ties God's blessing to human faithfulness in ways that connect their worship of God to the human society they create. According to Torah, that society must exhibit God's justice and righteousness, especially in its care for those who are vulnerable. Jesus's summary of the law's two commandments—love of God and of neighbor—fits squarely within the framework of Second Temple Judaism.

Non-Jews today sometimes think that Jews in Jesus's day saw the Torah as a burdensome (if not impossible) list of rules and regulations required to earn God's favor. But ancient sources paint a far different picture. For one thing, Jews such as Jesus embraced the covenant—with its provisions for life together—as a gift, rather than a burden. For another thing, they tried to

FIGURE 3.4: GRACE AND LAW IN RABBINICAL JUDAISM

If the NT is your only source for understanding the role of Jewish law in Jewish thought, you might miss the fact that, far from a burden imposed as a way to earn God's favor, **Torah** sets the terms for living in relationship with a God who first blesses and calls the people Israel.

As E. P. Sanders points out in *Paul and Palestinian Judaism* (Philadelphia: Fortress, 1977), many rabbinical writings assume that "obedience to the commandments is the consequence of the prior election of Israel by God" (85). For instance, R. Joshua b. Karha interprets Deuteronomy 6 to say the "yoke of the kingdom of heaven" precedes the "yoke of the commandments" (*Berakot*, 2:2). That is, Torah comes as a response to the free gift that is God's call of the people Israel. Likewise, Rabbi Simeon ben Yohai interprets the commandments as the result of accepting God's kingship, not the way to earn God's favor. As one tradition has God put it, "Already before I gave them the commandments I advanced them the rewards" (Jacob Z. Lauterbach, *Mekhilta de-Rabbi Ishmael: A Critical Edition*, vol. 1 [Philadelphia: Jewish Publication Society, 2004], 294).

YOUR TURN: What role do rules play in your life today—personal, social, religious, or otherwise? When are rules a gift? What makes them a burden?

follow the law in gratitude for God's steadfast love, not to earn it. (See Figure 3.4.) In fact, Torah has built-in systems for restoring relationships with God and the wider community when people break its rules.

Cultic Practice: Temple

Those systems have a lot to do with the fourth prominent feature of Second Temple Judaism: the physical structure of the Jerusalem temple. While prayer and study of Torah took place in **synagogues** scattered throughout Palestine and beyond, sacrifices could only be performed by the priests in the temple. That made this structure ground zero for Jews, right up until the year 70 CE, when the Roman army leveled the city. (See Figure 3.5.)

The significance of the temple in Jesus's day is hard to overstate. For one thing, its exclusive role in Judaism made it a unifying place for Jews throughout the ancient world. Each year, Jews would set aside savings to fund pilgrimages to Jerusalem, where they'd purchase animals that the temple priests would then slaughter on their behalf. These pilgrims thus strengthened their sense of belonging to the spiritual people Israel and their devotion to the one God associated with the one temple. **Philo of Alexandria** put it this way: "Since God is one, there should be also one Temple" (*Spec Leg* 1.67).

FIGURE 3.5: MODEL OF THE JERUSALEM TEMPLE IN JESUS'S DAY

A scale model of Herod's Temple Mount is on display in Jerusalem at the Israel Museum. The view pictured is from the eastern Mount of Olives.

Within the temple complex, the most sacred space was located in its in-nermost sanctuary, the **holy of holies**. Tradition taught that YHWH's very presence lived there, behind an elaborate curtain. Among humans, only the high priest could enter this part of the temple, and only once a year on the Day of Atonement. When Gospel traditions say this curtain was torn at the moment of Jesus's death, they're implying that God's presence has broken through the sacred boundaries long preserved in the temple's architecture (see Mark 15:38; Matt 27:51; Luke 23:45).

The first-century temple also served a sociopolitical role in the context of Roman occupation. Around the time of Jesus's birth, the Roman client king **Herod the Great** renovated and expanded the temple's rather modest structure. This investment in the temple's infrastructure went a long way to-ward appeasing the priests and Jerusalem's ruling class. It signaled that Rome sanctioned their way of life, boosting the Jerusalem economy along the way. But an important upshot lies behind the Gospel stories of Jesus's death, since Jerusalem's Jewish leaders had aligned themselves, even if awkwardly, with Roman rule. More than just a religious center, the temple served as a hub of political power as well.

To summarize, Judaism in Jesus's day was deeply rooted in the belief that the *one God* had chosen the *people Israel* to live in a special *covenant relationship* that would ultimately bear God's blessing to the world. They responded to this call by devoting themselves to God and thus to each other by keeping the terms of that covenant found in the Torah. No matter where they lived, Second Temple Jews saw themselves as one people, worshipping one God, with *one temple* serving as their home base.

Review and Reflect

- What are the four defining markers of Second Temple Judaism?

- How does the concept of "covenant" convey the practice and beliefs you find here?

PALESTINIAN JUDAISM

Jews living in Jesus's native Palestine enjoyed proximity to Jerusalem, majority status, and historic ties to the land that strengthened their Jewish identity. But Palestinian Jews also contended on a daily basis with the realities of life under Roman occupation. For them, foundational claims about YHWH's power stood in tension, if not outright conflict, with the evidence of Roman economic and military might throughout the land. The NT story of Jesus, a first-century Palestinian Jew, unfolds against the backdrop of these socio-religious and political dynamics.

The Roman occupation of Palestine began decades before Jesus's birth, when the Roman general **Pompey** conquered the region for Rome in 63 BCE. Of course, the people of that land were well-acquainted with life under foreign rule. In some ways, it was the only constant in their long and storied past. Even before the Babylonian exile, the Assyrians had seized the northern territory known as Samaria. After the Babylonians came and went, the population continued to live as subjugated people. (See Figure 3.6.)

On the one hand, some foreign rulers took a tolerant approach toward native inhabitants. The **Persians**, for instance, liberated the Judeans from captivity in Babylon and even helped to finance the rebuilding of the Jerusalem temple the Babylonians had burned to the ground. On the other hand, the Syrian ruler **Antiochus IV Epiphanes** ruled with a heavy hand. Under his aegis, policies put in place aimed to erase Jewish identity and culture at every turn, especially through strict measures intended to prevent Torah observance.

FIGURE 3.6: A REPEATEDLY OCCUPIED LAND

With only a handful of exceptions, the land of Palestine has been occupied by foreign powers for most of the last three millennia. The list of empires that have come and gone is extensive: Neo-Assyrians, Babylonians, Persians, Macedonians, Ptolemies, Seleucids, Romans, Byzantines, Umayyads, Abbasids, Crusaders, Turks, Ottomans, and British. Today, native Palestinians even see Israel as an occupying power. Not all of these conquering empires have been equally harsh on the people living in the land. Still, post-colonial critics have shown that imperial governments often rule by using the conquered people and their land to the empires' advantage. Often they have deployed strategies that constrain the people's mobility, economic opportunity, and access to natural resources. They also sometimes impose laws or other social mechanisms designed to erase a people's culture, language, and identity. All of these forces were in play during the Roman occupation of Palestine in the first century CE.

YOUR TURN: Learn a bit about colonialism, either in the Middle East or elsewhere. How do military occupations or foreign rule affect life on the ground for the people of colonized territories?

Not surprisingly, those who saw themselves as part of God's covenant people negotiated life under foreign rule in different ways. Some took a pragmatic approach that prioritized self-preservation. Others were more ideological and fomented outright revolt. The first-century Jewish historian **Josephus** describes four first-century groups, or "parties," of Palestinian Jews who represent, in broad terms, these different responses to Roman rule. All of these groups show up, at least implicitly, in the NT landscape.

The **Sadducees** came from Jerusalem's privileged elite and were closely associated with the temple establishment. Of the four groups, they accommodated the Roman occupation with greatest ease. The Sadducees were also the most conservative group in several respects. For one thing, they upheld the authority of Jewish law (Torah)—especially its mandates for sacrifice—but rejected later interpretations by the rabbis, whom they deemed too progressive. They followed a strict interpretation of scripture that left no room for new-fangled ideas such as resurrection or the afterlife or a coming judgment that had crept into popular Judaism. In short, the Sadducees prioritized peace with Rome and drew a traditional line in the sand.

Josephus calls a second group known as the **Pharisees** the "party of the people." Of the four groups, the Pharisees enjoyed the widest popular support. They also appear most frequently in the NT Gospels, perhaps because so much of Jesus's story takes place in the countryside (Galilee) rather than the urban center (Jerusalem). After all, the Pharisees (also known as the "rabbis") worked mostly at the grassroots level to help regular people remain faithful amid the contingencies of daily life.

What did the Pharisees care most about? They tried to make Jewish practice more viable by interpreting Torah in light of changing circumstance. They haggled with each other over questions about what constituted "work" on the Sabbath. They also had a lot to say about what it meant for regular people, not just the priestly elite, to live in a state of religious purity. For them, purity only sometimes concerned moral conduct. More often, it had to do with preserving life's sacredness from contamination by things like bodily fluids. To be "unclean" didn't mean you were bad or evil in any way, but it did entail a separation from the community. In most cases, though, the Pharisees made ritual cleansing broadly available to people.

If the Sadducees merged religious and political interests, the Pharisees separated the two realms. For them, scrupulous personal piety served as antidote to a less-than-ideal political context. Some Pharisees took comfort in the notion that God's justice would soon prevail on earth and that the day of the Lord would bring resurrection to the faithful. In the meantime, they modeled dynamic conversations about what it means to obey Torah in daily life.

In different ways, both Sadducees and Pharisees accepted the Roman occupation of Palestine, at least in the short run. But two other groups actively resisted it. The **Essenes**, Josephus tells us, took a more sectarian stance. They withdrew from mainstream society to ensure that their communities lived uncorrupted by the religious and political powers they associated with the forces of evil. (Scholars broadly associate the Essenes, with the community that lived at Qumran by the Dead Sea.) These tight-knit collectives often operated within strict parameters of conduct as they awaited the coming "day of the Lord." Their resistance came in the form of an alternative social order that, they thought, reflected God's rule, not Rome's—or Jerusalem's, for that matter. (See Figure 3.7.)

Josephus calls a fourth group, quite fittingly, the **Fourth Philosophy** (or **Zealots**). These were the insurgents who kept inciting active, armed resistance to the Roman occupation. Like the Essenes, they thought God's kingdom would soon arrive on earth. But rather than waiting in a state of purity for God's angelic forces to start a holy war, the Zealots thought they were God's agents on earth. Josephus mentions several of their uprisings, and the NT book of Acts names two leaders, **Theudas** and **Judas the Galilean** (Acts 5:36-37). Sometimes, these figures were called "messiahs" ("anointed ones") because some thought God had "anointed" them to bring about regime change. Historians think Jesus was executed by the Romans because they viewed him in this light, as a credible threat to the occupying army (see Mark 14:48).

FIGURE 3.7: SECTARIANS IN OUR WORLD

What comes to mind when you hear the word *sect*? It's a term that designates a wide range of groups that share a common feature with the first-century Essenes and with one another: they separate themselves from dominant culture, either physically or in their conduct. Some sects embody a deliberately peaceful, communitarian vision. The Amish come to mind in this regard. After a gunman shot ten students in Lancaster County, Pennsylvania, the community response of forgiveness shocked much of the nation. One member explained it this way: forgiveness "is so ingrained in our heritage that it's part of our character."

The Branch Davidian community that went up in flames in Waco, Texas, represents another modern-day version of sectarianism. Its leader, David Koresh, was convinced that a showdown with government officials was the beginning of the end of the world. The stockpile of weapons on the compound led to its destruction.

YOUR TURN: What's the relationship between religion and culture for sectarian communities? What do they most value? Why?

The Zealots learned about Roman power the hard way, and with dire consequences for the wider Jewish population. In the century after Jesus's death, two revolts altered the landscape of Palestinian Judaism and so shaped the emerging Christian movement and the NT itself. First came the **Jewish War**, which began in 66 CE, when Zealots took over the temple precinct from Jewish leaders. The insurgency they inspired elicited a heavy-handed response from the occupying power: in April of 70 CE, during the Passover festival, the Roman army leveled the Jerusalem temple, effectively dismantling the sacrificial system based there. A second uprising led by a figure known as **Bar Kochba** spanned 132–35 CE. Roman officials had had enough. This time, they deported a large number of Jews from the land and so diluted the Jewish presence in Palestine.

The early Christian movement and its literary footprint in the NT emerged alongside a Judaism that was reinventing itself by necessity. With the temple's destruction, religious authority shifted away from the Sadducees and toward the Pharisees. The rabbis' adaptable, even conversational, approach to Jewish tradition provided the conceptual flexibility required once the physical center lay in rubble. To this day, Judaism as rabbinical Judaism has proven resilient across place, time, and host culture.

At the same time, the forced migration of Jews made Judaism an increasingly diasporic religion—that is, a tradition observed by people scattered throughout civilization, rather than concentrated in one place. Though Jerusalem remained a place of mythic, deeply spiritual importance, Jews throughout the Mediterranean and beyond no longer looked to Jerusalem as home in any physical sense. Only in the last century has the Jewish spiritual identity merged again so closely with a geographic location.

Review and Reflect

- What are the four main groups in Palestinian Judaism? Describe their defining traits.

- Consider the different responses to the foreign rule of "God's people." Which one seems most effective to you? Most appealing? Most problematic? Why?

DIASPORA JUDAISM

Even before the Bar Kochba revolt, Jews lived in communities throughout the ancient world, from the Mediterranean rim to East Africa to the Far East. They had migrated at different times and for different reasons, but they worshipped YHWH and followed Torah while living far from Palestine. In fact, most of the NT was originally written for early Christian communities whose members had come partly from the Jewish diaspora.

Why is this the case? According to Acts, those who told people about a crucified and raised Jewish Messiah first shared this "good news," understandably, at Jewish synagogues. The strategy was a pragmatic one. After all, Jews were well-acquainted with prophetic hopes for God's coming kingdom, and even with the possibility of resurrection in bodily form. True, the so-called messiah's death on a Roman cross constituted a "stumbling block" (see 1 Cor 1:23) to most mainstream Jews, but at least some found the stories about Jesus compelling and convincing.

Diaspora Judaism is an important part of the NT's backdrop for other reasons as well. Jews throughout the Greco-Roman world modeled a dynamic engagement with wider culture that Christians imitated early on. In fact, we'll see that the Apostle Paul's own conversation patterns mimic those from the diaspora Judaism to which he belonged. Like his Jewish peers, Paul explains distinct elements of his message in terms that are familiar to contemporary culture.

Diaspora Jews held strictly to their singular devotion to YHWH as their Lord and God. Often, civic leaders exempted Jews from requirements associated with state-sanctioned religion, such as the worship of the emperor as god.

And just as the Babylonian exile strengthened Jewish identity through such practices as circumcision, dietary laws, and the Sabbath, first-century diaspora Jews maintained these "boundary markers" to promote both group solidarity and individual identity within non-Jewish culture.

At the same time, writers such as **Philo of Alexandria** freely integrate Hellenistic thought into Jewish beliefs. For instance, Philo equates the Stoic notion of *logos* (see below) with Jewish law. Other Jewish writers link Torah to wisdom traditions from Egypt and other cultures, while apocalyptic writers incorporate dualistic views of both Manichaeism and Greek philosophy in their assessment of the current battle between good and evil forces. Finally Platonic distinctions between flesh and soul appear in Jewish writings that weigh the possibility of life after death—a concept almost entirely absent from the Jewish scriptural canon.

> ### Review and Reflect
>
> - Describe key challenges diaspora Jews faced in relation to their wider host culture.
>
> - In what ways does the dominant culture in which we live shape us?

THE GRECO-ROMAN WORLD

Like their Jewish counterparts, NT writers converse with the wider Greco-Roman world by both adopting and reframing the terms, concepts, and values of popular culture. But what is the "Greco-Roman" world? What did its religious landscape look like? And how do the main features of this ancient setting connect with our study of the NT?

Scholars use the phrase *Greco-Roman world* to signal first-century Mediterranean culture's hybrid nature. It combines the **Greek** (or **Hellenistic**) cultural influences with the sociopolitical landscape of the **Roman Empire**. Together, these forces shaped daily life for those living in the region's urban centers, where Christianity first took root.

Hellenization as Cultural Template

Scholars trace the impact of Hellenism to a Macedonian ruler named **Alexander the Great**. Despite a relatively short career (336–323 BCE), Alexander's impressive territorial gains (see Figure 3.8) brought an ambitious

FIGURE 3.8: ALEXANDER'S CONQUERED LANDS

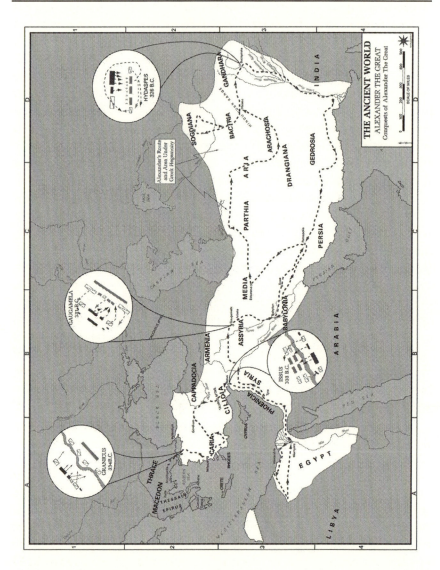

(and successful) cultural agenda as well. In other words, he captured not just land and people but also the hearts and minds of conquered societies. Alexander wasn't Greek himself, but tradition says he slept with a copy of Homer's classic, *The Iliad*, under his pillow—as if by osmosis he'd absorb Achilles's valiance. (I don't recommend this strategy for exam preparation, by the way.) Later, the Greek philosopher **Aristotle** was Alexander's personal tutor.

Clearly, this Macedonian was enamored with all things Greek. As a result, his Hellenizing impulse touched most aspects of urban life: he instituted Greek as the common tongue for all territories; he built gymnasiums, theaters, and public baths to shape shared civic spaces; and he endorsed religious devotion to the Greek gods found in Vergil and Homer.

This process of **Hellenization** lived on after Alexander died. Though the geographic reach of Macedonian power was short-lived, the lasting impact of his cultural influence is hard to overstate. The adoption of a shared language led scholars to translate Jewish scriptures into Greek. This translation, known as the **Septuagint** (**LXX**), was the Bible for most of the first-century CE diaspora Jewish population we discussed above. Alexander's also responsible for the fact that the NT itself was originally written in Greek.

Beyond language, Alexander's legacy made Greek academic disciplines the core curriculum for the ancient world. If you learned the Pythagorean theorem in geometry class, you can thank (or blame) Alexander. Greek philosophy gained a currency that lived on as well. As we'll see below, people living in the Roman Empire often embraced the worldviews and values promoted by Plato, Aristotle, the Stoics, and the Epicureans, to name a few. Finally, public works projects established the Greek *polis* (city-state) as a model for urban centers.

In many ways, the Roman Empire used Alexander's accomplishments as a scaffolding or template of its own. Rather than introducing a novel set of gods or values or institutions, the Romans often repurposed these elements of Hellenistic culture. For instance, the Greek god Zeus was renamed as Jupiter, but with little change in character or role. Let's turn attention now to the distinctive influences that the Roman Empire brought to bear on the NT world.

The Roman Pluralism Project

Roman mythology traced the empire's origins to the story of **Romulus and Remus**, twins who descended from both Latin and Greek heritage (and so were "Greco-Roman" themselves). As a republic, Rome expanded its political footprint outward from the Italian peninsula during the last three centuries before the Common Era. Over that time, the Roman Senate was marked by political intrigue that culminated with the assassination of Julius Caesar in 44 BCE. Just over a decade later (in 27 BCE), his grandson Gaius Octavius took the title **Caesar Augustus** in a power grab that imposed political stability from on high. Over time, the empire continued to rule a large portion of the Mediterranean region, building roads and aqueducts that tourists can still see today.

To keep conquered nations in check, imperial officials struck a balance between "hard power" and "soft power." The "hard power" came in the form of military occupation, as well as economic control through taxation. "Soft power" leveraged the influence of local leaders to lure conquered peoples to acquiesce to rather than resist Roman rule. These allies profited from their support for Rome, to be sure, but their complicity with the empire also protected local populations from Roman reprisal, which often came through violence. As part of this awkward dance, Rome struck a pluralistic stance toward the variety of religions and worldviews embraced by those in its colonies. In this way, Rome gave just enough latitude and autonomy to keep them mostly in check.

What did that pluralistic approach entail? Think of the Roman Empire as something of a "cafeteria plan," when it came to different responses to questions about the nature and meaning of human life. If you've been on a college campus, chances are you've walked into a dining hall full of options. In many cases, you don't even have to choose: you can have pizza, French fries, some salad, a cookie, and ice cream all on the same swipe. In the same way, people in the first-century Mediterranean world didn't have to select one and only one religion or philosophy. They could subscribe to Stoic principles for daily living, pray to the god Asclepius for healing when sick, and offer sacrifices to local deities to ensure a vibrant economy.

Members of the early Christian movement stood out from this approach. Like their Jewish counterparts, they pledged their allegiance to one and only one God. Yet our exploration of the NT in its context will expose the ways they borrowed from their neighbors when it came to specific religious practices and morals. As a foundation for that study, let's acquaint ourselves with the range of voices involved in the Roman pluralism project.

Religious Devotion

In every place and time people look to the sacred to find meaning in— and sometimes alter—their daily lives. When a loved one is sick, a crop fails, or natural disaster strikes, humans often try to explain or fix conditions by supernatural means. Even in our contemporary world where science and reason have called religion into question, times of trial sometimes find thoroughly secular people lighting candles and murmuring heart-felt prayers.

This impulse operated freeform in the ancient world, where people often thought of gods as capricious forces at work for both good and ill. As a result, ancient religious devotion had a lot to do with offering sacrifices, prayers, and other practices that would win the favor of divine power in desperate circumstances. This devotion was personal and social, individual and communal, local and global.

FIGURE 3.9: HINDU HOUSEHOLD WORSHIP ("PUJA")

Hinduism affirms that the one god takes almost endless forms. Most Hindu households have a shrine to one form (*murti*) of god and conduct daily worship there. Pictured is a home shrine devoted to three "forms" of god: Rama, Sita, and Lakshmi, displayed during a spring Hindu festival that celebrates the birthday of Rama.

Households in the Greco-Roman world generally had their own array of gods to whom they paid tribute. Through prayer and sacrifice, family members petitioned household gods to ensure the family's physical and fiscal well-being. Sometimes known as *daimonia,* these gods weren't associated with evil, as the term might suggest. Rather, they oversaw specific aspects of human life, from food supply to health care. (See Figure 3.9.)

Communities, too, shared devotion to civic gods charged with protection of a village from disease, natural disaster, or other hardship. Of course, such suffering was commonplace in the ancient world; just because a village honored a guardian god didn't mean they wouldn't experience a plague or flood. But such tragedy only intensified religious devotion, on the assumption that prayer and sacrifice could win back the gods' favor and reverse societal misfortune.

As the Roman republic became an empire, officials increasingly enforced a form of religious devotion to the human emperor as a god, or at least as the gods' chosen representative. Inscriptions from the ancient world call Caesar the "savior of the world," and state-sanctioned religion soon became an institutionalized way of declaring one's allegiance to "god and country." In other words, what we might call "patriotism" and religion became indistinguishable from each other.

Besides the emperor, other figures appeared to be human agents of divine power. Some earned reputations as miracle workers. Philostratus, for instance, records the life of **Apollonius of Tyana** in terms that share much in common with Jesus's story. Born to a mother who'd been visited by an angel, Apollonius showed wisdom even as a young child. In adulthood, this "Son of God" excelled as a wise teacher, gathered disciples, and performed miracles. He was executed by Roman officials, and some followers told others they'd seen him afterward, in bodily form. Besides Apollonius, other figures such as **Asclepius** and **Dionysus** bore evidence of a divine-human union as they mediated the gods' healing powers on earth.

These kinds of divine emissaries sometimes inspired devoted groups of people to form what scholars call **mystery religions**. By definition, these groups remain just that: mostly a mystery. That's because they observed secret rituals they weren't allowed to share publicly. (If you're in a fraternity or sorority, you may be familiar with similar prohibitions against sharing handshakes or initiation rites.) One ancient novel, *The Golden Ass*, describes an initiation rite into the cult of the goddess **Isis** that features the motif of death and resurrection. (See Figure 3.10.) Early Christian gatherings were often seen as another mystery religion, though they didn't prescribe secrecy.

It's important to remember that the religious options we've discussed were not mutually exclusive. Someone initiated into a mystery religion probably had a shrine to the god of the pantry in her home. Those who worshipped the local gods also paid homage to the emperor as divine son. The pluralism of the ancient world freely mingled religious traditions as a way of negotiating life in the Roman Empire.

Philosophical Worldview

Besides religious options, the Greco-Roman world offered many philosophies—thanks again to Alexander's Hellenizing strategy—that brought meaning and purpose to personal and sociopolitical life. NT writers often mention philosophical concepts and ethical systems in their effort to translate the significance of a Jewish Messiah for the wider world. Let's consider some of the most popular and influential of these ancient philosophies.

Greek philosophy traces its roots to **Socrates**, a prominent public intellectual from fifth-century BCE Athens. Socrates made a career of wandering in the *agora* (marketplace) asking pointed questions that college curriculums today associate with critical thinking: On what basis do you stake your claims

FIGURE 3.10: SECRET INITIATION IN *THE GOLDEN ASS*

In his *Metamorphoses* (also called *The Golden Ass*), the second century CE Roman writer Lucius Apuleius narrates an initiation into the cult of the goddess Isis, and in some detail. But he stops short of divulging its mysterious rites, acknowledging that their secrecy is inherent to the initiation itself:

> And now, diligent reader, you are no doubt keen to know what was said next, and what was done. I'd tell you, if to tell you, were allowed; if you were allowed to hear then you might know, but ears and tongue would sin equally, the latter for its profane indiscretion, the former for their unbridled curiosity. Oh, I shall speak, since your desire to hear may be a matter of deep religious longing, and I would not torment you with further anguish, but I shall speak only of what can be revealed to the minds of the uninitiated without need for subsequent atonement, things which though you have heard them, you may well not understand. So listen, and believe in what is true. I reached the very gates of death and, treading Proserpine's threshold, yet passed through all the elements and returned. I have seen the sun at midnight shining brightly. I have entered the presence of the gods below and the presence of the gods above, and I have paid due reverence before them. (Apuleius, *The Golden Ass*, A. S. Kline, trans. 11:23. https://www.poetryintranslation.com/PITBR/Latin/TheGoldenAssXI.php#anchor_Toc353982295)

YOUR TURN: Based on what Apuleius does say in *Metamorphoses*, what do you learn about this mystery religion? What would you still like to know? Why?

to truth? Have you thought about what you haven't thought about? What's the relationship between the way we think and the way we live? Socrates challenged many settled assumptions associated with tradition and reportedly said, "The unexamined life is not worth living." His student **Plato** recounted these conversations in his *Dialogues*, in which Socrates distinguishes himself as a true "agnostic" because he admits what he *doesn't* know. For Socrates, wisdom lies in recognizing the limits of our knowledge, for instance, on the question of what happens after we die. Many saw Socrates's strategy of asking questions, rather than regurgitating others' views, as provocative and even dangerous. Like Jesus centuries later, he was executed as an enemy of the state, even though he posed no direct threat to the political order.

After his death, Socrates's legacy left an important foundation for other "lovers of wisdom" (from *philo* = love + *sophia* = wisdom) to explore questions about truth, beauty, and meaning in ways that went beyond conventional approaches of whimsy and fatalism. In the **Allegory of the Cave**, for instance,

FIGURE 3.11: EFFORT AND EASE IN HATHA YOGA

In American culture, **yoga** has become a popular means of strength training and stretching. But many who practice yoga have little understanding of its ties to **Hindu** thought. Like the Stoics, the Hindu tradition of **Hatha Yoga** promotes alignment with a metaphysical force. In yogic practice, that alignment is both physical and spiritual. Patanjali's *Yoga Sutra* puts it this way: "By lessening the natural tendency for restlessness and by meditating on the infinite, posture is mastered" (*The Yoga Sutras of Patanjali*, trans. Sri Swami Satchidananda [Yogaville, VA: Integral Yoga Publications, 2005], 2.47). Hatha yoga thus combines effort and ease, using the breath as a tool for settling into bodily postures and for accessing the life force that animates us.

YOUR TURN: Learn a bit more about yoga's Hindu roots. How does yoga link the physical to metaphysical alignment?

Plato uses metaphorical language to convey the view that the sensory human experience is a mere shadow of the reality that is comprised of eternal forms beyond the physical world. Plato's body-soul dualism hovers over the ancient world—and emerging Christianity—for centuries. Plato's student **Aristotle** (384–322 BCE), in turn, emphasized perception as the channel to understanding. Aristotle advocated the use of deductive reasoning, and his robust ethical teachings nudged people beyond self-interest in ways that have reverberated down through Western culture.

Soon after Aristotle's death, a movement called **Stoicism** emerged based on the teachings of **Zeno** (336–263 BCE). This school of thought was wildly popular in the first-century Mediterranean world and shows up across the NT writings, from John's Gospel to the letters of Paul. You may have heard the term *stoic* describe someone who faces life's vicissitudes calmly and with little emotion. Stoicism itself cultivates personal discipline and self-control as habits that help people tap into the divine spark within each human. In Stoicism, the *logos* is the force that gives coherence and meaning to the universe. The goal of a Stoic way of life is to live out of that divine center, rather than to be tossed by the whims of human circumstance. (See Figure 3.11.)

Epicureanism offers a dramatically different response to life's vagaries. Named after **Epicurus** (342–270 BCE), this philosophy is more down to earth in some respects. Since the material world is perishable by nature, Epicurus taught, it's better to indulge physical desires along the way. (Many college students are modern-day Epicureans!) At the other end of the spectrum, the philosophy known as **Cynicism** deems the material world as ultimately unsatisfying. Rather than indulging themselves, its adherents, Cynics, voluntarily gave up their resources and livelihood and lived in dependence on the magnanimity of others. In Jesus's day, this meant a subtly subversive resistance to Roman society, where opulent wealth served as a barometer of how well people were doing. Scholars detect Cynic influence, for instance, in Gospel stories about some elements of Jesus's own ministry (see e.g., Mark 6:7-13).

This sampling from the Greco-Roman "cafeteria plan" introduces some of the more popular philosophical options in the first-century Mediterranean world. Of course, most people weren't professional philosophers. Instead, they picked up pieces of Stoic or Platonic thought because it was in the air. Remember, too, that religious devotion and philosophical worldviews often went hand in hand. One Stoic named **Cleanthes** penned the "Hymn to Zeus" that provides a theological basis for the human-divine kinship that lay at the heart of Stoicism. (See Figure 3.12.)

FIGURE 3.12: HYMN TO ZEUS

Here is a portion of the Stoic poet Cleanthes's "Hymn to Zeus":

> Most glorious of immortals, Zeus
> The many named, almighty evermore,
> Nature's great Sovereign, ruling all by law
> Hail to thee! On thee 'tis meet and right
>
> That mortals everywhere should call.
> From thee was our begetting; ours alone
> Of all that live and move upon the earth
> The lot to bear God's likeness.
> Thee will I ever chant, thy power praise!
>
> For thee this whole vast cosmos, wheeling round
> The earth, obeys, and where thou leadest
> It follows, ruled willingly by thee.
> But, Zeus, thou giver of every gift,
> Who dwellest within the dark clouds, wielding still
> The flashing stroke of lightning, save, we pray,
> Thy children from this boundless misery.

("Hymn to Zeus," in *Hellenistic Religions*, trans. Frederick C. Grant [New York: 1953], 152–54)

YOUR TURN: What kinds of claims does this poet make about Zeus? Can you connect them to claims people make about God or other gods?

SUMMARY

We know by now that the NT didn't appear in a vacuum. Nor were its contents originally addressed to twenty-first-century American Christians— or non-Christians, for that matter. In this chapter, we've explored the wider religious and political landscape in which the Gospels, letters, and other texts took shape. Their resolute focus on a Palestinian Jewish Messiah named Jesus emerges in dynamic conversation with both Judaism (Second Temple and rabbinical) and the Greco-Roman world. As they address communities embedded in a decidedly non-Christian culture, the NT writings explain Jesus's significance by engaging popular religious and cultural views. By knowing a bit about the "pop culture" of the ancient world, we're better equipped to grasp their distinctive claims.

Review and Reflect

- Explain the term *Greco-Roman world.* Name and explain three religious and three philosophical traditions that were popular in first-century Mediterranean society.

- Reflect on the "hybrid" or "both/and" approach to religious and philosophical worldviews. Where do you see people today combining religious and political devotion or religious and philosophical worldviews?

GO DEEPER

Boring, M. Eugene, Klaus Berger, and Carsten Colpe. *Hellenistic Commentary to the New Testament.* Nashville: Abingdon Press, 1995.

Cohen, Shaye J. D. *From the Maccabees to the Mishnah.* 2nd ed. Louisville, KY: Westminster John Knox, 2006.

Magness, Jodi. *Stone and Dung, Oil and Spit: Jewish Daily Life in the Time of Jesus.* Grand Rapids, MI: Eerdmans, 2011.

Meyer, Marvin, ed. *The Ancient Mysteries: A Sourcebook of Sacred Texts.* Philadelphia: University of Pennsylvania Press, 1999.

Rives, James. *Religion in the Roman Empire.* Maldon, MA: Blackwell, 2007.

Chapter Four

What Are the Gospels?
Truthful Stories

CONVERSATION STARTERS

- What features of the Gospels help us take them on their own terms?

- How does "truth telling" in the ancient world differ from "truth telling" today?

- What are the Synoptic Gospels, and why do scholars study their literary relationship?

- What is the main hypothesis used to solve the Synoptic Problem?

- What are the other possible solutions to the Synoptic Problem?

- How does source criticism help us study the Synoptic Gospels? What about John?

If you want to record an important event today, all you have to do is whip out your phone and snap a few pictures or a video. If you hear someone say something memorable, you might Tweet it right then and there. We live in a world where we usually have at our fingertips all we need to capture any moment that stands out as fun, poignant, or otherwise memorable.

It's easy to look to the Gospels for a similar, MyStory-like account of Jesus's life, death, and resurrection. After all, we know there were eyewitnesses to most parts of his very public career. It's natural to assume that both his close friends and the crowds that followed him around were taking notes;

if not literally, at least they were paying close attention to him. It's not surprising that many read the Gospels as straightforward, real-time accounts of Jesus's first-century story.

But the truth is that even the Gospels don't claim to tell stories that are factually accurate, in scientific or historical terms. They don't reveal their authors (the titles were added many decades later), and they don't claim to be divinely inspired. What is more, the four NT Gospels regularly disagree on matters great and small: they name different days for Jesus's death, different disciples, and different women who appear at the empty tomb, for instance.

If they're unconcerned with accuracy or with their own authority, the Gospels *are* concerned with questions of truth at a deeper level. Each story relates episodes from Jesus's earthly mission that cast him in a particular light, as the Jewish Messiah who's come to reveal the ways of God's reign on earth. They're interested in questions such as these: What do his words and actions tell us about God and God's power? If Jesus was God's special agent of that power, why did he die on a Roman cross? And what does it mean to follow him in changing times? These questions probe beneath the stories' details to examine their meaning.

They're also the kind of questions that leave room for more than one answer. In fact, we have already seen that the process of canonization used more of a "both-and" than an "either-or" framework. That's because the early church valued truth more than fact. As we've noted, the inclusion of four Gospels, not one, makes the NT conversation inherently pluralistic. As a canon, the NT assumes the value of different, and sometimes competing, accounts of Jesus's life, death, and resurrection.

This chapter will equip us to enter into this lively conversation. As a first step, we'll consider the Gospels as a particular kind of ancient literature. We'll also explore how these stories would have been heard by their first audiences, located in the first-century Mediterranean world. Next, we'll trace how the four Gospels' similarities and differences help explain their literary relationship to one another. Finally, we'll explain our approach in the following chapters, as we consider each Gospel's distinctive message for its own place and time.

ORAL TRADITIONS: PASS IT ALONG

If the Gospels aren't factually accurate accounts of Jesus's career, what are they? Several observations will help us take the Gospels on their own terms. The first is this: *the Gospels were written decades after Jesus died.* Why is this such an important detail to ponder? Think back to your favorite childhood memory. Where were you? Who else was there? What happened? Who said what to whom? If you had to write your version of the story, you'd likely use some creative license to fill in the details you simply don't remember. When our family sits around a table and recalls a shared memory, we won't agree on all the details. We might merge two or more visits to Grandma's house into one or disagree about what car Dad was driving when he wrecked.

Simply put, those stories that we recall can mean different things to different people, and that meaning—that truth—is sometimes loosely tied to the facts surrounding those stories. Even in a world where factual accuracy can be confirmed in a flash, we tend toward stories that confirm truth claims that make sense to us, and we often arrange "facts" around them.

In this sense, we're not so far from the world in which the Gospels were written. Their writers ("evangelists") relied on **oral traditions**, or stories that were told, and reshaped, over the decades since Jesus's career. How does this affect how we read the Gospels? Anthropologists offer helpful insights about the nature and function of oral traditions. They tell us that stories survive by oral transmission when people think they preserve a lesson, worldview, or episode that adds to life's meaning in the present moment. They also tell us that, as stories pass from one group to another, their basic contours remain the same, while their details shift freely. In many cultures, storytelling provides an organic way to adapt a tradition's meaning to the context in which it's told. (See Figure 4.1.)

To understand the Gospels' background in oral tradition begins to make sense of their similarities and differences. Sure, these stories preserve *some* reliable facts about Jesus's life, death, and resurrection. They may even be based on eyewitness accounts. But the Gospels are also full of conflicting details. Those differences come partly from the fluid nature of oral tradition, but they also have to do with the truth claims each evangelist wants to stress.

BIASED ACCOUNTS: ON A MISSION

That leads to a second observation that will help us take the Gospels on their own terms: *the Gospels are biased accounts of Jesus's story, intended to promote his legacy and agenda in the post-resurrection age.* In our world, voices across the political spectrum encourage us to consider the bias that's implicit in stories told as "news." That bias grows out of the writer's (and news organization's) values and priorities. Fox News generally treats Republican leaders more gently than Democratic leaders, while the reverse is the case with MSNBC. Postmodern theory has, in many ways, led us to a "post-fact" world, in which we're more likely to cite (or create) "facts" that fit our chosen truth.

Of course, bias isn't necessarily a bad thing. What parent doesn't think her newborn is the most beautiful baby ever? I'm a UNC basketball fan, which colors my view of both Duke (even though I went there as well) and,

FIGURE 4.1: ORAL TRADITION IN PERU

One anthropologist who has spent time in the Peruvian town of Huilloc reports that oral tradition is valued even more highly than written accounts among community members when it comes to preserving their foundational stories. He reports:

> The Quechua town where I lived in Peru isn't an outright nonliterate population, but most of the women and the older men were nonliterate. . . . Among the nonliterate community members, oral tradition is . . . very important for learning about the town history, community values, belief systems, etc. When I was conducting my project on myths, almost every participant told me to talk to the *viejitos* (old men) because they were the ones with arsenals of sacred narratives to share. Telling stories in the native language was very important, as the Quechua language is associated with the Quechua ethnic identity is associated with community history. Many shared myths in Spanish for my sake, but they made a point to express the importance of speaking Quechua to preserve community tradition and identity. (From author's correspondence with anthropologist Ben Bridges. Used with permission.)

YOUR TURN: What's the difference between oral and written stories? Why might some communities value oral tradition more highly than written accounts?

at times, the officials. Bias only becomes a problem when we don't see its influence on our perspectives, our actions, and our world. Recognizing the bias in play in our own lives and world helps us understand the partisan nature of the Gospels as well. That doesn't make them less valuable or meaningful. Instead, it equips us to take them on their own terms, as narratives crafted for audiences trying to live out their loyalty to Jesus and his mission. Each Gospel draws selectively from both oral tradition and earlier written accounts, cherry-picking sayings, deeds, and attributes that portray Jesus in a certain light. But they do so from a deeply sympathetic perspective. Their aim is not to present all the evidence for and against the case for Jesus as Jewish Messiah. Each evangelist writes, instead, as a committed insider who interprets Jesus's story for those who've already aligned themselves with his messianic mission.

WORDS ON TARGET: CONTEXTUAL RELEVANCE

This leads to a third observation about the Gospels: *most scholars agree that the evangelists crafted Jesus's story as contextually relevant messages for particular communities living in particular places and times.* Mark's Gospel emphasizes following in Jesus's way of the cross and calls for endurance because it probably addresses a persecuted community. Matthew depicts Jesus's faithful interpretation of Torah for an audience of mostly Jewish believers. Luke writes for a more cosmopolitan setting and, many think, subtly challenges the Roman Empire's socioeconomic and militaristic values. John reframes Jesus's mission in personal and spiritual terms that provide clear boundary lines for a community increasingly set apart from the Judaism to which it once belonged.

These summaries offer just a snapshot of how the Gospels pitch Jesus's story to believers living in a place and time far removed from ours. By shifting the questions we're asking away from factual accuracy and toward truth claims, we'll explore these four different accounts as distinctive reports that share some common features along the way. In doing so, we'll listen in to each voice on its own terms, as well as the animated conversation that together they create.

WHAT THE ANCIENTS SAY

Students are sometimes surprised to learn what ancient writers have to say about their own craft. The three examples that follow offer insights about ancient authors' views about writing history, biography, and Gospel. Notice how transparently and honestly they treat questions of accuracy, bias, and context.

Thucydides: On Writing History

Several centuries before Jesus lived, the Greek historian **Thucydides** (460–395 BCE) chronicled events related to the Peloponnesian War. As an official historian, he took his task seriously. Thucydides explains his use of oral tradition this way:

> With reference to the speeches in this history . . . [it was] difficult to carry them word for word in one's memory, so my habit has been to make the speakers say what was in my opinion ***demanded of them by the various occasions***, . . . adhering as ***closely as possible to the general sense*** of what they really said. And with reference to the narrative of events . . . my conclusions have cost me some labor from the ***lack of coincidence between accounts*** of the same occurrences by different eye-witnesses, arising sometimes from ***imperfect memory***, sometimes from ***undue partiality*** for one side or the other. (Thucydides, *History of the Peloponnesian War*, vol. 1, trans. C. F. Smith [Cambridge: Harvard University Press, 1920], Loeb Classical Library, 1:22, emphasis added)

FIGURE 4.2: EYEWITNESS TESTIMONY

Eyewitness testimony has long been trusted as reliable evidence in our justice system. But with the dawn of new technologies such as DNA testing and body cameras, we are beginning to understand just how subjective, and flawed, firsthand reports can be. Indeed, organizations such as the Innocence Project and the Equal Justice Initiative reexamine convictions—especially of those sentenced to death—in light of new, more reliable evidence. Perhaps surprisingly, about three-quarters of all convictions overturned through DNA and other scientific evidence were originally based on eyewitness accounts. More than a third of those cases relied on more than one eyewitness. Memory, it turns out, can be shaped through all kinds of influences.

YOUR TURN: Have you ever witnessed an accident or other event and reported it differently than another witness? What's the significance of this tendency for our study of the Gospels?

Thucydides doesn't hide the fact that his account isn't completely factual. His words show us the gap between ancient and contemporary history. Part of his history, for instance, includes speeches that have been reconstructed from memory, which he admits can't be trusted in every detail. Who can recall a speech word-for-word on first hearing? But Thucydides makes another important point. His editorial approach both preserves the "general sense" of a speech and selects "what was demanded" by the context, in his own opinion. He thus acknowledges his inaccuracy, his bias, and the importance of context—all while conveying the main speaker's main gist.

On his report of the war's key events, Thucydides writes with similar candor, openly conceding how hard it is to deal with competing reports. He blames their contradictions on two things. The first has to do with the kind of "imperfect memory" that crops up when people mix up details in family stories, on the witness stand, or about national events. (See Figure 4.2.) But Thucydides also acknowledges that stories of even important national events are inherently biased, since people's "undue partiality" shapes their accounts of what happened. He takes these factors into account in his best effort at telling a true story.

Plutarch: On Writing Biography

Another renowned author living closer to the time of the Gospels explains how he composes authorized biographies of famous people. This is how **Plutarch** (45–120 CE) describes his intention and approach to preserving the life stories of world leaders:

It being my purpose to write the lives of Alexander the king, and of Caesar, . . . the multitude of their great actions affords so large a field that I were to blame if I should not by way of apology forewarn my reader that I have chosen rather to ***epitomize the most celebrated parts*** of their story, than to insist at large on every particular circumstance of it. . . . . I must be allowed to give my ***more particular attention*** to the marks and indications of ***the souls of men.*** (Plutarch, *The Life of Alexander the Great,* trans. John Dryden [New York: Random House, 2004], 3, Modern Library, emphasis added)

For starters, Plutarch notes that his is a selective task. After all, the noteworthy figures he portrays have accomplished far too many "famous actions" to include them all. He can't tell the whole truth, so he chooses the most relevant parts.

But how does he prioritize? Even more intriguing is Plutarch's description of how he tells each "life." He chooses stories that "epitomize" the "souls of men" he depicts. That means his biographies are "biased" in two respects. For one thing, he's writing state-sanctioned accounts—some would call it propaganda—intended to elevate the memory of a great leader for posterity. His bias means he accentuates the positive, to say the least. In addition, Plutarch operates through his choice of material to make the case for the story he wants to tell. What's important to note, though, is that he doesn't claim to be unbiased or thorough; he's forthcoming about the purpose of his project, which is to portray his subjects in a certain, positive light.

Papias: On Writing a Gospel

Fortunately for our study, an early church leader weighs in on the process and purpose of Gospel writing. Within decades after the first Gospel was composed, a bishop of Hierapolis named **Papias** (60–130 CE) describes an evangelist's work in these words:

Mark, having become the ***interpreter*** of Peter, wrote down ***accurately***, though not indeed in order, ***whatsoever he remembered*** of the things done or said by Christ. For he neither heard the Lord nor followed him, but afterward, as I said, he followed Peter, who adapted his teaching to the ***needs of his hearers***, but with no intention of giving a connected account of the Lord's discourses, so that Mark committed ***no error*** while he thus wrote some things ***as he remembered them.*** (Eusebius, *Ecclesiastical History*, 3.39.15, in The Nicene and Post-Nicene Fathers, Second Series, ed. Alexander Roberts et al. [Peabody, MA: Hendrickson, 1996], vol. 1)

This excerpt, preserved by a church official centuries later, lays bare Mark's approach to Gospel writing. For one thing, Papias describes Mark as Peter's "interpreter" (or "translator"). Why would Peter need a translator? As we noted in chapter 1, Jesus and his closest companions spoke Aramaic, not koine Greek. Papias offers a helpful reminder that the evangelist's first task is to translate Jesus's story into the common tongue of the wider Greco-Roman world. If you've ever translated from one language to another, you know there's lots of interpretation that happens along the way.

Like Thucydides, Papias openly admits that the Gospel itself contains plenty of factual errors. Not only does Mark leave material out of this account, but also the story's chronology is not to be trusted. Why would a church leader say such things about a document whose content he endorsed? Simply put, he didn't equate *truth* with *fact*. That's how he can insist there's "no error" in the narrative as it appears, despite its inaccuracy!

Perhaps most importantly, Papias exposes the evangelist's *purpose* in writing: to tailor authentic stories to address the contingencies (or "needs") of the audience. In other words, Mark adapts Peter's best recollections (oral tradition) to deliver a "word on target" for his first hearers. That means that, if we're to read the Gospels on their own terms, we must to look for clues that will help us understand the evangelist's audience.

Review and Reflect

- Name and explain the three traits of the Gospels. Connect each one with an excerpt from an ancient writer discussed here.

- Reflect on the task of writing down shared memories. How does your own experience of memory-making relate to what you're learning about the Gospels?

THE GOSPELS: BASELINE OBSERVATIONS

Where do we look for those clues? Scholars begin with careful investigation of the Gospels themselves. Rather than glossing over the differences among them, we'll take great care to notice where the stories agree with one another, where and how they diverge from one another, and where they intersect in more complex ways. Several broad observations frame our investigation of the similarities and differences among the Gospels:

- **A Common Plotline**: The four Gospels share a "big picture" story. They all recount the life, death, and resurrection of a man named

Jesus, whom they all call the Christ. In all four Gospels, Jesus earns a reputation as teacher ("rabbi") and healer, and he attracts quite a following—both a close-knit "band of brothers" (the disciples) and large crowds as well. In all four Gospels, Jesus dies at the hands of the Roman occupying army during the Passover celebration in Jerusalem. And in all four Gospels, women who hope to prepare his dead body for burial find it missing from the tomb where it had been placed when he died.

- **"One of These Things Is Not Like the Others"**: Of the four Gospels, John differs most dramatically from the other three. This account is an outlier in several respects. For instance, Jesus's career lasts not one but three years, and he travels to and from Jerusalem several times along the way. The content of his message shifts radically as well: Jesus has little to say in John about the "kingdom of God"— his favorite topic in the other three Gospels—and he has much, much more to say about himself. (The phrase "I am" appears about forty times in this Gospel.) In John, Jesus dies not on Passover (as in the other three Gospels) but on the day of preparation that precedes it.

- **The Shortest Gospel**: Though the first three Gospels tell a similar story, Mark is much shorter and lacks many key passages and teachings. Mark doesn't mention Jesus's birth, includes only a handful of teachings and parables, and, in its earliest form, ends abruptly, lacking any instances of post-resurrection encounters.

- **The Sayings Overlap**: Matthew and Luke have the most material in common. Not only do they both include much of Mark's broad narrative outline, but also they fill it in with teachings that overlap. Both tell the story of Jesus's birth to Mary and Joseph. They both include versions of Jesus's Sermon on the Mount, the Lord's Prayer, and other sayings not found in either Mark or John.

- **Going Their Own Way**: Despite these common features, Matthew and Luke often diverge in their details. In Matthew, for instance, an angel visits Joseph, while Luke's story reports two angel visits—one to Elizabeth (Mary's cousin) and one to Mary herself. These two evangelists also present Jesus's genealogy differently: Matthew traces it through Joseph, back to Abraham, while Luke traces it through Mary, back to Adam (the first human being in the biblical story).

Together, these observations suggest that some literary relationship exists among the Gospels—especially among the three **Synoptic** (literally, "seeing together") **Gospels**—that is, Matthew, Mark, and Luke. In other words, they share too much common material to explain as a matter of coincidence, or even as reliance on similar traditions. Scholars think it's highly likely that authors composed Matthew, Mark, and Luke by citing one another as sources. The question is, who used whom?

THE SYNOPTIC PROBLEM: "WHO USED WHOM?"

Over the last two hundred years, scholars have used **source criticism** to analyze the literary relationships among the Gospels, especially the Synoptic Gospels. They're interested in questions such as these: Which Gospel came first? What other sources did the evangelists use? What are we to make of the similarities and differences noted above? These are the questions that lie behind the **Synoptic problem**, a term that explores what sources the synoptic evangelists used when composing their Gospels.

To solve this problem, critics investigate the variables and their relationships, much as you'd tackle a challenging math problem. The approach is also fairly scientific, in that it assesses the evidence and tries to make sense of it through an emerging hypothesis. To see the evidence "under the microscope," scholars use a **Gospel synopsis**, which sets related passages side by side in columns on the page. This makes more visible the precise ways in which the stories converge and diverge. (See Figure 4.3.) Let's walk through the step-by-step discovery that charts source critics' inquiry.

A Literary Relationship: Detecting Plagiarism

First, we need to determine whether or not there's a literary relationship among the Synoptic Gospels. After all, isn't it possible that the overlapping passages only agree by coincidence? If two evangelists are both telling the same story, which they heard from oral tradition, couldn't their agreement simply be happenstance? Of course, anything's possible, but in this case, the patterns of **verbatim agreement** indicate it's highly likely that one evangelist copied another.

In our world, patterns of verbatim agreement are a telltale sign of plagiarism. It's a word that gives professors fits and can spell academic trouble for students who use sources without giving due credit. Outside the academic setting, some people lose their jobs over plagiarism, while others simply lose public esteem. Some kinds of plagiarism are treated as theft. Copyright lawyers make a fortune ensuring that artists don't "steal" profitable song lyrics

FIGURE 4.3: GOSPEL SYNOPSIS: AN EXAMPLE

Here's a synopsis of one passage that appears in the three Synoptic Gospels:

Matthew 27	Mark 15	Luke 23
33 And when they came to a **place called Golgotha (which means Place of a Skull)**, 34 they **offered him wine** to drink, mixed with gall; but when he tasted it, he would not drink it. 35 And when they had crucified him, they divided his clothes among themselves by **casting lots**; 36 then they sat down there and kept watch over him. 37 Over his head they put the charge against him, which read, "This is Jesus, **the King of the Jews.**" 38 Then two bandits were crucified with him, **one on his right and one on his left. 39 Those who passed by derided him, shaking their heads 40 and saying, "You who would destroy the temple and build it in three days, save yourself! If you are the Son of God, come down from the cross." 41 In the same way the chief priests also, along with the scribes** and elders, **were mocking him, saying,** 42 **"He saved others; he cannot save himself. He is the King of Israel**; let him **come down from the cross now, and we will believe** in him. 43 He trusts in God; let God deliver him now, if he wants to; for he said, 'I am God's Son.'" 44 The bandits **who were crucified with him also taunted him** in the same way.	22 Then they brought Jesus to the **place called Golgotha (which means the place of a skull).** 23 And they **offered him wine** mixed with myrrh; but he did not take it. 24 And they crucified him, and divided his clothes among them, **casting lots** to decide what each should take. 25 It was nine o'clock in the morning when they crucified him. 26 The inscription of the charge against him read, "**The King of the Jews.**" 27 And with him they crucified two bandits, **one on his right and one on his left. 29 Those who passed by derided him, shaking their heads and saying, "Aha! You who would destroy the temple and build it in three days,** 30 **save yourself, and come down from the cross!" 31 In the same way the chief priests, along with the scribes, were also mocking him among themselves and saying, "He saved others; he cannot save himself.** 32 Let the Messiah, **the King of Israel, come down from the cross now, so that we may see and believe.**" Those **who were crucified with him also taunted him.**	33 When they came to the place that is called The Skull, they crucified Jesus there with the criminals, one on his right and one on his left. 34 Then Jesus said, "Father, forgive them; for they do not know what they are doing." And they **cast lots** to divide his clothing. 35 And the people stood by, watching; but the leaders scoffed at him, saying, "**He saved others**; let him save himself if he is the Messiah of God, his chosen one!" 36 The soldiers also mocked him, coming up and **offering him sour wine,** 37 and saying, "If you are the King of the Jews, save yourself!" 38 There was also an inscription over him, "This is **the King of the Jews.**" 39 One of the criminals who were hanged there kept deriding him and saying, "Are you not the Messiah? Save yourself and us!" 40 But the other rebuked him, saying, "Do you not fear God, since you are under the same sentence of condemnation? 41 And we indeed have been condemned justly, for we are getting what we deserve for our deeds, but this man has done nothing wrong." 42 Then he said, "Jesus, remember me when you come into your kingdom." 43 He replied, "Truly I tell you, today you will be with me in Paradise."

YOUR TURN: Choose two similarities and two differences among these three accounts and reflect on their significance.

from each other. That's because we see our creative activity (words, music, art, and so on) as personal property that others can't use without proper citation or even compensation. Though the ease of the "copy/paste" option makes plagiarism enticing, it still carries a stigma and sometimes hefty consequences.

In the ancient world, though, plagiarism was a routine and accepted practice. Ancient historians such as Josephus weave other sources into their work without attribution. Usually, this practice is obvious to discerning readers, who detect a change of writing voice, sentence structure, or word choice, for example. Not only did Josephus and his contemporaries lack an MLA style guide, but they also brought a different mind-set to the use of sources. In the ancient world, to incorporate another's written product into one's own work was to show highest esteem for it. In a similar way, the verbatim agreement among the Gospels simply means that one or more of the evangelists thought an earlier account merited repeating, with adjustments, for a new audience.

Besides verbatim agreement within shared passages, scholars detect literary dependence among the Synoptic Gospels because they tell stories in similar order, even when the stories themselves don't require the sequence. Remember, it's a given for Papias that Mark's Gospel isn't in chronological order. But especially the first two Gospels, Matthew and Mark, march in lockstep through the episodes they both include.

Mark as Middle Term

If you scan your eyes down a Gospel synopsis, you'll see quite clearly that the second Gospel serves as the "middle term" between the other two Synoptic Gospels, and not just because it occupies the center column among the three. It's also the literary common denominator that the other two Synoptics share. This phenomenon works at both the micro (within passages) and macro (across the Gospels) levels.

Within the **triple tradition**—Gospel episodes included in Matthew, Mark, and Luke—the patterns of agreement indicate that Matthew and Luke line up most closely where Mark shares the same content. Let's take one example of Mark as middle term. If you examine Mark 2:22 in a Gospel parallel, you'll find that Mark ends with these words: "new wine is for new wineskins." Both Matthew and Luke include this exact language, but they both find it an insufficient ending, adding new material that differs from each other. Matthew says that "people pour new wine into new wineskins so that both are kept safe" (Matt 9:17). Luke goes in an entirely different interpretive direction: "No one who drinks a well-aged wine wants new wine, but says, 'The well-aged wine is better'" (Luke 5:39). This shows that Matthew and Luke agree more closely where Mark is present in the conversation.

Such a **pattern of alternating support** also characterizes the sequence of stories shared among the three Synoptic Gospels. This has to do with the macro level of narrative order. On the one hand, when they include a scene that also appears in Mark, Matthew and Luke generally place it at the same point in the Gospel that Mark does. Sometimes, they alternate which scenes from Mark they choose. Thus these two Gospels alternate in their support of Mark because they take turns using parts of Mark. On the other hand, when Matthew and Luke tell a similar story that's *not* in Mark, it usually shows up in entirely different places in the unfolding narrative.

Markan Priority

Mark's role as a middle term among the three Synoptic Gospels suggests two possible hypotheses for the literary relationship they share. Either Mark came first and served as source for Matthew and Luke (the dominant view), or Mark used Matthew very selectively, abbreviating it into a much slimmer volume. What evidence convinces most scholars of **Markan Priority**, or the view that Mark came first?

For one thing, Mark is shortest in length among the three Synoptics and leaves out the other Gospels' beginnings (birth stories), endings (post-resurrection appearances), and significant material in between. On a common-sense level, it's easier to conceive of Matthew and Luke adding stories than it is to understand why Mark might deliberately omit them. And here's a curious feature: when Mark does tell stories found in Matthew and/or Luke, Mark's version is usually longer. That shows that Mark tends to be more long-winded in conversation style, rather than an author who "cuts to the chase," casting details to the recycle bin.

A second factor that supports Markan Priority concerns this evangelist's writing style. When compared with Synoptic peers, Mark lacks literary panache. It's as if its author is just learning to write in Greek. Much as a middle-schooler might string sentences together with little sophistication, Mark begins many sentences with "and." Mark can also be repetitive, using more words than necessary even to convey a simple thought. In general, Mark's syntax and word choices are often awkward and plodding. None of this indicates that Mark is first among Synoptics, of course. But when Mark's stories appear also in Matthew or Luke, they're told in much more refined and fluid prose. That makes it more plausible that Matthew and Luke polished their source (Mark) and less plausible that Mark downgraded the quality of Matthew's (or Luke's) writing.

Third, differences in content among the Synoptic Gospels support Markan Priority. In a number of cases, changes appear that reflect the passing of time. As we'll see, Mark's message gives the impression that God's kingdom is about to appear on earth—really, any day now (see e.g., Mark 13:32-37). Though the message about God's coming kingdom still plays a part in Matthew and Luke, these Gospels convey much less urgency and often deliberately shift focus to the here and now (see e.g., Luke 19:11).

Another set of changes related to Jesus himself indicates to most scholars that Mark came first. The term ***Christology*** refers to the characterization of Christ: What's his nature? His relationship to God? His main concerns and attributes? Of the three Gospels, Mark's Christology emphasizes Jesus's human features. After all, he loses his temper, he takes two tries to heal a blind man, and he repeatedly pleads with God to intervene and save his life. In several places, Matthew and Luke downplay Jesus's humanity and associate him more closely with God. But we know, historically speaking, that the claim Jesus was divine emerged only after time passed. (This question became a matter of vigorous debate three hundred years later—a fact that shows it was far from settled in the first century.) As a result, Mark's lower Christology makes more sense as an earlier, not later, account of Jesus's life, death, and resurrection.

The Double Tradition

So far, we've reviewed evidence that points toward Markan Priority and the associated claim that it served as a source for both Matthew and Luke. We turn now to the Gospel material shared by Matthew and Luke but not found in Mark. After all, about 220 verses that mostly feature Jesus's sayings appear in this **double tradition**. Sometimes, we can see *verbatim* (word-for-word) agreement between the two Gospels (see e.g., Matt 23:37; Luke 13:34), which points to a literary relationship, rather than mere coincidence.

But what kind of relationship? Scholars consider two main possibilities. The first and simpler proposal is that Luke used Matthew as a source. Most scholars think that these evangelists operated without knowledge of each other's work and look for other possibilities to account for the double tradition material.

Q Is for Quelle ("Source")

That leads to the last step in the consensus view. If Matthew and Luke wrote independently of each other, how might we explain the double

FIGURE 4.4: WHAT'S IN Q?

By definition, the contents of Q include the Gospel material found in Matthew and Luke but not in Mark. Here are a few of the familiar teachings that may have come from this hypothetical source:

The Beatitudes

Love your enemies

Golden Rule

Warning against judging others

Familiar parables, such as the parable of the wise and the foolish builders, the lost sheep, the wedding feast, and the talents

The Lord's Prayer

Wisdom teaching referencing the "birds of the air" and "lilies of the field"

YOUR TURN: Have you heard of any of these sayings or parables? How would you describe their importance in Christianity today?

tradition, or the material they share? May I introduce a hypothetical source called **Q** (for *Quelle,* the German word for "source")? To be clear, no one's located an ancient copy of Q—what a dream discovery that would be. Instead, Q exists as a hypothesis, reconstructed in the minds of scholars and comprising Gospel material found in Matthew and Luke but not in Mark. What makes Q such a compelling part of the solution is that it helps explain what we otherwise can't. (See Figure 4.4.)

Far-fetched as this hypothetical document might sound at first, we have good reason to think such a source *could* have existed. For instance, the **Gospel of Thomas**, discovered among the Nag Hammadi writings mentioned in chapter 1, features only Jesus's teachings. If Q did exist, it was a different version of this kind of gospel. Thus the discovery of Gospel of Thomas makes the Q hypothesis plausible if not ultimately provable. (See Figure 4.5)

The Special Sources: "M" and "L"

So far, we've accounted for Gospel material shared by Matthew and Mark, Luke and Mark, and Matthew and Luke. But what about those passages found

FIGURE 4.5: GOSPEL OF THOMAS

Among the noncanonical gospels, the Gospel of Thomas is perhaps best known. Though most scholars date this collection of sayings to the second century, a few think it contains versions of Jesus's teachings that predate the canonical Gospels. In any case, it differs from them in terms of literary genre: it's made up only of sayings and so lacks any narrative account of Jesus's life, death, or resurrection.

From the start, the Gospel of Thomas reads as a collection of sayings rather than a story. Some of its teachings are similar or even identical to teachings found in the canonical Gospels. Here's how it opens:

> These are the secret sayings which the living Jesus spoke and which Didymos Judas Thomas wrote down. And he said, "Whoever finds the interpretation of these sayings will not experience death."
>
> Jesus said, "Let him who seeks continue seeking until he finds. When he finds, he will become troubled. When he becomes troubled, he will be astonished, and he will rule over the All."
>
> Jesus said, "If those who lead you say to you, 'See, the kingdom is in the sky,' then the birds of the sky will precede you. If they say to you, 'It is in the sea,' then the fish will precede you. Rather, the kingdom is inside of you, and it is outside of you. When you come to know yourselves, then you will become known, and you will realize that it is you who are the sons of the living father. But if you will not know yourselves, you dwell in poverty and it is you who are that poverty." ("The Gospel of Thomas," in *The Nag Hammadi Library*, ed. James M. Robinson, trans. Thomas Lambdin, rev. ed. [San Francisco: HarperCollins, 1990]; available online at http://earlychristianwritings.com/text/thomas-lambdin.html).

YOUR TURN: What do you notice about this opening series of sayings? What makes a "sayings gospel" different from one of the canonical Gospels?

in Matthew and Luke that "go their own way" entirely? After all, both Gospels tell the story of Jesus's birth, but they do so in very different ways. Both Gospels report encounters with a risen Jesus, but their accounts contradict each other. In Matthew, Jesus tells the disciples to go to Galilee, where he meets them on a mountain and gives them further instruction (Matt 28:10, 16-20); in Luke, Jesus tells the disciples to stay in Jerusalem until they're "furnished with heavenly power" (Luke 24:49).

Between these book-ends, Matthew and Luke include teachings that are unique to each Gospel. The good Samaritan story, for example, appears only in Luke (Luke 10:25-37). Likewise, Jesus's diatribe against the Pharisees appears only in Matthew (Matt 23:1-36). This observation leads to the final step in the mainstream solution to the Synoptic problem. Scholars think that, besides using

Mark and Q as sources, Matthew and Luke both drew from their own special sources, called **M** and **L** respectively. As with Q, scholars reconstruct these reputed sources from the special material found in the Gospels themselves.

THE SYNOPTIC SOLUTIONS: THE FOUR SOURCE HYPOTHESIS AND ITS ALTERNATIVES

If you've followed the bread crumbs through these six steps, you've arrived at the most widely accepted hypothesis used to solve the **Synoptic Problem**. First proposed by B. H. Streeter almost a century ago, the **Four Source Hypothesis** has largely stood the test of time as the most likely explanation for the Synoptic problem. Here's the Four Source Hypothesis in a nutshell: Matthew and Luke both used two sources, Mark and Q, but they did so independently of each other. In addition, they each used a source of their own, M and L respectively. Thus the four sources—Mark, Q, M, and L—together comprise the content found in the Synoptic Gospels. (See Figure 4.6.)

Keep in mind that this hypothesis depends on the evangelists' sense of **editorial freedom**. Already, we've seen that the evangelists both emend (change) and amend (add to) their sources, based on a variety of motives ranging from stylistic improvement to correction of inaccurate details to a preferred theological message. This freedom occurs both within passages and in the choices about material to include in the Gospels. For instance, Mark's story of a two-staged healing of a blind man (Mark 8:22-26) appears in neither Matthew nor Luke, even though Matthew includes about 90 percent of Mark's content. Scholars attribute the later evangelists' glaring omission to theological motives, since Mark seems to qualify Jesus's healing power.

In the scholarly conversation, even the most convincing hypothesis has its detractors. Today, two main alternatives to the Four Source Hypothesis retain meaningful minority support among source critics. Let's summarize each one briefly.

The Griesbach Hypothesis

Early church tradition assigned Matthew primacy among Gospels—both as the earliest and as the most important church teaching. That's why it's first in the NT canon. Today, some scholars continue to support **Matthean Priority**, or the view that Matthew came first. The **Griesbach Hypothesis**, named for its main modern proponent, claims that Mark and Luke drew

FIGURE 4.6: FOUR SOURCE HYPOTHESIS

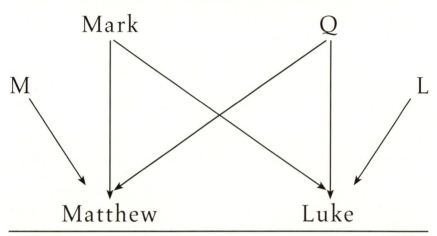

The Four Source Hypothesis diagram is the most broadly held solution to the Synoptic Problem. Notice the four sources, M, Mark, Q, and L. Scholars think Matthew and Luke each used three of these written documents as the basis of their gospel stories.

their material from Matthew. Mark thus condensed Matthew, taking a "just the facts, ma'am" approach. Luke exercised artistic liberties, carefully selecting and adapting Matthew's story to suit his audience. The Griesbach Hypothesis has two main points in its favor. First, it follows the earliest impulse of church leaders who, generally speaking, knew more about the origins of the Gospels than we do. Second, it doesn't require a hypothetical source (such as Q) to make sense of the similarities and differences. As we've noted, though, most scholars simply find it hard to understand both Mark's omission of so much of Matthew's story and Mark's clumsy presentation of it.

Mark without Q

The **Mark without Q hypothesis** agrees with the Four Source Hypothesis on the question of Markan Priority and on the premise that Matthew and Luke used Mark as a source. Its difference lies in how it accounts for the double tradition material. In this view, Luke combined elements of *both* Mark *and* Matthew with Luke's own special material. Like the Griesbach Hypothesis, it's a simpler approach, since it accounts for the Synoptic relationship on the evidence at hand, without positing a hypothetical source. It also helps to explain some of the more troubling instances in the Gospels that don't quite fit the Four Source Hypothesis.

Objections to the "Mark without Q" solution are two-fold. First, while Luke follows Mark's narrative outline, the double tradition material appears scattered freeform throughout this Gospel. Why would Luke, scholars ask, follow Mark so closely but disregard the settings to which Matthew has assigned this material? (One scholar has proposed Luke *does* follow Matthew's order, but in reverse, as if winding up the scroll from back to front.) Second, since verbatim agreement in the double tradition varies widely, scholars wonder why Luke would copy Matthew carefully in some places but edit Matthew freely elsewhere.

Review and Reflect

- Describe the investigation that leads to the Four Source Hypothesis. What are the four sources, and how are they used?

- Of the three hypotheses discussed here, which seems most compelling to you and why? What's the greatest weakness of your preferred hypothesis?

"ONE OF THESE THINGS IS NOT LIKE THE OTHERS": JOHN AS OUTLIER

So far, we've treated the first three canonical Gospels as a set. These Synoptic accounts agree with one another—both broadly and, at times, in great detail—across the span of Jesus's earthly career. But what about John? Did the writer of the last among the four canonical Gospels know of or use any of the others? It's a question that's trickier to answer than we might expect.

As we'll see, John does share a few stories with the Synoptic Gospels. Perhaps the most important example comes from John 6, where Jesus feeds a crowd of five thousand (John 6:1-15; cf. Matt 14:13-21; Mark 6:30-44; Luke 9:10-17). It's one of only a handful of stories that appear in all four Gospels. What's even more striking is this: as in Mark and Matthew, John follows this episode with an account of Jesus walking on the water. The shared sequence leads scholars to think that John knew Mark (and/or Matthew) or perhaps used the same source Mark used.

In addition, John names many of the characters who play important roles in the other Gospels. Besides the twelve disciples, two women named Mary and Martha (found only in Luke) appear also in John, though in a different narrative setting. In fact, where John does share details with any of the Synoptics, it's most often Luke whose story overlaps.

Though most scholars think John was written independently of the Synoptic tradition, some propose that the latest author may have used the Synoptics' sources or even—very selectively—parts of Luke. In particular, Luke's last few chapters resemble John's more than they do Mark's. In any case, we'll see in chapter 8 that the Fourth Gospel (another name for John) was probably written in several different stages. Such a complex process behind its composition makes it possible that earlier versions relied on sources related to the Synoptic Gospels.

"SO WHAT?" INTERPRETIVE PAYOFF

This chapter has set the stage for our study of the NT Gospels by inviting you to think quite carefully about what the Gospels are and how they're related to one another. But what's the payoff? How will this information affect how we read the Gospels, the questions we'll explore, and the possible answers we'll consider?

For one thing, the first half of the chapter has unearthed assumptions that many students bring to the Gospels. Think about it. Many people—both Christians and non-Christians—assume the Gospels represent something like four travelogues, as if Jesus's disciples were taking notes at every turn in his career (including, oddly enough, those times when he was apart from them). Once we reflect on the nature of oral tradition, the passing of time, and the way ancient writers approached their task, we begin to appreciate the Gospels on their own terms. Though they do retain some interest in historical fact (we'll return to this question in chapter 9), the Gospels mainly tell Jesus's story in ways that connect it to the communities they address decades later.

As we'll see, we can use the Four Source Hypothesis to expose each Synoptic Gospel's particular features, and thus its particular message for a particular setting. By using a Gospel parallel, we can ask such questions as these:

1. How do Matthew and Luke treat the material found in Mark? What do they change, and what do they omit?

2. How do Matthew and Luke cast the teachings they share—ostensibly from the Q source—in a particular light?

3. What does their special material (M and L) show us about these Gospels' main concerns?

We can ask similar questions of Mark and John as well. Since we don't have access to their sources, it's harder to infer their editorial patterns. But we will detect their tendencies in terms of style and thematic content. In each case, we'll try to make sense of the text in conversation with its contexts—literary, religious, and sociopolitical.

SUMMARY

By now, I hope it's clear that the academic study of the NT isn't just a thought experiment devised to entertain nerdy biblical scholars. Whether or not this sacred tradition is sacred to you, you're probably well-aware of the Bible's role in our world. You may endorse or deeply resent that role. In either case, to read the Bible responsibly in our world requires reading it in its own world, and on its own terms. For starters, that means remembering that the Gospel writers cared much less about factual accuracy than about telling true stories—stories imbued with meaning designed to help people see the world, and their own lives, in a certain light. That makes these Gospel stories conversation starters more than lists of ideas to believe in. As we move into the Gospels themselves, we'll listen in on that ancient conversation between the evangelists and their audiences. We'll also happen upon the conversation they generate among believers, as well as with the wider world. Are you ready to dive in?

> ### Review and Reflect
>
> • What makes John's literary relationship to the Synoptic Gospels hard to figure out?
>
> • How will you read the Gospels differently because of what you've learned so far?

GO DEEPER

Carroll, John T. *Jesus and the Gospels: An Introduction*. Louisville, KY: Westminster John Knox Press, 2016.

Goodacre, Mark. *The Synoptic Problem: A Way through the Maze*. London: Sheffield Academic Press, 2001.

Henderson, Suzanne Watts. *Christ and Community: The Gospel Witness to Jesus*. Nashville: Abingdon Press, 2014.

Stein, Robert H. *Studying the Synoptic Gospels: Origin and Interpretation*. 2nd ed. Grand Rapids, MI: Baker Academic, 2001.

Streeter, B. H. *The Four Gospels*. London: Macmillan, 1924.

Chapter Five

What Is God's Kingdom?
Gospel of Mark

CONVERSATION STARTERS

- What's the Jewish apocalyptic worldview, and why is it important for understanding Mark?

- Who wrote Mark and what kind of community did it address?

- What sets Mark's story apart?

- What does Mark have to say about God's coming kingdom?

- Why does Mark end so abruptly?

As we turn to the Gospels, we begin not with Matthew, which appears first in the NT, but with Mark. Why? As we saw in the last chapter, scholars think that it's the earliest written account of Jesus's life, death, and resurrection and that it served as a literary source for the other Synoptic Gospels. In other words, Mark's our starting point partly because we think it was the starting point for at least two other NT Gospels as well.

For centuries, Mark was mostly ignored by those curious about who Jesus was and what his mission was about. After all, Mark lacks many favorite sayings and stories found in the other Gospels. Mark has no birth story, nor, in its earliest version, any reports of people encountering the risen Jesus. It's also missing such familiar passages as the Lord's Prayer and much-loved parables such as the story of the prodigal son and the good Samaritan. Both its writing style and its message are a bit rough around the edges: its Greek is unpolished, and Mark's Jesus sometimes sounds like a moody hothead who spars with opponents and lambastes even his closest friends. For all these reasons, this earliest Gospel has been *almost* dispensable in the life of the church.

But not quite. Early church leaders such as **Papias** valued Mark because they thought it preserved Peter's version of Jesus's career. From the beginning, Mark took its place among the emerging canon of four Gospels, even if ancient interpreters rarely mention it. But the rise of modern scholarship has brought a renewed interest in Mark. When source critics determined Mark came first, some readers have considered its portrait of Jesus more true to life and less tainted by theological editing. Today, scholars take a more skeptical view of Mark's objectivity. Still, modern and postmodern critics detect in Mark a literary artistry long overlooked.

As we turn to each Gospel, we'll start by acquainting ourselves with the worldview that shapes its message. In Mark's case, that means laying out the contours of Jewish apocalyptic thought. Next, we'll situate the Gospel in its original setting, noting scholars' views about Mark's author and audience, as well as the conversation between them. Then, we'll trace Mark's story, pointing out dominant themes and striking features along the way. As we'll see, Mark portrays Jesus as the Messiah whose mission points at every turn to the "good news" that God's kingdom is taking root in the world. We'll conclude by listening to the Gospel's overarching claims in conversation with its first-century audience, as well as with those in similar circumstances across place and time.

WHAT'S MARK'S WORLDVIEW? JEWISH APOCALYPTIC THOUGHT

To make sense of Mark—especially its keen interest in "God's kingdom" (Mark 1:15)—scholars often point to its background in Jewish apocalyptic thought. This is not to deny its Hellenistic features, such as the resemblance between Jesus and such divine men as **Apollonius of Tyana**. But for Mark, Jesus's gospel story is first and foremost rooted in the soil of his native Jewish tradition. In particular, Mark frames this story as an apocalyptic drama.

But what does *apocalyptic* mean? You've probably heard (or even used) the phrase "sign of the apocalypse" in casual conversation—as in, "My professor's cancelled the final exam: a sign of the apocalypse." In popular discourse, the apocalypse entails the (very violent) end of the world as we know it. How does that fit with ancient Jewish thought? It's only part of the picture.

Let's get our bearings by covering some basics. The word *apocalypse* trans-literates the Greek *apocalypsis*, which means "unveiling" or "revelation." In the first century, the term designated a literary genre marked by visions of the heavenly realm that had been revealed to a prophetic writer. Though Revelation is the only full-length apocalypse in the NT, the apocalyptic worldview shows up across the NT, beginning with Mark.

Indeed, Jewish writings that aren't technically apocalypses often use an apocalyptic framework to interpret present reality. Together, they set the stage for our reading of Mark. When you read "apocalyptic" here, think not "catastrophe" but "revelation," not disaster but hope. That hope comes from a linear sense of time as it unfolds toward its end goal: an ideal age. (In this sense, apocalyptic thought is also **eschatological** because it looks toward the "end.") Here are the main steps in this apocalyptic and eschatological timetable. (See Figure 5.1.)

1. "Things Are Bad and Getting Worse": Those who see the world through an apocalyptic lens are hyper-aware of the evil that lurks all around. Jewish apocalyptic writers often say they're living in the *present evil age*. For now, they say, evil forces have infiltrated God's good creation and hold it captive through harmful tactics: personally, in cases of physical and spiritual disease; socially, in structures that divide and conquer; and cosmically, in natural disasters. This age, they say, is something of a battlefield between good and evil, and it *seems* as if evil is winning.

2. "Hang On; Hope (Judgment Day) Is Coming": Most people think of judgment day in ominous terms. But those steeped in Jewish apocalyptic thought look with hope toward the *day of the Lord*. Why? The answer has to do with the kind of judgment it brings. In Jewish tradition, God's trademark values of justice and righteousness promote the well-being of creation—at the personal, social, and cosmic levels. The day of the Lord, in this view, will establish God's priorities on earth, once and for all. This is good news for those who've been faithful along the way. After all, judgment day brings two possible outcomes: salvation (or "liberation") from the present evil age on the one hand, or eternal destruction of evil on the other. Why is this hopeful? Think about it. Most people are pretty sure it's the others who're missing the mark, not themselves!

3. "Free at Last": On the other side of judgment lies the *age to come*, when God's kingdom will prevail "on earth as it is in heaven" (Matt 6:10 NRSV). In this "new creation," God's saving power

FIGURE 5.1: JEWISH APOCALYPTIC WORLDVIEW

This diagram shows the linear progression implied in the Jewish apocalyptic worldview. In many writings, even the dead are raised up to stand before God (or God's agent) in judgment. To be "saved" is to enter into the age to come, where evil has lost its power. Thus, the drama presses toward the restoration of a "new creation," returning the world to its idyllic state described in Genesis 1–2.

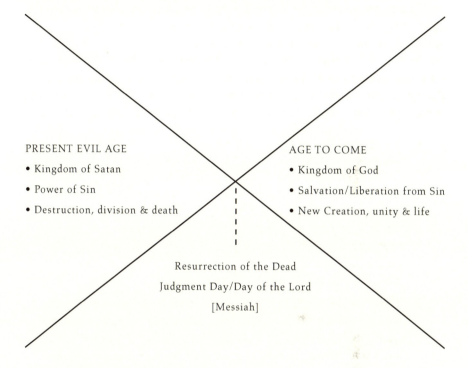

PRESENT EVIL AGE

- Kingdom of Satan

- Power of Sin

- Destruction, division & death

AGE TO COME

- Kingdom of God

- Salvation/Liberation from Sin

- New Creation, unity & life

Resurrection of the Dead

Judgment Day/Day of the Lord

[Messiah]

YOUR TURN: In what settings might the promise of a coming judgment day (or day of the Lord) be "good news"? Why?

finally renews the cosmos so that it flourishes on every level. That power engenders a kingdom of life, not death' and human and cosmic wholeness, not suffering. It's a divine kingdom characterized by justice and righteousness that ensures peace within human community and in relationship to God.

This schema is called "revelation" because it discloses what's really real, which is not human power that rules by force but divine power that rules by generativity and life. The day of the Lord brings God's power fully to light. In some (but not all) Jewish texts, an individual figure called by such names as *messiah, human one,* and *chosen one* plays a pivotal role in judgment and then presides as agent of God's kingdom in the new creation. (See Figure 5.2.)

As we'll see, early Christian writers adapted this script to contend with two competing aspects of their reality. On the one hand, they believed that *Jesus was the Messiah,* the one who showed forth God's sovereign power on earth. On the other hand, their daily existence still included sickness, hostility, and death—all signs that *evil was still loose in the world.* Like other writers, Mark sees the present moment as a sort of meantime, poised between the demise of the present evil age and the full disclosure of God's kingdom on earth. If loyalty to that kingdom brings suffering—both to Jesus and to his followers—Mark's story declares the "good news" that God's power will soon prevail and invites hearers to bear faithful witness to that power along the way.

WHO WROTE MARK? AND FOR WHOM? THE AUTHOR AND AUDIENCE OF MARK

Like all four NT Gospels, Mark was written anonymously. By the late second century CE, church leaders linked this Gospel to the **John Mark** who joined both Peter and Paul (Phlm 24; Col 4:10; Acts 12:12-15) and who, they thought, translated Peter's "recollections" into koine Greek for Roman Christians. Historians are reluctant to take these claims at face value, since they are late and not verifiable.

The Gospel offers tantalizing if competing clues about its author's religious identity. Clearly, Mark (we'll use this name for the evangelist) recounts Jesus's mission against the backdrop of Jewish scripture, citing it both directly and indirectly. Yet, the evangelist is less than proficient in using that tradition. For instance, Mark opens with a citation attributed to Isaiah that's really a collage of verses found in three different biblical books: Exodus, Isaiah, and Malachi (see Mark 1:2-3). Later, Mark overgeneralizes Jewish practice by claiming that "all the Jews" wash their hands before meals (see Mark 7:3). Still, the Gospel situates Jesus and his disciples squarely within Palestinian Judaism.

Mark's audience, though, apparently lived outside of Palestine, even if some of them were Jewish. The Gospel itself, especially Mark 13, suggests that the community was targeted by both religious and political officials for their commitment to Jesus the Messiah. If scholars agree about their persecuted status, opinion about their location generally divides around two main possibilities. The minority opinion follows ancient church tradition to link

FIGURE 5.2: MESSIAH(S) IN JEWISH APOCALYPTIC THOUGHT

Jewish apocalyptic texts depict **messianic** characters in different ways and call them by different names. The term *messiah* means "anointed"—that is, officially designated for a divinely appointed purpose. In the **Tanakh** (Jewish scripture or Old Testament), prophets, kings, and priests are all "anointed" as part of their commissioning. By Jesus's time, the messiah had come to be associated with the establishment of God's kingdom on earth. But expectations about this messiah (or messiahs, as we'll see) were far from uniform. Let's take a look at three textual glimpses of key figures who serve on God's behalf.

Daniel 7: This apocalyptic vision reports the deposing of earthly kings from their place in the heavenly throne room. In their place, "one like a human being" arrives from earth (often translated as "Son of Man" or "Son of Humanity") to assume a throne alongside the Ancient One. Daniel doesn't use the term *messiah*, but it's clear this figure shares power with God and presides over the establishment of a divine reign on earth (see Dan 7:1-27).

Dead Sea Scrolls: Among the Scrolls are documents that set forth the views of a community that expects God's angels to defeat the wicked rulers any day. Both the Community Rule and the Manual of Discipline apparently expect not one but two messiahs, one "from Aaron" (priestly) and one "from David/Israel" (political) (see 1QS 9:10-11; cf. CD 14:18-19; 19:10-11).

Psalms of Solomon: This text envisions a political messiah who comes to power by way of violent conquest and establishes God's kingdom in Jerusalem (see *PsSol* 17:21-46). This messiah tramples the opposition and establishes a righteous rule for the faithful.

Simply put, there's no set messianic script within Jewish apocalyptic thought. In fact, some texts look forward to God's kingdom without designating a specific figure to implement it. And when messiahs do appear, they tend to be human, not divine.

YOUR TURN: Read one of the passages mentioned here. How is its messiah (or messianic figure/s) similar to or different from Mark's?

---

the Gospel with Rome, where the **Emperor Nero** used Christians as scapegoats for a devastating fire in the capital city (64 CE). In this context, Christians were not just tortured and killed but crucified as well.

Today, most scholars think this Gospel first addressed a community closer to Palestine during the **Jewish War** (66–73 CE). We know that the Jewish insurgency in Jerusalem brought a spill-over effect throughout the region. Roman officials were concerned about possible uprisings elsewhere, which made Jewish leaders wary of those in their midst who might put Jews on Rome's watch list. Caught in the middle were communities like Mark's, whose devotion to the Jewish Messiah and the kingdom he heralded probably made them easy targets for those in power.

Taken together, these possibilities make it likely the Gospel was written in the late 60s or early 70s CE, perhaps for those suffering the fallout of the Jewish War in nearby Syria. More than three decades had passed since Jesus's death. But his legacy remained alive and well, echoing down into the next generation of believers. Drawing on oral and probably some written sources, the evangelist interprets Jesus's messianic career in narrative form. Mark's story of a crucified and risen Jesus imbues their suffering with meaning and hope. If this Gospel is a story about Jesus—and that it is—it is also a story about any who would "come after" him and pay the price for doing so.

Review and Reflect

* Describe the main features of Jewish apocalyptic thought. How does it make sense of human suffering?

* What's your view of the "apocalypse"? How do you understand that term differently now?

WHAT'S THE "GOOD NEWS" IN MARK? THE GOSPEL OF GOD'S KINGDOM

From the outset, Mark tells the "good news of Jesus Christ" (Mark 1:1 NRSV). The term *good news* (Greek: *euangelion*) is often translated "gospel." In Mark, this term heralds the dawn of God's kingdom and liberation from evil. As the Christ, the one anointed to wield God's power on earth, Jesus plays the leading role in that coming kingdom. For Mark, though, that "good news" extends beyond his life, death, and resurrection to his mission's afterlife in the witness of those who would "take up their cross, and follow" (Mark 8:34).

Literary critics detect two main parts to Mark's Gospel that are flanked by opening and closing scenes. (See Figure 5.3.) The first half takes place mostly in the north, in and around Galilee and its trademark "sea" (which is really a lake). The second half moves toward the south, arriving in Jerusalem, the matrix of religious and political power in the Palestine of Jesus's day. Along the way, the story makes little geographic sense. Scholars think that's

FIGURE 5.3: OUTLINE OF MARK

Prologue: In the Wilderness (1:1-15)

God's Kingdom in Word and Deed (1:16–8:26)

 In and around Galilee (1:16–4:41)

 To the Other Side and Back Again (5:1–6:52)

 Among the Gentiles (6:53–8:21)

A Gospel Hinge: Healing Blindness, Take Two (8:22-26)

God's Kingdom on the Way of the Cross (8:27–15:47)

 Passion Predictions and Discipleship (8:27–10:52)

 Passion narrative in Jerusalem (11:1–15:47)

Epilogue: Empty Tomb and beyond (16:1-8, 9-20)

---

because Mark stitches together a patchwork of sources with little regard for their chronological accuracy. Let's follow the unfolding story step by step.

Prologue: In the Wilderness (Mark 1:1-15)

The first few lines of any Gospel provide important clues about what will follow. Mark opens abruptly, with John's baptism of Jesus in the Jordan River. These early verses establish two vital aspects of Jesus's background: his story's roots in *biblical tradition* (Mark 1:2-3) and his ties to an *apocalyptic prophet* named John the Baptist (Mark 1:4-11). John calls people to prepare for the "day of the Lord" (Mal 4:5) by confessing their sins and expressing their loyalty to God through baptism. Along comes Jesus, who answers John's call. But Jesus's baptism is no ordinary cleansing. (See Figure 5.4.) As he comes out of the water, a Spirit descends on him along with a heavenly voice that pronounces him "my Son, whom I dearly love; in you I find happiness" (Mark 1:11). Thus Mark uses Jewish scripture to confirm Jesus's privileged status from the outset (see Isa 42:1; Ps 2:7). (See Figure 5.5.)

Unlike the other Synoptic Gospels, Mark mentions Jesus's temptation in the wilderness only in passing (Mark 1:12-13; cf. Matt 4:1-11; Luke 4:1-13).

FIGURE 5.4: BAPTISM AS RITUAL CLEANSING

Many people today think of baptism as a uniquely Christian practice that confers insider status either on infants born to Christian families or on those who deliberately choose to identify with a Christian community. But the story of Jesus's baptism by John reminds us that baptism was a form of ritual cleansing in Second Temple Judaism. Immersion in a ritual bath was a standard part of Jewish life in first-century Palestine. Archeologists have discovered small pools used for ritual immersion in homes from the time, and ritual cleansing remains a part of Jewish life to this day.

Other religious traditions promote ritual washing as well. Hindus wash in the sacred Ganges River, especially at death. They also see daily bathing as a ritual practice that restores bodily purity. Not all traditions require full-body washing. Before prayer, Muslims practice *wudu*, or sacred washing, described this way in the Qur'an:

> You who believe, when you are about to pray, wash your faces and your hands up to the elbows, wipe your heads, wash your feet up to the ankles and, if required, a wash your whole body. If any of you is sick or on a journey, or has just relieved himself, or had intimate contact with a woman, and can find no water, then take some clean sand and wipe your face and hands with it. God does not wish to place any burden on you: He only wishes to cleanse you and perfect His blessing on you, so that you may be thankful. (Sura 5:6)

YOUR TURN: Have you participated in any form of ritual bathing? What's your understanding of its meaning or significance? How does Christian baptism differ from the kinds of baptism mentioned here?

This early skirmish with Satan and John's subsequent arrest lead quickly to Jesus's first public appearance. His inaugural sermon is notably brief: "Now is the time! Here comes God's kingdom! Change your hearts and lives, and trust this good news!" (Mark 1:14-15). Mark thus provides a thesis for the Gospel, as Jesus points the way to that kingdom and invites others to trust in its power.

God's Kingdom in Word and Deed (Mark 1:16–8:21)

Several thematic features shed helpful light on this Gospel's message about God's kingdom, disclosed through Jesus's words and deeds. In essence, the Gospel's first half offers early glimpses into the messianic mission that leads, in the second half, to Jesus's death and resurrection in Jerusalem. Along the way, he engages others in both conversation and action.

FIGURE 5.5: ADOPTIONIST CHRISTIANITY

Some early believers found in Mark's Gospel evidence that Jesus had been "adopted" as God's son at his baptism. This view, known as "adoptionism," emerged in the second century CE and was especially popular among Jesus's Jewish followers. After all, Judaism's monotheistic devotion to the one Lord God left little room for other divine beings, especially a human one. **Adoptionists** thought Jesus was a righteous man whose exemplary faith qualified him for messianic status and that he was designated as God's Son at his baptism. This group, sometimes identified with the **Ebionites**, even had their own gospel, known to us through the fourth-century CE writer Ephiphanius. He describes the view this way: "Jesus was begotten of the seed of a man, and was chosen; and so by the choice of God he was called the Son of God from the Christ that came into him from above in the likeness of a dove." (Epiphanius, *Panarion* 30.16.4, *The Apocryphal New Testament*, trans. Montague Rhode James [Oxford, 1924], 10)

YOUR TURN: Make the case for an "adoptionist" understanding of Jesus based on Mark's Gospel.

Discipleship: A Mixed Review

At the story's outset, Jesus calls four fishers as companions and co-laborers on his mission (Mark 1:16-20). For all the Gospel's interest in Jesus, he's far from a "lone ranger." As they "fish for people" (Mark 1:17), the disciples (literally, "learners") do the things that Jesus does. Once commissioned as **the Twelve,** they, too, proclaim the good news of God's kingdom in word and deed (Mark 3:13-15; cf. 6:7-13).

But Mark doesn't gloss over the disciples' flaws, as if using the most favorable filter on SnapChat. More in Mark than in other Gospels, Jesus's followers are dim-witted and thick-headed. They simply don't seem to understand. This motif of **incomprehension** takes many narrative forms. Jesus chastises their lack of faith when they panic in a storm at sea (Mark 4:40). When Jesus asks the disciples to feed a hungry crowd, they protest at first, seeing the problem through the lens of scarcity rather than God's kingdom provision (Mark 6:35-36). Later, they misunderstand Jesus's metaphorical teaching about the yeast of the Pharisees and Herod and ask about literal bread (Mark 8:14-21).

Interpreters view this theme of incomprehension from many angles. Some see the disciples as literary foils to Jesus. That means their ignorance further highlights Jesus's supreme wisdom. Others think Mark uses this negative characterization to critique some in Mark's audience who likewise misconstrue Jesus as a superhero who's something of a show-off. Another common view is that Mark thought no one could understand Jesus's

FIGURE 5.6: MIRACLE WORKERS IN JESUS'S WORLD

In chapter 2, we mentioned Apollonius of Tyana, a well-known first-century CE miracle worker. Similarly, Josephus describes a man named "Onias the circle-maker" with these words: "Now there was one named Onias, a righteous man and beloved of God, who, in a certain drought, had once prayed to God to put an end to the intense heat, and God had heard his prayer and sent rain" (*Antiquities*, 14.2.1). And the Mishnah (*Berakot*, 5:5) describes the effective healing prayers of a rabbi named Hanina ben Dosa.

YOUR TURN: If Jesus was "one among many" known in the first century for miraculous powers, how does that affect your reading of Gospel miracle stories? Why?

significance until after his death and resurrection. It's possible, too, that the disciples' misunderstanding has more to do with their own calling to full-fledged trust than with their beliefs about Jesus's identity. In any case, Mark's story preserves the disciples' faithful participation in Jesus's mission right alongside their halting human lapses.

Deeds of Power: Restoration and Faith

You may be surprised to learn that Mark barely mentions Jesus's teaching ministry. (A red-letter edition of this Gospel uses very little red ink.) Instead, Jesus appears especially in Mark's first eight chapters as a hyperactive miracle worker, doling out God's restorative power at every turn. He casts out demons, heals sick people, feeds thousands with a handful of food, and even tames violent winds and seas. Readers today sometimes think these stories prove that Jesus was God-on-earth in a unique way, but ancient sources tell us that others were known for their abilities to suspend the laws of nature. (See Figure 5.6.)

If these miracles don't set Jesus apart from his peers, why does Mark include them? For Mark, they're evidence that God's kingdom is at hand—and in the very hands of Jesus. He's Messiah because he's the designated agent of divine power, and these stories make that case a compelling one. Sometimes, Jesus effects personal healing, as when he cures Peter's mother-in-law (Mark 1:32), cleanses a leper (Mark 1:40-45), makes a paralytic walk again (Mark 2:1-12), raises a little girl from apparent death and stems a woman's twelve-year flow of blood (Mark 5:21-43), and expels a demon from a Gentile girl (Mark 7:24-30). But personal restoration brings social and economic restoration as well. Typically those who faced physical or mental illness were kept apart from the community, in order to prevent contagion. Those suffering leprosy, demon-possession, and blood flow remained outside the social structure and the economic support it provided. Jesus wields divine power not just for personal well-being but for social restoration as well. (See Figure 5.7.)

There's also a cosmic dimension to Jesus's restorative power. In several instances, Jesus displays divine authority over the created order. He calms a stormy sea twice (Mark 4:35-41; 6:45-52); he multiplies scarce provisions to feed two different crowds (Mark 6:30-44; 8:1-10); and he even walks on water without sinking (Mark 6:45-52). Thus Jesus deploys authority over the natural world to show that God's life-giving power is at work through him.

FIGURE 5.7: FEMINIST READINGS OF MARK 5:21-34 AND MARK 7:24-30

Feminist scholars have noted Jesus's unconventional interaction with women in two key stories in Mark. In the first, a woman who's been bleeding for twelve years dares to seek healing by touching his clothes—a physical contact that was prohibited by Jewish law. Here's what Laurel K. Cobb has to say about this encounter:

> In the world of first-century Palestine, reproductive health complications and illnesses would have been the leading cause of death for women. Today, we don't talk about reproductive illnesses, although over fifteen million women suffer debilitating infections and injuries during pregnancy and childbirth. The woman, however, tells Jesus the "whole truth," the only instance in the Gospels where the gospel writers give to one of the crowd the agency of speaking the "truth." . . . What whole truth of pain and suffering would desperate women relate today if they had a chance and were not afraid of the repercussions? (*Mark & Empire: Feminist Reflections* [Maryknoll, NY: Orbis, 2013], 82)

Two chapters later, Mark includes a story in which a Syrophoenician woman, marginalized by gender, ethnicity, and culture, boldly violates social protocol to challenge Jesus's initial refusal to offer help. Elizabeth Schüssler Fiorenza sees in Mark's story a pattern of "Christian faith as a combative, argumentative, and emancipator praxis that seeks the well being of all," and she sees this woman as "apostolic 'foremother' of all Gentile Christians" (*But She Said: Feminist Practices of Biblical Interpretation* [Boston: Beacon Press, 1992], 160–63).

YOUR TURN: Reread both passages from the woman's viewpoint. What does each woman's interaction with Jesus in a male-centric world contribute to the Gospel story?

In Mark, **faith** plays a key role in activating that power. The Greek word *pistis*, which can also be translated as "belief" or "trust," indicates deep-seated dependence more than intellectual belief. Mark never mentions faith *in* Jesus, as if believing *ideas* about Jesus's identity is this author's main concern. Rather, faith in Mark means reliance on God's sovereign power as it's mediated *by* Jesus. For Mark, those who cast allegiance with God's kingdom, revealed in Jesus, become active participants in it.

Two examples illustrate how faith relates to divine power in Mark. First, Jesus pronounces forgiveness—and thus healing—for a paralyzed man, not because of *his* faith, but because *his friends* trust enough in Jesus's curative power to find a way, against the odds, to lay him at Jesus's feet (Mark 2:5). Later, Jesus says a bleeding woman's "faith has healed" her (Mark 5:34) because she's risked grasping at the fringe of his cloak. Both stories prioritize trusting behavior over spoken beliefs. When Mark blames Jesus's inability to heal people in Nazareth on their "lack of faith" (Mark 6:6, author's translation), we infer they didn't act in ways that open them to God's power operative through Jesus.

Revelation and Secrecy

Amid the frenzied activity of the Gospel's first half, the narrative pace pauses for an extended teach-in. In Mark 4, Jesus tells a series of **parables**, illustrative stories that explain complex ideas in familiar terms. Together, the parables in Mark 4 answer these questions: If God's kingdom has approached, why does resistance lurk around every corner? And how should people live in the meantime? Jesus answers these questions not with theological jargon but by spinning tales from the farmer's world—tales about planting and harvesting, adverse soil conditions, and the organic growth that God alone gives.

The sower parable tells of a farmer whose day in the field seems only marginally successful, since much of what he plants lands on infertile ground (Mark 4:1-9). Jesus explains this story by citing the prophet Isaiah. The disciples, he says, have been entrusted with the "mystery" (or "secret"; Greek: *mysterion*) of God's coming kingdom, so they can recognize its power in the world. But to outsiders, Jesus's ways remain perplexing—and deliberately so (see Mark 4:11-12; cf. Matt 13:13; Luke 8:10; Isa 6:9-10).

Modern scholars see this saying as part of the **messianic secret** motif that recurs throughout Mark. Elsewhere, Jesus forbids people and demons to reveal his identity (see Mark 1:34, 45). Later, he'll shut down the disciples as well (Mark 8:30). Yet for Mark secrecy and hiddenness are meantime conditions in an apocalyptic story that's all about revelation. And both Jesus and his disciples keep bringing the good news to light (Mark 4:22). Ultimately,

FIGURE 5.8: RETHINKING THE MESSIANIC SECRET

Careful readers of Mark have long been perplexed by this Jesus who goes around "shushing" whoever recognizes him. One scholar named Wilhelm Wrede proposed an elaborate explanation for this motif. Wrede suggested that Mark invented it to explain what he inferred as a conceptual gap between Jesus's followers (who didn't think Jesus was the Messiah) and post-resurrection believers (who did). In this line of thinking, the reason people didn't know Jesus was the Messiah is simple: Jesus told whoever caught wind of the news not to tell anyone. (To be clear, Wrede didn't think Jesus enforced secrecy; he thought Mark told the story to make it sound that way.)

But is there a simpler explanation—one that doesn't rely on several layers of speculation? Is it possible that Mark preserves an authentic aspect of Jesus's earthly career? Might Jesus's exclusive faith in God led him to avoid public acclaim that focused on his own status and to redirect attention and glory toward God?

YOUR TURN: Based on Mark's Gospel and what you've learned about its setting in Jewish apocalyptic thought, do you think Jesus suppressed word that he was "Messiah"? Why or why not?

Mark's Jesus says it will prevail not through human effort but mysteriously, as if "all by itself" (Mark 4:28)—or rather, by God's good care. (See Figure 5.8.)

Resistance as Spiritual Conflict

In Mark, Jesus's work as advance agent of God's kingdom elicits vigorous resistance from the forces whose conventional power he challenges. That resistance takes many forms: spiritual, religious, and political. Though the conflict will come to a head in the Gospel's second half, Mark lays the groundwork of opposition early in the story.

For all the confusion about Jesus's identity, one group clearly recognizes both him and his power: the "demons" or "unclean spirits." Sensing his authority, they lash out: "What have you to do with us, Jesus of Nazareth? Have you come to destroy us? I know who you are. You are the holy one of God" (Mark 1:24). Throughout Mark, evil forces that hold people captive both discern Jesus's divine power and launch a counterattack. But Mark's Jesus sees his work as a search and seizure mission; he's "tying up the strong person" (Mark 3:27)—that is, Satan's forces—at every turn.

Opposition arises from religious leaders as well. In historical terms, Mark exaggerates Jewish leaders' concerted efforts to undermine Jesus. Often in this Gospel, it's the **Pharisees** (sometimes called the "rabbis") who take issue with Jesus or his disciples (see e.g., Mark 2:24). But while some rabbis probably did engage Jesus in vigorous debate—as he did them (see Mark 7:9-13)—claims about their conspiring against him likely reflect tension in Mark's setting more than Jesus's (see Mark 3:6).

Mark signals that Jesus threatened political leaders as well. Sometimes the **Herodians**—local political leaders authorized by the Roman occupying force—appear in allegiance with the Pharisees (besides Mark 3:6, see 8:15). In addition, Mark includes a flash back account of Herod's beheading of John the Baptist (Mark 6:14-29). In a literary sense, this gruesome feast that features John's head on a platter contrasts sharply with God's miraculous provision in the wilderness (see Mark 6:30-44). But this account also shows how religious and political concerns converge. After all, John's call for religious renewal challenged the status quo and those whose power derived from it.

A Gospel Hinge: Healing Blindness, Take Two (Mark 8:22-26)

At the center of Mark's Gospel lies an odd story about Jesus healing a blind man in not one but two tries. At the narrative level, this passage pivots from thematic interest in Jesus's miracle working (Mark's first half) to increasing focus on his death on a Roman cross (Mark's second half). Geographically, the story shifts from Galilee to Jerusalem. But this two-staged healing also works metaphorically. After Jesus's first attempt, the man can see, but his vision is blurry (see Mark 8:24). Interpreters think this awkward middle step toward clear sight may indicate that Jesus's deeds of power are only part of the Gospel story; to "see everything clearly" (Mark 8:25) is to recognize God's power in the way of the cross as well. This more subtle point may have been lost on Matthew, who deliberately omitted the passage.

> ### Review and Reflect
>
> • Name and explain the four main themes found in Mark's first half.
>
> • Choose two themes, and reflect on how they connect to the Gospel's interest in God's coming kingdom.

God's Kingdom in the Way of the Cross (Mark 8:27–15:47)

Mark's second half divides into two main parts: a central section organized around three **passion predictions**; and the **passion narrative** itself. (The term

passion refers to Jesus's suffering.) Throughout these chapters, Mark's story explains Jesus's death as part of the unfolding apocalyptic drama disclosing God's power taking root on earth. This claim, of course, turned on end expectations of God's coming kingdom. After all, crucifixion signaled powerlessness, not power. Mark's story works deliberately to show that Jesus's way of the cross ultimately shows the way of life-giving power.

Passion Predictions (Mark 8:27–10:52)

In Mark's central section, Jesus predicts his death and resurrection three times. Each time, he presents his destiny as a pattern for followers. Thus Mark highlights two main points about this "way of the cross": (1) Jesus's death on a Roman cross is part of God's plan to liberate the world from evil; and (2) that plan involves not just Jesus but also those who join in his messianic movement.

As far as we know, the notion of a *suffering* messiah was unprecedented in Jewish apocalyptic thought. Jewish traditions expect messianic figures to trounce their foes, not to be killed by them. (See Figure 5.9.) It's no wonder, then, that Mark repeats Jesus's passion prediction three times, as if to underscore the necessity of Jesus's death. This section opens by facing the question head-on. Once Peter names him as the Messiah, Jesus responds in two ways: he insists they not tell anyone (Mark 8:30), and he says he must "suffer many things," including rejection and death (Mark 8:31). Understandably, Peter rebukes Jesus for this ominous forecast; in response, Jesus calls Peter "Satan" because he sees things in human, not divine, terms (Mark 8:32-33).

The precise details of Jesus's predictions (see also Mark 9:31; 10:33-34) are probably **ex eventu** prophecy. This term that refers to "forecasting" the future after the fact, and with full benefit of hindsight. Remember, Mark writes decades after Jesus's death. Yet prophets across place and time know their bold challenges to those in power can put their lives on the line. (See Figure 5.10.) That leads to Mark's second main point in this section: Jesus's destiny is neither unique nor exclusive. It constitutes part of the disciples' job description as well. Like their lord, Jesus's followers will "say no to themselves," forfeiting self-interest, self-protection, and self-gain as they, too, "lose their lives" for the gospel (see Mark 8:34-36). True greatness, Jesus teaches, can be seen among those who are "least of all and the servant of all" (Mark 9:35; cf. 10:43-44). Together, both Jesus and those who "come after" him put God's kingdom on display when they exert power to liberate rather than constrain (Mark 10:45).

Along with the way of the cross, these chapters portray Jesus's lofty status and his resolute allegiance to God's kingdom. In the **transfiguration** story,

FIGURE 5.9: REDEMPTIVE SUFFERING IN JEWISH TRADITION

Though it's true that Jewish messiahs typically don't suffer, a number of texts interpret faithful suffering in a redemptive light. Mark and the other evangelists rely heavily on such interpretations to understand Jesus's crucifixion as part of God's restoration of the world. Let's consider a few of the traditions that articulate this view:

Isaiah's suffering servant (Isa 52:13–53:12): When his followers wanted to make sense of Jesus's death, many quickly turned to a familiar passage in the prophetic oracles of Isaiah. There, God's servant was disfigured, despised, and suffered. Read in context, the "suffering servant" is God's faithful people who've suffered defeat at the hands of the Babylonians and been exiled far from home. Isaiah holds out hope that God's using this calamity, which comes as a result of a corrupt society, to restore wholeness to God's people.

Daniel's wise ones (Dan 12:1-4): Like Mark, the OT book of Daniel is steeped in apocalyptic thought. Scholars think it addresses faithful Jews who're resisting the harsh Syrian occupation in the mid-second century BCE. Like Mark, Daniel insists that suffering is both part of the divine drama and their penultimate, not ultimate, fate. Daniel doesn't mention a messiah per se, but it does promise that, at the day of the Lord, the ones who are "skilled in wisdom" (Dan 12:3) not only will be vindicated but also will inspire righteousness among their peers. Thus Daniel's message situates the present hardship in a broader landscape of redemption and hope.

Maccabean martyrs (2 Macc 7): Written about the same setting as Daniel, 1 and 2 Maccabees provide a straightforward account of the armed resistance led by Judas Maccabeus and his brothers. This chapter recounts a series of showdowns between the oppressive human ruler and seven brothers devoted to "the king of the universe" (2 Macc 7:9). Not only do they suffer physical death because they put their "whole trust in the Lord" (2 Macc 7:40 NRSV), but also their sacrifice ultimately brings liberation from the Syrian force.

YOUR TURN: What connections do you see among these examples of redemptive suffering and Mark's story?

Jesus takes three disciples atop a mountain, where they watch as he changes dramatically in appearance while he converses with Moses and Elijah (see Mark 9:2-13). The episode ends with a heavenly voice again declaring Jesus as God's beloved Son (see Mark 9:7; cf. 1:11). This passage thus situates Jesus within Jewish tradition and legitimizes his message.

Other stories in this section depict Jesus's concern for vulnerable members of his social and religious setting. For instance, he delivers an evil spirit

FIGURE 5.10: A MODERN-DAY "PASSION PREDICTION"?

It's not uncommon for those who challenge the status quo to sense a palpable threat to their lives. The night before he was shot and killed in Memphis, Tennessee, Martin Luther King Jr., delivered a sermon called "I Have Been to the Mountaintop." In it, he uttered these words: I've seen the promised land. I may not get there with you. But . . . we, as a people, will get to the promised land!" It was the first time he had publicly acknowledged the possibility that his life would be cut short.

YOUR TURN: What convictions and actions did Martin Luther King Jr., share with Jesus? Can you think of other public figures targeted for taking similar stands in similar ways?

from a young boy (Mark 9:14-29) in response to a father's honest plea; he warns against those who cause "little ones" to stumble (Mark 9:42); he takes a strong stand against divorce, a practice that left women in dire economic straits (Mark 10:2-12); he blesses children (Mark 10:13-16); and he challenges a man with "many possessions" to invest his treasure on behalf of the poor (Mark 10:17-27). Mark's Jesus repeatedly takes the side of society's "little ones" and encourages others to do likewise. He also notes that following in his ways entails no small personal cost (Mark 10:28-31).

Passion Narrative (Mark 11:1–15:47)

Even before any of the NT Gospels appeared, stories of Jesus's last week in Jerusalem probably circulated as written accounts. Scholars think Mark draws material from these earlier sources, emphasizing certain features in the process. Here we consider both the historical setting of the passion story itself and Mark's distinctive way of spinning it.

The Setting: In Jerusalem, at the Passover

All four NT Gospels say Jesus died in Jerusalem during the Passover feast. Why did he die, there and then? Understanding Jesus's death in its original sociopolitical setting is vital to understanding the Gospels' religious claims about it. Ancient writers say Jewish pilgrims numbered in the hundreds of thousands during the annual Passover celebration in Jerusalem. This population surge made Roman officials wary, so they did what ruling powers do: they beefed up

Figure 5.11: From Jerusalem to Ferguson

If you followed events in Ferguson, Missouri, in the summer of 2014, you understand something of the dynamics in play in Jerusalem during the week of Jesus's crucifixion. In both cases, gathered crowds were met with military force. In both cases, officials justified their arms and boots on the ground as a strategy designed to keep the peace.

> **YOUR TURN:** Imagine you were a Roman soldier deployed to Jerusalem during the Passover. What might you have been worried about or looking for? What kinds of threats might you have been trained to subdue?

their police force. The Roman governor even left his resort-like home by the Mediterranean to keep a close eye on the crowds. (See Figure 5.11.)

Besides their sheer numbers, Passover pilgrims set Roman authorities on edge for symbolic reasons as well. After all, Passover commemorates the central Jewish myth of God's miraculous rescue of the enslaved Hebrew people living under an oppressive Egyptian Pharaoh (see Exod 1–15). Over time, this story gave rise to a springtime religious festival that celebrates God's saving power over foreign rulers. Passover's subversive message of hope for those living under military occupation wasn't lost on the Romans.

Besides its symbolic power, Passover also revved Jerusalem's economic engine. For pilgrims, Passover was expensive; they saved all year to pay for costs associated with travel, as well as with the sacrifices required to participate in temple worship. For Jerusalem's leaders, Passover brought an influx of cash, as the institution and its guardians profited from such religious tourism. Thus it wasn't only the Romans who had a vested interest in keeping the peace during Passover. Native religious leaders, too, had little patience for those whose delusions of liberation might erupt into outright revolt.

Jesus's Prophetic Challenge

Mark's passion narrative begins with two scenes that portray Jesus as a contentious troublemaker in the eyes of political and religious leaders. First, he stages a dramatic entry into Jerusalem, riding on a donkey and so reviving prophetic hopes for God's coming kingdom (Mark 11:1-11; cf. Zech 9:9-17). The political implications of this act are clear to the crowds, who praise this king "who comes in the name of the Lord" (Mark 11:9; cf. Ps 118:25-26). They hope Jesus might end Roman rule and reclaim the Holy City for their God.

A second overtly prophetic act takes place not on the city's fringe but at its geographic and spiritual heart: in the temple courtyard, the center of religious commerce (Mark 11:15-19). Jesus assails those who have made the temple a "den of robbers" (Mark 11:17 NRSV; Jer 7:1)—that is, a place where those in power profit from the devotion of those who can least afford it. Using a literary device called **intercalation**, Mark surrounds this story with another one in a "sandwich" effect: he curses a fig tree as a metaphorical indictment on the religious leaders who, he thinks, oppose God's kingdom (Mark 11:12-14, 20-26).

Mark's passion narrative includes prophetic teaching as well. Once again, Jesus turns aside from frenzied activity to point out signs that God's kingdom is near (Mark 13:1-37). Scholars call Mark 13 the **little apocalypse** because its literary features resemble full-volume works such as John's Revelation. In this chapter, Jesus predicts that the temple will soon lie in rubble and that cosmic events such as earthquakes will precede the impending end of the present evil age. He also explains that social and cosmic upheaval unfold as an organic part of God's renewal of the world. His followers, Jesus says, will face persecution by religious and political officials, but they will be "saved" from such palpable evil power if they endure "until the end" (Mark 13:13). Once again, historians think the details included in this prediction come from Mark, not Jesus. As *ex eventu* prophecy, Mark's Jesus interprets the harsh realities faced by Mark's community as an inevitable part of the apocalyptic script.

Jesus's Opponents

The opposition to Jesus that first appears early in Mark gains momentum in Jerusalem. Among Jewish leaders who oppose Jesus, Mark mentions several groups working in coalition to thwart the uprising they fear he's stirring. **Chief priests**, the **legal experts**, and the **elders** grill Jesus about his authority (Mark 11:27-33). **Pharisees** and followers of **Herod** align interests to pose a question about paying the Roman tax (Mark 12:13-17). And **Sadduccees** try to stump Jesus with a question about the resurrection, which they didn't believe in (Mark 12:18-27). Mark uses this battery of informal interrogations to show that Jesus was a marked man.

Ultimately, a vigilante crowd detains Jesus and delivers him to a gathering of religious leaders called the **Sanhedrin** (Mark 14:55). There, the **high priest** hones in on the real issue: "Are you the Christ, the Son of the blessed one?" (Mark 14:61), which Jesus answers in the positive. Jesus's interrogator calls this response blasphemy, a charge typically reserved for pronouncing the divine name, which Jesus does not do. In any case, the Jewish leaders hand Jesus over to Pilate, who has authority to execute him.

Historians depict **Pontius Pilate** as a ruthless official who had no qualms about eliminating a potential security threat. In Mark, though, he seems easily swayed by both Jewish leaders and the crowd. Why does Mark tone down Pilate's culpability, a trend that only continues in the other Gospels? Perhaps Mark writes in a setting where Jesus's followers are already under suspicion of Roman officials; by attributing Jesus's death mostly to Jewish leaders, Mark may have protected his audience from further reprisal. In any case, Mark probably does preserve vestiges of the awkward collaboration between religious and political officials. Jesus thus plays the scapegoat for both, as his death serves to keep the peace of Jerusalem. Notably, the crowd—not religious or political officials—ultimately seals Jesus's fate with these words: "Crucify him!" (Mark 15:13-14).

Jesus and Women

As they have elsewhere in the Gospel (see Figure 5.7), women play an important role in Mark's passion narrative. Once again, they appear as models of devotion to Jesus and the divine economy he promotes. In one passage, he contrasts a poor widow's meager offering (about "a penny") with the vast sums given by the rich (men). In Jesus's view, the woman has "put in more" than those who give "out of their spare change" (Mark 12:41-44). Her gift becomes an object lesson to illustrate the sacrificial servanthood Jesus embodies and promotes throughout Mark.

FIGURE 5.12: GARDEN OF GETHSEMANE

Garden of Gethsemane

In another story, Mark again weaves together contrasting stories by means of intercalation. The account of an unnamed woman who anoints Jesus lies sandwiched between reports of intrigue that will lead to his death (Mark 14:1-11). Jesus's companions chastise the woman for her extravagance, but Jesus affirms her enduring legacy: "wherever in the whole world the good news is announced, what she's done will also be told in memory of her" (Mark 14:9). Thus Mark elevates the woman's self-offering as the gospel in miniature. Like Jesus, she's invested her life in the disclosure of God's kingdom.

A Suffering Jesus

Among NT Gospels, Mark portrays Jesus in the most human light, and in the passion narrative, that humanity is in full view. Two stories in particular highlight Mark's keen focus on Jesus's suffering. The first occurs in the **garden of Gethsemane**, where Jesus and his disciples go after their Passover meal. (See Figure 5.12.) As Jesus prays, he's gripped by anxiety and despair

FIGURE 5.13: SUFFERING IN BUDDHISM

Like Christianity, Buddhism squares up to the human experience of suffering. But this Eastern religious and philosophical tradition approaches the question of suffering from a different angle than Mark. Buddhism's four "noble truths" are as follows:

1. To live is to suffer.

2. Suffering comes from desire.

3. To end suffering, end desire.

4. To end desire, follow the eightfold noble path.

That path includes eight practices—from "right intention" to "right speech" to "right action" to "right meditation"—that release people from their desire for life to unfold in a certain way. In other words, Buddhists think of suffering as a state of mind, and for the enlightened, an unnecessary one. Mark's Gospel takes a different tack: a certain kind of suffering is an inevitable part of the faithful life, but righteous suffering isn't the end of the story. It always leads to redemption and hope.

YOUR TURN: How do you think about suffering? What do you learn from Mark and from Buddhism? Do you agree with either? Both? Neither? Why?

(Mark 14:33). Compared with the other Gospels, Mark's Jesus shows much more visceral emotion, prostrating himself as he prays, "Abba, Father, for you all things are possible. Take this cup of suffering away from me. However—not what I want but what you want" (Mark 14:36). It's an internal conversation marked by candid struggle and willing submission that puts very human flesh on Jesus's faith (cf. Mark 9:24).

A similar kind of faith emerges from Jesus's last words on the cross in Mark. Hanging in agony, he cries, "My God, my God, why have you left me?" (Mark 15:34). Though the words seem to end Jesus's life on a note of despair, they come from a psalm that moves from desperation to praise (see Ps 22). This **cry of dereliction** preserves Jesus's human plight of suffering even as it hints—through subtle scriptural allusion—at the hope of redemption. For Mark's Jesus, there's no way around suffering, but the way through suffering for God's kingdom leads to new life. (See Figure 5.13.)

Epilogue: The Empty Tomb (Mark 16:1-8)

Text critics tell us that the earliest versions of Mark end with three women fleeing the empty tomb in "terror and dread" and in fearful silence (Mark

FIGURE 5.14: THE SHORTER AND LONGER ENDINGS OF MARK

Ancient manuscripts of Mark end in different ways: some at 16:8, others with just an extra verse (called the "Shorter Ending"), others with an extensive conclusion found in 16:9-20 (the "Longer Ending"), still others with both the Shorter and the Longer Endings. What do these later additions say, and why do scholars think they're not original to Mark?

The Shorter Ending (Mark 16:9) was probably the last one added—perhaps four hundred years after Mark was written. In this brief statement, the women do indeed tell Peter "all of the young man's instructions." Then, Mark ends this way: "Afterward, through the work of his disciples, Jesus sent out, from the east to the west, the sacred and undying message of eternal salvation. Amen." The language used here is alien to the Gospel itself and belongs more naturally to the language of later Christian tradition.

The Longer Ending (Mark 16:9–20) appeared fairly early in the transmission process. It's mentioned in the late second century CE, even though the earliest and most reliable manuscripts lack it. What's more, it includes key features from the other three canonical Gospels: the Great Commission from Matthew; Jesus's appearance to two disciples and snake-handling powers from Luke; and the condemnation of non-believers from John. Scholars think it's an attempt to make Mark's ending conform to the other Gospel accounts that were recognized as authoritative at the time.

> **YOUR TURN:** Read both endings. What do these later additions tell you about the scribes' mind-set and concerns? What does Mark's Gospel gain or lose with these endings?

16:8). It's possible—some think likely—that the Gospel's last verses were lost early in the transmission process. But Mark 16:9-20 was clearly added later. This ending appears in most Bibles today in square brackets that designate it likely didn't belong to the original Gospel. It's a helpful reminder of how fluid the textual tradition was, since scribes felt free to add a more palatable conclusion to the story. (See Figure 5.14.)

Many literary critics think Mark 16:1-8 perfectly suits the aura of mystery and ambiguity that permeates the preceding fifteen chapters, where we find bumbling disciples, two-staged healings, and perplexing statements. So it's possible—some think likely—that Mark meant to leave readers hanging, literally, in mid-sentence. (In the Greek, Mark 16:8 ends with the conjunction *for*, as unnatural a syntax in Greek as it would be in English.)

The story of the empty tomb itself is fraught with creative tension. The male disciples are nowhere in sight; instead, three women—Mary Magdalene, Mary the mother of James, and Salome (Mark 16:1; cf. Matt 28:1; Luke 24:1; John 20:1)—set out to perform the Jewish ritual washing for final burial. To their surprise, they find the "very large stone" that had sealed the temporary tomb rolled away and a young man dressed as an angel sitting inside. Their response is not joy but alarm, but the messenger directs them to "go, tell his disciples, especially Peter, that he is going ahead of you into Galilee . . . just as he told you" (Mark 16:7; cf. 14:28). The promise of a post-resurrection reunion, though, remains just that: an unfulfilled promise, hanging in the air.

MARK'S MESSAGE

Over time, readers have turned to other Gospels to fill in details about Jesus's identity and his earthly mission. On its own, Mark leaves many unanswered questions surrounding this man called the Christ and the first followers who joined in his ministry. But remember, Mark's original audience had *only* this story. For them, its message explained Jesus's life, death, and resurrection in ways that imbued their own experience with meaning and hope. We turn now to Mark's particular features and their import for the persecuted community it first addressed.

Imminence

Mark stands out from its canonical peers for its heightened sense of urgency. Besides a frenetic narrative pace that shifts abruptly from one scene to another, the story itself is mostly action. There's little time for Jesus to deliver a lecture or invite measured reflection. God's kingdom looms near, and this imminence colors Mark's whole story. Why the rush?

Most scholars trace at least some of this imminence back to Jesus himself. Many historians think Jesus thought time was short, that his own generation would see the coming "day of the Lord." Others think it was Jesus's followers who introduced this motif and that Mark carried it forward. Regardless of its origins, Mark's story is fraught with a sense that a regime change is at hand.

That's likely due to Mark's own landscape a few decades after Jesus's death. Mark 13, in particular, "winks and nods" at an audience beset with conflict, persecution, and chaos (see e.g., Mark 13:14). What Mark's Jesus predicts for the future is playing out for them in living color. As we've noted, their persecution may have come as ripple effects from the Jewish War in Palestine. After all, this community was probably "in the neighborhood," both geographically (perhaps in Syria) and religiously through their devotion to a Jewish Messiah, a title that was often associated with insurgency. Mark interprets their suffering, like Jesus's, as an inevitable part of the power play that messiahship entails in Jewish apocalyptic thought. If they find themselves targeted by religious and civic authorities, they're simply taking up that cross and following a crucified Lord. More than that, they can rest in the good news that, no matter their present circumstance, God's kingdom—and with it, liberation from all evil forces—will soon prevail.

Trust

Within this short-term timeframe, Mark encourages hearers to reaffirm their loyalty to God's coming kingdom. More than just the belief *that* Jesus is the Christ, Mark's story inspires faith *in* God's alternative world order and its power to renew and restore all of creation. Of course, Jesus models full-fledged dependence on God's power, as its anointed agent on earth. But his followers, too, play a part in mediating divine authority. They launch out on Jesus's behalf (Mark 6:7-13) and participate in feeding the crowds (Mark 6:30-44). In several cases, women exemplify the faith Jesus promotes (e.g., Mark 5:25-34; 7:24-30; 12:41-44; 14:3-9). In Mark, those who cast their allegiance with God's power find it brings well-being to those in need.

For Mark's community, these instances of "power sharing" may have inspired renewed trust in God's power, especially when the present world order seemed to be winning. At the same time, Mark's portrait of the disciples' faulty, sporadic faith offers a narrative reminder that the dawn of God's coming kingdom doesn't ultimately depend on human effort or understanding. After all, the women at the tomb relay Jesus's post-resurrection promise to "go ahead" of those who've denied and abandoned him (Mark 16:7). It's Jesus's durable trust, in both God and those he's drawn into his mission, that's the defining mark of this story.

Suffering

Above all, this Gospel acknowledges explicitly what Mark's community full well knows: those who trust the good news of God's coming kingdom will suffer backlash from conventional powers-that-be. As we've seen, such push-back appears from the Gospel's outset, when opponents conspire to bring about Jesus's demise. But it looms even larger in the second half, as Jesus teaches his disciples about the cost of following him and then meets his own destiny in Jerusalem.

It is important to note that Mark's message neither minimizes nor glorifies human suffering, as if promoting martyrdom for its own sake. Jesus agonizes both in the garden of Gethsemane and on the cross; his suffering is real, and poignant, and full of pathos. But it's a certain kind of suffering—the kind that comes organically from Jesus's allegiance to God's kingdom and its values, rather than Rome's. He plays by God's rules, not theirs. And he dies as a result.

But suffering isn't the last word of this Gospel—neither for Jesus nor for Mark's community. It's set within the wider horizon of God's saving ways. Mark's apocalyptic worldview leaves no doubt that God will win in the end— and soon. At the empty tomb, three women learn that Jesus's tragic death has given way to new life. And so the Gospel ends with this paradox: they flee in stunned silence, but Mark's audience knows the rest of the story.

SUMMARY

This earliest Gospel is also roughest around the edges. In it, Jesus appears as a messianic prophet who points urgently to God's kingdom. His words and deeds show that this kingdom operates not by coercive force but by bringing life and wholeness, exerting divine power to liberate the world from evil's grasp. In Jerusalem, Jesus dies at the hands of the very power he resists. But the empty tomb, and the promise of his post-resurrection presence, end the Gospel on a note of understated but resolute hope. Throughout the story, Jesus draws others into his messianic mission, calling disciples not just to follow him but to disclose the mystery entrusted to them—the mystery that God's kingdom is loose in a world still plagued by suffering. Written decades later for a persecuted community, this Gospel tells the story of a Lord who shares their plight and fills it with ultimate meaning. It ends with the promise that suffering gives way, through hope, to life.

Review and Reflect

- Why did Jesus die, according to Mark's story? Name two details from the Gospel's second half that illustrate your response.

- How does Mark's emphasis on Jesus's suffering connect to Mark's community? How does a story about suffering also offer hope?

GO DEEPER

Dowd, Sharyn E. *Reading Mark: A Literary and Theological Commentary on the Second Gospel.* Macon, GA: Smyth and Helwys, 2000.

Harrington, Daniel J. *What Are They Saying about Mark?* Mahwah, NJ: Paulist Press, 2005.

Leander, Hans. *Discourses of Empire: The Gospel of Mark in Post-colonial Perspective.* Atlanta: SBL Press, 2013.

Levine, Amy-Jill, ed. *A Feminist Companion to Mark.* Cleveland, OH: Pilgrim Press, 2004.

Malbon, Elizabeth Struthers, ed. *Between Author and Audience in Mark: Narration, Characterization, Interpretation.* Sheffield, UK: Sheffield Phoenix, 2009.

Maloney, Elliott C. *Jesus' Urgent Message for Today: The Kingdom of God in Mark's Gospel.* New York: Continuum, 2004.

Chapter Six

What Is Righteousness?
Gospel of Matthew

CONVERSATION STARTERS

- How does rabbinical Judaism inform Matthew's Gospel?

- Who wrote this Gospel? And for whom?

- What kind of "righteousness" does Matthew promote?

- What does Matthew say about "the church"?

- Who's in? Who's out? And on what basis?

Though most scholars today think Mark was written earlier, the Gospel of Matthew has long appeared in first place among the NT Gospels. Ancient Christian writers favored Matthew in their sermons and commentaries, perhaps because it often reads like an instruction manual for Christian living. Today, many Christians find an ethical ground zero in the Sermon on the Mount featured in this Gospel. All of this wins Matthew acclaim, among some readers, as the clearest and most complete account of Jesus's life, death, and resurrection in the NT.

Matthew's twenty-eight chapters make it the longest NT Gospel. But it's not just Matthew's length that qualifies this story as first among equals for many. It's also the kind of material Matthew features, as well as the Gospel's methodical approach. For instance, Matthew organizes Jesus's teachings according to themes such as righteousness and discipleship. Matthew also

116

clarifies Mark's mystery (e.g., Matt 13:10; cf. Mark 4:10), softens Mark's criticism of the disciples, and corrects Mark's errors in grammar, geography (e.g., Matt 8:28; cf. Mark 5:1), and scriptural citation (e.g., Matt 12:4; cf. Mark 2:26).

Another feature makes Matthew particularly well-suited to church teaching: its explicit interest in the church. In fact, it's the only Gospel to use the word *ekklēsia* ("church") to designate the gathered group of Jesus's followers. (In the ancient world, the Greek term *ekklēsia* referred to public meetings devoted to a wide range of social, political, and religious concerns.) Only in Matthew does Jesus name Peter as the "rock" on which "I'll build my church" (Matt 16:18); only in Matthew does Jesus offer a code of conduct for addressing disputes that arise within the church (Matt 18:15-20).

At the heart of Matthew's message lies the dominant value of righteousness that Jesus both embodies and inculcates. It's a concept deeply rooted in Jesus's own Jewish tradition. In Matthew's story, it's the leading marker of God's kingdom. Jesus fulfills this righteousness, heeding the "law and the prophets" in their promotion of bedrock values of "justice, peace, and faith" (Matt 23:23). In turn, this Jewish Messiah inaugurates a kingdom of righteousness that his followers, too, both reflect and promote.

Matthew walks a fine line with respect to Judaism. This Gospel both stresses Jesus's Jewish roots and forges a distinction between Jesus and his competitors, the rabbis often called "legal experts and Pharisees" in Matthew. Over time, Christians have used Matthew's vitriol against these leaders to legitimize anti-Jewish attitudes and policies. But while we can't overlook Matthew's hostile rhetoric—just read Matthew 23, for example—we'll try to understand this Gospel in its first-century context. In its own socioreligious setting, Matthew appeared as a conversation partner in a family squabble, as Judaism reinvented itself after the temple's destruction by the Roman army. To read Matthew on its own terms is to listen in on this vigorous exchange with the Pharisees who were shaping the future of Judaism, even as a small splinter group cast their loyalty with a Jewish Messiah. Who were these Pharisees, in Jesus's and Matthew's day?

WHAT'S MATTHEW'S WORLDVIEW? RABBINICAL JUDAISM

If Mark's setting forged that Gospel in the fires of apocalyptic thought, Matthew recounts Jesus's story in conversation with **rabbinical Judaism**. This is the form of Jewish practice and belief that gained influence in the late first century CE and persists to this day. To understand Matthew, then, let's explore this kind of Judaism.

With the temple's destruction in 70 CE, the landscape of Palestinian Judaism (which we considered in chapter 3) shifted in historic ways. The **Sadducees**, who had negotiated an uneasy alliance with Roman officials, had lost the confidence of both the occupying power and the people. The basis of their religious authority—the temple and its sacrificial system—lay in rubble. That left a vacuum of religious power. But who would fill it? Among the groups we discussed in chapter 3, neither the **Zealots** (the **Fourth Philosophy**) nor the **Essenes** were in a position to reform Judaism. After all, the first group had stoked the uprising that brought Jerusalem's defeat, and sectarian groups were far from mainstream religious players.

That left the **Pharisees** as the natural heirs to religious authority, for many reasons. Also known as the "rabbis," this group had made their mark on the landscape of Palestinian Judaism mostly outside the halls of power in Jerusalem. (Josephus reports a noteworthy exception to this pattern, when the Pharisees grew so popular among the people that Queen Alexandra yielded power to them during her reign, which spanned 76–67 BCE.) Yet the Pharisees had gained a widespread following because they were, quite simply, the party of the people in that they equipped the faithful for righteous living in daily life. Moreover, their Torah-centered approach to piety was innately adaptable to changing circumstance, anchored as it was in oral and written tradition rather than geographic or cultic location.

The Gospels give the impression that the Pharisees were overly scrupulous in their rule-following. But other Jewish sources sometimes portray them as what we might call "flaming liberals." When the Qumran community's Damascus Document, for instance, says they "sought easy interpretations, chose illusions, [and] scrutinized loopholes" (CD 1:18-19), the description isn't intended to be a compliment. What are we to make of these competing claims? Perhaps it's best to consider the sources. Both the Gospels and the Damascus Document come from sectarian groups who were at odds with the Pharisees' interpretation of Torah. Both resented their popular sway. That made them more likely to disparage this competing form of Jewish practice.

Rather than taking these detractors' words at face value, let's consider how the Pharisees describe themselves. A collection of their teachings known as the **Mishnah** dates to around 200 CE, but scholars agree it preserves oral traditions from Jesus's day and so offers a helpful window into the rabbinical school of thought that would soon leave its indelible imprint on Judaism. The sayings in the Mishnah cluster around such topics as how to keep Sabbath, how to maintain purity in the course of daily life (with an entire section

Figure 6.1: A Rabbinical Conversation

The Mishnah preserves over three hundred differences between the views associated with two first-century rabbis, **Hillel** and **Shammai**. In general, Shammai is the stricter and Hillel the more lenient interpreter. Perhaps not surprisingly, Hillel's interpretation gained authority over time. Here's an example of the kind of disagreement that appears in the Mishnah:

The school of Shammai says: In the evening all people should recline and recite [Shema], and in the morning they should stand, since it says [in the verse (Deut. 6:7)], "And when you lie down and when you arise." But the school of Hillel says: Each person may recite it in his usual way (posture), since it says [this], "And when you walk on the road." If so, why does it say "and when you lie down and when you arise"? —[It means:] at the time when people are lying down, and at the time when people are arising. Said Rabbi Tarfon: "I was once traveling on the road, and I reclined to recite [Shema] in accordance with the view of the school of Shammai, and [by doing so] I put myself in danger of [attack by] bandits." They [the other Sages] said to him: "You would have deserved to be guilty for your own fate, since you went against the view of the school of Hillel." (Mishnah, *Berakot*, 1:3)

YOUR TURN: Reflect on the value of such conversation about religious instruction. Why do you think people tended to find Hillel's views more compelling?

devoted to women's menstrual cycle), and how to observe religious holidays within the context of an agrarian society.

If you've only met the Pharisees through the lens of the Gospels, you might be surprised by some of rabbinical Judaism's prominent features. For one thing, the Pharisees don't present the Torah as a burden at all. Instead, they delight in it as sheer gift. It's a covenant that frames healthy relationships—both within human society and with God—as its ethics and rituals connect human life to the Creator.

Another feature of rabbinical Judaism is its conversational nature. Rather than a doctrinal code, the Mishnah captures animated discussions about how to follow Torah. If you know anything about Hegel's dialectical philosophy, you'll find it in full measure in the Mishnah: one rabbi spouts a thesis; another responds with an antithesis; ultimately, a synthesis incorporates elements of the exchange and also transcends them. (See Figure 6.1.)

All of these features positioned the Pharisees as prominent voices when the future of Judaism was up for grabs. Even before 70 CE, an academy at **Javneh** (Jamnia) had trained rabbis in this interpretive approach. Established by a disciple of **Rabbi Hillel** named **Johanan ben Zakkai**, the school provided a safe haven for those fleeing the embers of the Jewish War. There, a wide variety of Jewish leaders gathered together around the question of Jewish identity and practice. It was, so to speak, time to circle the wagons.

Sociologists of religion tell us that moments of crisis and reinvention such as this one up the ante on questions about group boundaries: Who's in, who's out, and who gets to decide? In the late first century CE, some Jewish leaders applied these questions to followers of a Messiah named Jesus. Since most Jews weren't convinced the messianic age had begun, this belief became a sticking point on the question of Jewish identity. That led to tension, at least in some Jewish communities, between those who cast their loyalty with Jesus Christ and those still awaiting the Messiah.

This dynamic is important to keep in mind as we turn to Matthew. In this Gospel, Jesus is a "new Moses" who exhibits and teaches about righteousness at every turn. If Moses bears authoritative witness to Torah in Jewish scripture, Jesus is its authoritative interpreter for Matthew. In this Gospel, Jesus is the Jewish Messiah, the one to whom the "law and the prophets" point. But Matthew's resolute insistence on Jesus's authority also pits Jesus against Jewish leaders more pointedly than the other Synoptic accounts. It's a Gospel devoted to shining light on Jesus's superiority over the competition, who aren't always painted in the most glowing (or historically accurate) light.

WHO WROTE MATTHEW? AND FOR WHOM?

As we've noted, all of the Gospels were written anonymously. Scribes added the title "Gospel According to Matthew" decades later, based on the Gospel's association with one of Jesus's named disciples (see Matt 9:9; 10:3). It's unlikely, though, that a Palestinian Jewish tax collector would number among the educated elite who could write such polished Greek. It's even less likely that he would have lived long enough to compose this Gospel. After all, the Four Source Hypothesis suggests Matthew was written in the 80s CE; in any case, the narrator implies the temple's been destroyed (see Matt 21:41; 22:7; 24:15-16). So it's out of convenience that we'll refer to the evangelist as "Matthew" throughout our discussion.

What, then, can we say about this Matthew and the Gospel's intended audience? For one thing, this evangelist may have belonged to the Jewish scribal tradition, a small group of men trained to preserve sacred texts. Remember, with a literacy rate hovering well below 20 percent in the ancient Mediterranean world, the ability to read and write was rare. But because Second Temple Judaism so valued scripture (mostly Torah, but other writings as well), these "legal experts" played a prominent role in sustaining religious identity.

Matthew's interest in Jewish sacred tradition permeates this Gospel. For one thing, only in Matthew does Jesus mention "every scribe who has been trained for the kingdom of heaven" (Matt 13:52 NRSV). This training entails intimate knowledge of Jewish scripture, which Matthew cites freely and explicitly. Often the author includes a **fulfillment citation** as a verbal clue connecting Jesus's story to Jewish expectation. Consider this example: "Now all of this took place so that what the Lord had spoken through the prophet would be fulfilled" (Matt 1:22). This Gospel makes explicit what Mark only suggests: all of Jewish scripture points to the Jewish Messiah named Jesus.

If Matthew writes as a highly trained Jewish scholar, most of the Gospel's first hearers were probably Jewish as well. Not that they were a homogeneous group. Some—perhaps non-Jewish—members may have wanted to set aside Torah altogether (see Matt 8:8-10). Matthew's opening genealogy includes four Gentile women (Matt 1:1-17), which may indicate the presence of non-Jews among its target audience. Finally, the Great Commission that is the Gospel's grand finale (Matt 28:16-20) sends disciples out to "all nations," using the same Greek term that's often translated "Gentiles."

On the location of this community, ancient tradition and modern historians together point to the Gospel's origins in Antioch, Syria. Not only was there a robust Jewish community there, but the book of Acts says that Antioch quickly emerged as a base for the early Christian movement outside of Palestine and that Jesus's followers were first called "Christians" in this city (Acts 11:26). Finally, **Ignatius of Antioch**, an early and prominent bishop, alludes to this Gospel by about 110 CE.

Of course, Antioch in the first century CE was part of the Roman Empire, so this Gospel interprets Jesus's story in conversation with imperial values as well. Jesus's family flees the state-sanctioned massacre of small children (Matt 2:16-18), a policy implemented by Herod the Great, who ruled on Rome's behalf. In the end, of course, Jesus dies on a Roman cross. More subtly, Jesus's way of righteousness challenges the basic Roman social order, based on separation and stratification. Matthew's community would have known better than most Christians today just how inherently political was the movement to which they'd committed their lives.

Matthew's message distinguishes Jesus's way of righteousness from rabbinical interpretations favored by the mainstream Judaism of the day. But rather than rejecting Jewish law, Matthew's Jesus intensifies its demands. This Gospel is no "Judaism Light." As one who has come "not to abolish" the law and the prophets "but to fulfill" them (Matt 5:16), Matthew's Jesus is a "new Moses" who points to a way of life that's both deeply ethical and eschatologically significant.

WHAT'S THE "GOOD NEWS" IN MATTHEW? THE "RIGHTEOUS ROAD"

Matthew compliments Mark's Gospel by incorporating about 90 percent of its content, but not without significant editorial input along the way. If Mark tells a story that's rough around the edges, Matthew organizes Jesus's career neatly into thematic sections and clarifies many confusing elements found in Mark. Matthew also leaves little to inference. Clues such as the fulfillment citations mentioned above, as well as clear narrative markers at the end of each main part of the story (Matt 7:28; cf. 11:1; 13:53; 19:1; 26:1), guide the Gospel's audience through the story. All of these features mean that Matthew emerged, early in Christian tradition, as the most teachable Gospel.

Matthew's structure (see Figure 6.2) features book end sections that frame the Gospel: Matthew 1–2 recount Jesus's backstory (from his family tree to his birth in Bethlehem), while concluding chapters tell of his death, resurrection, and post-resurrection appearance. Sandwiched in between lie five major sections that combine Jesus's messianic activities with his extended teachings. Of the five, four take place in and around Galilee, while the last begins as Jesus heads toward Jerusalem (see Matt 19:1). Scholars think this five-part structure casts Jesus as a "new Moses," since the Torah is composed of five books.

Prologue: Matthew's Birth Narrative (Matt 1:1–2:23)

Matthew opens with a page from ancestry.com—a genealogy that traces Jesus's lineage back through some of the heroes of Jewish tradition. In Greek, Matthew calls this genealogy Jesus's "genesis," which is also the name of the first book in Jewish scripture. Tellingly for the rest of the Gospel, the opening verse signals that Jesus is the Davidic Messiah that the Jewish "children of Abraham" have long awaited (Matt 1:1).

FIGURE 6:2: OUTLINE OF MATTHEW

Prologue: Birth Narrative (1:1–2:23)

Jesus's Ministry in and around Galilee:

Book One (3:1–7:27): Narrative + Discourse

Book Two (7:28–10:42): Narrative + Discourse

Book Three (11:1–13:52): Narrative + Discourse

Book Four (13:53–18:35): Narrative + Discourse

Book Five (19:1–25:46): Narrative + Discourse

Passion Narrative (26:1–28:15)

Epilogue: Great Commission (28:16-20)

Besides these important identity markers, the genealogy offers noteworthy clues about Matthew's Gospel. For one thing, Matthew organizes the generations leading up to Jesus into groups of fourteen, a strategy mentioned explicitly in Matthew 1:17. Why fourteen? Scholars think Matthew uses an ancient practice called **gematria** that signifies meaning by way of numerical code. As with the Roman numerals we learned in elementary school, Hebrew letters also represent numbers. The three letters that make up David's name in Hebrew add up to fourteen, which leads many scholars to think Matthew's stressing Jesus's messianic ties to David (see 2 Sam 7:12-16). If Matthew has to force fit the biblical story into this scheme of fourteen, that simply reminds us that this biblical author privileges meaning over accuracy.

Matthew's genealogy also assigns key roles to four women in a list otherwise dominated by men. Matthew names Tamar, Rahab, Ruth, and the "wife of Uriah" (Bathsheba in 1 Sam 11) as birth mothers in Jesus's story. Why these women? We can only speculate, based on a few observations. For one thing, at least three of them are non-Israelite women whom God uses at strategic points in the biblical story. Intriguingly, all four women deploy their sexuality in ways that protect either them or their offspring (or both). Many interpreters have inferred that Matthew includes these women from the Gospel's outset to signal the expansive reach of Jesus's messianic movement.

Matthew again uses the word *genesis* to introduce the story of Jesus's birth (Matt 1:18). Many familiar parts of the Christmas pageant are missing in Matthew's version. Here, no angel visits Mary; no one travels to Bethlehem; no innkeeper puts the holy family out back in an animal shed; and no shepherds visit the newborn child. Matthew's story is leaner, and a bit harsher, than Luke's.

What does Matthew emphasize? For one thing, Joseph plays a prominent role as Jesus's (earthly) father. Joseph, not Mary, hears from an angel, who visits him in a dream. Joseph, not Mary, is instructed to name the child "Jesus," which means "he saves." After Jesus's birth, an angel warns Joseph to escape with his young family to Egypt, because of King Herod's sinister plans. Finally, an angel tells Joseph to return to Nazareth, rather than to Bethlehem, implying that Bethlehem was their original home. Matthew also conveys an interest in Joseph's righteousness, a theme that appears throughout the Gospel. One of the first things Matthew says about Joseph is that he was a "righteous man" (Matt 1:19), meaning that he followed Torah faithfully.

Besides Joseph, the birth narrative has much to say about the power play Jesus's arrival in the world introduces. The passage's other main character (besides Jesus) is King Herod. The Roman Senate appointed **Herod the Great** "king of Judea" in 37 BCE. He served in that capacity, as client king (native leader authorized by the empire) until his death in 4 BCE. Tourists in the Holy Land today can still see evidence of his massive building projects, designed both to impress his own people and to enhance Roman power in the region. Born to a family from Idumea (known as Edom in the Hebrew Bible), Herod's family had converted to Judaism when their land was conquered a century earlier. Many Palestinian Jews questioned his nominal devotion to Jewish law.

In Matthew's story, Herod is so threatened by Jesus's international acclaim—three foreign officials have come to pay their respects—that he resorts to mass slaughter of children around Bethlehem under age two. Though we have no historical record of such an edict, Josephus reports that Herod's regime freely used violence to control the occupied people. Matthew uses Herod's character to make two important points. First, Matthew lays the groundwork for the sharp contrast between God's kingdom and Rome's. Second, the massacre provides a pretext for Joseph and his family to take refuge in Egypt. This geographic location links Jesus to Moses, the one who led the ancient Hebrew people out of slavery in Egypt in Exodus. Matthew makes the connection explicit by saying this part of the story fulfills Jewish scripture: "I have called my son out of Egypt" (Matt 2:15; cf. Hos 11:1). In all these ways, Matthew's opening chapters set the stage for the five books that follow.

Book One: Jesus as the New Moses (Matt 3:1–7:27)

Matthew's first major section begins where Mark begins: in the wilderness, with John the Baptist. As will be the case with each major section, Matthew combines traditions found in Mark with stories and sayings from Q and M. At every turn, we see Matthew's editorial tendency to shape the message of Jesus Christ in ways that comport with Jewish belief and practice.

When it comes to Jesus's baptism and temptation, both Matthew and Luke fill out Mark's barebones account, inserting material scholars attribute to Q. Though both portray John as a firebrand preacher who calls his onlookers "children of snakes," only Matthew identifies them as "many Pharisees and Sadducees" (Matt 3:7; cf. Luke 3:7). Also distinctive to Matthew is Jesus's insistence that his baptism is necessary "to fulfill all righteousness" (Matt 3:15). Already, Matthew sets Jesus apart from the Jewish leaders who represent a competing brand of righteousness in the religious marketplace.

After the baptism, Matthew reports Jesus's testing in the wilderness and his move from Galilee to Capernaum—noted only in this Gospel—to fulfill Jewish prophecy (see Matt 3:12-16; cf. Isa 9:1-2). As in Mark, the inaugural act of Jesus's public ministry finds him recruiting four fishers who will join in his messianic mission. Matthew ends this section with an expanded report about Jesus's preaching and healing ministry (Matt 4:23-25; cf. Mark 1:39).

Jesus's first major **discourse** (extended body of teachings) in Matthew is perhaps his most famous: the **Sermon on the Mount** (Matt 5:1–7:27). The material found here mostly appears in Luke as well and so probably derives from Q. But Matthew combines these disparate sayings into something of an inaugural address that includes such well-known teachings as the Beatitudes, the Lord's Prayer, and the Golden Rule. (See Figure 6.3.)

But this sermon also features some of Jesus's most challenging sayings, such as the command to "love your enemies" (Matt 5:44), to "stop collecting treasures for your own benefit on earth" (Matt 6:19), and to "be perfect . . . as your heavenly Father is perfect" (Matt 5:48 NRSV). Early generations of believers apparently took these teachings at face value. Many refused military service since Jesus taught them to love, not kill, their foes. Over time, interpreters have often toned down, and spiritualized, the sermon's contents, making them more amenable to Christian war-making and consumerism. (See Figure 6.4.) Still, these teachings retain a vital place in the canon for many Christians. They also offer a window into a lively conversation with the rabbinical Judaism emerging in Matthew's day. What is it about Jesus's kind of righteousness that Matthew highlights?

FIGURE 6.3: PLURALISM AND THE GOLDEN RULE

Most religious traditions incorporate teachings that sound a lot like the Golden Rule. Sometimes, the injunction to care for others appears as a negative prohibition against doing something you wouldn't want others to do to you. In other cases, including Matthew's Gospel, the teaching appears as a positive mandate to treat others as you'd like to be treated. Here are a few examples:

Hinduism: "This is the sum of duty: do not do to others what would cause pain if done to you" (*Mahabharata*, 5:1517).

Confucianism: "Do not do to others what you do not want them to do to you" (Doctrine of the Mean); "What I do not wish men to do to me, I also wish not to do to men" (*Analects*, 15:23).

Judaism: "That which is despicable to you, do not do to your fellow, this is the whole Torah, and the rest is commentary, go and learn it" (Babylonian Talmud, *Shabbat*, 31a).

Islam: "None of you [truly] believes until he wishes for his brother what he wishes for himself" (Hadith 13, Imam "Al-Nawawi's Forty Hadiths).

Pima (Native American) tradition: "Do not wrong or hate your neighbor. For it is not he who you wrong, but yourself."

YOUR TURN: What similarities and differences do you detect among these sayings? How do these common sayings promote cooperation across religious difference?

To Fulfill the Law and the Prophets

Matthew never uses the term *new Moses* to describe Jesus, but careful readers will catch the connection throughout the Gospel. This section opens with just such a cue. Matthew says Jesus "went up a mountain" (Matt 5:1), an echo of Moses's journey up Mount Sinai, where Exodus says God gave him the Torah. (Deuteronomy names Mount Horeb as the location.) This close connection between Jesus and Jewish tradition continues throughout the sermon.

For instance, the **Beatitudes**—the blessings that begin the sermon (Matt 5:3-12)—promote traditional Jewish values such as righteousness, mercy, and peace. Like the Jewish prophets, these sayings attend to the well-being of the oppressed. Indeed, Jesus reiterates his deeply Jewish bearings explicitly: "Don't even begin to think that I have come to do away with the Law and the Prophets. I haven't come to do away with them but to fulfill them" (Matt 5:17).

FIGURE 6.4: CAN CHRISTIANS SERVE IN THE MILITARY?

That may sound like a preposterous question if you live in a country (like the US) where many people link worship of God to patriotism. Have you seen the "God, Guns, Country" bumper sticker? But for the first three hundred years after Jesus, Christian writers consistently spoke out against military service among believers. Why? For one thing, to serve in the Roman army was considered idolatry, since it entailed the worship of civic gods in place of the Lord God. For another thing, many theologians took a strong stand against killing other people—even enemies. Here are a few examples:

Lactantius: "A just man may not be a soldier" because "killing itself is banned" and "killing a human being is always wrong" (*Divine Institutes*, 6.20).

Tertullian: "The Lord, by taking away Peter's sword disarmed every soldier thereafter. We are not allowed to wear any uniform that symbolizes a sinful act."

Origen: "Christians are not to participate in war, even if they are just wars" (*Against Celsum*, 8.73).

YOUR TURN: Learn a bit about Just War Theory. Then argue both for and against Christian military service.

Likewise, Jesus interprets Jewish tradition through a series of *antitheses*, a term that refers to the rhetorical practice of contrasting conventional teaching (a thesis) with new instruction (an antithesis). Six times in the Sermon, Jesus says, "You have heard that it was said . . . but I say to you" (Matt 5:21-22, 27-28, 31-32, 33-34, 38-39, 43-44). He doesn't deny or tame the demands of Jewish law; he intensifies them, claiming for instance that even unspoken anger subjects a person to divine judgment (Matt 5:22).

On the question of religious ritual, too, the Sermon on the Mount stands squarely within Jewish tradition. Both Jesus's and Matthew's Jewish contemporaries took for granted that almsgiving, prayer, and fasting—topics addressed in Matthew 6:1-18—expressed devotion to the Lord God. (See Figure 6.5.) What he criticizes has to do with showy religiosity, not the practices themselves. (See Figure 6.6.)

Greater Righteousness

If the sermon connects Jesus to Moses, it also distinguishes him from those Matthew calls the "legal experts [or scribes] and the Pharisees" (Matt

FIGURE 6.5: THE LORD'S PRAYER IN A NEW LIGHT

Most Christian churches today include the Lord's Prayer in worship on a regular basis. In New Zealand, the Anglican Church's Prayer Book includes a version of the prayer influenced by native Maori and Polynesian cultures. Read Matthew 6:9-13, and then reflect on these words:

Eternal Spirit,
Earth-maker, Pain bearer, Life-giver,
Source of all that is and that shall be,
Father and Mother of us all,
Loving God, in whom is heaven:

The hallowing of your name echo through the universe;
The way of your justice be followed by the peoples of the world;
Your heavenly will be done by all created beings;
Your commonwealth of peace and freedom
sustain our hope and come on earth.

With the bread we need for today, feed us.
In the hurts we absorb from one another, forgive us.
In times of temptation and test, strengthen us.
From trial too great to endure, spare us.
From the grip of all that is evil, free us.
For you reign in the glory of the power that is love,
now and forever. Amen.

(*New Zealand Prayer Book: He Karakia Mihinare o Aortearoa* [San Francisco: Harper Collins, 1997], 182)

YOUR TURN: How does this version both reflect and reinterpret Matthew's version of the Lord's Prayer?

5:20). This phrase, which occurs eleven times in this Gospel, probably works as a cipher for the rabbis in Matthew's day. Though Jesus likely did converse with religious leaders, historians think his strident, combative tone here conveys disputes among Jews in the late first century CE that revolve around Jesus's messianic status as a dividing line within Jewish communities.

What kind of righteousness does the sermon promote? Jesus's radical ethics lie at the heart of this teaching. For one thing, Jesus prioritizes ethical concerns over religious devotion as he interprets Torah. For Second Temple Jews like Jesus, the Decalogue (or Ten Commandments) combined

FIGURE 6.6: RELIGIOUS PRACTICE:
AN ABRAHAMIC OVERLAP

If both Jewish and Christian tradition affirm the practice of prayer, fasting, and almsgiving (generosity to the poor), so, too, does their younger sibling Islam. Of Islam's Five Pillars (five required practices), three overlap with this Jewish and early Christian list:

Salat is daily prayer, observed five times a day by most Muslims (Indian Muslims known as Ismailis pray only three times a day).

Zakat is the giving of alms to the poor in an effort to promote economic justice. Notably, gifts to support the upkeep of a mosque or other institution don't count toward zakat. Only money that helps the poor is recognized by this pillar.

Sawm is fasting, both at ritual celebrations such as the season of Ramadan and for personal purification.

YOUR TURN: Have you ever participated in any of these religious practices in your own tradition or worldview? How do they shape the lives and mind-sets of believers?

love of God (expressed through "piety") with love of neighbor (expressed through "righteousness"), in just that order. (See Figure 6.7.) Many inferred that those who love God inevitably love other human beings as well. In an intriguing twist, the sermon flips the order of these concerns, addressing ethics first and religious practice second. Matthew even uses the word *righteousness* for religious practices typically called "pieties."

Another interpretive strategy highlights the weight of Torah's demands for Matthew. Jesus places what the rabbis call a "fence around the law" by restricting attitudes and actions that might lead down the slippery slope toward breaking the law itself. That's why Jesus charges even the "man who looks at a woman lustfully" (Matt 5:27) with adultery. He also bans divorce (Matt 5:32), which is legal in the Torah, and forbids any spoken pledge (Matt 5:34). (See Figure 6.8.)

Sometimes, the sermon illustrates "greater righteousness" by way of negative example. Tax collectors, Gentiles, and hypocrites all provide case studies in how *not* to live. Both tax collectors and Gentiles, Jesus says, take a tribal approach to human relationships: they love those who love them and greet only those of their own group (Matt 5:46-47). For their part, hypocrites follow Torah in order to enhance their reputation or status. They perform religious

FIGURE 6.7: THE DOUBLE COMMANDMENT
IN HELLENISTIC JUDAISM

Jewish writers who were Jesus's rough contemporaries often referred to a "double commandment" to love God ("piety," or *eusebeia*) and neighbor ("righteousness," or *dikaiosynē*). Philo thinks each of the "two tablets" that make up the Decalogue fit these two concerns (see *Spec.*, 1:42). Josephus uses similar terminology when referring to the commandments (see *Ant.* 8:120–21). He writes that love for God generates love for humanity (*Ag Ap*, 2:170–71). Matthew's Gospel turns the tables, giving primary focus to righteousness—or ethical care for others—as leading evidence of devotion to God.

YOUR TURN: In your view, which takes precedence: love of God or love of neighbor? Why?

duties when others are watching, so that they'll be praised, seen, and heard by others (Matt 6:2, 5, 7, 16).

First and Foremost God's Kingdom and God's Righteousness

For Matthew, righteous living affects the human relationship to possessions as well. Jesus doesn't cite the commandment against coveting others' goods (Exod 20:17; Deut 5:20-21), but he does take on the question of treasures. Rather than "collecting treasures for your own benefit" (Matt 6:19), serving wealth as a god (Matt 6:24), or worrying over what to eat or wear (Matt 6:25), Jesus channels desire in a different direction: toward "God's kingdom and God's righteousness" (Matt 6:33). For Matthew's Jesus, either people trust God, or they trust their own capacity to provide for themselves. This binary choice appears in story form to end the sermon. Jesus describes two different homes, built on two different foundations. When adversity hits, one rests on "bedrock" (Matt 7:25), while the other's "completely destroyed" (Matt 7:27).

The righteousness described in this sermon is not for the faint of heart. Jesus claims it's the harder, countercultural way of living (see Matt 7:13-14). But as Jesus's signature teaching in this Gospel, it casts a vision for an alternative world order called God's kingdom or the "kingdom of heaven" that offers, in Matthew's view, the only way to true life.

Book Two: Workers for the Harvest (Matt 7:28–10:42)

The crowds are awestruck by Jesus's sermon, but he quickly moves on. The next two chapters recount Jesus's miraculous deeds, much as they're

FIGURE 6.8: THE SERMON ON THE MOUNT AND #METOO

Lutheran pastor Katya Ouchakof offers this reflection on Jesus's teachings in Matthew 5, in light of the #metoo movement:

> In Matthew 5:27-30, Jesus affirms the humanity and agency of women in a revolutionary way. He tells men that the very act of looking at a woman as an object of sexual desire is equivalent to breaking one of the Ten Commandments.
>
> In today's society, sexual indiscretions by men against women are rarely prosecuted and often not even believed. Women are condemned both for speaking out and for keeping silent. Men continue to assault women, often with little or no legal, social, professional, or political consequences.
>
> Jesus makes it very clear that the problem is with the men who objectify women— not with the woman who finds herself mistreated. If a man treats a woman as a sexual object, his actions have nothing to do with what she was wearing or whether she was drunk or how long she kept silent or how young they were at the time. If a man sexually disrespects a woman, Jesus requires one simple thing: Cut off the offending part of your body. Men, whatever part of you it is that is causing you to lust, chop it off! It might be your eye or your hand, though I'm guessing it's something else.
>
> Whatever is causing your sin—because, yes, it is sin, and it cannot be dismissed with a "boys will be boys" or "locker room talk" excuses—whatever causes your sin needs to be excised from your body. It is better to enter paradise without one of your "members" than for your whole body to be thrown into hell.
>
> Jesus says that women are humans who deserve respect. They are not sexual objects put on earth for the pleasure of men. His claim was revolutionary in antiquity and still is counter-cultural today.

(Conversation shared with permission.)

YOUR TURN: Reread Matthew 5:27-30 and write a letter to your son about the connection between Jesus's teachings and the #metoo movement.

---

described in Mark. Along the way, Jesus's disciples watch as he uses divine power over illness, demons, and even nature's force. Meanwhile, Jesus adds others to his sphere of influence—first a legal expert (Matt 8:19) and then, in a story unique to this Gospel, a tax collector named Matthew (Matt 9:9). (Though Matthew is one of the named disciples in Mark, this story seems to revise Mark's account of Jesus's recruitment of Levi, son of Alphaeus. Cf. Mark 2:14-17.)

These narrative encounters lead thematically to a series of discourses about discipleship, often taken from Mark. Jesus laments the "size of the harvest" (Matt 9:37) and so solicits laborers to extend his messianic mission. Like Jesus, the disciples are given "authority over unclean spirits," as well as the ability "to heal every disease and every sickness" (Matt 10:1; cf. Mark 6:7, 13). Like Jesus, they proclaim the nearness of the kingdom of heaven (Matt 10:7; cf. Mark 3:14).

Several differences from Mark bring Matthew's concerns (and setting) into clearer view. For one thing, Matthew intensifies Jesus's teachings about the rejection and persecution the disciples will inevitably face. Mark tells them simply to walk away from any unwelcoming community, but in Matthew, Jesus pronounces harsh judgment on those cities that refuse to listen to the disciples' message (Matt 10:15; cf. Mark 6:11). Matthew also repositions predictions about persecution to make it a more central part of the disciples' job description (Matt 10:16-23; cf. Mark 13:9-13). Finally, Jesus encourages the disciples not to fear (Matt 10:26, 28, 31) and promises "a prophet's reward" (Matt 10:41) to those who welcome his emissaries.

Matthew also makes more explicit than Mark the likeness between Jesus and his students. For instance, only Matthew's Jesus says, "Disciples aren't greater than their teacher. . . . It's enough for disciples to be like their teacher" (Matt 10:24-25). In rabbinical Judaism, students carry forward their rabbi's legacy. Matthew presents Jesus as an ideal rabbi whose disciples honor him by being like him. That said, the disciples operate neither of their own accord nor on their own behalf, for Matthew. After all, the reward for caring for them comes "because they are my disciples" (Matt 10:42).

Book Three: The One Who Is to Come (Matt 11:1–13:52)

Matthew's third major section combines traditions from Mark and Q, with a particular Matthean twist. If Jesus has appeared as authoritative rabbi and miracle worker to this point in the Gospel, his messianic identity comes into sharper focus here, and the theme of coming eschatological judgment dominates his teachings.

The question of Jesus's identity arises when an imprisoned John the Baptist sends his followers to ask, "Are you the one who is to come?" (Matt 11:3). Rather than a direct answer, Jesus points to the evidence at hand: his deeds of restorative power, which fit the markers of the messianic age (Matt 11:4-6; see Isa 61:1). What's more, he identifies John with "Elijah who is to come" (Matt 11:14), the biblical figure Jewish tradition associates with the dawn of the messianic age (Mal 4:5).

More than just Messiah, Matthew's Jesus fits a number of other roles known in Second Temple Jewish literature. He's the "Human One" (Matt 11:19), personified Wisdom (Matt 11:19), God's servant (Matt 12:18), and "Son of David" (Matt 12:23). In a sense, Matthew collapses all of these faithful figures into the person of Jesus. Taken together, they encompass many attributes and actions associated with God's anointed one, from judging, to instruction, to wielding God's power on earth. It's fitting, then, that Matthew concludes the narrative section with Jesus reframing family values on the basis of faithfulness to God rather than human heredity (Matt 12:46-50); in a brusque move, Jesus shuttles aside his mother and brothers to adopt his disciples as those who constitute his true family.

The discourse that follows draws from Mark's parables chapter (Mark 4:1–34), but Matthew adds a story found only here: the weeds among the wheat (Matt 13:24–30; 36–43). In this story, weeds appear overnight in a field of wheat, and fieldworkers ask the landowner if they should gather them (Matt 13:28). The response—"let both grow side by side until the harvest" (Matt 13:30)—brings into focus the coming judgment. As Jesus explains, "The Human One will send his angels, and they will gather out of his kingdom all things that cause people to fall away and all people who sin. He will throw them into a burning furnace. People there will be weeping and grinding their teeth. Then the righteous will shine like the sun in their Father's kingdom" (Matt 13:41-43; cf. Dan 12:3).

This parable illustrates two points that Matthew makes throughout this Gospel. First, the message about righteousness arises out of a thoroughly eschatological framework. That is, if Jesus points to God's kingdom in the present, its final disclosure will bring a judgment that sifts evil from good, righteous from unrighteous. Second, the judging task belongs not to Jesus or his followers in the present but to God and God's agents at the end. In the meantime, his disciples take up the task of scattering good seed (see also Matt 7:1-5).

Book Four: On This Rock (Matt 13:53–18:35)

Within Matthew's next major section, two passages highlight the evangelist's signature interest in the church, a word found only in this Gospel. For you, *church* may refer to a building with a tall steeple or tower, or perhaps to an organization that includes ordained clergy, a governing board, and sometimes even a national or global office. Matthew uses the word in a much simpler way. In Matthew, a church is more like a "small group"—a gathering of those who orient their lives around the kingdom of God that Jesus has inaugurated.

What does Matthew's Gospel have to say about church? The word first appears in a conversation between Jesus and the disciple named Simon Peter (Matt 16:13-20). When Jesus asks, "Who do you say that I am?" Simon answers, "You are the Christ, the Son of the living God." Only in Matthew does Jesus then call Simon the "rock" (Greek: *petros*) on whom he'll build the church. For Matthew, Peter's legacy is central to the emerging Christian movement.

Even more, Matthew assigns Peter a level of authority that rivals Jesus's own. Jesus gives him the "keys of the kingdom of heaven," which means Peter's ability to "fasten" and "loosen" *on earth* will affect *heavenly* matters, rather than the other way around. Matthew thus portrays an earthly church, led by Peter, that's endowed with divine authority. (Notice that all the jokes about St. Peter as main bouncer at heaven's pearly gates seem to miss the point.)

The other passage that mentions the church illustrates the authority Jesus assigns to Peter (Matt 18:15-20). Here, Jesus commends a deliberate process of conflict resolution in the church that begins with a one-on-one conversation between offended and offending parties. Wrongdoers are given several chances to make amends, but in the end, those who refuse to do so will be treated as if they were "a Gentile and tax collector"—that is, as an outsider. In Matthew's story, Jesus endows church leaders—represented by Peter—with the capacity to set boundary markers that promote unity within the gathered community.

Book Five: Justice, Peace, and Faith (Matt 19:1–25:46)

Matthew's fifth section relates Jesus's approach to Jerusalem. When he crosses the Jordan River, he's following a common traffic pattern for those traveling from Galilee (in the north) to the holy city. (See Figure 6.9.) It will take him two more chapters to arrive at his destination, but the landscape of his death is now on the horizon (see Matt 20:17-20).

The material in this section plays a culminating role in differentiating Jesus's "righteous road" from other religious leaders. For instance, Jesus levels weighty charges against the legal experts and the Pharisees (Matt 23:2) in front of a growing crowd. This chapter-long tirade appears only in Matthew. As we've noted, scholars think this extended invective grows out of dynamics playing out in Matthew's late first-century CE setting. Several pointed claims here credential Jesus as authoritative interpreter of Torah.

For one thing, Jesus assails "blind guides" (e.g., Matt 23:16) who promote Torah observance for their own benefit and corrupt its intended role: to create a just society. As Jesus puts it, they neglect Torah's "more important matters" such as "justice, peace, and faith" (Matt 23:23). He also berates

FIGURE 6.9: JESUS'S TRAVEL FROM GALILEE TO JERUSALEM

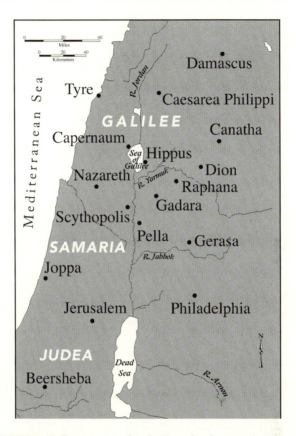

YOUR TURN: Following Matthew's Gospel, plot Jesus's itinerary from Galilee to Jerusalem, using this map. What do you notice about his journey?

concern with external appearance while they're "full of pretense and rebellion" on the inside (Matt 23:28).

Besides this negative assessment of his competitors' leadership, Jesus engages in a bit of self-promotion of his own, calling himself his audience's "one teacher" (Matt 23:8, 10). This probably works at two levels. In the Gospel, that audience is his disciples. But Matthew's post-resurrection audience probably heard this instruction as directed toward them.

If Jesus has harsh words for Jews who comply with Torah but don't reflect its values, he also holds out hope for Gentiles who don't follow Torah explicitly but bear witness to justice, peace, and faith. The section's concluding story

135

looks toward the eschatological judgment of "all the nations," a judgment at which the Human One and his angels will preside (Matt 25:31-46). Jesus's story uses the image of separating the "sheep from the goats"—that is, those who'll enter God's kingdom from those who'll "go into the unending fire."

On what basis will such judgment take place? Not surprisingly for Matthew, it's on the basis of righteousness. For Jews, of course, Torah points the way to righteousness. But in this Gospel, even non-Jews can be called "righteous" when they care for "the least of these brothers and sisters of mine" (Matt 25:40). Once again, Matthew's message about righteousness is both ethical and eschatological.

Passion Narrative (Matt 26:1–27:66)

On the matter of Jesus's end game, Matthew's Gospel follows Mark's account closely. Still, a few elements distinguish this account of Jesus's last week. For one thing, Matthew downplays the role in Jesus's death played by the Roman governor Pontius Pilate. Only in Matthew does Pilate's wife warn him to steer clear of "that righteous man" (Matt 27:19). This makes Pilate something of a reluctant peacemaker: he's afraid that he'll either disappoint his wife or start a riot if he lets Jesus off scot-free. And only in Matthew does Pilate say he's "innocent of this man's blood" (Matt 27:24). As a result, culpability for Jesus's death shifts to the Jewish leaders, as well as to the clamoring crowds who become their pawns.

Matthew also revises Mark's account by including cosmic events that accompany Jesus's death. Not only does the temple curtain tear when Jesus takes his last breath (as it does in Mark), but Matthew mentions an earthquake that released from their tombs "many holy people who had died" (Matt 27:52). These features may sound strange to modern readers, but they're standard fare in apocalyptic writings of Matthew's day. Jesus's death launches the kind of resurrection that signals the dawn of God's life-giving power on earth.

Epilogue: The Resurrection and Great Commission (Matt 28:1-20)

Matthew concludes on a note that fits many of the features we've discussed above. Remember, Mark's Gospel leaves readers hanging; the women have been entrusted with a message for the disciples to meet Jesus in Galilee, but they're frozen in stunned silence. Matthew brings the story to a neater resolution. The eleven remaining disciples do indeed reconnect with a risen Jesus on a mountain in Galilee, where he delivers this closing commission: "I've received all authority in heaven and on earth. Therefore, go and make disciples of all nations, baptizing them in the name of the Father and of the Son and of the Holy Spirit, teaching them to obey everything that I've commanded you. Look, I myself will be with you every day until the end of this present age" (Matt 28:18-20).

Once again, Jesus's authority is shared authority, as he equips his followers to extend the reach of his mission to all nations. In addition, the emphasis on instruction fits Matthew's portrait of Jesus as preeminent interpreter of Torah. Finally, the promise of Jesus's continued presence "until the end of this present age" signals their perpetual dependence on the living Lord.

Review and Reflect

- What role does "righteousness" play in Matthew's Gospel? Give three examples of its importance and meaning.

- Reflect on the conversation with Jewish leaders that lies behind Matthew. How does this Gospel convey Jesus's interpretation of Torah with theirs?

MATTHEW'S MESSAGE

In Matthew's Gospel, Jesus has much to say about the kind of righteousness that befits the kingdom of heaven. Though we may associate righteousness with prude religious conduct or sinlessness, Matthew's message takes a different tack. Righteousness in Matthew has more to do with what Jesus calls the "more important matters of the law": justice, peace, and faith. We conclude this chapter by summarizing the main points Matthew's Jesus makes with respect to this "righteous road."

Fulfillment

From the opening genealogy, Matthew stresses over and over again that Jesus is a *Jewish* Messiah. The fulfillment citations insist that Jewish scripture points toward Jesus, and the ways he's described—from Messiah, to Human One, to rabbi, to prophet—mostly fit the cast of characters that decorate the Jewish literary landscape. True, the Gospel hints at God's rejection of Jewish leaders and their replacement by Gentiles in God's plans for salvation (e.g., Matt 8:10-13; 21:33-45; 22:1-14). But Jesus's generally positive acclaim in mostly Jewish regions shows that Matthew assumes the movement is deeply embedded in Judaism.

Yet, from the outset, Matthew also shows that part of this Jewish script means drawing non-Jews into its way of righteousness. Even Jesus's lineage features Gentiles—and women at that! Near the Gospel's end, the judgment of "the nations" (found only in Matthew; Matt 25:31-46) illustrates that Torah's vision of righteousness can be followed quite apart from Jewish law. In this story, it's not a matter of non-Jews becoming Jewish; these righteous Gentiles reflect Torah's values without naming them as such.

This universalizing impulse probably reflects Matthew's late first-century setting. As we've noted, scholars think Matthew's audience was predominantly but not exclusively Jewish. Matthew thus reads those Gentile believers into Jesus's story and even more strikingly, into the backstory of his family tree. The Gospel concludes, too, with a Great Commission that sends Jesus's Jewish followers out into the world, to "make disciples of all nations" (Matt 28:19) by teaching them his deeply Jewish way of righteousness.

Righteousness

In Matthew, the term *righteousness* refers both to human behavior and to a status that qualifies people for salvation at the day of the Lord. In other words, this righteousness has both an ethical and an eschatological dimension. That means many find Matthew to be the most exacting Gospel among its canonical peers. There's a rigor to this righteousness and little concern with the kind of grace many associate today with Christian faith.

What kind of ethical standards does Jesus lay out in Matthew? They're rooted in Torah but go beyond following a checklist of rules and regulations. The messianic vision Jesus casts has more to do with living together in covenant community. That means building a social order marked by a love for God that's inseparable from love for other people, especially society's most vulnerable. For Matthew's Jesus, this kind of righteousness goes above and beyond what Torah requires in the strictest sense to embody its "important matters" of justice, peace, and faith.

This way of righteousness also transcends tribalism. After all, even God cares for the "righteous and unrighteous" (Matt 5:45). Where it divides insider from outsider—and divide it does—the line separates on the basis of human conduct, not religious or ethnic identity. Eschatological judgment looms large in Matthew, and it will bring much "weeping and grinding of teeth" (Matt 8:12; 13:42, 50; 22:13; 24:51; 25:30) to those deemed "evil" or "unrighteous" at the "end of the age" (Matt 13:49). Meanwhile, Matthew issues a call to follow Jesus's way of righteous concern for the weak and to reserve final judgment for God (see Matt 7:1-5; 13:24-30).

If this rigorous ethical standard and its eschatological importance sound harsh, remember that Matthew's audience probably heard this message as a minority religious group devoted to a way of life that was under siege. Their loyalty to a Jewish Messiah located them at the fringe of the social order. Both Jewish neighbors and civic officials likely looked askance at their notions about a "kingdom of heaven" that would soon rule the world. The cataclysmic outcome of the Jewish War—itself stoked by a different version of messianism—made Matthew's audience an easy target for scorn and even outright persecution. In this setting, Matthew reiterates Jesus's authority in ways that support their ethical framework and hold out hope for their vindication at the "end of the age" (Matt 13:49).

The Church

Matthew's explicit interest in the church shows that this way of righteousness is the hallmark not just of individual lives but of the gathered community. This community, this Gospel insists, finds its coherence not in a shared ethnic identity or socioeconomic status, but in devotion to doing God's will (Matt 12:50). Their allegiance to God and God's righteousness makes Jesus's followers a subversive contingent, since they cast their loyalty not with the empire or its minions, but with the "kingdom of heaven."

But this community isn't exactly sectarian in nature. They don't simply withdraw from wider society, refusing to participate in its systems entirely. Instead, they're sent out into the world as "workers for [God's] harvest" (Matt 9:38). Initially, they labor among the "lost sheep, the people of Israel" (Matt 10:6), promoting Jesus's interpretation of Torah in a marketplace of rabbinical options. But Matthew's Great Commission also extends the disciples' reach beyond Judaism; they are to "make disciples of all nations" (Matt 28:19). Ultimately, they pave the way for the "end of the present age" (Matt 13:40), which Jesus describes this way:

> The Human One will send his angels, and they will gather out of his kingdom all things that cause people to fall away and all people who sin. He will throw them into a burning furnace. People there will be weeping and grinding their teeth. Then the righteous will shine like the sun in their Father's kingdom. Those who have ears should hear. (Matt 13:41-43)

SUMMARY

Matthew writes as a scribe "trained as a disciple for the kingdom of heaven" (Matt 13:52). Conversant with Jewish tradition, this evangelist tells Jesus's story as its supreme fulfillment, with a laser-like focus on Torah's important matters of justice, peace, and faith. In Matthew, Jesus appears as a "new Moses" whose interpretation bests the rabbis who are his conversation partners. But Jesus is more than mere teacher; he's God's Messiah who lays the groundwork for the coming kingdom of heaven and will return as eschatological judge. In his earthly ministry, Jesus inculcates God's wisdom on matters of righteousness and engages disciples who bear his power and witness "until the end of this present age" (Matt 28:20). For Matthew's audience, it's a demanding message that's also shot through with hope.

Review and Reflect

- Explain the three main themes found in Matthew. Illustrate each one with a passage from the Gospel.

- If you only had Matthew as a source for Jesus's meaning, what would you take as most important? What would be lacking?

GO DEEPER

Allison, Dale C. *The New Moses: A Matthew Typology*. Minneapolis: Fortress, 1993.

Boxall, Ian. *Discovering Matthew: Content, Interpretation, Reception*. Grand Rapids, MI: Eerdmans, 2014.

Carter, Warren. *Matthew: Storyteller, Interpreter, Evangelist*. 2nd ed. Peabody, MA: Hendrickson, 2004.

Levine, Amy-Jill. *A Feminist Companion to Matthew*. Cleveland, OH: Pilgrim Press, 2004.

Powell, Mark Alan. *Methods for Matthew*. New York: Cambridge University Press, 2009.

Chapter Seven

What Is Salvation?
Gospel of Luke

CONVERSATION STARTERS

- What sets Luke apart from the other NT Gospels?

- How does Luke tell a Jewish story for a Gentile audience?

- What's the relationship between "religion and politics" in Luke?

- What kind of salvation does Luke portray?

- How does Luke expand and extend the Gospel story?

If Matthew's Gospel is rooted firmly in Jewish soil, Luke tells this salvation story for those mostly outside Jesus's religious tradition. But that doesn't make Jesus less Jewish in this Gospel; far from it. Indeed, Luke deliberately traces Jesus's Jewish heritage, portraying him as a prophet in word and deed. In this Gospel, Jerusalem is a focal point for Jesus's career and a base for the followers he leaves behind. But like biblical prophets before him, Jesus extends the good news of God's kingdom to "all peoples" (Luke 2:31)—that is, to the Gentiles. More than the other Synoptic Gospels, Luke tells Jesus's story in conversation with the wider Greco-Roman world.

This third canonical Gospel contains many of Christian tradition's most familiar and well-loved stories. Only Luke reports the angel Gabriel's visit to Mary with word of an unexpected pregnancy. Only Luke features her beautiful prayer known as the **Magnificat**. Only Luke recounts cherished parables such as the good Samaritan and the prodigal son. Only Luke includes Jesus's post-resurrection "reveal" to two travelers walking to Emmaus.

Luke stands apart from its NT counterparts in other ways as well. For one thing, this Gospel belongs to a larger, two-volume collection. The **Acts of the Apostles** extends Luke's Gospel story beyond Jesus's ascension, a story Acts repeats. Luke's sequel tracks Jesus's followers as they carry forward his messianic mission and expand its reach throughout the Mediterranean world. (We'll consider Acts in chapter 10.)

Luke is also the only evangelist who self-identifies as a bona fide historian. Remember, ancient historiography had less to do with accuracy than with authenticity and meaning. From the outset, Luke explicitly acknowledges that other, unidentified sources lie behind this account (see Luke 1:1-4). According to the Four Source Hypothesis, those sources include Mark, Q, and L, which designates Luke's special material. Luke also situates Jesus's story as part of the wider history of the ancient world, naming rulers and providing historical markers along the way.

This Gospel shares with its Synoptic conversation partners the broad contours of Jesus's story as well as many details. But Luke also takes more editorial liberty than Matthew does. As a redactor, this evangelist both adds and changes parts of the story to make it fitting for its own place and time. As we'll see, Luke invites a cosmopolitan audience to rethink the values and priorities that order the Greco-Roman culture they inhabit. To understand Luke on its own terms—as a story about the Jewish Messiah who brought God's salvation to the whole world—let's consider some of the aspects of the cultural context Luke so artfully engages.

WHAT'S LUKE'S WORLD LIKE? GRECO-ROMAN SOCIETY

Already, we've discussed in some detail the pluralistic bent of the Greco-Roman world (see chapter 3). First-century Mediterranean culture offered a marketplace of religious and philosophical options that coexisted rather amicably. In terms of religious pluralism, Greco-Roman society took a "both/and" approach. You could worship the goddess Isis as a member of a mystery cult and pay homage to the emperor as god to fulfill your civic, patriotic duty. (Because of their strict monotheism, Jews were exempt from religious devotion to Caesar, though they sometimes faced persecution for being outliers on this score.) Religious commitments were rarely exclusive and were generally considered harmless—even beneficial—as long as they supported social and political protocol.

Let's consider some elements of the cultural milieu that Luke's Gospel engages, both directly and more subtly. Take the term *savior*. For millennia, Christians have assumed that Jesus is the one and only savior, a point Luke certainly promotes. But Luke's view was far from the dominant one in a world that applied the term freely to various religious and political figures. For instance, the **Priene Calendar Inscription** (ca. 9 BCE) heralds the birth of the Emperor (Caesar) Augustus with these words:

> Providence, which has ordered all things and is deeply interested in our life, has set in most perfect order by giving us Augustus, whom she filled with virtue that he might benefit humankind, sending him as a **savior**, both for us and for our descendants, that he might end war and arrange all things, . . . and since the birthday of the god Augustus was the beginning of the good news [or "gospel"] for the world that came by reason of him. (V. Ehrenberg and A.H.M. Jones, *Documents Illustrating the Reigns of Augustus and Tiberius*, 2nd ed. [Oxford: Clarendon Press, 1955], 82)

Other sources call such gods as Asclepius "savior," as well as "healer" and "lord." Saviors channeled divine blessing in the here and now rather than securing an eternal status in the afterlife. As we'll see, Luke reframes the term to apply it in an exclusive way to Jesus, who brings a different kind of salvation.

The social and political order of Luke's Greco-Roman setting forms another part of the backdrop for this Gospel story. Generally speaking, the first-century social order rested on a clear hierarchy, which was closely linked to economic status. (See Figure 7.1.) Historians report that the gap between the "haves" and the "have-nots" was extreme: about 90 percent of the Roman Empire's inhabitants lived in poverty, while less than 5 percent enjoyed what we might call Kardashian wealth. A patronage system worked to mitigate the effects of such a stratified society. Those with abundant resources—the **patrons**—cared for needy **clients**, who in turn pledged a certain loyalty to their provider. It's not hard to see that such a social system normalized economic inequality.

Social inequality also fell out along gender lines. In the ancient world, women were considered less fully human than men, as if they'd failed to develop in utero. Though women could be Roman citizens, they couldn't vote or serve in office. Their proper place was within the domestic realm of home and hearth, and their value depended on the man who was their **paterfamilias**, or "father of the family." This "family" extended beyond parents and their children to include (unmarried) adult daughters, as well as any servants or slaves. According to many ancient writers, this orderly, hierarchical household promoted an orderly society.

FIGURE 7.1: HINDU CASTE SYSTEM

One tradition in Hinduism affirms a stratified society according to "caste" or class. Here's an excerpt from the Manu smrti, or "Laws of Manu" (ca. 100–300 CE): "For the sake of the preservation of this entire creation, [Purusha], the exceedingly resplendent one, assigned separate duties to the classes which have sprung from his mouth, arms, thighs, and feet."

The text goes on to specify four classes in descending order of rank:

• Brahmans (priests)

• Kshatriyas (warriors)

• Vaishyas (merchants)

• Shudras (servants)

A fifth caste, the "untouchables," refers to the lowest caste in Hinduism today. Twentieth-century visionary and prophet Mahatma Gandhi (1869–1948) railed against the caste system in general and "untouchability" in particular, dubbing the "untouchables" as Harijans, or "friends of God."

> **YOUR TURN:** Are there "castes" in our Western society? On what basis do people fall within a social class or "caste"? What's the appeal of the traditional Hindu view that social order comes from knowing one's caste and fulfilling its calling faithfully? What's the danger?

Another social code encompassed and supported the hierarchy of the Greco-Roman world: the system of **honor** and **shame**. In Luke's setting, honor depended both on circumstance—age, gender, physical ability, wealth, ethnicity—and on conduct. Indeed, you could enhance your honor by cultivating certain virtues, such as generosity, self-control, and religious devotion. Shame derived from any form of weakness, from physical impairment, to mental or emotional instability, to criminal activity, to simple misfortune. (See Figure 7.2.)

Luke both adopts and reframes the prevailing value system of this first-century Mediterranean setting. On the one hand, Luke's Jesus sometimes embodies the Stoic ideal of self-control. And like other miracles workers in the Greco-Roman world, his divine power is on full display in Luke. On the other hand, Luke consistently highlights ways in which Jesus subverts social norms. He violates protocol when it comes to his eating habits, and he regularly associates with people on the bottom side of the social order. Ultimately, Jesus's shameful destiny—his execution on a Roman cross—proves necessary to God's plan of salvation, which brings his vindication and ascension to heaven.

FIGURE 7.2: HONOR, SHAME, AND THE PROSPERITY GOSPEL

New Testament scholar Dustin Ellington teaches at a seminary in Zambia, where he challenges widespread embrace of the "prosperity gospel," the view that physical and material well-being convey God's blessing. He writes:

> African churches need to wrestle with the tendency to give the greatest esteem to believers who are successful, wealthy, and powerful in ways that are in tension with Christian teaching. As one who trains pastors in Zambia, I frequently hear of social shame that accompanies Christians who lack financial means.
>
> I know a seminary student from Zambia who, with his wife, spent two weeks without any meals. All they had in their cupboard were teabags and sugar, so that's what they had each day. He said he couldn't tell his extended family or friends and ask for help because it would seem that he's not qualified for ministry, or not really even a Christian, because he obviously wasn't blessed. A real person of faith, and a real Christian, would have plenty. There was a lot of shame for him because of the stigma of poverty in a social world impacted heavily by the prosperity gospel. God gives physical blessings now to those who are truly his children, and to those who obey him. . . .
>
> This attitude suggests a deep misunderstanding of the Christian God and the Christian gospel. Rooted in the incarnation and crucifixion, the concept of power-in-weakness arises from the foundation of the Christian faith. (From personal correspondence. Used with permission.)

YOUR TURN: How and where does the "prosperity gospel" appear in your own setting? Choose a passage from Luke that challenges it.

WHO WROTE LUKE? AND FOR WHOM?

Like all the evangelists, the author of this Gospel is unknown to us. Within a century of its writing, though, tradition associated this story with a figure named Luke—probably "Luke, the dearly loved physician" mentioned in Colossians 4:14 and in two other letters attributed to the Apostle Paul (see Phlm 24; 2 Tim 4:11). This identification gave the Gospel an apostolic pedigree, which was an important part of establishing its authoritative, canonical status. (Paul was considered an apostle even though he wasn't one of Jesus's original followers.) In addition, several passages in Acts imply that its writer accompanied Paul on his voyages, though Luke is never named in that book. Scholars have pointed out noteworthy discrepancies, though, between Acts and Paul's own letters, leaving the question of authorship wide open.

What can we say about Luke? For reasons discussed below, we take this author to be a gifted writer among the educated elite. Luke was also probably a Gentile, perhaps a **God-fearer**. This term refers to non-Jews who worshipped the Jewish God but didn't comply with all of Torah's mandates such as dietary restrictions and circumcision. It's a "middle ground" relationship to Judaism that fits this Gospel's keen interest in Jewish sacred tradition on the one hand and the inclusion of Gentiles in God's redemption on the other (see e.g., Luke 2:30-31; 4:16-30).

Identifying Luke's intended audience is, at first glance, a bit easier for this Gospel than for the others. After all, Luke explicitly names its recipient as "most honorable **Theophilus**" (Luke 1:3). But scholars don't know whether Theophilus was a real person or a generic stand-in for any "god lover," which is what the name means in Greek. In either case, the detail implies that Luke crafted this story for (mostly) Gentiles. In terms of social location, the community probably spanned the economic scale but almost certainly included some wealthier members, since the Gospel seems concerned to level the playing field with respect to resource allocation.

Of all Gospels, Luke is least attached in tradition to a particular place. Both Antioch and Ephesus have been named as plausible settings, but any cosmopolitan, urban setting in the Mediterranean is an equally good guess. In the end, Luke tells the story of Jesus's life, death, and resurrection in terms that would have been familiar in such a sophisticated setting. At the same time, Luke works sometimes subtly to turn cultural assumptions and values upside down.

Review and Reflect

- Explain two specific Greco-Roman values that Luke's story turns upside down.

- Reflect on Luke's interest in telling a *Jewish* story for a mostly *Gentile* audience.

WHAT'S THE "GOOD NEWS" IN LUKE? SALVATION IN THE HOUSE

Among the Gospels, Luke exhibits the most sophisticated writing style, in terms of form and content. Even English translations convey its narrative elegance, and scholars have noted that the Greek text mimics the **Septuagint**

FIGURE 7.3: OUTLINE OF LUKE

Prologue and Infancy Narrative (1:1–2:52)

Galilean Ministry (3:1–9:50)

Travel Narrative (9:51–19:27)

Passion Narrative (19:28–23:56)

Empty Tomb and *Epilogue* (24:1-53)

Note: The italicized items contain the "special material" found only in Luke. (In chapter 4, we saw that scholars call this material "L.") Notice that this Gospel intersperses sections of this special material with sections that feature stories and teachings found in Mark and Matthew.

and other refined ancient writings. The Gospel's literary sophistication fits the evangelist's high-minded purpose of offering a polished, "carefully ordered account" of Jesus's story (Luke 1:3).

In terms of narrative setting, Luke begins and ends at the **Jerusalem temple** (Luke 1:8; 24:53) and pivots toward Jesus's destiny in Jerusalem about mid-way through the Gospel (Luke 9:51). Thus Luke locates this story squarely within a spiritual geography associated with God's revelation to the Jewish people. As one scholar put it, this Gospel also positions Jesus's life, death, and resurrection "in the middle of time"—between God's activity in Jewish scripture (see e.g., Luke 1:1; 4:21; 24:27) and the story of Acts, where Jesus's "witnesses" extend his messianic mission "in Jerusalem, in all Judea and Samaria, and to the end of the earth" (Acts 1:8). Luke's audience is in it, we might say, for the long haul.

In weaving various sources together, this author departs more radically from Mark than Matthew does. (See Figure 7.3.) In fact, Luke includes only about half of Mark's content (compared with 90 percent found in Matthew). Notably, Luke omits meaningful spans of Mark, sections scholars call the **Great Omission** (Mark 6:45–8:20) and the **Little Omission** (Mark 9:41–10:12). Luke also includes about 220 verses shared with Matthew (probably from the Q source) interspersed throughout the narrative. And fully one-half of this longest canonical Gospel is made up of content found nowhere outside of Luke. Both Luke's editorial treatment of the sources included and the special material will shed light on the particular features of Luke's message.

Prologue and Infancy Narrative (Luke 1:1–2:52)

Unlike the other NT Gospels, Luke opens with an explicit statement of purpose (see Luke 1:1-4). In this prologue, we find pointers to wider Gospel concerns. For instance, the first verse calls Jesus's ministry "the events that have been fulfilled among us" (Luke 1:1). Luke is less formulaic than Matthew about *how* Jesus's story fulfills Jewish scripture. Instead of proof texts and fulfillment citations, Luke tells stories about Jesus that echo episodes found in Jewish scripture (e.g., Luke 7:11-17; cf. 1 Kings 17).

Luke's prologue also confirms what scholars have deduced through source criticism: this Gospel relies on earlier sources that relate the reminiscences of firsthand witnesses. Notice that Luke doesn't dispute the legitimacy of these earlier versions. Yet they must leave something to be desired, since Luke says this account offers an unprecedented "soundness of the instruction" to its audience (Luke 1:4). Truth, even for Luke, runs deeper than factual accuracy.

As we've noted, Luke's birth narrative shares very few details with Matthew's. (See Figure 7.4.) In both, a boy named Jesus is born in Bethlehem (in the southern region of Judea) to Mary and Joseph; in both, the family is from Nazareth (in the northern region of Galilee), where Jesus grows up. Beyond these common claims, the specifics diverge significantly. A simple comparison sheds light on central aspects of Luke's message.

While Matthew focuses on Joseph as a "righteous man," Luke places **Mary** front and center in Jesus's backstory. The angel Gabriel appears to Mary, not Joseph, to deliver news of her pregnancy and the child's promising destiny. Though she responds initially in disbelief, the angel reassures her: "The Holy

FIGURE 7.4: JESUS'S BIRTH IN MATTHEW AND LUKE

Visit any church's Christmas pageant, and you'll find details that have been combined from two very different stories. Here are some examples of those differences:

Matthew	Luke
Joseph plays the leading role	Mary plays the leading role
Wise men from the East visit the family	Shepherds visit the family
Joseph dreams of an angel	Angel visits Mary
Family flees to Egypt	Family takes Jesus to Jerusalem

YOUR TURN: Reread one of the birth stories (from either Matthew or Luke). What impressions does this story, on its own, convey? What's missing?

FIGURE 7.5: MARY IN THE QUR'AN

The Qur'an names an entire chapter after Mary (Sura 19) and even echoes Luke's account of the visit Gabriel pays to her:

> And mention in the Scripture Mary, when she withdrew from her people to an eastern location. She screened herself away from them, and We sent to her Our spirit, and He appeared to her as an immaculate human. She said, "I take refuge from you in the Most Merciful, should you be righteous." He said, "I am only the messenger of your Lord, to give you the gift of a pure son." She said, "How can I have a son, when no man has touched me, and I was never unchaste?" He said, "Thus said your Lord, 'It is easy for Me, and We will make him a sign for humanity, and a mercy from Us. It is a matter already decided.'" (Sura 19:16-21)

YOUR TURN: Learn more about Mary in Islam. How do views about her fit with or differ from Christian views? (Remember, both traditions include a wide range of perspectives.)

Spirit will come over you and the power of the Most High will overshadow you" (Luke 1:35). Mary's willing acceptance of her role establishes her as a model of the kind of faith this Gospel will promote. (See Figure 7.5.)

Mary's song, known as the **Magnificat**, praises God "my savior [who] has looked with favor on the low status of his servant" (Luke 1:47-48). In Luke, salvation has much to do with God's liberation for those on the bottom of the social order. Echoing **Hannah's Song** (see 1 Sam 2:10), Mary's words celebrate God's favor for the lowly: "[God] has pulled the powerful down from their thrones, and lifted up the lowly. [God] has filled the hungry with good things and sent the rich away empty-handed" (Luke 1:52-53; cf. 1 Sam 2:4-5). Both women, it turns out, give birth to prophets who'll challenge those who profit at the expense of those who are in need.

Other details in the opening chapters invert, and subvert, conventional notions about worldly power. Only Luke notes that Jesus's first crib was an animals' trough (Luke 2:7). In Luke, it's not the elite dignitaries who gain a private audience with the newborn baby but shepherds, straight from the fields. True, this infant Jesus is a king who will "reign over Jacob's house forever" (Luke 1:33), but already Luke signals the unconventional kind of kingdom he'll institute.

Luke hints at a reversal of religious status as well, when Jesus's parents present him for ritual dedication at the Jerusalem temple. There, a "righteous and devout" man named **Simeon** recognizes the infant as "the Lord's Christ" (Luke 2:25-26). But while traditional messianic hopes prioritize the Jewish people within God's restoration of the world, Simeon first mentions non-Jews as beneficiaries of God's saving activity: "My eyes have seen your salvation. / You prepared this salvation in the presence of *all peoples*. / It's a light for revelation *to the Gentiles* and a glory for *your people Israel*" (Luke 2:30-32, italics added). For Luke, Jesus's messianic mission is fundamentally inclusive; non-Jews are on par with the people called Israel within God's sweeping salvation. It's yet another reversal of fortune that will characterize this Gospel story.

Still, Luke's narrative leaves no question about Jesus's Jewish heritage. For instance, Luke establishes Jesus's relationship to the Jewish apocalyptic prophet **John** even before either one is born. Only this Gospel says these are related by blood (their mothers are cousins), and John's father Zechariah heralds his son's role as "prophet of the Most High . . . [who'll] go before the Lord to prepare his way" (Luke 1:76).

The concluding scene of Luke's birth narrative returns to the Jerusalem temple. As faithful Jews, Jesus's parents make their annual pilgrimage to the Holy City to celebrate the Passover, the festival that will serve as backdrop to Jesus's last week there. When their twelve-year-old goes missing, his parents find him at the temple, "sitting among the teachers, listening to them and putting questions to them" (Luke 2:46). He explains that it was necessary for him to be in his "Father's [that is, God's] house" (Luke 2:49). For Luke, Jesus's formation as Christ, Son, and prophet takes place within the structures of his native religious tradition.

Jesus's Galilean Ministry (Luke 3:1–9:50)

As Jesus steps into adulthood, Luke combines material from Mark and Q with passages found only in this Gospel. In short order, Jesus is baptized by John; a genealogy traces Jesus's lineage back to "Adam son of God" (Luke 3:38); Satan tests Jesus's loyalty to God in the wilderness; Luke summarizes Jesus's early missionary activities; and Jesus preaches an inaugural sermon at his hometown synagogue in Nazareth. Taken together, these passages set the stage for Luke's portrait of a prophet whose way of salvation proves both liberating and unsettling.

Luke's editorial concerns appear throughout the traditional material found in this section. Like Matthew, Luke inserts John's call to repentance (Q material) within Mark's sparse account of Jesus's baptism. But while Matthew highlights eschatological judgment, Luke subtly shifts attention to the meantime. When the crowds ask, "What then should we do?" (Luke 3:10), John tells the wealthy and powerful to leverage their positions toward the good of others (see Luke 3:10-14). As we'll see, this Lukan twist fits well with the Gospel's wider interest in economic justice.

Likewise, Luke's genealogy differs in important ways from Matthew's. Though Luke's version of Jesus's family tree includes no women—not even Mary—Luke traces Jesus's ancestry beyond the Jewish patriarch Abraham to "Adam son of God" (Luke 3:38). This shift universalizes Jesus's messianic significance, connecting this Jewish Messiah to all of humanity. It also subtly affirms the divine image imprinted, from the beginning, on Adam and his offspring (see Gen 1:27).

As in the other Synoptics, Jesus's first public speech serves as a thesis statement for his messianic career in this Gospel. In Mark, Jesus announces God's coming kingdom and calls people to repent and trust in God alone. Matthew's Jesus sounds like a New Moses who interprets Jewish law to promote "greater" righteousness. Luke relocates and embellishes Mark's story of Jesus teaching in Nazareth (cf. Mark 6:1-6) to portray Jesus as a Jewish prophet rejected by his own people.

In this scene, Jesus begins his public career by invoking the authority not of Torah but of the prophet Isaiah. These are the words he reads in his hometown synagogue:

> The Spirit of the Lord is upon me,
> > because the Lord has anointed [Greek: *echrisen*] me.
> He has sent me to preach good news to the poor,
> > to proclaim release to the prisoners and recovery of sight to the blind,
> > to liberate the oppressed, and to proclaim the year of the Lord's favor.
> (Luke 4:18-19; cf. Isa 61:1-2; 58:6)

Jesus thus self-identifies as the anointed one (that is, he's the Christ) and discloses the kind of salvation he brings: a reversal of fortune for those on the bottom side of the social order.

At first, the congregation marvels at his words. But the tide quickly turns toward rejection when Jesus hints that his mission will extend beyond the religious and ethnic bounds of "Israel." Jesus is on solid biblical ground, of course. He recalls for listeners that the prophets Elijah and Elisha by-passed needy Israelites to bring deliverance and life to outsiders. But in a hint about things to come, the crowd resolves to eliminate him from their midst. In this episode, Luke sets the stage for Jesus's disruptive, prophetic mission and its inevitable outcome. Bringing salvation to those at the margins—and beyond—will prove to be his undoing.

Most of Luke's story of Jesus's Galilean career comes from Mark and Q. Still, Luke edits and rearranges this material to target the Gospel's first audience. Let's consider some prime examples of Luke's distinctive spin.

Call to Discipleship (Luke 5:1-11)

In Mark, Jesus's first disciples respond to his simple command to "follow me" abruptly; they leave their lives and livelihoods without hesitation. Luke's account makes the story more plausible. First, Jesus joins them in their boat and miraculously enables them to haul in a record catch. Only when they're awestruck by his divine power does Jesus say they'll soon be "fishing for people" (Luke 5:10). Thus Luke supplies a clear rationale for the report that they "left everything and followed Jesus" (Luke 5:11).

Why such a change? For one thing, Luke's version of the story highlights Jesus's divine power in ways that echo Jewish scripture. For instance, God enlists Moses by first producing a spectacular scene—a burning bush that's not consumed (Exod 3). But Luke also emends the tale to fit an audience that may not have known these biblical precedents. They did know, though, stories about "divine men" such as **Apollonius of Tyana**, who wandered the countryside performing such deeds of power that disciples were drawn to him in droves. The proof, they might have said, was in the pudding: evidence of Jesus's power legitimized his authority; people followed him as a result. (See Figure 7.6.)

Sermon on the Plain (Luke 6:17-49)

Luke's Sermon on the Plain is shorter than Matthew's Sermon on the Mount and differs in ways that display this Gospel's thematic concerns. The scene itself takes on "a large area of level ground" where crowds from Jewish and non-Jewish regions have gathered. Already, Jesus levels the playing field for God's saving activity.

Luke's list of blessings also emphasizes the hearers' present, lived experience. Those who hunger and weep *now* will find their fortunes improved. But Luke addresses the other end of the social order as well, pronouncing a terrible outcome for those whose current conditions are marked by abundance and fame. (See Figure 7.7.)

Finally, Luke draws Jesus's teachings about loving enemies and nonjudgment sharply into focus. At the heart of the passage lies the command to "be compassionate just as your Father is compassionate" (Luke 6:36; cf. Matt 6:48).

FIGURE 7.6: BUDDHA'S TWIN MIRACLE AT SRAVASTI

According to Buddhist tradition, Siddhartha Gautama (the "Buddha," or "enlightened one") performed the "twin miracle" seven years after reaching his enlightened state. In this miracle, observers saw flames of fire and streams of water flowing out from his body at the same time, in different directions. Since fire and water are incompatible, their coexistence in one body constitutes this miracle. This story emerged in the context of a contest with other miracle workers and features important thematic ties to the miracle of Elijah in contest with the priests of Baal (see 1 Kings 18:20-40).

A fine example of a Greco-Roman Buddha from the finest collection of Asian art in Europe, "The Greek Buddhas of Gandhara," at the Musée Guimet in Paris. Note this image emphasizes both flames and flowing water from the "Twin Miracle" story.

YOUR TURN: What's a "miracle" in your opinion? Do you believe in them? Why or why not?

For Luke, forgiveness is central to Jesus's way; those who would follow him must bear witness to the unshakable foundation he has laid (Luke 6:46-49).

Jesus and Women (Luke 7:36–8:3)

The theme of forgiveness comes through loud and clear in another story Luke rather drastically revises. In Mark, a woman anoints Jesus during his last week in Jerusalem, as part of the drama that points to his death (Mark 14:3-9;

FIGURE 7.7: KENDRICK LAMAR FLIPS THE BEATITUDES

The Irish band U2's 2017 album *Songs of Experience* features a song titled "Get out of Your Own Way." The song concludes with rapper Kendrick Lamar's "spoken word" reversal of the gospel of Luke's beatitudes. "Blessed are the arrogant," he says, "for theirs is the kingdom of their own company." Check out the full lyrics and note Lamar's ironic critique of contemporary culture in light of Jesus's teachings.

YOUR TURN: Reread Luke's "sermon on the plain," and then listen online to "Get out of Your Own Way." Why might U2 have concluded their song with these lyrics?

cf. Matt 26:6-13). In Luke, a woman anoints Jesus even before he turns toward Jerusalem. Rather than anticipating Jesus's burial, the woman's lavish act of devotion serves in Luke as an object lesson on great love and forgiveness.

Only Luke identifies the woman as a sinner (Luke 7:37). Since the encounter takes place at a Pharisee's home, her appearance is doubly problematic: both her gender and her religious status would make her unwelcome at the meal. But Jesus overrides her exclusion, not by forgiving her, but by saying that she's *already* forgiven. He explains, "This is why I tell you that her many sins have been forgiven; so she has shown great love. The one who is forgiven little loves little" (Luke 7:47). In other words, her extravagant care for him belies her sinner status. As if to reaffirm the positive role of women in Jesus's movement, Luke credits female patrons mentioned only in this Gospel (Luke 8:1-3). These named women, in addition to "many others," break through the typically male-dominated patronage system to invest "their resources" (Luke 8:3) in Jesus's mission.

Review and Reflect

- Explain three ways in which Luke's Gospel stands out from the other Synoptic Gospels.

- Luke's been called the "social justice" Gospel. Give two examples that highlight Luke's concern with leveling the playing field within the wider social order.

Travel Narrative (Luke 9:51–19:27)

In Luke, Jesus sets his sights on Jerusalem fairly early in the story. He's just predicted his destiny twice in rapid succession (Luke 9:21-22, 44) when

Luke writes that he "determined to go to [literally, "set his face toward"] Jerusalem" (Luke 9:51). Such deliberate intention makes Jesus seem unflinching in his resolve to meet his fate. This verse constitutes an important turning point in the Gospel. The section that follows, called the **travel narrative**, features a dense array of stories belonging to the L source. Let's notice some of the prominent themes that emerge here.

Emphasis on the "Now"

If Mark's Jesus fixes his gaze mostly on the horizon, pointing to the first signs of God's coming kingdom, Luke is much more concerned with the here and now. Such a shift makes sense in light of the fact that Luke probably writes a decade or more after Jerusalem's destruction. Those who'd thought this cataclysmic event might establish God's kingdom on earth had been sorely disappointed. And though Luke doesn't edit out all future eschatological hope, the present implications of Jesus's messianic mission are front and center in Luke's special material.

Only Luke, for instance, reports Jesus's sending of seventy missionaries (Luke 10:1-12, 17-24; some manuscripts say "seventy-two"), expanding the scope of the twelve apostles' journey (cf. Luke 9:1-6; Mark 6:6b-13; Matt 10:1-14). Not only does the group grow in number, but their cosmic impact swells as well. Jesus assesses their results this way: "I saw Satan fall from heaven like lightning. Look, I have given you authority to crush snakes and scorpions underfoot. I have given you authority over all the power of the enemy. Nothing will harm you" (Luke 10:18-19).

In the battle between good and evil, Satan suffers a heavy blow at the hands of Jesus's minions. Luke thus signals a broad-based participation in Jesus's defeat of malevolent forces both during Jesus's earthly career and as a part of the meantime reality that will unfold in Acts.

Luke's interest in the present appears more explicitly elsewhere. For instance, in a saying unique to Luke, Jesus chastises those who don't "know how to interpret the present time" (Luke 12:56), as if they're caught up in the past or future rather than in the "now." In a similar vein, Luke's Jesus warns against those who link God's coming kingdom to "signs that are easily noticed." Instead, he says, "God's kingdom is already among you" (Luke 17:20-21). (See Figure 7.8.)

Finally, two stories that conclude the travel narrative drive home the importance of the present time in Luke. When a tax collector named **Zacchaeus** welcomes Jesus into his home, he resolves to make amends for his ill-gotten gain. He even promises to give half of his wealth to the poor and to make

FIGURE 7.8: GOSPEL OF THOMAS

The noncanonical Gospel of Thomas renders this traditional saying in this way:

Jesus said, "If those who lead you say to you, 'See, the kingdom is in the sky,' then the birds of the sky will precede you. If they say to you, 'It is in the sea,' then the fish will precede you. Rather, the kingdom is inside of you, and it is outside of you. When you come to know yourselves, then you will become known, and you will realize that it is you who are the sons of the living father. But if you will not know yourselves, you dwell in poverty and it is you who are that poverty." (Gos. Thom. 3; trans. Lambdin; see http://www.earlychristianwritings.com/text/thomas-lambdin .html)

YOUR TURN: Reflect on the connections and differences between Luke and the Gospel of Thomas on the view of the kingdom of God.

four-fold restitution to those he's defrauded. In response, Jesus says, "Today, salvation has come to this household" (Luke 19:9). For Luke, salvation has much to do with setting things right—even in an economic sense—in the here and now.

In the next passage, Luke introduces the **parable of the pounds** this way: "Jesus told them another parable because he was near Jerusalem and they thought God's kingdom would appear right away" (Luke 19:11). This story features an absent lord who has entrusted his slaves with resources they're expected to invest wisely while he's away. Luke uses the story to show that the delay of God's kingdom has introduced a meantime when Jesus's followers should invest by expanding its footprint.

Social Reversal

What does that kingdom look like? Luke's special material portrays a social, economic, and religious world order that subverts the dominant systems of Greco-Roman culture. Already, we've seen these concerns appear in the Gospel's opening chapters, through Mary's song and Jesus's inaugural sermon. Within the travel narrative, several stories engage hearers in a conversation that turns conventional values on end.

Luke challenges gender-laden assumptions in an account of Jesus's visit to the home of two sisters, **Mary and Martha** (Luke 10:38-42). While Martha tackles expected domestic chores, Mary sits "at [Jesus's] feet." This is code

FIGURE 7.9: MEAL ETIQUETTE THEN AND NOW

In the ancient world, good table manners were vital to ethical living. Philosophers often weighed in with guidelines called "symposium laws," a term that referred to the time following the meal itself, when entertainment of all types took place. People's social rank (gender, social class, etc.) often made a difference in whether or not they were included at all, in their position at the banquet, and in whether they reclined or sat upright for the gathering. Sometimes, ancient writers urged moderation in food and drink. Generally speaking, the ethical motivation for etiquette grew out of a concern for civil discourse: no volatile political discussions or personal attacks, they urged. (See Dennis E. Smith, "Greco-Roman Meal Customs," *ABD*, 4:650–53.)

Today's fast-food culture may make us less focused on good table manners, but special settings—celebrations or professional gatherings, for instance—can call for a bit more attention to meal etiquette. A website that carries forward the work of the late Emily Post, contemporary guru of social protocol, even offers seminars on table manners based on this claim: "Eating a meal with others is a veritable minefield of potential blunders and gaffes. . . . If you're planning to dine with work colleagues, superiors or clients, it's wise for you to be fully versed in dining etiquette." (See https://emilypost.com/lifestyle/online-dining-etiquette-course/.)

> **YOUR TURN:** How does whom we eat with and how we eat together relate to the social order in our own place and time? Have you ever crossed social boundaries to eat with someone from a different culture or background? How did that experience affect you?

language for the posture of discipleship, a role usually confined to men. When Martha complains about Mary's negligence, Jesus rebuffs her, insisting that Mary has chosen the "better part" (Luke 10:42). Luke thus suggests a new social order that includes women, along with men, in the circle of Jesus's disciples.

In the ancient world, social protocol around meals encoded the stratification of different social classes. Typically, eating with those outside of one's designated status constituted a violation of the very morals on which imperial power rested. (See Figure 7.9.) But Jesus explicitly defies this norm when he says that those who give banquets (that is, the wealthy) shouldn't invite their peers; they should invite "the poor, crippled, lame, and blind" (Luke 14:13). In the very next passage, he likens such a banquet to the "great dinner" that symbolizes the kingdom of God (Luke 14:15-24).

Luke's Jesus also challenges religious tribalism that privileges groups based on religio-ethnic pedigree. Luke uses geography to make this point, as Jesus travels to Jerusalem "along the border between Samaria and Galilee" (Luke 17:11). In Jesus's day, Galilean Jews mostly avoided passing through

Samaria, even if it was the most direct route to Jerusalem. (See Figure 6.9.) Who were the Samaritans, and why would Galilean and Judean Jews show them such disdain?

Second Temple Jews generally saw **Samaritans** as half-breeds, because they traced their heritage to ancient Israelites who had intermarried with other groups for generations. In Jewish tradition, Samaria was the name for the northern kingdom of biblical Israel defeated by the Assyrians in 722 BCE. Its inhabitants were seen as part of the ten lost tribes of Israel. Over time, the Samaritans continued to follow Torah and live in covenant relationship with the Lord God. But they weren't Jewish, because, instead of worshipping in Jerusalem, they had their own temple on **Mount Gezirim**. Jerusalem's religious leaders deemed Samaritans ritually impure and unfaithful to the Jewish covenant.

Against this backdrop, the story of the **good Samaritan** (found only in Luke) challenges stereotypes associated with this group (Luke 10:29-37). In this parable, Jesus tells of a man violently attacked on the desolate road from Jerusalem to Jericho—a road used by Judeans to avoid Samaria. He then contrasts the reactions of two Jews, a priest, and a Levite, who cross the road to avoid the man, with a Samaritan, who shows him mercy (Luke 10:37). It's the Samaritan, Jesus says, who proves to be a neighbor to the man in need. In this way, Luke redraws lines around insider status: rather than ethnic or religious identity, the mark of a neighbor is lavish mercy toward those in need.

In Luke, God's kingdom also reverses the present social order when it comes to the economic divide between the "haves" and the "have-nots." One parable calls a man who builds bigger barns to store his enormous surplus of grain a fool (Luke 12:13-21). Already, we've noted that Jesus links Zacchaeus's salvation to his decision to reallocate his assets toward both those he's defrauded and poor people in general.

Another Lukan parable contrasts an unnamed rich man with a poor man named **Lazarus** (Luke 16:19-31), who lives just outside the gate to the rich man's estate. Proximity on earth, though, brings a chasm in the afterlife. While the rich man is tormented by fire, Abraham tends to the poor man. Now it's the rich man's turn to beg—this time for a way to get word back to his remaining family members to change their ways. But Abraham responds, "If they don't listen to Moses and the Prophets, then neither will they be persuaded if someone rises from the dead" (Luke 16:31). That is, the rich brothers should know their own religious tradition—and follow it! Jesus the Jewish prophet thus challenges the prevailing value system that honors the wealthy and neglects the downtrodden.

Repentance

Luke's emphasis on God's kingdom as a present reality that reverses the social order leads to a third theme that receives special emphasis in this section: **repentance**. In Luke, Jesus insists there's still time to throw off the world's oppressive systems and find salvation—or be found by it—in God's merciful regime.

At the heart of the travel narrative, Luke includes a series of three parables about repentance: the lost sheep, the lost coin, and the lost son. Together, they form a narrative reply to religious authorities' concern that Jesus "welcomes sinners and eats with them" (Luke 15:2). It's a charge that recurs throughout the Gospel and one that Luke reframes as a badge of Jesus's honor rather than his shame. The restoration of "one sinner who repents" (Luke 15:7, 10 NRSV) brings nothing short of heavenly joy—and sometimes even a great party.

The third in the series, the **parable of the prodigal son** (Luke 15:11-32), may be the most familiar and most widely interpreted story in the NT. (See Figure 7.10.) In this tale, an older son brazenly demands his inheritance long before his father dies. He squanders every last penny on a prolonged bender and hits rock bottom. The son's "aha" moment comes when he sees that his father's animals are better off than he is. So he vows to return home and beg for mercy. But even *before* he utters the first word of his well-rehearsed speech, his father spies him in the distance and runs to greet the lost son.

Like the stories of the sinful woman and Zacchaeus, this parable portrays repentance quite apart from religious performance or even self-abasing guilt. In Greek, the word *metanoia* has both a mental and a physical dimension. Repenting means adopting a new way of seeing the world and then living into that new reality. Once the prodigal son sees his father's provision, he turns toward home, where he finds gracious welcome. In conventional terms, the father's response is shameful. After all, the son had effectively pronounced a death wish on his father. But Luke's world again redefines honor in terms that attend to the least and the lost and draw the lines of social inclusion in terms of mercy rather than merit.

Review and Reflect

- How does the travel narrative build on themes emphasized earlier in the Gospel? Give two examples.

- Reflect on Luke's treatment of salvation and repentance. What features stand out for each term?

FIGURE 7.10: THE PRODIGAL SON THROUGH MIDDLE EASTERN EYES

New Testament scholar Kenneth Bailey points out several ways in which the father in the Parable of the Prodigal Son defies expectations for a "traditional oriental patriarch."

- The first violation of social protocol comes when the younger son demands his portion of the estate, even while his father is living. In essence, Bailey says, the son is pronouncing a death wish on the father.

- Second, the father gives the inheritance to his son, even though, as Bailey explains, Jewish practice in Jesus's day included "method of punishing any Jewish boy who lost the family inheritance to Gentiles . . . called the '*qetsatsah* ceremony.' . . . From that point on, the village would have nothing to do with the wayward lad."

- Third, when the father runs to reconcile with his son, he ignores social convention. "Traditional Middle Easterners, wearing long robes, do not run in public," says Bailey. "To do so is deeply humiliating."

- Fourth, the father honors the prodigal with a banquet, perhaps celebrating what Bailey calls "the father's costly efforts at creating shalom."

- Finally, the father takes the initiative in reconciling too with the elder son, an act that "goes beyond what a traditional patriarch would do."

("The Pursuing Father" by Kenneth E. Bailey, *Christianity Today*, October 26, 1998)

YOUR TURN: Reflect on Bailey's reading of this parable in the context of Middle Eastern culture. What details seem more striking to you now? Why?

In Jerusalem (Luke 19:28–23:56)

The travel narrative leads ultimately to Jerusalem. Luke's account of Jesus's last days follows Mark's passion narrative closely. Still, several features stand out in Luke's version of the story. Luke never assigns saving power to Jesus's death, for instance. Only Luke mentions two cups and one loaf in the Last Supper account. And only Luke includes Jesus's trial before Herod. At some points, Luke shares more with John than with the other Synoptic Gospels. Let's consider some key features that emerge from a careful study of Luke's passion narrative.

Prophetic Judgment

Throughout Luke, Jesus plays the part of prophet. From his first appearance in his hometown synagogue, throughout the Galilean ministry, and as he's headed toward Jerusalem, this Galilean Jew issues a clarion call to repentance and promises salvation from social and religious structures that stymie human flourishing. His arrival in Jerusalem brings the culmination of a prophetic career that leads inevitably to rejection and death (see Luke 13:31-35).

Luke's interest in Jesus's prophetic role appears in key places throughout the passion narrative. For one thing, Luke inserts a prophetic lament over Jerusalem (Luke 19:41-44) between Jesus's entry into Jerusalem, on the one hand, and his condemnation of the temple economy on the other. In this Lukan passage, scholars see evidence of Luke's own historical setting, since the verses predict Jerusalem's defeat using details from the emperor **Titus's** siege of the city in 70 CE (Luke 19:43). Notably, though, Jesus attributes that defeat not to the Romans but to Jerusalem's leaders, who have not recognized "the time of [their] gracious visit from God" (Luke 19:44). Once sentenced to death, Jesus revisits the theme of impending judgment—and devastation—that will come in its wake (Luke 23:28-31).

Luke also intensifies Jesus's prophetic critique by relocating and amending Jesus's teaching on greatness (Luke 22:24-30; cf. Mark 10:41-45). For one thing, Luke places the passage just before Jesus's arrest and so sets up a stark contrast between conventional and divine power. In addition, Jesus calls out the "kings of the Gentiles" (rather than "rulers," as in Mark) and mocks the notion that they're "friends of the people" (Luke 22:25). In Luke's telling, this passage challenges imperial propaganda that promoted Roman officials as benevolent patrons. Finally Luke adds a Q saying about the royal power conferred on both Jesus and his followers: they, not the Roman officials, wield ultimate authority to judge (Luke 22:30).

In Matthew, Jesus's prophetic critique mostly targets Jewish leaders. But the reach of judgment in Luke draws political authorities into the mix. Indeed, Luke adds a trial before **Herod Antipas**, tetrarch of Galilee, as Pilate's way of appeasing the crowd. Both Pilate and Herod are moved more by the crowd's vehemence than by any sense of Jesus's clear and present danger. Luke ends the brief encounter by noting that Pilate and Herod forged a friendly alliance over this episode (Luke 23:12). Their mutual assent to the crowds' wishes only solidifies, in Luke's view, the coalition of religious and political powers conspiring against this prophet.

———

Divine Necessity

More than in either Mark or Matthew, Luke tells the story of Jesus's last days as if he's in full knowledge of—and compliance with—God's will. Already, the Gospel has hinted at the necessity of Jesus's death in Jerusalem (see Luke 9:51; 13:33). But Luke revises Mark's account to show that Jesus willingly participates in a divine plan that overrides human choice.

In Luke, Jesus's visit to the **Mount of Olives** is less marked by human anguish than in Mark's account. (Luke doesn't mention Gethsemane, perhaps because the Gospel's audience wouldn't have known about this particular garden.) Here, Jesus prays not three times but only once: "Father, if it's your will, take this cup of suffering away from me. However, not my will but your will must be done" (Luke 22:42). Most scholars think the next two verses, which mention an angel's visit and Jesus's profuse perspiration, were added later, since they aren't found in the earliest and most reliable manuscripts. Without them, this passage portrays a Jesus who's very much in charge of, and fully compliant with, his destiny.

Compared with the other Synoptics, this Gospel emphasizes Jesus's innocence as he hangs on a Roman cross. Luke alone includes Jesus's interaction with the two criminals hanging beside him. While one joins in the crowd's mockery, the other insists Jesus has done "nothing wrong" (Luke 23:41) and calls his death a miscarriage of justice. In Jesus's last words, too, Luke portrays a willing martyr. Rather than the cry of dereliction found in Mark and Matthew, Luke's Jesus utters a different psalm as his last words: "Father, into your hands I entrust my life" (Luke 23:46; cf. Ps 31:5). Finally, the soldier who names Jesus as God's son in Mark pronounces him innocent in Luke—a verdict confirmed by Luke's report of the crowd's repentance (Luke 23:47-48). Together, these editorial touches highlight the notion that God's will unfolds as an innocent man is put to death.

Empty Tomb and Epilogue
(Luke 24:1-53)

Luke draws to a close with a version of Mark's empty tomb story, followed by two encounters with the risen Lord. Once again, details in Luke's account fit the Gospel themes we've discussed so far. For one thing, angelic figures who greet the women remind them of the divine necessity of Jesus's death, along with the promise of his resurrection (Luke 24:6; cf. 9:22, 44). This implies they heard the earlier prediction and thus assigns women a prominent role among Jesus's disciples. Even if the male disciples dismiss word of the empty tomb as "nonsense" (Luke 24:11), the reader knows the women have been entrusted with this good news.

After their report, Jesus appears twice to his followers. In the first encounter, two travelers—one named **Cleopas**—are walking to **Emmaus**, grieving their Lord's death and their dashed hopes for Israel's redemption (Luke 24:21). They're also baffled by the women's reports about the empty tomb. Jesus joins them, incognito at first, and reminds them of the necessity of "these things" (Luke 24:26) and uses "all the scriptures" to prove his point. Finally, they recognize the risen Jesus not through his teaching but through the breaking of the bread, and he vanishes from their sight.

Jesus then appears to his disciples with evidence that confirms his bodily resurrection. He points out his mortal wounds, and he eats a meal, as only bodies can do. Finally, he instructs them, too, about the biblical warrant for the events. Before he departs, he entrusts them with a message of repentance and forgiveness to be proclaimed "to all nations, beginning from Jerusalem. You are witnesses of these things" (Luke 24:47-48). Finally, he tells them to await heavenly power from the Father (Luke 24:49), a promise that paves the way for the opening of Luke's sequel in the book of Acts.

Meanwhile, the Gospel concludes, after Jesus has ascended to heaven, with the disciples in Jerusalem, "continuously in the temple praising God" (Luke 24:53). It's a fitting end to a story that stresses Jesus's own Jewish tradition. Like their Lord, his witnesses begin their inclusive mission by their own full participation in that tradition. That full participation, it turns out, will unfold in detail in Acts.

Review and Reflect

- What sets Luke's version of the passion narrative apart from the other NT Gospels?

- Consider the Gospel's conclusion. How does it prepare the way for the story of the early church that we'll find in Acts?

LUKE'S MESSAGE

As the first of a two-part series, Luke depicts Jesus as a Jewish prophet, the Messiah, and Savior whose mission belongs to God's inexorable redemption of all nations. Thus this story is fraught with religious motifs, such as salvation, repentance, forgiveness, and God's will. But Luke's message is one that carries important sociopolitical implications as well. As Messiah, Jesus institutes a new age of God's reign *right alongside* the Roman imperial power. For Luke, these are not separate but (un)equal spheres of authority, as if Jesus distinguishes between religious and political concerns. In part, it is Jesus's prophetic challenge to the sociopolitical status quo that makes him vulnerable to its death-dealing ways. But for Luke, Jesus's story lives on after the cross—not just in the risen Lord who ascends to the heavenly throne room, but also in the community of his followers who likewise become prophetic witnesses to God's saving power. What elements of that witness does Luke most stress for the Gospel's first hearers?

"Beginning from Jerusalem"

If Matthew writes for a mostly Jewish audience, insisting that the movement's inclusion of non-Jews fulfills scripture, Luke takes a complementary approach. Luke reminds a mostly Gentile audience that Jesus's story belongs to God's unfolding revelation in Jewish scripture. Luke's context makes good sense of this shift. As we'll see in our study of Paul's letters and the book of Acts, believers in Jerusalem and the wider Mediterranean didn't always agree on what it meant to follow a Jewish Messiah. At least some Jewish followers thought that Gentile converts should comply with Jewish law to a "T." Meanwhile, some Gentile believers denied the validity of Jewish tradition altogether.

Luke steps in with something of a middle-ground position. This Gospel neither imposes all of Jewish law on a Gentile audience nor removes Jesus's story from its Palestinian Jewish landscape. Instead, Luke points, from start to finish, to the ways in which God's saving activity in the world—beginning with Adam, not Abraham—culminates in the story of this Prophet-Messiah Jesus. Jerusalem thus takes on vital importance as the sacred place associated with this revelation. It's also for Luke the ground zero from which that revelation continues to unfold through Jesus's followers after the resurrection.

"Poor, Crippled, Blind, and Lame"

More than any other Gospel, Luke sets the scene of Jesus's story deliberately within the first-century CE Mediterranean world. Luke writes as a historian after all; Jesus's story is no mere "once upon a time" fairytale. Luke names those in power and may even address the Gospel story to a recognized official, "most excellent Theophilus."

But Luke's story brings a challenge to the values and systems that define that world. Women appear as prominent followers, active disciples, and even benefactors, when the empire's social code linked their identity mostly to their father or husband and their social role to domestic matters. Luke's Jesus also turns on end popular notions of honor and shame, assigning a place at God's royal banquet to the "poor, crippled, blind, and lame," while the affluent are called fools and consigned to eternal flames of misery.

For Luke, this scheme of reversal is no novelty on Jesus's part. It's simply a matter of following Jewish prophetic tradition, from Elijah and Elisha onward. They, too, warned against the kind of wealth that isolates the "haves" from the "have-nots." They, too, protested the kind of tribalism that locates evil among groups that don't belong, in an ethnic or religious sense, to the dominant group. In the divine kingdom Jesus launches, it's those at the margins who take pride of place.

"Witnesses of These Things"

Both Mark and Matthew associate Jesus's message about the coming kingdom of God with future eschatological judgment. In Mark, that means waiting as if on tiptoes for this imminent regime change. For Matthew, the coming harvest may be delayed, but the promise that God will sort out the righteous from the unrighteous still looms large over the Gospel story.

Luke doesn't eliminate this future dimension entirely. But this Gospel does shift its focus to the meantime. "What then should we do?" is the question that frames this Gospel (see Luke 3:10), and Luke's answer grows out of what Jesus does: hanging out with sinners and tax collectors, healing the sick, preaching a message of forgiveness that's more alluring than combative. More than once, Luke's Jesus says he's come to "seek and save the lost" (see e.g., Luke 19:10).

Luke's expansion of the gospel story lays an emphasis on the witness of Jesus's followers. Like the Samaritan, like the faithful women, and like repentant Zacchaeus, disciples are invited to live generously, even as profligates of grace and material generosity. They're charged with boundless forgiveness, with the breaking down of social distinction and stratification. For Luke, these are the deeds through which Jesus's way of salvation brings welcome, forgiveness, and divine delight.

SUMMARY

Luke extends the scope of the gospel story for a cosmopolitan setting. Written in sophisticated Greek, this Gospel engages the wider Greco-Roman world, framing Jesus's career as part of the Jewish story that now encompasses "the nations." Luke depicts Jesus as an innocent but rejected Jewish prophet whose critique of imperial norms leads, inevitably, to his crucifixion on a Roman cross. But more than the other Synoptic Gospels, Luke highlights the expanding community that carries forward Jesus's earthly priorities after his death. God's kingdom is already among them (see Luke 17:20-21), as seventy (-two?) missionaries participate in Satan's fall from the sky "like lightning" (Luke 10:18). More than that, Luke's place in the NT canon is a prequel to the story of Acts, where Jesus's apostles continue his demonstration of God's kingdom in word and deed. Stay tuned!

Review and Reflect

- What makes Luke a thoroughly Jewish story? What makes it fitting for a Gentile audience?

- What invitation might Luke's first hearers detect in this story? How might they have connected their lives and commitments to it?

GO DEEPER

Borgman, Paul. *The Way According to Luke: Hearing the Whole Story of Luke–Acts.* Grand Rapids, MI: Eerdmans, 2006.

Carroll, John T. *Luke: A Commentary.* New Testament Library. Louisville, KY: Westminster John Knox Press, 2012.

Levine, Amy-Jill, ed. *A Feminist Companion to Luke.* Cleveland, OH: Pilgrims Press, 2004.

Nadella, Raj. *Dialogue Not Dogma: Many Voices in the Gospel of Luke.* New York: T&T Clark, 2011.

Reid, Barbara E. *Choosing the Better Part? Women in the Gospel of Luke.* Collegeville, MN: Liturgical Press, 1996.

Vinson, Richard B. *Luke.* Smyth & Helwys Bible Commentary. Macon, GA: Smyth & Helwys, 2008.

Chapter Eight

What Is the Word?
Gospel of John

CONVERSATION STARTERS

- What makes John different from the other NT Gospels?

- Who wrote John? And for whom?

- How does John fit the literary patterns of Hellenistic Judaism?

- Why does this Gospel sound so hostile toward "the Jews"?

- What's the role of Jesus's signs in John?

- What concerns dominate Jesus's Farewell Discourse?

Called the "spiritual Gospel" by the ancient writer Clement of Alexandria, the fourth canonical Gospel stands out from its peers in striking ways. For one thing, about 90 percent of its contents appear nowhere else. Like the Synoptic Gospels, its narrative arc begins with John the Baptist and ends with appearances of the risen Jesus. But along the way, John features a different chronology (Jesus's ministry spans three years, not one) and a different itinerary (Jesus travels between Galilee and Jerusalem repeatedly throughout this Gospel). And this Gospel weighs in on important matters such as faith, the kingdom of God, judgment, and salvation from a decidedly different point of view.

Readers today are drawn to John for many reasons. For one thing, many of its claims have become central for practicing Christians. John says belief in Jesus is the way to eternal life (see John 20:31), a notion unparalleled in the other Gospels. Only in John does Jesus speak of being "born again" (or "anew," John 3:3). Only here does Jesus approach the kind of divine status that will emerge in later doctrines such as the Nicene Creed and the Trinity. More than any other Gospel, John's Jesus promotes love as a core value. And we can credit John with the spiritualized—and depoliticized—view of the kingdom of God that's so common among Christians today. All of these elements make this Gospel a great fit for many readers.

But as serviceable as John's narrative has proven to be for those within the Christian tradition, its language can sound divisive, even offensive, to those outside it. Two examples make this point. The Gospel's portrait of "the Jews" is notoriously harsh. In one conversation with Jewish peers, Jesus calls them children of "your father . . . the devil" (John 8:44). John's passion narrative also intensifies the blame it places not just on Jewish leaders, but on "the Jews" who repeatedly clamor for Jesus's death. Over the last two millennia, John's Gospel has supplied literary fodder for Christian anti-Semitism that has sometimes flared into tragic conflagration. (See Figure 8.1.)

More broadly, this Gospel draws a clear line between insiders and outsiders based on belief that Jesus is the Messiah (or "Christ"). John paints the world in stark contrasts, as a sort of zero-sum religious landscape: either you're a believer (you win!) or you're not (you lose!). John's Jesus isn't "*a* way"; he's "*the* way" who alone gives access to the Father (see John 14:6). The Gospel's strident tone leaves little room for "seekers," "nones," or devout people of other traditions, shutting down conversation across difference more than opening it up.

Both John's insider appeal and its apparent disdain for outsiders make good sense in light of the Gospel's first-century CE setting. In this chapter, we'll consider the Gospel's message in conversation with the wider religious and philosophical milieu to which it belongs. We'll also consider how this particular take on Jesus's story spoke to a community that had likely been shunned for their devotion to Jesus. Reading John from their socioreligious location will help us take this complex, compelling, and occasionally brash story on its own terms.

WHAT'S JOHN'S SETTING? HELLENISTIC JUDAISM

Scholars today widely recognize that John's Gospel bears the marks of conversation with **Hellenistic Judaism**. The term refers to patterns of Jewish

FIGURE 8.1: MEL GIBSON'S *THE PASSION OF THE CHRIST*

Mel Gibson's 2004 blockbuster movie, *The Passion of the Christ*, is based mostly on John's Gospel. Several features of the film led a joint committee of representatives from the United States Conference of Catholic Bishops and the Anti-Defamation League to issue a statement of concern about the movie's portrayal of Jews and Jewish leaders. The movie, it claims, presents Jesus "as having been relentlessly pursued by an evil cabal of Jews, headed by the high priest Caiaphas, who finally blackmailed a weak-kneed Pilate into putting Jesus to death."

Because this "storyline [has] fueled centuries of anti-Semitism within Christian societies," the committee claims, the movie itself has "potential for undermining the repudiation of classical Christian anti-Semitism" that's been unfolding in recent decades. (See John T. Pawlikowski, "Christian Anti-Semitism: Past History, Present Challenges; Reflections in Light of Mel Gibson's *The Passion of the Christ*," *Journal of Religion and Film* [February 2004].)

But not everyone—Jew or non-Jew—agreed with these groups' assessments. Gibson says he intended only to tell the "truth" and that "if anyone has distorted Gospel passages to rationalize cruelty towards Jews or anyone, it's in defiance of repeated Papal condemnation. The Papacy has condemned racism in any form" (Thomas Rosica, "Don't Take the Wrong Message," *Globe and Mail*, February 2, 2014; https://www.theglobeandmail.com/opinion/dont-take-the-wrong-message/article741892/)

YOUR TURN: How does the Holocaust affect how we read Gospel accounts of Jesus's death—and the role Jewish leaders play in those accounts?

belief and practice forged in the context of the Greco-Roman world. Remember, **Alexander the Great**'s Hellenizing agenda of the fourth century BCE had left a lasting imprint on the Mediterranean world to which both Jesus and John's Gospel belonged (see chapter 3). Here we'll note a few ways in which this Gospel deploys conventions and concepts familiar in Hellenistic Judaism to tell Jesus's story.

John begins with a hymnic Prologue that probably circulated on its own before its inclusion as the Gospel's opening passage (John 1:1-18). As we'll discuss below, it traces Jesus's origins not to Bethlehem or even to biblical figures like Abraham (as in Matthew) or Adam (as in Luke) but to something called the word (Greek: *logos*). But what is this word? For Greek philosophers called **Stoics**, the *logos* was the operating principle that ordered the universe. Much Stoic teaching involves living in harmony with this cosmic "logic."

Hellenistic Judaism both adopted and adapted this concept of *logos*, identifying its with God's wisdom. Many Jewish texts personify that wisdom, sometimes as Lady Wisdom. (The word for "wisdom" in both Hebrew and Greek is feminine.) In Proverbs, she's the first of God's creative acts and serves alongside God as a cocreator (Prov 8:30). In some Hellenistic Jewish writings, Wisdom makes her home among God's people—often in Jerusalem (see Sir 24:8-12), and sometimes in Torah's teachings. Elsewhere, she searches in vain for a place to live on earth and returns to heaven lamenting that failure (see *1 Enoch* 42). Against this backdrop, John's Prologue registers a radically new claim that the word *has* found a home—in a human being named Jesus.

A second feature common in Hellenistic Jewish texts that's prominent in John is the use of **symbolism**. The first-century CE writer **Philo of Alexandria** consistently read Jewish scripture at a symbolic, rather than literal, level. For Philo, even circumcision—the defining "mark" of Jewish men— was mostly a symbolic practice. Throughout John, the symbolic meaning of Jesus's words overrides the literal; thus, he says, "I am the bread of life," without promoting cannibalism. A discussion with Nicodemus about being "born anew" (see John 3:1-21) contrasts Jesus's symbolic teachings with his student's flat-footed question about "[entering] the mother's womb for a second time" (John 3:4). Quite simply, it's impossible to read John literally.

John's strong pattern of **dualism** also reflects literary patterns found among Hellenistic Jewish writings. Our conversation about Mark's apocalyptic worldview introduced the notion of the world as staging ground for a cosmic conflict between good and evil as prelude to God's end-time reign on earth. The Fourth Gospel retains a dualistic framework, but with a twist: it's less eschatological, as if moving toward a culminating point in history, and more focused on the world as it exists in an "eternal now." For John, the cosmos is like a magnetic field charged by opposing forces such as light and darkness, truth and falsehood, spirit and flesh. Though some of these binary pairs play a role in Jewish apocalyptic thought, John's treatment of them leans toward Hellenistic worldviews such as **Neoplatonism**, with its preference for essence (spirit) over forms (flesh).

In these and other ways, this Gospel relates its message about Jesus the Jewish Messiah through the linguistic and conceptual currency of its own pop culture. But John doesn't just map Jesus into Hellenistic Judaism wholesale. Instead, this Gospel appropriates familiar terms to convey Jesus's identity and mission. Convinced that Jesus was anointed to reveal God's way, John sketches a story filled with signposts that point to the abundant life Jesus promises.

WHO WROTE JOHN? AND FOR WHOM?

As with the other NT Gospels, no one knows who wrote John. Second-century CE traditions credit one of Jesus's original twelve, **John of Zebedee**, with authorship, identifying him as the disciple "whom Jesus loved" and who presents his own eyewitness account (John 13:23; cf. 19:26; 21:20-24). But Acts 4:13 says John was "uneducated" and thus illiterate, a claim that fits his fishing profession. Other early church writers attribute the Gospel to a different figure, known as **John the Elder,** who they think also wrote three letters (1, 2, 3 John), as well as the book of Revelation. Scholars today find little evidence to confirm or deny that someone named John wrote this Gospel, though most think it preserves some early, firsthand reports.

The question of this Gospel's authorship is notoriously complex. After all, John is full of literary seams that indicate it's a patchwork of various sources pieced together over time—and sometimes clumsily. What do those seams look like? Consider one example. After an evening with his disciples, Jesus says, "Get up. We're leaving this place" (John 14:31). But the next verse introduces three more chapters of teachings before the group departs. Partly following these clues, scholars have detected several sources combined in John: a **signs source,** a **discourse source**, and a **passion source**.

John's complicated compositional history leads scholars to see this Gospel as the product of a school of thought more than an individual author. Why is this important? As we'll see, the form of John we read today weaves together diverse voices as it tells Jesus's story. That's why many interpreters call John the **Fourth Gospel,** downplaying the notion of a single writer behind its message. In this chapter, we'll use this term interchangeably with "John" to refer to the Gospel.

Though it incorporates earlier material, the John found in today's NT is clearly the latest among canonical Gospels, dating to the end of the first or beginning of the second century CE. From John's vantage point, the urgent hopes for God's coming kingdom have faded over time. As a result, this Gospel reinterprets the apocalyptic message found in the Synoptic Gospels. For the most part, John *spiritualizes* Jesus's message, toning down hopes for God's deliverance from the powers of the present world order. Jesus's kingdom, he says, is decidedly "not from this world" (John 18:36 NRSV). In addition, John *personalizes* Jesus's message of salvation by promising eternal life on the basis of individual belief. Both of these adaptations have made John a favorite among evangelical Christians over time. (See Figure 8.2.)

Early interpretive traditions associate John with a church in Ephesus, but there's no independent support for this claim. What can we say about John's audience? The Gospel was written in Greek and occasionally translates Aramaic words, which points to a location outside Jesus's Palestinian landscape. Its Hellenistic worldview fits a cosmopolitan setting, since Alexander's influence mostly affected urban areas. But beyond these broad observations, we know little about the precise location of its audience.

FIGURE 8.2: DEVELOPING THOUGHT FROM SYNOPTICS TO JOHN

The Fourth Gospel reflects several shifts in thinking about Jesus and his followers from the Synoptic Gospels. Let's consider a few of those changes:

Synoptics	John
Jesus promotes faith in God, God's kingdom, or the "good news" that God's at work to renew the world.	John's Jesus says "belief in the Son" is what secures eternal life (e.g., John 3:36).
God's judgment will take place on the "day of the Lord," when the Son of the Human arrives to secure the world for God's rule.	John's Jesus says, "Now is the time for judgment of the world" (John 12:31).
Portrays Jewish leaders as Jesus's opponents, both in the Galilee and in Jerusalem.	John broadens the critique to apply to "the Jews" (e.g., John 5:18).
"Salvation" has to do with God's coming deliverance of the world from the forces of evil that currently hold it captive.	In John, "eternal life" concerns what individuals secure both now and in the future—a dimension of existence that's in tune with God, even in the midst of surrounding adversity.

YOUR TURN: Reflect on the relationship between the messages found in the Synoptic Gospels and John. What role might the passing of time play in the shaping of these messages?

The Gospel does show pointed interest in the community's relationship to Judaism, even if the nature of that relationship varies widely in the story. On the one hand, Jesus and his disciples appear as observant Jews in this Gospel, traveling back and forth to Jerusalem to worship in the temple. John also features stories in which Jewish people believe Jesus is their awaited Messiah (e.g., John 8:31; 11:45).

At the same time, John uses the phrase "the Jews" to designate outsiders or even opponents of Jesus's mission. Indeed, questions about Jesus's identity often lead to debate and division (see e.g., John 10:19). Three times in John, people are banned from the synagogue precisely because they believe in Jesus as Jewish Messiah (John 9:22; 12:42; 16:2). Historically, such an exclusionary practice is anachronistic, since the impulse to separate Judaism from messianic movements appeared only after the Jewish War. (See Figure 8.3.) (Remember, Jewish messiahs typically inspired armed revolt against Rome.) Even more notably, Jesus calls Jews who don't believe in him children of "the devil" (John 8:44). Ultimately, "the Jews" convince a reluctant Pilate to execute Jesus (John 19:12).

FIGURE 8.3: EIGHTEEN BENEDICTIONS AND APOSYNAGŌGĒS?

Historians broadly agree on two points about the exclusion of Christ-believers from Jewish synagogues. First, it didn't happen during Jesus's lifetime; the Greek word *aposynagōgēs*, translated as "put out of the synagogue," is sheer anachronism in John. Second, though there was no systemic expulsion of Jesus's post-resurrection followers from their Jewish communities, some Jewish texts identify "Nazarenes" (believers in Jesus of Nazareth) among those called "heretics." One passage from the **Eighteen Benedictions**, called the "Curse Against the Heretics" (**Birkat Ha-Minim**), includes these words: "For the apostates let there be no hope. And let the arrogant government be speedily uprooted in our days. Let the *noẕerim* [Nazarenes] and the *minim* [heretics] be destroyed in a moment. And let them be blotted out of the Book of Life and not be inscribed together with the righteous. Blessed art thou, O Lord, who humblest the arrogant." (See jewishvirtuallibrary.org/birkat-ha-minim.)

Historians think the Eighteen Benedictions were added to synagogue liturgy sometime in the late first or early second century CE. Several ancient Christian writers indicate that synagogue leaders considered Christian beliefs blasphemy. Among them, Justin Martyr, Origen, Epiphanius, and Jerome all allude in some way to the cursing of Jesus and his followers (Nazarenes), sometimes explicitly within synagogue prayers. Read more about the Birkat Ha-Minim here: lawrenceschiffman.com/the-benediction-against-the-minim/.

YOUR TURN: Imagine that you're a Jew who's convinced Jesus is the Messiah. How might you have responded if you went to the synagogue and heard the leader recite a curse against believers? Why?

How are we to understand John's portrait of "the Jews"? Historians think John's community ultimately saw themselves as outsiders to Judaism. In their worldview, Jesus is one of *them*, not one of "the Jews." In any case, it's important to note that even John doesn't decry "the Jews" in a wholesale way; rather, it's those who reject Jesus—regardless of religious or ethnic identity—who fall under the Gospel's condemnation.

Together, the Gospel's complex array of sources and inconsistent portrait of Judaism leads scholars to detect three stages in both the community's relationship to Judaism, captured at three stages in the Gospel's literary formation:

1. **Stage One: Insider Status**

   Significant parts of John portray Jesus and his followers as full participants in Jewish life and practice. These Gospel elements stress Jesus's worship of the one true God and relate several visits to the Jerusalem temple.

2. Stage Two: Rejected Status

A second set of sources casts Jesus's messianic status as a litmus test for believers' relationship to the wider Jewish community. These episodes include narrative flash points, when Jewish officials deliberately target Jesus's followers for exclusion.

3. Stage Three: Outsider Status

Later revisions to the Gospel intensify and broaden the scope of its anti-Jewish rhetoric. In this final phase, the Gospel offers its most scathing indictment not just of Jewish leaders but of "the Jews" as a discrete group. The perspective fits a community that's completely separate from mainstream Jewish life.

Note that each stage in John's composition retains, rather than retracts, earlier material. As we read it today, John preserves an unfolding conversation about the relationship between Jesus and Judaism and its impact on believers in later generations. Scholars agree that it's impossible to pinpoint a particular place and time when Judaism and Christianity parted ways. We also can't say for sure who caused the division. The Fourth Gospel, though, preserves a glimpse of that messy religious divorce. For its community, belief in Jesus *as Messiah* had become a polarizing issue that set them apart from their native religious landscape. The Gospel thus undergirds their conviction that Jesus is the way to abundant life, even if it's a costly one.

Review and Reflect

- Name and explain two features of Hellenistic Judaism that appear in the Fourth Gospel.

- Reflect on the different stages of John's composition. What caused the tension between Jewish believers in Jesus and Jewish nonbelievers?

WHAT'S THE "GOOD NEWS" IN JOHN? WORD BECOME FLESH

John's structure (see Figure 8.4) breaks neatly into two main halves. After a Prologue (John 1:18) that traces Jesus's origins back to "the beginning" (John 1:1), the first major section relates both events and extended teachings from Jesus's public ministry. In John Jesus has a longer earthly career (three

FIGURE 8.4: OUTLINE OF JOHN

Prologue (1:1–18)

Book of Signs (1:19–12:50)

Book of Glory (13:1–19:42)

    Farewell Discourse (13:1–17:26)

    Passion Narrative (18:1–19:42)

Epilogue (20:1–21:25)

    Original Gospel Conclusion (20:1-31)

    Later Addition (21:1-25)

---

years, not one) and travels freely between Galilee and surrounding regions and Judea and Jerusalem. The Gospel's second half slows the story's pace to a crawl. At a final meal with his disciples, Jesus offers something like a last will and testament that spans five chapters. After the passion narrative that follows, John's Epilogue probably combines two different sources—both of which feature encounters with the risen Lord.

Prologue: John 1:1-18

Like the other Gospels, John begins by tracing Jesus's origins. But while Mark links Jesus's earthly ministry to an apocalyptic prophet, and Matthew and Luke locate Jesus's place in the family tree of Jewish tradition, the Fourth Gospel reaches back even further. Echoing the opening phrase of Genesis, John begins this way: "*In the beginning* was the Word" (John 1:1; see Gen 1:1). Interpreters have long found in this statement evidence of Jesus's pre-existence with God. As Christian doctrine developed over time, church leaders turned this passage as biblical support for the Son's divine nature and origins.

Read in its pluralistic context, though, John's Prologue differentiates between the word (or *logos*) and the human Jesus in whom that word came to dwell. Already we've seen that Hellenistic Jews often associated the *logos* with wisdom, Torah, and sometimes God's cocreator. What's unprecedented in John is the claim that God's *logos* has made a home in human flesh, specifically in Jesus, God's only son (John 1:14, 18).

This bold statement hovers over the rest of the Gospel, as Jesus reveals God's word through both deeds and teachings. Along the way, he radiates a "glory like that of a father's only son" (John 1:14). Yet even John's "high Christology" consistently distinguishes between Jesus and God, in that Jesus's glory points back to the Father. In addition, Jesus imparts God's *logos* to those he leaves behind. They, too, will bear God's glory for the world to see.

Book of Signs (John 1:19–12:50)

Jesus's public ministry in John features several stories and characters found in the Synoptic Gospels. Here, too, he teaches, heals, and performs nature miracles. We meet Peter, the renamed "Simon, son of John" (John 1:42), along with other disciples. Mary and Martha also appear again, this time imploring Jesus to raise their dead brother, Lazarus (John 11:1). As he has in the Synoptics, Jesus heals an official's son (John 4:46-54) and provides food in the wilderness just before walking on water (John 6:1-21).

Yet the first half of John departs in significant ways from Matthew, Mark, and Luke. Indeed, plenty of key Gospel stories are missing from this account: Jesus's baptism by John, his parables, and the story of his transfiguration, for instance. What *does* John add to the NT conversation about Jesus's public ministry? The Fourth Gospel has much to say about Jesus's identity as God's Messiah and the importance of believing in his unique revelation of God's truth. Let's turn to three key facets of the Gospel's first half.

Jesus's Signs

In the Synoptic Gospels, signs play an ambiguous role at best. There, it's Jesus's detractors who demand a sign (see e.g., Matt 16:1; Mark 8:11; Luke 12:54), as if none of his miracles count as evidence of his messianic status. As a rule, the synoptic writers portray this request as evidence of their insufficient faith. By contrast, John assigns a positive meaning to signs as proof positive for Jesus's messiahship.

The Fourth Gospel relates seven specific signs throughout this section, though the narrator mentions that many more aren't reported here (e.g., John 2:23; 6:2). (See Figure 8.5.) Jesus's first sign takes place at a wedding in the village of Cana, in Galilee. After he miraculously turns jars of water into fine wine, the narrator explains that this first sign "revealed his glory, and his disciples believed in him" (John 2:11). In this Gospel, Jesus's signs confirm his divine agency and his identity as the Messiah in a public way. In turn, they

Figure 8.5: Jesus's Seven Signs in John

Here are the seven signs or miracles of Jesus found in John's Gospel. Except the first and the last in the list, these miracles appear in some form in at least one Synoptic Gospel:

1. Water changed into fine wedding wine at Cana (John 2:1-11)

2. Official's son healed at Capernaum (John 4:46-54)

3. Paralytic healed at Bethesda (John 5:1-15)

4. Five thousand fed (John 6:5-14)

5. Jesus walks on water (John 6:16-24)

6. Blind man healed (John 9:1-7)

7. Lazarus raised from the dead (John 11:1-45)

YOUR TURN: Choose one of the signs that appears in a Synoptic Gospel and compare the two different accounts. What tendencies do you see in John, compared with its companion version?

elicit two responses: many believe in him, but others detect danger in his messianic posturing and begin to plot against him (John 11:45-53).

Jesus's Itinerary

In the Synoptic Gospels, Jesus's messianic mission takes place mostly in and around the region called Galilee, to the north of Jerusalem. There, he flies under the radar of religious and political officials as he builds a movement devoted to God's coming reign. The Fourth Gospel relates Jesus's public ministry quite differently, in several respects. For one thing, Jesus's itinerary in John varies from the synoptic accounts. John's Jesus doesn't wait until the end of his life to go to Jerusalem. He travels back and forth between Galilee and Jerusalem repeatedly, usually to celebrate one of the major Jewish festivals. John *seems* to mention three separate Passovers during the course of Jesus's career (John 2:13; 6:4; 11:55), implying a longer public ministry than the Synoptic time line suggests.

Jesus's frequent visits to Jerusalem fit this Gospel's bolder, more forthright account of his public ministry as well. In John, he's no backwater preacher at the margins of the social order, demurring and evasive when asked about who he is or what he's up to. He's a rabble-rouser from the start, provoking temple authorities early in his career rather than during his last week (see John 2:13-22). As a result, John intensifies Jesus's mounting conflict with Jewish leaders (see John 11:45-53).

Another distinctive feature of Jesus's career in John is his ministry in **Samaria**. Remember, Galilean Jews typically traveled *around* Samaria to get to and from Jerusalem, even though it's right on the way. Mark's Jesus prohibits the disciples from entering the region (Mark 10:5). Luke reports Samaritan rejection of Jesus, because he was headed for Jerusalem (Luke 9:53) but also features the parable of a "good Samaritan." Only in the Fourth Gospel does Jesus actually go *into* Samaria. What's more, his encounter with a Samaritan woman not only convinces *her* that he's the Messiah but also makes her the first successful evangelist to appear in this Gospel (John 4:39-42).

Jesus's Identity

Perhaps what stands out most about John is Jesus's consistent attention to his own identity and calling. In the Synoptic Gospels, Jesus almost never speaks openly about himself. Others recognize him as Son of God or Messiah, but he's slow to acknowledge his identity. Sometimes—especially in Mark—he even silences those who would spread his acclaim.

Against this backdrop, John's Jesus can sound like a self-absorbed egomaniac. Rather than belief in God and God's kingdom, he solicits belief in himself (e.g., John 3:16). In addition, Jesus uses the phrase "I am" to identify himself over forty times in the Fourth Gospel. Together, these "**I am" statements**, found only in John, forge Jesus's intimate ties with God. How do they do so? In the Torah, God says to Moses, "I Am Who I Am" (Exod 3:14), implying to some interpreters that God's proper name is "I am." Sometimes, Jesus uses the cryptic clause to identify himself, as he does when he says that "before Abraham was, I Am" (John 8:58; see also 4:26; 6:20; 8:24, 28; 13:19; 18:5-6, 8). Elsewhere, the words introduce metaphors that convey who Jesus is or what he's about: "I am," he says, "the bread of life" (John 6:35, 48), "bread . . . from heaven" (John 6:41), "the light of the world" (John 8:12; 9:5), "the gate of the sheep" (John 10:7, 9), "the good shepherd" (John 10:11, 14), "the resurrection and the life" (John 11:25), "the way, the truth, and the life" (John 14:6); and "the true vine" (John 15:1). Notably, in Jewish scripture, most of these metaphors refer to God.

Besides the "I am" statements, John forges close ties between Jesus and God in other ways as well. Let's consider some examples. When we meet someone new, we often ask, "Where are you from?" In John, it's a question that Jesus answers at every turn, and the answer is neither Bethlehem nor Nazareth (cf. John 7:27). He's "from above" (John 3:31; 8:23); he "comes from heaven" (John 6:58); he's decidedly "not from this world" (8:23). What's more, he's come to do the "will of the one who sent" him (John 4:34) and so that "the world might be saved through him" (John 3:17). In John, the whole point of his miraculous signs is to confirm that "the Father sent me" (John 5:36-37; 6:29, 57).

Indeed, Jesus remains mystically united with the Father during his earthly career in John. In what scholars think is one of John's earlier sources, Jesus says he "can't do anything by himself except what he sees the Father doing" (John 5:19). Elsewhere, he insists that his instruction isn't his own but comes from the one "who sent me" (John 7:16). When he claims that "I and the Father are one" (John 10:30), Jesus signals unmistakable union with God that onlookers find blasphemous (John 10:31).

On the question of Jesus's status as Messiah, too, the Book of Signs is much more straightforward than the Synoptic Gospels. In John, people quickly recognize Jesus as Messiah, and he openly confirms it (see e.g., John 1:41; 4:25-26). Only those who don't heed the signs of his divine origins mistake him for a messianic pretender (see John 7:25-31), a notion he actively rebuts.

But John's Jesus doesn't self-promote for his own benefit. He does so to inspire belief in him and, through him, abundant life (or, "life to the fullest"; John 10:10). If you've ever watched a football game, you might recognize "John 3:16" from the ubiquitous end-zone signs. This iconic verse is, for many Christians, the gospel in a nutshell: "God so loved the world that he gave his only Son, so that everyone who *believes in him* won't perish but will have eternal life" (italics added). As John's Jesus puts it, "Now is the time for judgment of this world" (John 12:31; cf. 5:27-28), a judgment-based belief in Jesus as the Messiah (see John 20:31).

Review and Reflect

- Choose three examples this Gospel uses to illustrate Jesus's special relationship to God. Be sure to notice differing perspectives.

- Reflect on the various views that already appear in the Fourth Gospel. What does this diversity of thought show about the community or the school of thought that compiled John?

BOOK OF GLORY (JOHN 13:1–19:42)

John's second half itself divides into two parts: a lengthy **Farewell Discourse** that spans Jesus's last meal with his disciples (John 13:1–17:26) and John's **passion narrative** and its aftermath (John 18:1–19:42). In both sections, John showcases Jesus's glory as he imparts teaching to his own and displays God's love to the world. Much of the material throughout these chapters is found only in John. Let's consider the main points John makes in this section.

Farewell Discourse

The Synoptic Gospels say Jesus spent his last evening with his disciples celebrating the **Passover** feast. Though they differ on some details, Matthew, Mark, and Luke all depict this meal as a Last Supper, in which Jesus says the bread and cup symbolize his own body and blood. Scholars think his followers reenacted this memorial meal when they gathered after his death (see 1 Cor 11:23-26).

Once again, John's account diverges in important ways. For one thing, the last meeting takes place on the **day of preparation** for the Passover, not the Passover itself. John's chronology may be more accurate, since it's unlikely Jewish officials would conduct a trial on a holiday. (Remember, a day in the Jewish calendar extends from sundown to sundown.) In any case, the timing also fits John's theological aims. This Gospel sees Jesus as the "lamb of God" (John 1:29, 36) whose death on the preparation day provides the ultimate Passover sacrifice.

But the central symbolic act of the last evening together shifts in John as well. Though Jesus still shares a meal with his disciples, we find no mention of his body and blood represented in its elements. Instead, the supper serves as backdrop for the act of foot washing. Here, Jesus assumes the role of servant, even though Peter protests vehemently. After all, washing feet is the job of servants, not lords—at least in conventional society. It's a dirty task, and it requires the washer to kneel at the feet of the washed. But in John, Jesus presents this lowly job as "an example: Just as I have done, you also must do" (John 13:15). This symbolic act becomes an emblem of the sacrificial love that characterizes Jesus's messiahship in this Gospel.

Indeed, such servant-like love becomes in John the hallmark of believers as well. It's the "new commandment" that he delivers, as his end on earth looms near: "Love each other. Just as I have loved you, so you also must love each other" (John 13:34). The command to love isn't new; Torah already calls for love of both God and neighbor (see Mark 12:29-31; Matt 22:37-39; Luke 10:27). For John, Jesus's "new commandment" stresses the *sacrificial* nature of that love. When Jesus assumes the posture of servant to wash his disciples' feet and hints at his own impending death (John 15:13), Jesus establishes a pattern for discipleship (John 13:35).

Another feature of the Farewell Discourse is its view to the future. If John's first half emphasizes Jesus's *origins* with the Father, this section stresses his *destination*. From the outset, we read that "Jesus knew that his time had come to leave this world and go to the Father" (John 13:1), and he refers repeatedly here to his imminent departure. Like a beloved family member facing death, Jesus wants to get his affairs in order, to bequeath an inheritance to those he'll leave behind.

But that inheritance isn't a car or a bank account. It's Jesus's legacy of mystical union with God. Already, John has portrayed *Jesus's* intimate ties to God; he's "in the Father and the Father is in" him (John 14:10). In this section, John's Jesus mediates that same union with God to those who keep his commandments (John 15:10). For one thing, Jesus instructs his disciples to "remain in me" (John 15:4) even after his physical departure from earth. Using the image of a vine and its branches, he promises his perpetual presence as the source of the fruit his disciples will bear. Just as Jesus remains dependent on God, so, too, will the disciples rely not on themselves but on their spiritual union with him.

To enable this union with Jesus and with the Father, Jesus promises a **Companion** to accompany his disciples once he's gone. Also called the "Spirit of Truth" (John 14:17) and the "Holy Spirit" (John 14:26), this Companion will enable them to remain in Jesus when he's no longer physically present (John 15:4). It will pick up where Jesus left off, instructing disciples in the word that he's already entrusted to them and mediating God's way of abundant life.

In his closing prayer, Jesus imparts his union with God (John 17:23), his glory (John 17:22), and his message (John 17:8, 14, 20) to his disciples. His death will not end the disclosure of God's wisdom and power on earth. Jesus even says the disciples will "do even greater works than these" (John 14:12)! Ultimately, John presents the disciples as Jesus's successors sent out to reveal God's glory to the wider world: "As you sent me into the world, so I have sent them into the world" (John 17:18).

In John, that world is far from hospitable to either Jesus or his followers. John's sectarian perspective shines through in this regard. Jesus has chosen them "out of the world" (John 15:19). Like him, they don't "belong to the world" (John 15:19). Like him, they'll find it to be a hostile environment

---

181

when they carry forward Jesus's message. Jesus blames such hostility, in essence, on ignorance: "they don't know the Father or me" (John 16:3).

But unlike most sectarian texts, John doesn't cut ties to the world, as if to isolate and insulate the believing community from danger or contamination. To the contrary, Jesus prays *not* "that you take [the disciples] out of this world but that you keep them safe from the evil one" (John 17:15). In the end, despite the resistance they will encounter there, the world remains the target audience for Jesus's word and for the love of God disclosed in him (see John 3:16). In John's view, Jesus's followers should not be deterred in their efforts to reveal God's love; they must press on, Jesus says, "so that the world will believe that you sent me" (John 17:21).

Passion Narrative

From early in the Fourth Gospel, Jesus openly acknowledges his fate (see John 3:14). So it's not surprising that this Gospel's passion narrative portrays a Jesus who's at ease with his destiny and in full command of the plot that leads toward his death. Let's consider several distinctive features found in John's passion narrative.

Jesus in Command and Control

One Synoptic episode that's notably absent from John is Jesus's anguished prayer in the garden of Gethsemane. Matthew and Luke may tone down Mark's portrait of Jesus's inner turmoil, but John leaves it entirely out of the picture. This Gospel mentions that the arrest takes place in a garden (John 18:1-11), but Jesus doesn't agonize over his destiny ahead of time. Instead, he seizes the initiative, asking the soldiers whom they're seeking (John 18:4; cf. John 1:38), since he knows "everything" that's about to unfold.

Jesus also exerts a commanding presence when he interacts with both Jewish and Roman officials. In the Synoptic Gospels, he's rather cagey, giving mysterious, evasive answers that only stoke his interrogators' anger (e.g., Mark 14:61; 15:5). By contrast, John's Jesus is direct and to the point. He identifies himself, quite unflinchingly, to those who come to arrest him (John 18:6, 8); he reminds the high priest of his consistent pattern of transparent teaching (John 18:20); and he engages the Roman governor Pilate in two conversations that sound like banter between peers more than interrogation of a condemned criminal (John 18:33-38; 19:9-11). John's Jesus is clearly in charge of the unfolding events.

Even when Jesus hangs on the cross, he doesn't seem to suffer in John. Instead, he retains control of both his faculties and the narrative to the bitter end. He takes time to establish mutual family bonds between his own mother and his "beloved disciple" (John 19:26-27). He declares his thirst not because of human need but because he's following a biblical script (John 19:28). In place of the cry of dereliction found in Mark and Matthew, Jesus utters these last words: "it is completed" (John 19:30). As if he's putting his own finishing touches on his life, Jesus bows his head and willingly gives up his life. In John, Jesus is no passive victim caught up in a religious and political power play. He's a strong protagonist in a divine drama of sacrificial love, seen finally and fully on the cross.

A Heavenly Kingdom

Jesus's calm demeanor relates closely to John's reinterpretation of the kingdom of God as a framing concept for Jesus's career. As long as Jesus's mission is to establish an outpost of God's kingdom on earth, as he does in the Synoptic Gospels, his death retains an element of tragic defeat. Even if this defeat is "swallowed up" in the victory of the empty tomb (see 1 Cor 15:54), Jesus's death comes as a by-product of the present evil age. But for John, God's kingdom belongs to a different world order altogether; it's a spiritual, heavenly kingdom that's both at odds with the kingdom of this world and already triumphant over it.

The passion narrative underscores this point in a couple of ways. When Pilate asks Jesus if he's King of the Jews, Jesus says his kingdom isn't "from this world" (John 18:36). In some ways, it's an evasive answer, since he tacitly acknowledges that he *does* have a kingdom. But he also clearly differentiates between his own authority and Pilate's. Unlike Pilate's kingdom, Jesus's rule isn't secured by force; it's based on truth (John 18:37). Ultimately, Jesus reminds even Pilate that any power he wields has been "given to you from above" (John 19:11); it's God, in John, who's really in charge.

As in the other Gospels, Jesus dies under the banner "**King of the Jews**"— a detail historians think accurately captures the Roman warrant for Jesus's crucifixion. But more is made of the title in John than in the Synoptics. For one thing, Pilate repeatedly presents Jesus to the Jewish leaders as "your king" (John 19:14, 15)—a provocation that elicits their claim to have no king but the emperor. In the context of Passover, the Jewish festival that hails the Lord God as the one and only king, such a pronouncement is ironic, if not blasphemous. Only in John, too, do the chief priests ask for a change in the sign so that it reads, "This man said, 'I am the king of the Jews'" (John 19:21), as if to distance themselves further from Jesus's (divinely authorized) kingdom.

Jewish Culpability

Already, we've noted that John intensifies the conflict between Jesus and "the Jews" as well as their leaders throughout this Gospel. This tendency only gains steam in the passion narrative, where both Jewish officials and the crowds grow more vehement and hostile toward Jesus. First, John reminds us that the **high priest Caiaphas** carries out a plan hatched earlier, when he decided it's better for "one person to die for the people" (John 18:14; cf. 11:45-53). In John, the high priest's worldly, political calculations to save the people from Roman retaliation fold neatly into Jesus's heavenly authorized plan to save the whole world through sacrificial love.

As a group, "the Jews" play a rather forceful role in the events leading to Jesus's crucifixion. For one thing, it's "the Jews"—not their leaders—who cite a religious law that anyone claiming to be son of God should die (John 19:7). But they also make Jesus's execution a litmus test for loyalty to Rome and so use a savvy ploy to convince a reluctant Pilate to put Jesus to death. Finally, the chief priests put the matter bluntly: "We have no king except the emperor" (John 19:16). Those who've gathered to celebrate the Passover miracle of divine deliverance from oppression thus cast their lot with their Roman overlord. (See Figure 8.6.)

The Empty Tomb and Beyond (John 20:1–21:25)

Scholars think the last chapter of John's Gospel was added at an early stage in its transmission. We'll consider the two concluding chapters separately, highlighting how each draws Jesus's story to a fitting close.

Original Ending (John 20:1-31)

The Synoptic Gospels credit various women—**Mary Magdalene** is always among them—with discovering the absence of Jesus's body. But in John, Mary finds the stone rolled away and brings word to Jesus's male followers. The disciple "whom Jesus loved" beats Simon Peter in a footrace to the tomb and finds it empty. According to John, "he saw and believed" (John 20:8). Jesus's male disciples thus eclipse the females' role in pointing to his resurrection in John.

FIGURE 8.6: PASSOVER HAGGADAH FOR TODAY

Jews today continue to celebrate the **Passover** as reminder of God's liberating power—not just "once upon a time" in the exodus story, but in the course of human life today. This impulse to make the ancient story relevant to the contemporary setting is a defining feature of Jewish thought, especially within Reform Judaism. Families who gather for a Passover meal share a **Haggadah**, a liturgical script that applies the promises of scripture to today's world. One group called "Rabbis Organizing Rabbis" has written a contemporary Haggadah that connects the plight of immigrants in the US to the Hebrew people delivered from slavery in Egypt:

> This year undocumented immigrants still live in fear in the shadows of a broken immigration system. Next year may over 11 million aspiring Americans step into the light of freedom and walk the path towards citizenship.

> This year, our eyes are still clouded by the plague of darkness, as the Gerer Rav taught: "The darkness in Egypt was so dense that people could not see one another. This was not a physical darkness, but a spiritual darkness in which people were unable to see the plight and pain of their neighbors." Next year, may we replace darkness with light and truly see our neighbors and be moved to act with them to fix our broken immigration system.

> For discussion:

> Today, the Reform Jewish Movement is working to help create a commonsense American immigration process. How do your family stories connect to this historic moment?

> Think about your family history: What brought your family to this country? What did your family leave behind, and what opportunity did they seek? Does this help you understand today's immigrants? Why or why not? (See Religious Action Center of Reform Judaism, https://rac.org/sites/default/files/ROB%20seder.pdf.)

YOUR TURN: Reflect on the political implications of the Passover celebration. What makes Passover a "dangerous" story? Dangerous for whom?

This chapter includes three separate appearances from the risen Lord. In the first, Mary Magdalene thinks Jesus is a gardener until he calls her by name (John 20:16) and tells her to report the encounter to the disciples. In the second, Jesus enters the room where his disciples are gathered behind locked doors "for fear of the Jews" (John 20:19 NRSV). Rather than stoking that fear, he imparts both his peace and the promised gift of the Holy Spirit and puts his "his hands and his side" on full display (John 20:20). Finally, Jesus appears to Thomas, who'd missed the disciples' private session with Jesus and

FIGURE 8.7: CONVERSATIONS ABOUT JESUS'S BODILY RESURRECTION

John's emphasis on Jesus's post-resurrection body may offer a conversational counterpoint to those who downplayed Jesus's physical humanity in favor of his spiritual nature. As we'll see in both 1 Corinthians and 1 John, other NT voices insist that Jesus's resurrection was bodily, not just spiritual. But some noncanonical writings, such as the *Treatise of the Resurrection*, call the resurrection as a "transition to newness" rather than a bodily resurrection. Though this work probably comes from the late second century CE, it's likely that some believers in earlier generations explained Jesus's resurrection in similarly metaphorical, and spiritual, terms.

YOUR TURN: Read the *Treatise of the Resurrection* and John 20. How do these views of Jesus's resurrection differ? Which seems more compelling to you? Why?

was reluctant to believe their report. Jesus encourages him, too, to touch his wounds (John 20:27). Together, these stories emphasize that the risen Jesus is no mere ghost; he's walking around, in the flesh, before he returns to his Father (John 20:18). (See Figure 8.7.)

The chapter concludes with a fitting Gospel summary about its contents and its purpose: "Then Jesus did many other miraculous signs in his disciples' presence, signs that aren't recorded in this scroll. But these things are written so that you will believe that Jesus is the Christ, God's Son, and that believing, you will have life in his name" (John 20:30-31). But wait. The story doesn't end there. Scholars think this is one more literary seam that indicates the next—and final—chapter was added later.

Epilogue (John 21:1-25)

Besides the apparent literary seam found at the end of John 20, the style, setting, and content of John 21 all suggest that it's a later addition to the Gospel. Notice, for instance, that though John 20 takes place in Jerusalem, this chapter abruptly shifts location to Galilee, bringing it into closer agreement with the endings of both Mark and Matthew. Scholars think this signals a scribal concern to move the base of operations outside of Jerusalem and emphasize the movement's Galilean roots.

More significantly, the addition may contain a subtle reference to Peter's martyrdom, which took place in Rome in the 60s CE (John 21:18-19). Peter's conversation with the risen Jesus serves two main points in the story. First,

Jesus authorizes his leadership that's marked by caring for "my sheep." Second, Jesus confirms that Peter's death will bring glory to God, just as Jesus's death has. After an odd exchange about an (unfounded) rumor that the beloved disciple "would not die" (John 21:20-23), the chapter concludes by insisting on the validity of his testimony (John 21:24).

JOHN'S MESSAGE

As we read it today, the Fourth Gospel weaves together various sources that come from different stages in the life of a first-century believing community. Like the other canonical Gospels, John relates the story of Jesus and his disciples for those who see themselves as heirs to the mission entrusted to those first followers. As we've seen with the other Gospels, John's story gives hints about their reality on the ground. What elements of John's message can we better understand by connecting them to their earliest context?

Belief in Jesus

Was Jesus of Nazareth the Messiah, the Son of God, or not? By late in the first century CE, this question took on pointed significance as both Christianity and Judaism invented and reinvented themselves. Emerging leaders within rabbinical Judaism were likely wary of messianic delusions that God's kingdom would bring the end of Roman rule. After all, Jerusalem had suffered the brunt of the Jewish War as reprisal for an insurgency fueled by such claims. And though we have no evidence of official Jewish policy excluding Christians from the synagogue, John's not the only early Christian text to refer, at least obliquely, to this policy.

For John's first audience, belief in Jesus as Jewish Messiah had become a defining trait of belonging. Mark urges hearers to trust that God's kingdom will soon dawn; Matthew promotes a way of surpassing righteousness modeled by Jesus; and Luke casts a subversive vision for an upside-down sociopolitical order. While the Synoptics clearly portray Jesus as protagonist, their stories show limited interest in his divine identity per se. But John focuses in a laser-like way on the key importance of belief in Jesus's messianic status. The world of the Fourth Gospel thus divides neatly between insider and outsider—that is, between those who believe and those who do not.

For a small group at the margins of their community, such a decisive boundary marker played an important role in building social cohesion. After all, their views were far from mainstream; Jews and non-Jews alike mostly looked askance at the notion that God's son would die on a Roman cross or that God's kingdom had triumphed over worldly powers. The community's minority status only raised the stakes for their insistence on their truth as a zero-sum game. Under siege for their worldview, John's community doubled down on the ideology that had become their trademark. John's Gospel thus declares itself for Jesus's messiahship with vigor and strikes a tone that is, at times, strident in its opposition to foes.

Over time, Christians switched social roles, gaining a monopoly on political power that's lasted, in many parts of the world, to this day. Along the way, a message that originally strengthened a marginalized group has been redeployed by those in power to coerce, exclude, and even destroy. If belief in Jesus remains a defining trait of Christianity today, readers of the Fourth Gospel will benefit from taking its categorical, insider-outsider distinction as a message first crafted for those at the margins, rather than at the center, of power.

God's Word Become Flesh

Even for John, belief in Jesus is more of a starting point than the Gospel's chief concern. More important for the story are the ways Jesus both embodies God's *logos* and equips others to do so after his death. In an extended prayer for his disciples, Jesus recalls that he's given God's word to them (John 17:14). It's a gift that's not for them to hoard or even protect; it's a gift to be shared with the world. Indeed, Jesus prays for believers who come to faith as his disciples share that word (John 17:20). In other words, John's community continues to bear witness to God's *logos*.

How will they be able to convey that word to the world? Not through their own ingenuity or ability. They'll do so only when they remain connected to its source by participating in Jesus's mystical union with God. Jesus prays that his followers will unite with one another and with both Father and Son, "just as you are in me and I am in you . . . [and] that they also will be in us" (John 17:21). In this Gospel, Jesus's unity with God enables believers' unity with God as well. (See Figure 8.8.)

Way of Sacrificial Love

What does that unity entail? For John, it's evident in Jesus's way of sacrificial love. After washing his disciples' feet as a living example of his new commandment, Jesus says, "This is how everyone will know that you are my disciples, when you love each other" (John 13:35). If belief in Jesus is assumed among disciples, John's message suggests it leads in turn to a servant-like

FIGURE 8.8: ICON OF THE TRINITY

Andrei Rublev, *The Trinity*, also called *The Hospitality of Abraham*, fifteenth century

This fifteenth-century Russian icon depicts the three mysterious visitors to Abraham (see Gen 18:1-8) as the three members of the Christian Trinity: Father, Son, and Holy Spirit. Many art historians have noted two features that suggest the artist envisioned human participation in this dynamic relationship. First, the Holy Spirit (on the right) points to the empty spot at the table. Second, the small rectangular box may have been where a mirror invited viewers to "see themselves" at the table. (See Richard Rohr, *The Divine Dance: The Trinity and Your Transformation* [London: SPCK Publishing, 2016].)

YOUR TURN: Reread John 17. How does this prayer express a believer's relationship to God, Jesus, and the Spirit?

FIGURE 8.9: "WAY" IN CHINESE THOUGHT

"Way" (the *dao* or *tao*) is an important concept to Chinese worldviews, including Daoism (or Taoism), Confucianism, and Mohism and has a range of meanings. Daoism's foundational text, the *Dao de Jing* (or *Tao Te Ching*), opens with this line: "The Way that can be followed is not the eternal Way." In Daoist thought, "way" is all-encompassing: discerning the "way" isn't a matter of formula or equation; it's the metaphysical force that underlies everything—both sensate and spiritual. Daoism practices such as qigong, alchemy, and meditation are the tools for humans to grow more mindful of and live in keeping with this "way." Daoists generally believe the way is often obscured to humans by a focus on reason and technology. *Dao* is evident in nature and living in tune with Dao or the way is akin to "going with the flow" rather than resisting or engineering life's path.

Confucianism uses the same term quite differently. The *Analects of Confucius* present a "way of life" that actively cultivates virtues such as filial piety and sincerity. Education is vital to this "way," as deliberate training in character development and ethical living. Confucius thought that social chaos and public corruption in his day called for a more disciplined, coherent system of beliefs and practices that span domestic and public spheres.

> **YOUR TURN:** Reflect on Jesus's "way" of sacrificial servanthood in the Fourth Gospel. How is it like or unlike the concept of "way" in Chinese thought?

selflessness. In the Fourth Gospel, Jesus is "the way, the truth, and the life" (John 14:6), and his example of sacrificial love provides the paradigm for life with him. (See Figure 8.9.)

For John's audience, this way has proven costly indeed. It's evoked the world's hatred, exclusion, and perhaps even death (see John 16:2). Still, Jesus doesn't suggest his followers should cut and run, or hole up behind locked doors, or dismiss the world as irredeemable and dangerous. Instead, Jesus sends out his disciples on this way of sacrificial love, even into a hostile world. He's confident that, by remaining "in him," they'll do "greater works" (John 14:12) and "produce much fruit" (John 15:5). Along the way, John maintains, they'll live "life to the fullest" (John 10:10), both here and in the hereafter.

SUMMARY

The Fourth Gospel stands out in many respects. In it, Jesus appears as a larger-than-life Messiah who's out to show the world the way that leads to abundant life. His conversation style is more direct than in the Synoptic Gospels, and he's more openly self-assured—sometimes even confrontational. He also seems to have more of a direct line to the Father, who's sent him into the world, where the battle between good and evil, light and dark, truth and falsehood, rages on. Written for a community still wrestling with their identity—and with their relationship to their native Judaism—this Gospel draws clear boundary lines around those who believe in Jesus and, in him, find eternal life and a calling to share his word with the world. As they join in his mystical union with the Father, they, too, disclose the way of sacrificial love.

Review and Reflect

- Name and explain two main themes that appear in the Farewell Discourse.

- Reflect on John's passion narrative. How does it fit the rest of the Gospel, John's community, or the group of NT Gospels?

GO DEEPER

Brown, Raymond. *The Community of the Beloved Disciple*. New York: Paulist, 1979.

Clark-Soles, Jaime. *Reading John for Dear Life: A Spiritual Walk with the Fourth Gospel*. Louisville, KY: Westminster John Knox, 2016.

Kysar, Robert. *John the Maverick Gospel*. 3rd ed. Louisville, KY: Westminster John Knox, 2007.

Martyn, J. Louis. *History and Theology in the Fourth Gospel*. 3rd ed. Nashville: Abingdon Press, 2003.

Schneiders, Sandra S. *Written That You May Believe: Encountering Jesus in the Fourth Gospel*. Rev. ed. New York: Crossroad, 2003.

Chapter Nine

Who Was the Real Jesus of Nazareth?

CONVERSATION STARTERS

- What is the "quest for the historical Jesus"?

- What are the origins and history of this "quest"?

- What sources do historians consider as they reconstruct Jesus's career?

- How do scholars determine which evidence about Jesus is historically reliable?

- What are the consensus findings about Jesus's life, death, and resurrection?

By this point in our study, we know the Gospels provide neither eyewitness accounts nor accurate records of Jesus's career. Their authors and editors were much more interested in truth than in fact. We've come to see that instead of *reporting* Jesus's career with precision, each account *translates* the gospel story for a particular setting. To take each Gospel on its own terms is, in part, to recover a sense of how each author interprets the meaning of Jesus's mission for a believing community living in the first-century CE Mediterranean world.

But this approach to the Gospels opens up new questions: Do the Gospels have any historical basis at all? If so, is it possible to separate fact from fiction, accuracy from embellishment, historical details from theological

FIGURE 9.1: DID JESUS EXIST?

A handful of historians think Jesus's earthly career is sheer fabrication. On what grounds? They think the earliest sources (Paul's letters, for instance) don't prove Jesus's existence and that even later sources focus mostly on the believing community devoted to Jesus the Christ. Also suspect, in their view, are the very critical methods we discuss in this chapter: these scholars think they're simply too subjective, or subjectively applied to the evidence, to make them useful. If you're interested in learning more, check out Richard Carrier, *On the Historicity of Jesus: Why We Might Have Reason for Doubt* (Sheffield, UK: Sheffield Phoenix Press, 2014).

YOUR TURN: Research the question of Jesus's existence online after reading this chapter, paying attention to the kind of sources you find. What do you think? What are the strongest arguments for and against Jesus's existence?

development? The short answer to both questions is yes. The more complete answer is yes, but it's complicated. (See Figure 9.1.)

This chapter takes up complex questions explored in the field of NT scholarship devoted to the "quest for the historical Jesus." By definition, it's a modern quest. With the dawn of the Enlightenment in Europe, intellectual inquiry grew more scientific in its concern with facts and evidence. As a result, the nature of "truth" shifted away from spiritual or religious meaning and toward verifiable evidence. When it comes to the NT, that shift brought scrutiny to Gospel stories long taken for granted. People began to ask, understandably, about Jesus's miracles and even his resurrection. They saw differences in the Gospels in a new light and posed historical questions that had mostly gone unaddressed: Did Jesus see himself as Messiah and if so, in what way? If Jesus was Jewish, why does he sound so critical of his own tradition? Did all the Gospel stories really happen, or were they created later to embellish Jesus's reputation?

In a sense, the modern "quest for the historical Jesus" takes up concerns most contemporary readers harbor about the Gospels. As a scholarly pursuit, this quest provides critical tools that help us think carefully about those concerns. Regardless of your faith commitments or lack thereof, understanding this quest is part of reading the NT responsibly for our place and time.

We'll examine this topic in three steps. First, we'll highlight early pioneers in the "quest for the historical Jesus" as well as its development over the last two centuries. As we'll see, historians today both build on and expand earlier trends. Second, we'll turn to the question of methods, laying out the evidence at hand and the critical tools used to assess it. In this unfolding conversation, historians review sources from inside and outside the NT, weighing their contents according to established criteria. Thus we'll glimpse scholars' concerted effort to be as objective as possible in their assessment of historical validity. Finally, we'll touch on the quest's major findings—both points of broad consensus agreement as well as the more hotly debated points. By the end of the chapter, I hope you'll see both the value of this academic investigation and its limits.

Before we proceed, I want to reiterate a point made earlier in our study. The approach taken here neither requires religious commitment nor prevents it. Historians cited in our discussions include Christians, Jews, and secularists. Among Christians, they're both "liberal" and "conservative"—or somewhere in the wide middle between them. What they hold in common is not a religious or political ideology but a commitment to the historical investigation of a man named Jesus. They work hard to avoid confirmation bias, which is the human tendency only to consider evidence that supports one's views. They're also honest enough to admit that pure objectivity is an elusive aim. After all, even our most disciplined efforts at impartiality can't free us from the implicit biases that come from our own setting. That's why it's so important to see this inquiry, too, as conversation more than definitive pronouncement. As our discussion unfolds, pay attention to the questions this "quest for the historical Jesus" raises, as well as the questions it answers.

WHAT'S THE "QUEST," AND HOW DID IT BEGIN? A THOROUGHLY MODERN CONVERSATION

Since around the time of George Washington, scholars have examined the Gospels through lenses that fit modern historical concerns. They've read stories of Jesus walking on water and explained them away ("he was really walking in the surf at the edge of the sea") or dismissed them as fanciful tales. They've noticed the differences among the Gospels that we discussed in chapter 4 and tried to make sense of them. They've recognized that even the earliest Greek versions of the Gospels are far removed—in place, time, and language—from Jesus's career, and they've wondered what Jesus really said and did and how he understood his mission in life. In all these ways, modern readers of scripture have hinted at—or asked outright—questions about the historical reliability of the Gospel record.

An eighteenth-century German scholar named **Hermann Reimarus** was the first to take up this question in a serious and sustained way. Many credit him with launching what's called the **First Quest** for the historical Jesus. Reimarus saw Jesus as a failed political revolutionary who thought he would see God's liberation of Palestine from Roman rule. Others scholars followed Reimarus's lead, weighing in with attempts to make historical sense of the Gospel accounts. Those who wrote the "liberal lives of Jesus" focused on the social agenda of Jesus's teachings and their contemporary relevance, while others stressed Jesus's eschatological leanings and suggested that he was mistaken, misguided, or misunderstood.

At the turn of the twentieth century, Albert Schweitzer wrote a book called (in English) *The Quest for the Historical Jesus* that mostly surveys the landscape of the First Quest's findings. Schweitzer's two sweeping conclusions continue to guide historians today. First, he highlighted the subjective nature of the First Quest, linking each "take" on Jesus's story to the scholar's context and personal ideology. He showed, for instance, how Ernst Renan's Jesus would have been all too at home in Renan's nineteenth-century France. Schweitzer's assessment cautions us against portraits of a "historical Jesus" who is too familiar in our own place and time.

This wariness leads to Schweitzer's second main contribution, which is a portrait of Jesus's historical mission that continues to influence the conversation today. Schweitzer summarizes Jesus's career this way:

> [John t]he Baptist appears, and cries: "Repent, for the Kingdom of Heaven is at hand." Soon after that comes Jesus, and in the knowledge that He is the coming Son of Man lays hold of the wheel of the world to set it moving on that last revolution which to bring all ordinary history to a close. It refuses to turn, and He throws Himself upon it. Then it does turn; and crushes Him. Instead of bringing in the eschatological conditions, He has destroyed them. The wheel rolls onward, and the mangled body of the one immeasurably great Man, who was strong enough to think of Himself as the spiritual ruler of mankind and to bend history to His purpose, is hanging upon it still. That is His victory and His reign. (370–71)

For Schweitzer, Jesus's career didn't end the way he'd hoped. He is, on some level, a failed revolutionary. But Schweitzer doesn't take this outcome as tragedy, pure and simple. Instead, he concludes that Jesus's "mangled body" still hangs on the wheel of history, which he names both "victory" and "reign."

Schweitzer's findings about the subjective nature of the quest led most scholars to abandon the task, at least for a while. Interest in Jesus and the Gospels turned from history to theology, from social movements to personal religion. Then, in 1953, **Ernst Käsemann** reopened the question, insisting on the vital importance of historical inquiry. This concern grew out of Käsemann's context: he wrote as the world was waking up to the horrors of Nazi Germany, horrors in which Christians had widely participated either actively or through a conspiracy of silence. Partly by spiritualizing Jesus—and detaching him from his own sociopolitical landscape—scholars had sustained that complicity.

Historians whose work makes up the **Second Quest** took up Käsemann's challenge. Together, their inquiry produced a critical tool called the "criterion of double dissimilarity" (see below), which assigns historical legitimacy to Gospel traditions that fit neither Jewish patterns of thought and practice nor early Christian doctrine. Jesus's use of the title "Son of the Human" to refer to himself is an example of Gospel content that's considered authentic on the basis of this criterion. On the one hand, no Jewish text sees the "Son of the Human" as a messiah who operates within the historical, earthly realm. On the other hand, it's a title that grows less important for Christian writers over time, as "Christ," "Lord," and "Savior" gain favor.

A third wave of research on the historical Jesus has spawned even greater interest. Known together as the **Third Quest**, this group includes a wider range of conversation partners on several levels. For one thing, they're not all European or male. They also deploy a wider range of academic disciplines, drawing the social sciences and archaeology more deliberately into historical investigation. Despite diverse findings, the Third Quest consistently situates Jesus within his own Jewish context.

The Third Quest embraces two main approaches. The first focuses on the question of what Jesus really *said*—that is, his teachings. You may have heard of the **Jesus Seminar**, made up of more than 150 scholars and first convened in 1985 by Robert W. Funk. This group builds on earlier findings—the priority of Mark, the existence of Q, and the general tendency of legendary tales to grow over time—and rates traditions for authenticity using a system involving color-coded beads. (See Figure 9.2.) Members of the Seminar don't always agree on these judgments, but as a group, they exhibit these leanings:

1. In their work, Jesus appears more as a wise teacher than an end-time prophet.

2. They consider the noncanonical Gospel of Thomas to be an early and useful source.

3. They operate with a **"hermeneutic of suspicion"**—generally "suspecting" that traditions are inauthentic unless proven otherwise.

A second group of Third Questers explores what Jesus *did*—his and others' actions, the people he associates with, and his Palestinian Jewish context. E. P. Sanders laid important groundwork for this approach that begins with

FIGURE 9.2: THE JESUS SEMINAR

A group of scholars called the Jesus Seminar has played a part in shaping popular views of Jesus over the last few decades. Among them, John Dominic Crossan and Marcus Borg have spoken widely in churches and nonreligious settings, inviting people to "meet Jesus again for the first time," as the title of a Borg book puts it. For many, the Jesus Seminar's attention to Jesus's social location (especially Crossan) and his meta-religious mysticism (especially Borg) has helped people read the Gospels afresh. It's worth noting that even these two scholars' portraits of Jesus differ in important ways.

Here's the voting system the members of the Jesus Seminar have used to assess the historical authenticity of Jesus's sayings:

- *Red beads* indicated the voter believed Jesus did say the passage quoted, or something very much like the passage. (3 Points)

- *Pink beads* indicated the voter believed Jesus probably said something like the passage. (2 Points)

- *Grey beads* indicated the voter believed Jesus did not say the passage, but it contains Jesus's ideas. (1 Point)

- *Black beads* indicated the voter believed Jesus did not say the passage—it comes from later admirers or a different tradition. (0 Points)

Together, these findings lie behind *The Gospel According to the Jesus Seminar* (1999), which weaves together the most highly rated material from the sources. The Jesus Seminar's consensus view is that Jesus was more of a wise teacher and community organizer than predictor of apocalyptic doom. (In general, they think the apocalyptic sayings are later additions to the core traditions.)

YOUR TURN: If we're trying to understand what Jesus was all about, what's the benefit of focusing on his sayings? What's missing from this emphasis?

historically reliable features, including Jesus's ties to John the Baptist and his death as "King of the Jews." These scholars then situate Jesus's career in relation to his first-century social and religious world. Their findings lead them broadly to affirm these claims:

1. Jesus's proclamation of the "kingdom of God" is rooted in the soil of Jewish apocalyptic thought.

2. Jesus's reputation for spending time with "sinners and tax collectors," as well as his prophetic deeds in Jerusalem, defied socioreligious protocol in provocative ways.

3. Jesus's controversial words and actions were part of an "insider" conversation within Judaism, not an external critique.

Taken together, these two approaches work to deepen our understanding of the historical Jesus. Indeed, their findings overlap in important ways. For instance, both groups within the Third Quest require "authentic" sayings or deeds to fit credibly within Jesus's historical setting as a Palestinian Jew living under Roman military occupation. We'll turn to some of their findings after a closer look at the sources and methods their inquiry uses.

Review and Reflect

- What are the three main stages of the "quest for the historical Jesus," and what's one key contribution from each?

- Reflect on the ways in which our own contexts inevitably affect our own study. Should we try to be objective? Why or why not?

WHAT "RAW MATERIAL" DO HISTORIANS USE? THE QUESTION OF SOURCES

Any historical study depends on sources. If we want to learn about Nelson Mandela, for instance, we read newspaper articles about him, letters he wrote, and government documents pertaining to his anti-apartheid work. These primary sources come from his twentieth-century setting in South Africa and so offer a glimpse of the "reality on the ground" during his lifetime. But we'd also probably consult what we call secondary sources: historical analysis, biographies, and even harsh critiques of Mandela as a revolutionary leader. Both primary and secondary sources are biased sources, so the more diverse the perspectives we consider, the closer we get to historical authenticity.

Exploring questions about the "real Jesus" proves to be a more challenging task. After all, Mandela earned an international reputation early in his career. In his modern, literate world, observers often captured his words and actions on film or recording. And Mandela devoted much of his time in prison to writing an account of his career, published in his autobiography, *The Long Walk to Freedom*.

But neither Jesus nor his disciples captured his story in writing. Nor do public documents record any instances related to his life or death. Instead, those interested in preserving Jesus's memory did so mostly orally, telling stories and quoting pithy sayings. It's also problematic, from a historian's view, that the only detailed accounts of Jesus's career come from his supporters. After all, as noteworthy as Jesus became across the millennia, he remained historically insignificant during his own lifetime. As a result, the sources that inform historians' quest for the historical Jesus are both limited in scope and mostly biased in his favor.

But you wouldn't be reading this textbook if we had *no* sources. Scholars divide the evidence we have into two unequal groups: external and internal sources. On the one hand are **external sources**, which mention Jesus or the movement he left behind from an outsider's perspective. These sources are scant but helpful because their authors have little interest in promoting the Christian cause. **Internal sources**, on the other hand, clearly present Jesus in a favorable light. That bias doesn't diminish their value, but it does mean scholars scrutinize their claims quite closely. As we'll see, most evidence about the historical Jesus comes from these internal sources.

What's the Outsider Testimony? External Sources

For generations after his death, most people living in the Roman Empire hadn't even heard of Jesus. It's not surprising, then, that only a handful of non-Christian documents from the first and early second centuries CE mention Jesus or his followers. Scholars mainly use three external sources to confirm, from an outsider perspective, basic features of Jesus's career and the communities established in its wake.

The only external source that mentions Jesus himself appears in **Josephus's** *Antiquities of the Jews*, published at the end of the first century CE. This excerpt, known as the **Testimonium**, describes Jesus this way:

> About this time there lived Jesus, a wise man, *if indeed one ought to call him a man*. For he was one who performed surprising deeds and was a teacher of such people as accept the truth gladly. He won over many Jews and many of the Greeks. *He was the Christ.* And when, upon the accusation of the principal men among us, Pilate had condemned him to a cross, those who had first come to love him did not cease. *He appeared to them spending a third day restored to life, for the prophets of God had foretold these things and a thousand other marvels about him.* And the tribe of the Christians, so called after him, has still to this day not disappeared. (*Antiquities* 18.3.3)

Historians think early Christian scribes have modified this passage (the later additions are italicized here); its affirmation that Jesus was "the Christ" simply doesn't fit Josephus's decidedly Jewish worldview. But despite the likelihood that Josephus's words have been expanded to support Christian belief, scholars think the nonitalicized, neutral report is original, especially since Josephus elsewhere mentions James, the brother of Jesus (20.9.1), as well as John the Baptist (18.5.2). This makes even the bare-bones account invaluable. It confirms several Gospel features: Jesus's reputation as a wise teacher and miracle worker, his broad public appeal, his death on a Roman cross, and the movement that endured after his execution.

We can note briefly two other external sources that mention a new religious movement devoted to the worship of Christ. In one, a Roman governor of Bithynia named **Pliny the Younger** writes to the Emperor Trajan for guidance about judicial proceedings against believers. This letter, which dates to around 112 CE, says that Christians "sing a hymn to Christ, as to a god," that they adhere to a strong ethical code, and that they gather for a "common but innocent meal." It's their exclusive worship of Christ, and their resulting refusal to worship local and imperial gods, that makes them objects of state-sanctioned persecution.

The Roman historian **Tacitus** also mentions Christians in his discussion of a fire in Rome (64 CE). Writing decades later, sometime around 116 CE, Tacitus says that the **Emperor Nero** targeted Christians as a group to blame for the tragedy. (See Figure 9.3.) In this brief passage, Tacitus also confirms Jesus's execution under Pontius Pilate and alludes to the "mischievous superstition" that arose after Jesus's death, a term that helps us understand how early Christianity was viewed by mainstream culture in the second century CE.

Even these few external sources help to situate Jesus of Nazareth in the landscape of first-century CE Roman-occupied Palestine. Not only do they establish that Jesus existed as a human being on the stage of history (and not just a mythological character), but they also back up Gospel claims that he died in Jerusalem and that his followers were, surprisingly to outsiders, inspired rather than demoralized by his death.

Can We Trust the Insider Reports? Internal Sources

Apart from these three external sources, we're left with evidence that's clearly written by and for Christ-followers. By nature these sources are biased, since they presume or promote devotion to Jesus as the Jewish Messiah. Most appear in today's New Testament, though some scholars also think noncanonical texts such as the gospels attributed to Peter and Thomas preserve authentic details from Jesus's career. Here's a brief rundown of these internal sources and how they serve historical inquiry.

FIGURE 9.3: TACITUS ON NERO'S PERSECUTION

In 64 CE, a fire raged through the Roman capital, affecting ten out of the city's fourteen districts. Many blamed the great fire in Rome on Nero himself. Tacitus explains the emperor's response this way:

> Therefore, to scotch the rumor, Nero substituted as culprits, and punished with the utmost refinements of cruelty, a class of men, loathed for their vices, whom the crowd styled Christians.

> Christus, the founder of the name, had undergone the death penalty in the reign of Tiberius, by sentence of the procurator Pontius Pilatus, and the pernicious superstition was checked for a moment, only to break out once more, not merely in Judaea, the home of the disease, but in the capital itself, where all things horrible or shameful in the world collect and find a vogue.

> First, then, the confessed members of the sect were arrested; next, on their disclosures, vast numbers were convicted, not so much on the count of arson as for hatred of the human race. And derision accompanied their end: they were covered with wild beasts' skins and torn to death by dogs; or they were fastened on crosses, and, when daylight failed were burned to serve as lamps by night. Nero had offered his Gardens for the spectacle, and gave an exhibition in his Circus, mixing with the crowd in the habit of a charioteer, or mounted on his car. Hence, in spite of a guilt which had earned the most exemplary punishment, there arose a sentiment of pity, due to the impression that they were being sacrificed not for the welfare of the state but to the ferocity of a single man. (*Annals* 15.44)

Notice that Tacitus says the "scapegoating" strategy wasn't entirely effective. After all, the point was to pin blame for adversity on a vulnerable group. Typically, this approach uses a "single victim mechanism" as a release valve for society's pent-up angst over misfortune or chaos. But in this case, Nero seems so harsh in his treatment of Christians that Tacitus shows sympathy for them.

YOUR TURN: Where in our world do you see people or groups targeted as "scapegoats" for adversity? How does popular opinion toward marginalized groups reflect this scapegoating?

The earliest evidence available to historians today is **Paul's letters**, written around the middle of the first century CE. These texts predate the NT Gospels. (Remember, most scholars think Mark was written around 70 CE.) Perhaps surprisingly, Paul has very little to say about Jesus's Galilean ministry. Mostly, Paul interprets the meaning of Jesus's death and resurrection for groups of believers already devoted to him.

Paul's letters do allude to Jesus's teachings in a handful of passages. Two appear in his first letter to the Corinthian community. In his discussion about marriage, Paul appeals to those who are married not to separate, saying that this command comes from "not I but the Lord" (1 Cor 7:10; cf. Mark 10:2-12). Later in the letter, he mentions a tradition about a commemorative meal that he "received from the Lord" (1 Cor 11:23-26; cf. Matt 26:26-29; Mark 14:22-25; Luke 22:15-20). He even cites Jesus's command to "do this to remember me."

Elsewhere, both Paul and other NT writers offer instruction that echoes Jesus's teachings, even if they don't mention him specifically. Paul tells the Roman Christians to "bless those who persecute you" (Rom 12:14; cf. Luke 6:28) and to "love one another" (Rom 13:8; cf. John 15:34). A later letter attributed to James warns against both judging one another (Jas 4:11; cf. Matt 7:1) and planning for tomorrow (Jas 4:13-17; cf. Luke 12:16-21) and uses agricultural imagery to anticipate the "coming of the Lord" (Jas 5:7-8; cf. Mark 4:26-29). Clearly, both Paul and the author of James are acquainted with sayings found in the Gospels and, in the case of James, perhaps the Gospels themselves.

The NT Gospels serve as our most helpful sources for reconstructing the historically reliable aspects of Jesus's career, even despite their highly subjective nature. But what about the gospels not included in the NT? Do they tell the "real story," as Dan Brown's *Da Vinci Code* would have you believe? (See Figure 9.4.) For the most part, scholars think the noncanonical gospels as too far removed in place and time from Jesus himself to prove helpful for our study of the historical Jesus. But two exceptions to this general claim are worth noting. As we've noted, a meaningful minority of scholars think much of the Gospel of Thomas—made up only of Jesus's sayings—dates to the first century CE. (The majority opinion attributes it to a second-century gnostic school of thought.) In addition, a handful of scholars detect historically authentic traces in the Gospel of Peter, considered by most to be a second-century work.

WHAT LITMUS TESTS DO SCHOLARS USE? THE QUESTION OF CRITERIA

None of our sources goes back to Jesus himself, or even to his lifetime. Still, historians generally agree they combine authentic material with reports created or adapted to fit later circumstance or belief. That leaves an important set of questions: How do we determine what the "real Jesus" did or said or thought? How might we recover a historically accurate sense of how Jesus

FIGURE 9.4: DAN BROWN
AND THE NONCANONICAL GOSPELS

The Da Vinci Code is a best-selling novel by Dan Brown that makes bold claims about Jesus's historical career and personal life, including his marriage to Mary Magdalene (New York: Anchor, 2009). (It's also been made into a motion picture.) The story features a scholar named Sir Leigh Teabing who pronounces with authority on historical matters. Mainly, Teabing explains that the emperor Constantine spearheaded a conspiracy to name the four NT Gospels as authoritative even though the gnostic gospels are the "earliest Christian records" (245) that "speak of Christ's ministry in very human terms" (234). He also mentions the gnostic gospels of Mary and of Philip as reliable sources for Jesus's ministry. Scholars across the spectrum, though, agree that the gnostic gospels date to the second century and later. What's more, their depiction of Jesus is much less human than the NT Gospel accounts.

YOUR TURN: How do you separate fact from fiction when reading a novel? What leads readers to believe material that's presented as true within a fictional work?

understood his mission, what he said and did, or how his friends and foes saw him?

To answer these questions, scholars use several criteria to assess the historical reliability of the evidence. Together, these critical tools inject a measure of objectivity into what is admittedly a subjective task. To understand how these criteria work, let's begin with a thought experiment about something unrelated to Jesus.

Suppose you've offered to make dinner for a friend in her own home. You've even promised to bring your own groceries. To make matters a bit more complicated, your friend is a vegan celiac, which means she doesn't eat animal products and can't eat wheat, barley, or rye in any form. But you're up to the challenge.

It's time to fill a grocery bag with the items you'll use to prepare the meal. As you consider the possible ingredients, you judge each item based on the criteria your friend has provided. You'll leave chicken out of the bag, along with the Brie cheese and crackers you love. Maybe a vegetable stir fry? Think again: soy sauce usually contains wheat. Item by item, you weigh the possibilities and finally fill the bag with plenty of nourishing food: rice, some vegetable stock, salad makings, hummus, and asparagus. You head out the door with your critically examined bag of supplies for a vegan, gluten-free dinner.

In a similar way, the study of the historical Jesus entails deciding which items, from the "pantry" full of sources, to identify as authentic. Some of these tools lead us to *include* items from our ancient texts; others will help us decide what to *exclude*. Together, these criteria work to establish the likelihood that a tradition about Jesus is historically reliable. Let's take a look.

What's In? Positive Criteria

Multiple Independent Attestation

At first glance, the criterion of **multiple independent attestation** seems straightforward. It claims that an event or saying is more likely to be authentic if it appears in *two or more sources that aren't related to each other*. But it's not always easy to determine whether or not two sources are truly independent from one another. Some count the Gospel of Thomas as an independent source, while others think it combines traditions found in the Synoptic Gospels or the Q source. Most scholars think John was composed without reference to the Synoptics, but some suggest it borrows traditions found in Luke. Even if Paul's letters don't rely on the Gospels (remember, the letters are earlier), they may incorporate traditions that lie behind them.

Broadly speaking, though, scholars use separate sources as a system of checks and balances system to confirm historical likelihood of various traditions. They think Jesus probably prohibited divorce, since both Paul and Mark mention this teaching. That Jesus had a brother named James is also likely, since he's mentioned by Josephus, Paul, and the Gospels. And both Josephus and Tacitus confirm the central claim of various NT writings that Jesus died under Pontius Pilate, the ruling Roman official in Judea. Used with due caution, then, this criterion helps to identify several bare-bones facets of Jesus's career.

Criterion of Dissimilarity (or Embarrassment)

A second criterion, which gained prominence during the Second Quest, has to do with material that's out of step with either Palestinian Judaism or early Christian thought as it developed in the decades after his death. Already, we've seen that over time, the Gospels portray Jesus in an increasingly divine light and downplay his human nature. This tendency toward high Christology leads scholars to say that Gospel material that's stranger or more "embarrassing" is more likely authentic. Put differently, sayings and deeds that don't advance Jesus's reputation or promote his worship, the logic goes, probably have a solid basis in his historical career.

FIGURE 9.5: JESUS AND JOHN THE BAPTIST: IT'S COMPLICATED

Historians agree that John's appearance in Gospel accounts of Jesus's public ministry indicates that the two figures shared some relationship. But notice how the evangelists alter their versions of the story over time:

Mark 1:9	Matthew 3:13-15	John 1:32-34
	John baptizes Jesus, after protest from John:	John recognizes Jesus without baptizing him:
John baptizes Jesus, without further comment: "About that time, Jesus came from Nazareth of Galilee, and John baptized him in the Jordan River."	"At that time Jesus came from Galilee to the Jordan River so that John would baptize him. John tried to stop him and said, 'I need to be baptized by you, yet you come to me?' Jesus answered, 'Allow me to be baptized now. This is necessary to fulfill all righteousness.' So John agreed to baptize Jesus."	"John testified, 'I saw the Spirit coming down from heaven like a dove, and it rested on him. Even I didn't recognize him, but the one who sent me to baptize with water said to me, "The one on whom you see the Spirit coming down and resting is the one who baptizes with the Holy Spirit." I have seen and testified that this one is God's Son.'"

YOUR TURN: What's the significance of Jesus's baptism by John, in your view? What kind of relationship might it suggest?

Let's consider a couple of examples. Take the case of Jesus's baptism by John. In all four NT Gospels, John the Baptist paves the way for Jesus's earthly ministry. But over time, the nature of their interaction changes, rather dramatically. (See Figure 9.5.) In fact, the Fourth Gospel doesn't even mention Jesus's baptism, probably because it implies that Jesus counted himself among John's followers. This awkwardness suggests, on the **criterion of dissimilarity**, that Jesus was baptized by John.

Another key feature of Jesus's career—his crucifixion by Roman officials—passes this test. Why? Because the Gospels and other NT writings all directly acknowledge just how "embarrassing" the notion of a crucified messiah was. They know it's a destiny that's a riff on the messianic script, so they reinterpret Jewish scripture to explain it. Precisely because it doesn't fit Palestinian Jewish expectations, NT writers repeatedly justify the death of the one they call the Christ by insisting that he had to die in this way.

What's Out? The Negative Criteria

If the first two criteria work to include authentic traditions about the historical Jesus, the next two do the opposite. Together, they flag details of Jesus's story that are out of place historically. As some put it, these elements don't belong in our "bag" because they're not contextually credible—that is, they're not believable within the context of Jesus's own place and time. We'll consider these criteria as two kinds of **anachronism**.

Historical Anachronism

In many cases, the Gospels portray Jesus's relationship to Judaism and its leaders in ways that fit the late first century but not the decades when Jesus lived. Remember, the Jewish War brought a monumental crisis that forced Judaism to reinvent itself. After the temple's destruction in 70 CE, the Pharisees gained significant religious power that they hadn't held in Jesus's day. Scholars think his harsh verbal attack on them in Matthew 23, for instance, is anachronistic. It's not contextually credible within Jesus's religious landscape. Likewise, the Fourth Gospel's distinction between Jesus's followers and "the Jews" clearly reflects a historical setting that postdates Jesus's career, as does the practice of excluding believers from the synagogue. Only long after Jesus's death did Jews and Christians begin to think of themselves as separate groups.

Theological Anachronism

In a similar manner, historians omit from their portrait of the historical Jesus elements that reflect Christian ideas that developed much later. As we've noted, the Fourth Gospel's high Christology emphasizes belief in Jesus and his own declaration of divine origins. Historians think these details are anachronistic. Jesus's theological context was thoroughly Jewish and monotheistic: he called for faith in God, not in himself. Likewise, John's spiritualized and personalized notions of salvation reflect developing Christian thought rather than Jesus's own setting. Finally, historians find the gnostic gospels' interest in secret knowledge imparted to the spiritual elite to be anachronistic as well. That's why most scholars assign such works as the Gospel of Thomas to the second century, when this kind of theology took shape.

Review and Reflect

• What evidence do historians consider in their assessment of the "historical Jesus"? How do they weigh that evidence?

• Reflect on the criteria used to judge the historical reliability of sources. Which criteria seem most helpful? Why?

WHAT GOES IN THE BAG?
SOME CONSENSUS AGREEMENTS

Once we apply these criteria to our sources, we can identify a number of features of Jesus's career that belong to our "bag of ingredients" for the historical Jesus. Here's a list of items most historians would include.

• Jesus was a Jew from Nazareth in Galilee, the northern region of ancient Palestine.

• He had some association with the apocalyptic prophet John the Baptist and was probably baptized by him.

• He gained a reputation as a teacher (rabbi) and healer.

• He had a knack for teaching through the use of parables (illustrative stories).

• He traveled throughout the region of Galilee announcing the coming "kingdom of God" and calling people to radical trust in that one (Jewish) God.

• He shared meals with those at the bottom of the social and religious order.

• He went on Passover pilgrimage to Jerusalem, where he deliberately challenged the temple establishment in ways that made Jewish and Roman leaders uneasy.

• He was executed by Pontius Pilate, Roman governor of Judea, around 30 CE on a charge of insurrection, and died under the banner "King of the Jews."

• Some followers soon believed that he was raised from the dead.

Together, these fundamental aspects of Jesus's career constitute the "ingredients" for our understanding of the historical Jesus. But just as a grocery bag filled with rice, vegetables, and seasonings isn't quite a meal, neither does this list make coherent sense of Jesus's identity and purpose at the historical level. Let's weigh in, then, on some of the key questions that mark conversations about the historical Jesus.

WILL THE REAL JESUS PLEASE STAND UP?

We've considered the origins of the "historical Jesus" as a focus of academic study. We've reviewed the sources scholars rely upon and the criteria they use to weigh their authenticity. And we've noted features considered by many historians to be credible. Now let's turn to the end game. Who was Jesus, really? What was Jesus's driving concern? Why did he die? And what happened next? These are questions that a wide range of scholars—from the devout to the secular—have attempted to answer *on historical grounds*. In what follows, we'll distill their findings and weigh in on the conversation.

Who Was Jesus, Really? Rethinking Jesus's "Messianic Self-Consciousness"

For almost two millennia, Christians have used a range of terms to capture Jesus's identity: Christ, Son of God, Savior, and Lord, just to name a few. But who did *Jesus* think he was? Did he have, as scholars so clumsily put it, a "messianic self-consciousness"? Did he consider himself to be "very God of very God," as an early creed claims?

The sources themselves offer mixed messages on these questions. In Mark, Jesus is cagey, to say the least. He has little to say about his own identity, referring to himself as the "Son of the Human," an enigmatic title, and only once (and indirectly) as the "Christ" (Mark 14:62). By contrast, John's Jesus spouts "I am" statements and urges people to "believe in me." Many scholars think Jesus himself had little interest in his messianic identity and that it was only after his death that his followers hailed him as Messiah. Some think he saw himself mainly as an apocalyptic prophet, others as a mystical sage, and still others as a community organizer.

Other historians, though, find it hard to explain why Jesus's followers called him the Christ so soon after his humiliating death if he hadn't somehow thought of himself this way. After all, death by Roman execution wasn't exactly the telltale sign of the messiah in any Jewish text we know of. What's more, these scholars find some of Jesus's actions—such as his dramatic entry into Jerusalem—to be charged with messianic meaning. In a similar vein, Jesus's proclamation of the coming kingdom of God fits an apocalyptic vision in which a messiah might play a leading role.

One way to make sense of *both* Jesus's reticence about his identity *and* his messianic career is to reexamine the question of messiahship within Jesus's Jewish context. After all, there was no set script for the messiah in Second Temple Judaism. Diverse written traditions—from the Dead Sea Scrolls to Jewish scripture to *1 Enoch*—weigh in on the messianic role from a range of perspectives. Some associate this figure with religious authority, while others frame the role politically. Some depict the messiah as a specially designated human being, while others look for a quasi-divine being. In the first century, several leaders claiming to be messiahs appeared on the Palestinian landscape and rallied revolutionaries to rise up against Rome. In each case, the messiah is anointed as *agent of God's renewal of the world through God's just and righteous rule.*

That makes the messiah a mediator, not a self-interested rock star. As one tapped by God and endowed with divine authority, the messiah summons people to embrace God's vision of justice and righteousness. In Jewish thought, the messiah focuses on both God and the faithful community that will live together under God's authority.

Did Jesus have a "messianic self-consciousness"? He may well have. Perhaps ironically, the historical likelihood that he *didn't* call attention to his own identity fits well within the landscape of Jewish messianic thought. In his own religious context, an authentic "messianic self-consciousness" didn't automatically entail the kind of "messiah complex" we recognize today. Jesus's resolute concern to promote faith in God and to engender God's values in the social order coheres with Jewish hopes for a messianic age.

What Was Jesus's Driving Concern? Rethinking the "Kingdom of God"

If the historical Jesus had little to say about his own messianic identity, scholars widely agree he had a lot to say about the "kingdom (or reign) of God." Indeed, the concept likely served as something of a mission statement for his career. But what did he mean by that phrase? Today, people often associate the "kingdom of God" with heaven as a realm where faithful people go in the afterlife. But in both the Gospels and Palestinian Judaism, the term consistently carries a more earthly connotation. A line from the Lord's Prayer in Matthew makes this point clear: "Bring in your kingdom so that your will is done on earth as it's done in heaven" (Matt 6:10). In other words, the Gospel traditions suggest Jesus thought that, in and through his ministry, the heavenly reign of God was making its way into the world.

But that claim exposes another key issue that divides historical Jesus scholars today. Some stress the *social and political* implications of the kingdom of God and thus of Jesus's career. After all, "kingdom" is an inherently political word. Jesus's concern for and proximity to those at society's margins—the poor, the sick and possessed, women, children, and ostracized groups—lead many historians to view Jesus as a community organizer, challenging the social order from the bottom up. Though few scholars think Jesus was a true insurgent—at least in the violent sense we associate with that term—many see the movement he led as disruptive because of its challenge to the status quo.

Others see Jesus's pronouncements about God's kingdom in more *religious* than political hues. Some stress the mystical dimensions of Jesus's message as he models and cultivates direct experience of the divine presence in all people. Another, more dominant, hypothesis stresses the apocalyptic, and otherworldly, backdrop to Jesus's mission. As we've discussed, the Jewish apocalyptic schema anticipated a cataclysmic end to the present world order *before* God's renewal of the earth as a home for divine rule. The Gospels contain several sayings that seem to predict just such a historical turning point. Since this prediction passes the criterion of embarrassment test, these scholars say, Jesus may well have thought that God's kingdom would supplant Roman rule within his lifetime, or upon his death.

It's also possible that Jesus's promise of God's coming kingdom entailed *both* political and religious implications. After all, Jewish apocalyptic traditions often use ethereal, heavenly visions to address real social circumstance. Apocalyptic literature is, in most cases, resistance literature since it generally looks toward a just, divine kingdom that will liberate those suffering under the present world order. That makes it plausible—even likely—that Jesus's hopes for the coming kingdom of God were inherently religious, even mystical, even as they heralded the renewal of the socio-political order.

Why Did Jesus Die? Rethinking "Religion and Politics"

This is an important question to answer on historical terms. Indeed, one of the most solid ingredients in our bag of authentic details about Jesus's career is that he was executed by Roman authorities under the prefect Pontius Pilate. But the Gospels quickly shift responsibility from the Romans to Jewish leaders—an interpretive spin that has led to a long and dark history of Christian anti-Semitism.

Historians widely agree that Jesus died because he posed *either a real or perceived threat* to Roman power since he probably died under the mocking sign, "King of the Jews." His executioners wanted to make sure that anyone who promoted a different kingdom knew the destiny in store for them. They used his very public, utterly humiliating execution as a billboard for Roman power in occupied Palestine. In its Passover setting, Jesus's death on a Roman cross sent a loud and clear message to the hundreds of thousands of pilgrims gathered in Jerusalem: there will be no divine deliverance from Roman rule this time around.

What, then, are we to make of the role played by Jewish leaders in Jerusalem—and of Jesus's relationship to his own Jewish tradition more broadly? As we've noted above, the greatest contribution of the Third Quest is its insistence that Jesus's Jewishness *must* remain part of any plausible historical reconstruction. Though historians disagree on whether or not Jesus fully followed Torah, they stand together in the view that he was an observant Jew, through and through. We must understand even his disputes with other Jews as part of the lively, conversational nature of Judaism, not a rejection of his tradition per se.

To consider Jewish leaders' role in Jesus's death, recall that, in the context of Roman occupation, they had no power apart from the power granted by imperial officials. On the one hand, Roman authorities needed local leaders' support to maintain peace and security, so they afforded Jerusalem's ruling class a certain degree of privilege. On the other hand, Jewish leaders were well-aware of the sinister potential of Roman power. Any collaboration with Rome was probably geared toward keeping the Roman army at bay. It was a "you scratch my back while I scratch yours" relationship, with all the hard power in the hands of the Romans.

Historically speaking, Jesus of Nazareth was likely caught in the crosshairs of this awkward dance between two unequal partners. His message about God's coming kingdom, along with his prophetic critique of the temple establishment, was enough to convince many political and religious leaders that he posed a danger to the social and political order, especially in the Passover context. While the Gospel writers clearly exaggerate Jewish officials' complicity in Jesus's death, the Romans likely knew they had to enlist local authorities to isolate this renegade firebrand and eliminate him.

What Happened Next? Rethinking Resurrection

Let's be clear: there's no historically verifiable evidence that Jesus's fully dead corpse sprung to new life. Sure, all four Gospels tell a version of an empty tomb story that believers soon embraced, but scholars remain appropriately skeptical of the story's historical validity. What they can affirm, even historically, is his followers' *perception* that Jesus was raised from the dead. Outside the Gospels, Paul mentions this phenomenon when he writes to the church at Corinth. The risen Jesus, he says, "appeared to Cephas, then to the

Twelve, and then he appeared to more than five hundred brothers and sisters at once—most of them are still alive to this day, though some have died. Then he appeared to James, then to all the apostles, and last of all he appeared to me, as if I were born at the wrong time" (1 Cor 15:5-8).

As one secular scholar has put it, "something happened" that convinced a meaningful number of Jesus's followers that he was alive. Put differently, the Jesus movement that expanded even after the crucifixion makes no historical sense apart from the kind of encounter Paul relates.

The quest for the historical Jesus has been reluctant to address questions about the resurrection, and for good reason. There's much that we can't prove about the resurrection through deliberate, scientific inquiry. But it's worth noting that other messianic figures have appeared across time and place, most staking out a role in ushering in God's kingdom on earth. But their followers have quickly faded into the recesses of history. Only Jesus's movement continued to gain acclaim for their teacher and Lord, even before Christianity gained popular acclaim or political power. It's an oddity that historians grapple with to this day.

SUMMARY

Our historical review of Jesus's life, death, and even resurrection neither presumes nor precludes any religious devotion to him or to his God. We've tried to show the value of historical reconstruction for anyone curious about this shadowy figure whose name is invoked by people of diverse backgrounds and commitments today. To remove Jesus from his own first century, Jewish Palestinian context is to miss out on the Gospels' insistence the Jesus lived and died as a real human being in a particular setting. Those who are convinced of his saving significance in their own place and time will do well to begin reflection with the historical Jesus. Those who're simply curious about the origins of the Christian tradition will find in this study an intriguing benchmark for assessing its development over time.

Review and Reflect

- Name and explain three key insights that the "quest for the historical Jesus" offers.

- What makes the question of the "historical Jesus" important for our own place and time?

GO DEEPER

Aslan, Reza. *Zealot: The Life and Times of Jesus of Nazareth*. New York: Random House, 2013.

Ehrman, Bart D. *Jesus: Apocalyptic Prophet of the New Millennium*. New York: Oxford University Press 1999.

Fredriksen, Paula. *Jesus of Nazareth, King of the Jews: A Jewish Life and the Emergence of Christianity*. New York: Knopf, 1999.

Levine, Amy-Jill. *The Misunderstood Jew: The Church and the Scandal of the Jewish Jesus*. San Francisco: HarperOne, 2006.

Reed, Johnathan. *Archaeology and the Galilean Jesus: A Reexamination of the Evidence*. Harrisburg, PA: Trinity Press International, 2000.

Schweitzer, Albert. *The Quest of the Historical Jesus: A Critical Study of Its Progress from Reimarus to Wrede*. Translated by F. C. Burkitt. Baltimore, MD: Johns Hopkins University Press, 1998.

After Jesus, Then What?
Acts of the Apostles

CONVERSATION STARTERS

- Why do scholars think Luke wrote Acts as a sequel to the Gospel?

- In what ways does Acts build on and expand Luke's concerns and themes?

- What kinds of conversations do the apostles have with Jewish audiences and leaders? With non-Jewish audiences?

- What kind of "witness" do the apostles offer in Acts?

- How does Acts deal with the question of Gentile participation in a Jewish-based movement?

Among the evangelists, only Luke thinks the Gospel story needs a sequel. In our NT today, of course, the book of Acts follows John rather than Luke. But that's because the four Gospels became a self-contained collection early on. Acts appears as something of an addendum to the Gospels, which fits its canonical function as a bridge from the Gospels to the rest of the NT.

That bridge functions in several ways. For one thing, Acts serves as narrative transition from the story of Jesus to letters mostly addressed to believing communities. Acts reaches in both directions, echoing Luke's Gospel while introducing key issues—the movement's relationship to both Judaism and the wider Greco-Roman world, for instance—that mark the remainder of the NT.

Acts features many characters we've encountered in the Gospels and introduces us to others, especially Paul, who play a prominent role in what follows.

The book of Acts links the Gospels with the rest of the NT geographically as well. Jesus's story was set in Roman-occupied Palestine—mostly in and around its northern region called Galilee, with a final week spent in Jerusalem. The remaining contents of the NT address circumstances outside this home base. Acts helps to make sense of that shift, as it relates the church's rapid expansion beyond Palestine as part of God's plan from earliest days. Like Luke, Acts begins in Jerusalem, and its story often returns there. But unlike Luke, Acts ends in Rome, the center of imperial power. From Luke's perspective, that means the Gospel has reached the "end of the earth" (Acts 1:8).

Scholars agree that the book's traditional title, "Acts of the Apostles," is a misnomer. For one thing, Luke reserves the designation of "apostle" for Jesus's first circle of disciples (see Acts 1:21-22), while Acts focuses on the missionary journeys of Paul, who wasn't among them. But the title is misleading in another way as well. In Acts, it's God—along with God's Spirit—who is the main actor on stage. Humans appear mostly as willing participants in God's "acts" on earth.

Acts stands out for its purposeful conversation with the wider pluralistic world. The first few chapters are set in Jerusalem and feature a style that sounds a lot like the **Septuagint**. The apostles' speeches cite Jewish scripture abundantly in their case for Jesus's messiahship. Later in Acts, Paul's speeches to non-Jewish audiences use rhetoric that places him among the philosophers of the day. This crafty shift in style is just one example of the literary artistry found in Acts.

Our conversation about the author and setting of Luke's Gospel lies behind Acts as well. Thus we'll start this chapter with a reflection on the novelty of this companion story and its function in Luke's own world. We'll then trace some of the themes and details common to Luke and Acts before an extended discussion of the book's structure and contents. Finally, we'll consider the main parts of the message Luke conveys through the book of Acts.

WHY THE SEQUEL? THOUGHTS ABOUT THE AUTHOR'S INTENT

We don't know why the author of Luke considered the Gospel to be unfinished business, but that doesn't stop scholars from speculating about the writer's motivation. A variety of theories have circulated, and many of them probably contain an element of truth.

- Some read Acts as an **apology**. Used as a technical term, this word suggests a *deliberate and detailed defense* offered in response to some kind of challenge. The fact that that Acts treats Roman officials with respect—even leaving out of the story their execution of Paul—leads many scholars to think Acts was written in part to defend the early church against charges that it threatened imperial society.

- Another popular view is that Acts **explains a puzzle** that lies at the heart of the early church: though it originated as a "sect" within Judaism (see Acts 24:5, 14; 28:22 NRSV), the movement quickly expanded to include Gentiles. Luke's take on this shift appears in many episodes throughout Acts where Jewish rejection of the gospel message opens the mission to non-Jews.

- A third approach takes a more **pastoral view** of Acts and finds in it encouragement for those on "**the way**," as Luke often calls the movement (e.g., Acts 9:2; 18:25). In this reading, the story's interest in the Holy Spirit's activity and the early church's unity inspired its first readers as they navigated the movement's early decades.

These explanations envision a range of audiences—from suspicious outsiders to committed insiders. Chances are, Acts provided a widely accessible account of Christian origins for both kinds of interested parties. In any case, Luke continues Jesus's story into the post-resurrection age, as many of Jesus's words and deeds live on in the story of believers left behind after his death.

WHAT MAKES ACTS A SEQUEL? LITERARY TIES TO LUKE

Acts makes its relationship to Luke's Gospel clear from the start, where Luke names the same addressee—**Theophilus**—and mentions "the first scroll I wrote [concerning] everything Jesus did and taught" (Acts 1:1). The storyline of Acts also picks up more or less where Luke's Gospel left off, with the eleven remaining disciples in Jerusalem (not in Galilee, as the other Gospels tell it). Luke says that Jesus has told them not to leave the city (Acts 1:4).

Besides such explicit literary connections, Acts repeats both broad themes and precise details that appear in Luke. As in Luke, **Jerusalem** plays a distinctive role in the sequel's story. Like Luke, Acts emphasizes that Jesus's journey fulfills Jewish scripture. Other familiar themes from Luke show up in Acts as well: the disciples continue to stress the *salvation* and *forgiveness* the gospel brings; *outsiders* such as women, Samaritans, and Gentiles play important parts in the story; Acts repeats Luke's interest in *economic justice*; the sequel is God's plan for *universal redemption*; and the Holy Spirit activates *God's will* within the believing community.

Beyond these recurrent themes, details from Luke's Gospel recur in the lives of early church leaders, making Acts something of a "cover" of Luke. Here are a few examples of the parallels the author draws between Jesus and his followers:

- Jesus's ministry begins with the gift of the Spirit (Luke 3:22; 4:18); the disciples are "filled with the Holy Spirit" (Acts 2:4) on the day of Pentecost, at the outset of their own mission.

- Jesus is known as a miracle worker who heals and exorcises demons (e.g., Luke 6:17-19); the disciples gain a similar reputation (Acts 5:12-16).

- Jesus raises a widow's son to new life (Luke 7:11-17); both Peter (Acts 9:36-43) and Paul (Acts 20:10) raise people from the dead.

- Jesus heads to Jerusalem, knowing his destiny (Luke 9:51); Paul reaffirms his intention to go to Jerusalem, even if he faces death there (Acts 21:13; cf. 19:21).

- On the cross, Jesus commits his spirit into God's hands (Luke 23:46); as he's stoned to death, Stephen similarly prays, "Lord Jesus, receive my spirit" (Acts 7:59).

In these and other ways, Luke affirms that Jesus's story doesn't end at either the cross or the empty tomb. It continues on, through the animating power of the Spirit, in the witness of his followers. For Luke, the "good news" that has interrupted history at Jesus's birth continues to gain a following—and expand its footprint—long after his earthly career ends.

One more note about the authorship of Acts. Scholars have identified several episodes that suggest the writer joined Paul on several missionary outings (see Acts 16:10-17; 20:5-15; 21:1-8; 27:1–28:16). Together, they're called "**we passages**" because the narration shifts from third-person to first-person pronouns, with the author providing a firsthand account. Scholars account for these passages in two ways. Some say Luke incorporates these diary-like accounts as sources (we know that ancient historians often use others' writings without attribution). Others think that the author of Acts was indeed one of Paul's companions. In either case, historians generally date the book's composition to the 80s, based both on the fact that it claims to follow Luke and on its idealized portrait of early Christian conversations.

WHAT'S THE "REST OF THE STORY" IN ACTS? DEEP ROOTS, BROAD REACH

While Luke begins and ends in Jerusalem, Acts begins in Jerusalem but
ends in Rome. As a pair, both works establish the church's deep roots in Palestinian Judaism and underscore the gospel's global impact. (Remember, most
people living in the first-century Mediterranean world thought of "global
impact" in terms of the vast reaches of the Roman Empire.) Indeed, the structure of Acts reflects a progressively expanding mission, even as the story keeps
circling back to affirm ties to Jerusalem. (See Figure 10.1.)

Prologue: Power Unleashed (Acts 1:1–2:13)

The Gospel's opening chapter provides a smooth transition from the
"first scroll" by reviewing for the audience what's already happened. Jesus has
suffered and died, yes, but he's also reappeared to instruct his apostles about
the kingdom of God. His message? Sit tight, and wait for the coming Spirit.
When the apostles ask Jesus if he's "going to restore the kingdom to Israel
now" (Acts 1:6), he refuses to name "the times or seasons" (Acts 1:7). Instead,
he pronounces a promise that serves as their apostolic commission: "Rather,
you will receive power when the Holy Spirit has come upon you, and you will
be my witnesses in Jerusalem, in all Judea and Samaria, and to the end of the
earth" (Acts 1:8).

In this verse, Luke lets us know where Acts is going. Beginning in Jerusalem, the disciples will proclaim the gospel message in regions that lie farther
and farther afield. A small band of believers at the outset (Acts 1:12-14), they
replace Judas with a disciple named **Matthias** by casting lots (Acts 1:26)—a
glimpse of God's will "rigging" the story.

It turns out the apostles don't have long to wait. During the Pentecost
celebration that follows fifty days after Passover, God's Spirit shows up, with a
flair (Acts 2:1-13). Even if you haven't read Acts before, you may have heard

FIGURE 10.1: OUTLINE OF ACTS

Prologue: Power Unleashed (1:1–2:13)

Witnesses in Jerusalem (2:14–8:3)

Turning Outward toward Judea and Samaria (8:4–12:25)

A Global Mission (13:1–28:31)

    Paul's Missionary Travels (13:1–21:14)

    Paul Under Arrest (21:15–28:31)

---

of **Pentecost**, since it's long marked the church's "birthday" on the Christian liturgical calendar. Many practicing Christians don't realize, though, that Pentecost was and is a Jewish holiday (see Lev 23:15-21). In Acts, Jesus's apostles are observing Pentecost *as faithful Jews* when this story takes place.

Luke's account of what happens on that day is vivid and fanciful. The disciples hear a tornado-like sound and see columns of flames resting on one another (Acts 2:2-3). What's even more stunning is their immediate, Spirit-given ability to speak languages they haven't mastered—even some that didn't exist in the first century (Acts 2:4-11). No one knows what to make of such drama at first, though Luke says some think the apostles have been "full of new wine" (Acts 2:13). (See Figure 10.2.)

As we've noted, this gift of the Spirit echoes Jesus's own story (Luke 3:22; 4:1, 14, 18). The apostles now stand equipped for the mission that lies ahead. But this early episode in Acts also signals that mission will have a lot to do with translating the gospel message across all kinds of differences: religious, ethnic, geographic, and even linguistic. Rather than establishing a "host language" that everyone else must learn to speak, the apostles speak words that are intelligible to a wide variety of people on their own terms. It's a conversational style that honors each group's native language, rather than establishing a shared, dominant parlance. The gift of the Spirit at Pentecost also reverses the division created in the **Tower of Babel** story found in Genesis (Gen 11:1-9).

Witnesses in Jerusalem (Acts 2:14–8:3)

The first major section of Acts reports the apostles' activities in **Jerusalem**, as well as the range of responses they elicit. The apostles serve as "witnesses,"

FIGURE 10.2: THE MODERN-DAY PENTECOSTAL MOVEMENT

In our context, the word ***Pentecostal*** is an umbrella term for a form of Christianity that's emerged over the last century and across the globe. More than seven hundred denominations and close to three hundred million Christian identify as Pentecostal. These believers share with "evangelical Christianity" several core beliefs: the authority of scripture, the importance of personal salvation through belief in Jesus Christ, and the expectation of a second coming. What sets Pentecostals apart, theologically, is the importance they assign to the "baptism of the Spirit"—an experience rooted in the Pentecost story that continues among believers today. Those endowed with the Spirit have access to Jesus's healing powers, as well as the ability to "speak in tongues" (a practice called "glossolalia") or interpret messages from those who do.

Historians trace the roots of Pentecostal Christianity to the late nineteenth-century Holiness movement, a spirit-led religious revival that swept across England and North America. In 1906, an African American preacher named William Seymour launched the three-year Azusa Street Revival, which left a lasting imprint on Pentecostalism. Notably, the group's conservative theology led, in the early years, to a progressive social makeup. Pentecostal congregations brought people together of various races and backgrounds, and women played a leading role from the beginning. Pentecostals were also pacifists and promoted conscientious objection to military service. Over time, the movement has shifted toward segregated congregations, limits on women's leadership, and diminished resistance to violent conflict.

YOUR TURN: How does the Pentecost story in Acts fit with what you know (or can learn) about Pentecostalism?

providing testimony about Jesus the Christ to both crowds and officials. The many speeches found in Acts supply the verbal content of that testimony. But the apostles' witness can be nonverbal as well, as believers' conduct shows God's power at work in their midst. It's a power that's alluring to some and threatening to others. Let's consider some elements of the apostolic witness in Jerusalem.

Speeches to the Crowds and Jewish Officials

Peter serves as the movement's main spokesperson early in Acts. In a series of three speeches, he interprets Jesus's death and resurrection for different audiences in Jerusalem. His first speech is an **apology** (again, in the technical sense) to a large crowd. In it, he says Jesus's execution is part of "God's established plan and foreknowledge" (Acts 2:23). To make his case, Peter cites passages from the **Septuagint**, freely revising them to make his

FIGURE 10.3: JEWISH INTERPRETATION OF PSALM 110

Acts implies Peter's application of Psalm 110 to Jesus Christ is the only viable interpretive option. Within both Second Temple and rabbinical Judaism, though, we find a range of possibilities. Most commonly, interpreters read the psalm as an affirmation of David's royal position, and sometimes in conjunction with Abraham (since the psalm mentions Melchizedek; cf. Gen 14:17-20). But some traditions from the early centuries of the Common Era do read the psalm with a messianic mindset. For instance, both the Dead Sea scrolls and various midrashic texts associate the "staff" mentioned in Psalm 110:2 with a coming messiah. In addition, the Babylonian Talmud includes a teaching by Rabbi Nathan about messiahs in Zechariah:

> These are the two anointed ones, that stand by the Lord of the whole earth (Zech. 4:14). This is a reference to Aaron and the Messiah, but I cannot tell which is the more beloved. However, from the verse, The Lord has sworn and will not repent: Thou art a priest for ever after the manner of Melchizedek (Psalm 110:4), one can tell that the messianic king is more beloved than the righteous priest. (*Avot*, chap. 34).

YOUR TURN: Read Psalm 110 and Peter's speech (Acts 2:14-36, esp. 32-36). Write a response that challenges Peter's claim that Jesus is the Messiah, based on a different interpretation of Psalm 110.

---

point. He adapts an excerpt from Joel to convince the crowd they're living in the "last days" that Joel promised, since God's Spirit has been poured out on "all people" (Acts 2:17; cf. Joel 2:28). Peter also quotes a psalm to "prove" that, at the resurrection, God has named Jesus "Lord and Christ" (Acts 2:34-36; cf. Ps 110:1). (See Figure 10.3.)

Peter delivers two more speeches in this section. After he heals a beggar, Peter addresses a crowd gathered at **Solomon's Portico** (part of the Jerusalem temple) about the man's faith. He urges his audience to follow the beggar's example and "change . . . hearts and lives" (Acts 3:19; NRSV: "repent"). He sees this as preparation for the "restoration of all things" (Acts 3:21) promised by Moses and the other prophets. Notably, Peter's conversational style conveys that the crowds are insiders, since they're "descendants of the prophets" (Acts 3:25).

Peter's third and final speech in Jerusalem takes place before religious officials (see Acts 4:5-6, 8) and strikes a more contentious tone. With another apostle named John, he's been arrested for speaking about the "resurrection of the dead" (Acts 4:2). What makes this such a dangerous message? It's rooted in the soil of apocalyptic thought, an ideology that sometimes sparks religious rebellion. But rather than simply defending the apostles' nonviolent aims,

Peter goes on the attack, lambasting his accusers for causing Jesus's death and calling Jesus the "stone you builders rejected" (Acts 4:11; cf. Ps 118:22).

The section's lengthiest speech, though, comes from **Stephen**, a Hellenistic Jew appointed as a leader among believers (see Acts 6:1-6). Stephen has been accused of blasphemy (Acts 6:11), a charge confirmed only by false witnesses (Acts 6:13). His rambling defense retells the biblical story in detail, from Abraham, to Moses, and finally to David and Solomon. It covers mostly friendly and familiar territory but ends with a harsh prophetic critique: God has rejected the temple and its guardians, whose complicity in Jesus's death makes them "betrayers and murderers" (Acts 7:52). Stephen's speech incites an angry reprisal, and a mob stones him to death (Acts 7:54–8:1).

A Way of Life

The apostles' witness in Jerusalem extends beyond carefully crafted oratory to encompass their actions as well. As the Gospel anticipates (Luke 10:18), Jesus's followers continue to wield divine power in Jesus's name. Peter heals a beggar with a simple command that echoes Jesus's words to a paralytic: "rise up and walk" (Acts 3:6; cf. Luke 5:23). As they pray for boldness, the disciples ask God to perform miracles through them (Acts 4:30). The author summarizes their activity by noting the apostles' reputation for successful healings of the sick and demon-possessed (Acts 5:12-16; see also Acts 2:43), since even those who don't believe to speak "highly of them" (Acts 5:13).

Another facet of the believers' witness arises out of their life together. Luke includes two brief descriptions of the community, and both portray the group in idyllic terms. In the first, they "shared everything" (Acts 2:44), and they gathered at the temple and "demonstrated God's goodness to everyone" (Acts 2:47). A second report says it is believers' rejection of personal wealth that confirms their "powerful witness to the resurrection of the Lord Jesus" (Acts 4:33). Together, these glimpses resonate with Luke's Gospel, where Jesus brings "good news to the poor" and condemns the wealthy. (See Figure 10.4.)

The contrasting tale of **Ananias and Sapphira** brings a cautionary word about believers who don't fully "buy in" to Luke's ideal of redistributed wealth (see Acts 5:1-11). Together, a husband and wife conspire to hold back part of the proceeds from the sale of property, rather than giving it all to the community. Peter confronts them separately about the ruse, and both are struck dead as a result. For Luke, to be a believer is an all-or-nothing proposition that carries economic, as well as spiritual, implications.

Another brief glimpse of discord arises between Greek- and Aramaic-speaking disciples over the distribution of resources to the needy (Acts 6:1-6).

FIGURE 10.4: KOINONIA FARM

The countercultural model of "holding all things in common" wasn't just an experiment for the first century. In 1942, Clarence and Florence Jordan and Martin and Mabel England established the Koinonia Farm in rural Georgia, calling it a "demonstration plot for the Kingdom of God." Inspired by the witness of Acts, they formed a community based on four key teachings:

- Treat all human beings with dignity and justice.

- Choose love over violence.

- Share all possessions and live simply.

- Be stewards of the land and its natural resource.

Their aim was true ***koinonia***, the NT Greek term for deep partnership, and the founders' vision placed an emphasis on racial justice in the Jim Crow South, along with ecologically responsible farming.

The Koinonia community has changed over time. It dwindled in the 1950s, as intense harassment by the KKK and other white supremacist groups threatened its members. Later, the community's work on affordable housing planted the seeds for what became Habitat for Humanity, an international organization made famous through the support of President Jimmy Carter. The Farm still exists but no longer practices the "common purse" economic model. You can visit it today. See their website at www.koinoniafarm.org.

YOUR TURN: Spend some time on the Koinonia Farm website. How does their life together connect to our study of Acts? Name and reflect on a few details that stand out to you.

Even the distinction between the two groups reflects a breakdown of the Pentecost unity across linguistic difference. But there's also stratification: Jesus's original followers (who spoke Aramaic) seem to hold privileged status, while Greek-speaking believers (also called **Hellenists**) suffer second-class status. In Luke's telling, the apostles respond quickly and efficiently, appointing seven men—all Hellenists themselves—to ensure that all people receive adequate care.

A Polarized Response

In Acts, believers' speeches and their way of life constitute a witness that their Jerusalem neighbors can't ignore. Onlookers—both the people and their leaders—respond in various ways. On the positive side, Luke posts

FIGURE 10.5: BUDDHISM'S "THIRD JEWEL": THE SANGHA

Three "refuges" or "jewels" lie at the heart of Buddhist thought and practice: the buddha (enlightened one), the dharma (teachings), and the sangha (community). Though some schools of Buddhist thought apply the term *sangha* to all Buddhists, its roots lie in the monastic tradition, established at the movement's beginning. Tradition has it that the Buddha, named Siddhartha Gautama, gathered disciples and equipped them to perpetuate his teachings after his death. Like the apostles in Acts, members of the sangha (especially in Theravada Buddhism) depend on the wider community for their provisions. They adhere to a set of rules called the *vinaya*, which mandates abstinence in many forms: sex, food, and speech. Members of the sangha follow a daily rhythm of prayers, meditation, and chanting as well.

YOUR TURN: Reflect on the role of monastic communities within religious traditions. How do they differ from other kinds of religious communities?

impressive numbers to quantify the apostles' missionary success. After Peter's first speech, for instance, "God brought about three thousand people into the community" (Acts 2:41). Just two chapters later, the body of believers has grown "to about five thousand" people (Acts 4:4). The movement's momentum continues to build throughout the section; even outsiders, as we've seen, look favorably on the group.

At the same time, persecution of the apostles also gains steam as the story progresses. At first, Peter and John mostly take the fall for the community. They appear on the religious leaders' radar for the same reasons Jesus did: the crowds are captivated by the gospel message, and it's a message that the leaders fear might sow seeds of insurrection. Religious officials detain and interrogate the apostles and then try to impose a gag order against speaking to anyone "in this name" (Acts 4:17). When the apostles won't comply, the high priest sends them to jail, where an "angel from the Lord" sets them free under cover of darkness (Acts 5:19). This miraculous turn of events, along with the movement's growing appeal, leaves Jewish officials in a quandary.

One member of the council named **Gamaliel** makes a pragmatic plea to let things play out, without forceful interference. He likens the apostles' message about Jesus to the short-lived careers of two noted insurgents, **Theudas** and **Judas the Galilean**. Josephus says Judas led an uprising against Quirinius's census, around 6 CE, and Theudas appeared on the scene around 44 CE—about a decade *after* the setting of Gamaliel's speech. (This anachronistic detail reminds us that "history" for Luke doesn't always pass the fact-checking test.) Gamaliel points out that both revolts failed soon after their

FIGURE 10.6: SAMARITANS TODAY

Ancient Samaria constitutes much of what's called the "West Bank" in the Holy Land today, though the Samaritan population has now dwindled to fewer than one thousand people. Today's Samaritans affirm their theological ties to ancient Israel, but they name Mount Gezirim, not Mount Zion, as the proper place of worship. They also use the Samaritan Pentateuch, which differs from the Jewish Pentateuch in significant ways, and consider themselves "children of Israel" but not "Jews." Their ethnic status is murky in the nation-state of Israel. Those who live in Israel (outside of Tel Aviv) are Israeli citizens but not Jewish, unless they undergo conversion. Those who live in the West Bank at Kiryat Luza hold dual Israeli-Palestinian citizenship and are exempt from military service.

YOUR TURN: Explore the term *Samaritan* and *Samaria* in the Bible or online. What do you learn about this ethnic group and their relationship to Judaism ancient or contemporary?

leaders died. Unless this movement "originates with God" (Acts 5:39), he says, Jesus's followers will disperse. His argument leads to a mild reprimand: flogging and a ban on public speaking.

The stoning of Stephen escalates the intensity of persecution against the church in Jerusalem. Indeed, Luke says it's because of this "vicious harassment" that most believers left the city and "scattered throughout the regions of Judea and Samaria" (Acts 8:1). This wave of systemic oppression, in Luke's telling, only carries forward God's plan for the expansion of the church into the next stage.

Turning Outward toward Judea and Samaria (Acts 8:4–12:25)

That next stage takes the apostolic witness into nearby territories of **Judea and Samaria** (see Acts 1:8). Not only are these territories in geographical proximity—the city of Jerusalem lies within Judea—but they also constitute regional partners in Jewish sacred tradition. After all, Judea and Samaria were both part of biblical Israel, a kingdom united briefly under David and Solomon (ca. 1000–922 BCE). The Assyrian Empire's defeat of Samaria in the eighth century BCE paved the way for the rift between Jews (the name comes from "Judeans") and Samaritans that extended into Jesus's day. (See Figure 10.6.)

To name "all Judea and Samaria" as the site of the apostles' first missionary activity outside Jerusalem illustrates Luke's interest in crossing boundaries and repairing deep-seated hostilities. As Acts unfolds, very few scenes occur in either geographic location, though many of the cities named in these chapters are nearby. (See Figure 10.6.) Rather, Luke uses the terms symbolically to highlight the apostles' expansive calling. Indeed the leadership team expands as well, adding to the mix Hellenists such as **Philip** and even a converted adversary named **Saul of Tarsus**.

Philip first appears in Acts as one of the seven men designated to care for the Greek-speaking widows (Acts 6:5-6). It's Philip who takes the gospel message to Samaria. In some ways, the Samaritans have been prepared for Philip's arrival by a man named **Simon**, who's dazzled them with deeds he attributes to God's power. But Luke makes it clear that Philip is no magician in the conventional sense. He exercises authority over the natural world, not for his own benefit, but to mediate God's life-giving power to others.

Even when the apostolic mission moves beyond Jerusalem, it never leaves behind the influence of the "mother church." Hearing of Philip's success, Peter and John arrive in Samaria with a ringing endorsement, along with prayers and even the gift of the Spirit (Acts 8:14-17). Simon wants to purchase some of the apostles' power, but Peter condemns him for thinking he could "buy God's gift with money" (Acts 8:20). Luke doesn't tell us whether or not Simon heeds Peter's invitation to repentance, leaving interpreters to fill in the gap themselves. (See Figure 10.7.)

Philip returns to Jerusalem for a brief stay when an "angel from the Lord" sends him on an errand in the Judean wilderness, on the road to Gaza. Here Philip finds an **Ethiopian** official returning home from a pilgrimage to the Jerusalem temple. The man's an outsider on two counts: he's from the African continent, and he's a **eunuch** (a castrated male), which means he can't be a Jewish convert. Philip finds the man stumped by a passage from Isaiah 53 about a slaughtered lamb. He asks Philip, "Tell me, about whom does the prophet say this? Is he talking about himself or someone else?" (Acts 8:34). Philip seizes the opportunity to tell him Jesus's story, which leads the eunuch to request baptism at the first sight of running water. In Acts, religious identity is "fluid" indeed.

Case in point: the dramatic conversion of another man who's made a career out of persecuting the church, **Saul of Tarsus**. We've met him in passing, when Acts notes his tacit approval to Stephen's stoning (Acts 8:1). Now, while in route to **Damascus** to round up believers, Saul has a vision of the risen Lord that makes him an ardent advocate for the movement he's been trying to suppress. Once in Damascus, a disciple named **Ananias** baptizes him, and Saul starts telling everyone who'll listen that Jesus is "God's Son" (Acts 9:20). In Luke's telling, Saul soon travels to Jerusalem, where the apostles' initial wariness soon gives way to joy and welcome. (In chapter 11, we'll take a closer

FIGURE 10.7: SIMON MAGUS IN ANCIENT TRADITION

Though Acts leaves the question of Simon's repentance open, one fourth-century Christian calls this "Simon Magus" the "inventor of all heresy." It's an intriguing example of how free-wheeling interpretation—along with a case of mistaken identity—can quickly become "truth." Here are some steps along the way:

> Justin Martyr and Irenaeus (late second century) recount the story of Simon's career in Rome after he was rejected by Peter. They say he connected with a woman of ill repute named Helen and that he performed miracles that led to his veneration as a god. (Details in Justin's writing lead historians to think he's confused Simon's identity with that of a Sabine deity named Semoni Sancus.)

> The Acts of Peter, as well as the Acts of Peter and Paul (both late second century at the earliest), report a story of Simon's death, when he falls from the air after Peter and Paul have prayed during Simon's levitation session.

> Several ancient writers report that Simonianism—a group devoted to Simon's memory—featured objectionable interaction with demonic angels. The group has some gnostic leanings.

We don't know for sure what happened with Simon, but we do know this: he gains a reputation as a cipher for all false teachings, and all on the basis of a story that leaves lots of room for interpretation.

YOUR TURN: Why do you think Simon's story made him an easy target for interpreters? How does his story differentiate between magic and divinely ordained deeds of power?

---

look at Saul's conversion, as well as the irreconcilable differences between Luke's and Paul's accounts of what happened.)

The second half of Acts will feature Saul as main character (his name changes to **Paul** in Acts 13:9), but first Peter undergoes a conversion of his own. He's busy performing miracles—even a resurrection!—in **Lydda** and **Joppa** (to the northwest of Jerusalem) when he has a rooftop vision that opens the way for Gentiles. There, Peter spies a spread of animals that Jewish law designates as both clean and unclean. When a voice tells him to "kill and eat," he declines, in compliance with Torah's guidelines. But then he hears these words: "Never consider unclean what God has made pure" (Acts 10:15).

Peter soon learns the vision is about more than food. God directs a Roman centurion (that is, a Gentile's Gentile) named **Cornelius** to send for

Peter, and Cornelius's openness to the gospel convinces Peter that "God doesn't show partiality to one group of people over another. . . . He is Lord of all!" (Acts 10:34, 36). Though Paul will soon take the lead as missionary to the Gentiles (see Acts 9:15; Rom 1:5), Luke puts the first public declaration about including non-Jews on the lips of Peter. And when believers in Jerusalem hear the news, they respond by praising God (Acts 11:18).

Two other developments lay important groundwork for the unfolding story. First, we learn that many who've fled Jerusalem after Stephen's stoning (see Acts 8:1) find themselves in **Antioch**. When they preach, Luke tells us, they proclaim "the word only to Jews" (Acts 11:19), among whom they find a warm response (Acts 11:21). Antioch becomes a regional base of operations, and the Jerusalem leaders bring in Saul to instruct Antiochene disciples, who are called "**Christians**" for the first time in that city.

Meanwhile, political authorities turn up the heat on the Jerusalem church. One disciple named James (not Jesus's brother) is killed by **Herod Agrippa I**, the area's client king. Herod also detains Peter, who's again miraculously released from prison. Soon thereafter, Luke reports Herod's death in terms that both overlap and conflict with Josephus's account. Both writers report that Herod allowed people to call him a "god" and that he died as a result, but they disagree on how much time passed (see *Ant* 19:343–52; Acts 12:20-23). Luke says that such deliberate and defiant persecution only strengthens the movement (Acts 12:24).

> ### Review and Reflect
>
> • Name and explain three aspects of the apostles' "witness" in Jerusalem, Judea, and Samaria.
>
> • Reflect on Peter's vision about clean and unclean foods. How does this vision fit themes in Luke and the story of Acts?

A "Global" Mission (Acts 13:1–28:31)

The rest of Acts relates the church's story as it ventures out across the Mediterranean, and ultimately to Rome. Not that Jerusalem is left behind; far from it. Indeed, as Paul makes his way around the Roman Empire, he repeatedly returns to the city, seeking the endorsement of church leaders. Like Jesus himself, Paul ultimately stares down the authorities who want to eliminate him. As Paul takes center stage, Peter, James (Jesus's brother), and other apostles recede into the narrative background.

The structure of this section falls into two parts: Paul's Gentile mission (Acts 13:1–21:14) and his detention by authorities (Acts 21:15–28:31). Rather than an exhaustive account of this section, our discussion will highlight key moments that advance Luke's story.

Paul's Gentile Mission (Acts 13:1–21:14)

First Missionary Journey (Acts 13:1–14:28): The church at Antioch sends Paul and his companion **Barnabas** on a first tour of duty outside the region, beginning on the island of **Cyprus** and moving throughout Asia Minor, or modern-day Turkey. (See Figure 10.8.) This itinerary takes Paul not far from his native region of Tarsus.

Paul's first recorded speech takes place at **Pisidian Antioch**, where Jewish leaders have invited him to address the synagogue community. Like Peter, he affirms God's promises to "this people Israel," declaring that, through the house of David, "God brought to Israel a savior, Jesus" (Acts 13:23). That salvation, he explains, brings deliverance "from all those sins from which you couldn't be put in right relationship with God through Moses' Law" (Acts 13:38). Such denigration of Torah makes the leaders understandably irate. For Luke, their rejection fits God's plan (see Acts 13:46-47). This pattern—synagogue proclamation, Jewish rejection, Gentile conversion—recurs throughout Acts as if scripted by God's will.

A healing in **Lystra** gives Paul occasion for conversation with another religious tradition. There, the crowd interprets his divine power as evidence that the "gods have taken human form and come down to visit us!" (Acts 14:11). What is more, they call Barnabas **Zeus** and Paul **Hermes** (because he's wordy) and want to offer sacrifices. But Paul clarifies that they're mere humans, urging the crowd to "turn to the living God and away from such worthless things" (Acts 14:15; cf. 1 Thess 1:16). After all, he says, God's life-giving ways appear throughout the natural world. Even this rather Jewish-sounding appeal evokes a hostile response from some Jewish infiltrators, who stone Paul almost to death. Once again, such persecution in Luke's story is part and parcel of the faithful way of life (Acts 14:22).

The Jerusalem Council (Acts 15:1-35): Between Paul's first and second missionary journeys, a defining debate arises among church leaders: How much of Torah must Gentile believers follow? It's an understandable question, from both Jewish and non-Jewish perspectives. On the one hand, Jewish believers saw Jesus's messiahship in Jewish terms, so it made sense that baptized believers would become Jews. That meant following Torah, with its dietary

FIGURE 10.8: MAP OF PAUL'S MISSIONARY JOURNEYS

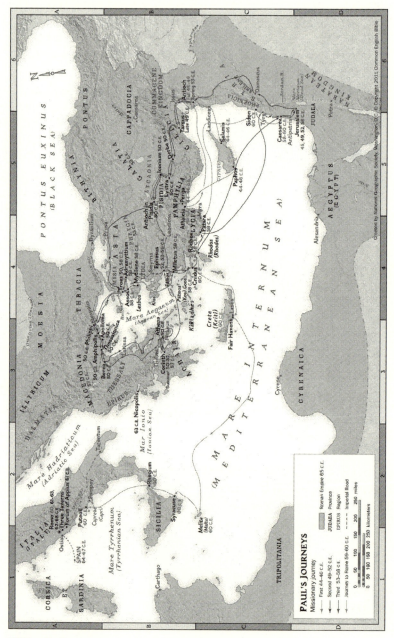

Wikimedia Commons

laws, sacred calendar, and—for men—circumcision. On the other hand, non-Jewish believers knew little about the biblical covenant with Abraham and (let's be honest) probably saw little value in undergoing such a painful and permanent physical procedure. Strategically, Paul saw the circumcision of Gentiles as a potential barrier for those who might otherwise be persuaded to join the movement. The first recorded church council, then, convened to hash out a consensus decision.

In Acts, Peter steps forward as the first proponent of a "Torah light" approach for the Gentiles, a position Jesus's brother James endorses. James says Gentiles should "avoid the pollution associated with idols, sexual immorality, eating meat from strangled animals, and consuming blood" (Acts 15:19–20). In other words, James applies Torah's own guidelines for non-Israelite residents of the land to non-Jewish members of the believing community (see Lev 17:8–18:30).

James's proposal wins immediate and broad-based support. Church leaders then send a delegation (Barnabas, Paul, Judas, and Silas) to Antioch and surrounding regions to deliver the verdict. Once again, Luke simultaneously confirms Jerusalem leaders' ultimate authority, depicts a harmonious and unified church, and affirms the Gentile mission.

Second Missionary Journey (Acts 15:36–18:22): Paul and Barnabas part ways over whether or not to include **John Mark** in their missionary journey. In place of Barnabas, Paul chooses **Silas** as companion for a tour that's planned as a check-up call on communities visited earlier (Acts 15:36). While in **Troas**, though, Paul has a nighttime vision of a "**man from Macedonia**" who asks him to visit that region. Several encounters from this journey stand out as critical to Luke's story in Acts.

Paul's first stop in Macedonia is at **Philippi**, a cultural, political, and economic hub of its region. When Paul searches out a place to pray on the Sabbath, he meets **Lydia**, the first woman mentioned among Paul's missionary efforts. She's both a "Gentile God-worshipper" and a successful merchant in her own right. Luke even portrays her as a head of household (Acts 16:14-15), and her home becomes a base of operations for Paul (Acts 16:40). (See Figure 10.8.)

While in Philippi, Paul encounters another woman as well: a slave-girl who earns a handsome income for her owners as a fortune-teller (Acts 16:16-19). When Paul exorcises her demon—and thus turns off her revenue stream—her owners are furious and have Paul and Silas detained for disrupting the local economy and undermining state-sanctioned religion (Acts 16:20-21). Though an earthquake sets them free, they use the occasion to speak the "Lord's word" to the jailer, whom they then baptize (Acts 16:30-33). City officials then release the pair, since they're Roman citizens.

FIGURE 10.9: THE ACTS OF PAUL AND THECLA

The positive responses to Paul from women in Acts and his letters give rise to a robust tradition that links his teachings about asceticism (see 1 Cor 7) to an early Christian "feminism" that liberates women from the constraints of marriage. A second-century text called "The Acts of Paul and Thecla" tells the story of how a woman named Thecla breaks her engagement in order to follow Paul's ascetic movement. Her family reports her to authorities, and she narrowly (and miraculously) escapes a death sentence. What would have been so dangerous about her failure to marry? To choose sexual abstinence, in the Greco-Roman world, entailed the violation of deeply held cultural norms that saw women's role mainly in terms of maintaining the household and bearing children. Thecla's "opting out" of this established protocol proves her faith in God.

YOUR TURN: Consider the view that sexual abstinence is freedom. Why do you think women in the first century might have found this interpretation of Paul's teachings appealing?

In **Thessalonica,** Paul returns to the synagogue and wins the following of some of its members, along with "a larger number of Greek God-worshippers and quite a few prominent women" (Acts 17:4). Others, though, claim that they're "turning the world upside down" (Acts 17:6 NRSV) by "naming someone else as king: Jesus" (Acts 17:7). This is an ironic charge, since it's Jewish leaders who affirm their allegiance to the emperor, rather than to God.

Paul's speech in **Athens** stands out on a number of grounds. For one thing, it's his only full-fledged address in Acts to a non-Jewish audience (cf. Acts 14:15-17). That means it provides Luke's take on how Paul translated the gospel message for those outside his own Jewish tradition. For another thing, though Rome was the political capital of the empire, Athens retained its vital significance as cultural and philosophical center for the Greco-Roman world. In other words, Paul engages his pluralistic world at its core, and on its own terms.

Luke notes that Paul's speech at the **Areopagus** comes at the invitation of philosophers who've engaged him in public debate. He first affirms the crowd's religious devotion but moves quickly to challenge their worship of idols. Rather than promoting a brand new religion, Paul redirects their worship, and even their philosophy, toward the one God. He sounds very much like one of their own—a philosopher or a poet—but his speech swerves at the end to announce a coming day of judgment, as well as the resurrection of the dead (Acts 17:31-32). In these details, he leaves behind the Gentile worldview to reaffirm a thoroughly Jewish and apocalyptic framework.

Paul's last stop on this journey is in **Corinth,** an economic engine for the empire, since it was strategically located between two ports. Here, Paul finds a Jewish couple named **Priscilla and Aquila** who've left Rome under **Claudius's edict**. Luke says the emperor had banned Jews from Rome, but other sources say the edict targeted Christians. Since most early Roman Christians were likely Jews, the lines of identity were not yet clearly drawn.

After rejection by Corinth's Jewish community, Paul leaves the synagogue and aligns himself with Gentile believers, using the home of **Titius Justus** as a base. Jewish officials ultimately engage the Roman proconsul **Gallio** in an effort to suppress Paul, but Gallio refuses to get involved in what he sees as a family squabble (see Acts 18:14-16). Paul stays in Corinth for eighteen months before leaving for home, accompanied by Priscilla and Aquila whom he leaves in Ephesus along the way. For his part, Paul touches base with the Jerusalem leadership before returning to Antioch.

Third Missionary Journey (Acts 18:23–21:14): As promised, Paul returns to **Ephesus** when he again sets out. During his prolonged stay in the city, Paul clarifies and strengthens the movement that Luke increasingly calls "**the way**" (see Acts 9:1-2; 18:25-26; 19:9, 23; 22:4; 24:14, 22). First, he finds believers whom **Apollos** (see e.g., 1 Cor 1:12; 3:6, 22) has baptized into "John's baptism" (Acts 19:3; cf. 18:24-28). Next, he performs deeds of power that contrast sharply with seven Jewish exorcists who try in vain to operate in Jesus's name. Once again, Luke stresses the dubious economic dimension of their practices. Finally, a silversmith named **Demetrius** targets Paul for disrupting the city's economic and religious status quo. Paul's message that idols aren't gods has caused the market built on commerce around the goddess **Artemis** to crash. A riot nearly erupts when the town clerk quiets the crowds.

The rest of Paul's voyage takes him on to Greece, back through Macedonia (including a stop in Philippi), and on to Troas. There, a man named **Eutychus** nods off and hurtles to his death during Paul's (long-winded) speech, but Paul revives him. At Miletus, Paul delivers a farewell speech that foreshadows his fate in Jerusalem: saying he won't return, he commends his own example of self-sufficiency and support for the weak (Acts 20:18-35). On the way to Jerusalem, Paul's entourage receives repeated warnings about his fate there. But Paul responds with these words: "I'm ready not only to be arrested but even to die in Jerusalem for the sake of the name of the Lord Jesus" (Acts 21:13). Like Jesus (see Luke 9:51), he stares down his destiny with unflinching resolve.

Paul under Arrest (Acts 21:15–28:31)

Paul lasts only seven days in Jerusalem before the crowds clamor for his arrest. From this point on, Paul remains under military detention by Roman officials, at the insistence of Jerusalem's Jewish leadership. This gives

Paul several occasions to defend himself before a variety of audiences: the Jewish people, the council, two governors, and the client-king and his wife. Throughout this series of apologies, Luke highlights several recurrent themes.

A Faithful Jew: Luke stresses Paul's impeccable credentials as a Jew (see also Phil 3:5-6). Born in Tarsus but raised in Jerusalem, Paul says he studied "the strict interpretation of our ancestral Law" (Acts 22:3) under **Gamaliel**. He's a Pharisee who comes from a long line of Pharisees (Acts 23:6), and he worships "the God of our ancestors" and follows the Law and written in the Prophets" (Acts 24:14).

According to Acts, Paul's devotion to Jesus the Messiah hasn't altered his compliance with traditional Jewish practice. The proof? He's had Timothy circumcised (since his mother was Jewish: Acts 16:3). He's cut his hair as part of a Nazirite vow (Acts 18:18; see Num 6:1-20). He purifies himself for temple worship (Acts 21:26; 24:18), and he presents alms and sacrifices according to Jewish law (Acts 24:17). In all these ways, Luke depicts Paul's adherence to Torah and rabbinical tradition.

Indeed, Paul insists that even his message of hope runs with—not against—the current of Jewish tradition. He notes rightly that many Pharisees looked for the resurrection of the dead at the day of judgment (Acts 23:7-8; 24:15). His teaching falls in line, he adds, with "the Prophets and Moses" who he claims announce "that the Christ would suffer and that, as the first to rise from the dead, he would proclaim light both to my people and to the Gentiles" (Acts 26:22-23). Clearly, Paul puts his own interpretive spin on Jewish scripture, since no known text combines these elements—Christ, suffering, resurrection, Gentile mission—into such a "prediction." For Luke, though, it's important to portray Paul's resurrection hope in lockstep with Jewish tradition.

A Respectable Roman Citizen: To a lesser degree, Luke depicts Paul as an upstanding, card-carrying citizen of the Roman Empire. For one thing, Paul's citizenship status earns him a degree of sympathy and admiration from the Roman officials who oversee his detention. Even the Roman tribune, **Claudius Lysius**, had to buy his citizenship; he's taken aback that Paul's been a citizen from birth and fears he's violated Roman protocol in the treatment Paul's suffered under his jurisdiction (Acts 22:27-29). At the judicial level, Paul's citizenship carries certain benefits. Among them, he can't be flogged when he's not been condemned, and he has the right to appeal to the emperor.

Besides Paul's legal rights, Luke points subtly to Paul's elevated socio-political position. He interacts with various Roman officials almost as their equals. From Claudius Lysius, to the governors **Felix** and his successor **Festus**, to **King Agrippa** and his wife **Bernice**, Paul appeals to those in charge in a spirit of mutual loyalty to Roman authority. The fact that Luke *names* each ruler shows the audience that Paul holds his own among bona fide authorities, even in their own halls of power. His appeal to Festus offers a sweeping denial of any guilt: "I've done nothing wrong against the Jewish Law, against the temple, or against Caesar" (Acts 25:8).

An Innocent Man: Like Jesus in Luke, Paul appears in Acts as an innocent man (see Luke 23:47). For one thing, proclaiming the resurrection is hardly a condemnable offense, much less a charge that warrants a death sentence. That leaves Paul's adversaries with the task of concocting charges that are patently false: they tell the Romans that he's a "troublemaker who stirs up riots among all the Jews throughout the empire [and] a ringleader of the Nazarene faction [who] even tried to defile the temple" (Acts 24:5-6), but the evidence is lacking.

As in the Gospel, Luke portrays imperial authorities as weak supporters of to Jewish leaders' machinations. Luke tells us that both the tribune and Felix are fearful—even though the Roman historian **Tacitus** paints a much harsher picture of the governor (see *History* 5.9). **Herod Agrippa II** states Paul's innocence outright (Acts 26:31). And when Paul arrives in Rome, he's treated with kid gloves and allowed to live under a form of house arrest, guarded by one soldier (Acts 28:16).

Luke wants to show that it's not just insiders who think Paul suffered a miscarriage of justice. His innocence, this story suggests, is clear to all; only those with a personal vendetta are really out to get him, and not with a cause that holds any merit. Like Jesus, Paul is caught in the crosshairs of jealousy and fear. Like Jesus, though, Paul is also caught in something much greater: the will of God.

An Evangelist to the Bitter End: After a dramatic storm at sea and shipwreck on the island of Malta, Acts ends with something of a whimper. Historians think Paul died in Rome long before Acts was written, but Luke leaves report of his execution out of the story. Instead, Acts ends with these words: "Unhindered and with complete confidence, [Paul] continued to preach God's kingdom and to teach about the Lord Jesus Christ" (Acts 28:31). Under house arrest in the seat of imperial, Gentile power, Paul remains an active witness to the gospel for all who will listen.

THE MESSAGE OF ACTS

From start to finish, Acts is the story of a messianic movement taking root across the Greco-Roman world. It's a history, in that Luke plots out God's activity in an account that features names, places, and known events—that is, within the concrete social and political realities of first-century Roman rule.

It's also a well-crafted drama, full of irony, touches of wit, intriguing characters, and fancifully spun stories. Mostly, though, this sequel to Luke shows how Jesus's messianic mission lives on among those who're inspired—literally, since they're filled with the Holy Spirit—to carry it forward. Luke makes meaning for them by recalling the church's earliest days, complete with challenges and successes. We'll highlight three dimensions of the story that Luke tells in Acts.

Jesus's Story, Remixed

Just as Luke's Jesus belongs to a long line of prophets before him, the early church takes its place as successor to his earthly mission in Acts. Its representatives advance *Jesus's message about God's coming kingdom* throughout this story. As "witnesses" to Jesus the Christ, both the original apostles and their coworkers (especially Paul) announce that Jesus's resurrection signals the coming reign of God, along with the judgment it brings. In Jesus's resurrection, God has not only vindicated him but also exalted him as "Lord and Christ" (Acts 2:36). That is, he has launched a new era in which God's power is palpably at work to bring forgiveness, restoration, and life.

As in the Gospel, the proclamation of God's kingdom—and Jesus's messianic role in it—goes hand-in-hand with *actions that display God's power.* Both the apostles and Paul dispense healing and even bring life out of death in Jesus's name. In distinction from other miracle-working characters, they do so not to seek glory or financial gain. Instead, they credit Jesus, in whose name they dispense divine power. Likewise, they embody relationships marked by the kingdom priorities Jesus has promoted in Luke: the inclusion of outsiders, such as women, Gentiles, and Samaritans, for instance, and the redistribution of resources to those in need.

Luke's harmonious depiction of the community and their leaders in these halcyon days is striking. Cynics might justifiably ask how "true" this rendition really is. Chances are Luke uses this story to cast a vision for life together that's winsome, compelling, and inspiring. We won't have to scratch far beneath the surface of Paul's letters to find a more discordant "reality on the ground." Luke opts, it seems, to set a high—if unrealistic—bar for what messianic community might look like.

It's God's Story, After All

In Acts, no character really "acts" on his or her own. God is directly involved on every page, plotting the itinerary, transporting characters from place to place, and sometimes disturbing the natural order for good. As the true protagonist of Acts, God shows up in many forms. In several cases, it's with fireworks, as when the "tongues of fire" descend at Pentecost, or when an earthquake shakes open Paul's prison doors, or when a lights-out storm finds him shipwrecked at Malta. At several key points in the story, God controls the narrative through visions. Peter sees comingled foods and learns that they're all "pure," a vision he translates into a more inclusive gospel message. Paul meets the risen Jesus in a mid-day flash of light, along with a voice that asks why he's sided with Jesus's persecutors. Elsewhere, either an "angel of the Lord" or the "Holy Spirit" plays an active role in informing disciples about God's plans or sometimes physically moving characters like pieces on a chess board (see e.g., Acts 8:39). Through these and other episodes, Luke reminds the audience that they're part of a drama that's playing out as a divine Director calls the shots.

That leads to another, related observation. For all of Luke's interest in naming historical figures who play a part in this story, even these governors, emperors, and high priests aren't really acting on their own. When Jewish leaders conspire against Paul, they're only doing so because the Holy Spirit said they had to reject Jesus so that salvation would open for the Gentiles (Acts 28:25-29). And though Roman officials find no fault with Paul, they send him on to Rome because circumstances have led him to make such a request. They're caught up in a narrative in which even powerful people exercise remarkably little agency.

Despite Resistance, Jesus Is Trending

The narrative arc of Acts pushes relentlessly toward success—numerical and otherwise. From the three thousand believers who join ranks with the messianic movement on Pentecost (Acts 2:41), to the "great number" of converts in Antioch (Acts 11:21), to Paul's effective missions to Syria and Cilicia (Acts 16:5), and even to Paul's appeal during his imprisonment in Rome (Acts 28:24), Acts depicts a movement that flourishes wherever it takes root.

This is true even, or perhaps especially, in the face of resistance. When Jewish leaders in Pisidian Antioch undermine Paul and Barnabas's witness, Gentiles embrace the message all the more eagerly. Paul causes quite a stir in Ephesus, but although he's run out on a rail, the nascent Christian community there thrives. He even uses jail time to evangelize his guard, whose family soon joins the Christian ranks.

Finally, the "church growth" model reported in Acts arises out of the movement's expansive charter. To be sure, Luke consistently reiterates the central importance of Jerusalem. Yet rather than safeguarding themselves behind locked doors, the disciples—even the Jerusalem leaders—redraw the boundaries around what it means to be a believer over and over again. This cultural adaptability serves the church well over time. While preserving a core loyalty to Jesus the Jewish Messiah, the movement promotes a way of salvation and forgiveness that crosses linguistic, geographic, ethnic, and social boundaries. It becomes a way of no distinction for all those who subscribe to the way of Jesus.

SUMMARY

In the book of Acts, the early believing community and its leaders carry forward Jesus's mission as it's portrayed in Luke's Gospel. With deep ties to the Jerusalem leadership, figures such as Peter and Paul take the "good news" about salvation into the wider Greco-Roman world. Along the way, they're buoyed by God's Spirit, which directs the story and endows believers with miraculous powers. They face rejection, as Jesus did, but that doesn't stymie their mission—far from it. Living together as people committed to Jesus's "way," the communities established throughout Acts lay the groundwork for a robust expansion of the gospel message—in word and deed—to the ends of the earth.

Review and Reflect

- Give examples of apostolic conversations with both Judaism and the wider Greco-Roman world in Acts.

- Reflect on Acts' portrait of Paul. Give three details that stand out for you, and explain their significance.

GO DEEPER

Gaventa, Beverly Roberts. *The Acts of the Apostles*. Abingdon New Testament Commentaries. Nashville: Abingdon Press, 2003.

Pervo, Richard. *The Mystery of Acts: Unraveling Its Story*. Santa Rosa, CA: Polebridge Press, 2008.

Rowe, Kavin C. *World Upside Down: Reading Acts in the Graeco-Roman Age*. Oxford: Oxford University Press, 2009.

Skinner, Matthew L. *Intrusive God, Disruptive Gospel: Encountering the Divine in the Book of Acts*. Grand Rapids, MI: Brazos, 2015.

Chapter Eleven

Who Is the "Apostle to the Gentiles"? Paul's Letters, Life, and Message

CONVERSATION STARTERS

- What are the three main groups of the Pauline Letters?

- Why might others have written letters in Paul's name?

- What do we know about the "historical Paul"?

- What are the main elements of his message?

- What reading strategies will help us take Paul's letters on their own terms?

Even before our study of Acts, you'd probably heard about Paul. For some Christians, Paul's understanding of Christ is more influential than the Gospel accounts of Jesus's messianic career. Without Paul, we wouldn't have more than half of the NT writings, and we wouldn't know phrases such as the "body of Christ" and "saved by grace through faith." We also wouldn't have any NT books that mention homosexuality or restrict women's role as church leaders. Some scholars go so far as to credit (or discredit) Paul with inventing Christianity as we know it.

Both inside and outside the church today, you'll find widely differing opinions about this first-century figure and his written legacy, found in the thirteen letters called the **Pauline corpus,** or "body" of Paul's letters. Many revere Paul and take these writings as authoritative guides for Christian living. Others are more skeptical, detecting in Paul's tone a smug arrogance that's at odds with Jesus's model of humility (see e.g., 1 Cor 11:1). Still others balk at passages used to undermine both female church leadership and LGBTQ rights.

No matter where you might fall on this spectrum, our study of the apostle and the Pauline Letters will likely challenge your assumptions. Over the next four chapters, we'll investigate the thirteen Pauline Letters on their own terms and in conversation with the wider world. We'll mine the literary and historical evidence to deepen our understanding of who Paul was, what changed his mind about Jesus, and the relationship he established with several believing communities around the Mediterranean. We'll examine both the letters he wrote and those he (more than likely) didn't, and consider why others might have written in his name.

We spent much of the last chapter discussing Luke's portrait of Paul in Acts. There, we set aside questions about Luke's historical accuracy, since we were more interested in Luke's story of how Paul's missionary activity extended the gospel to the "ends of the earth." This chapter takes up the question of the "historical Paul": Who was he? What did he believe? And what was his mission to the Gentiles about?

We'll explore the "historical Paul" in several stages. As we did with the historical Jesus, we'll begin with the question of sources. Which letters that *claim* to be written by Paul did Paul really write, and why do scholars question the authenticity of several NT letters written in his name? Once we identify which letters bear direct witness to Paul's experience and worldview, we'll highlight several key aspects of his career:

- The "revelation" that convinced him of Jesus's messianic role

- His sometimes-testy relationship to other Jewish believers

- His views about the Jewish people and Jewish law

- His mission to the Gentiles and the role of his letters in that mission

- His views about women

The chapter will conclude with some guidelines that will inform our study of Paul's letters in subsequent chapters.

FIGURE 11.1: PAULINE CORPUS

Authentic	Deutero-Pauline	Pastoral Letters
Romans	2 Thessalonians	1 and 2 Timothy
1 and 2 Corinthians	Colossians	Titus
Galatians	Ephesians	
Philippians		

WHAT'S THE "PAULINE CORPUS"?

Almost half of the books in the NT—thirteen out of twenty-seven—claim to be written by Paul. Together, these letters make up the **Pauline corpus**. (Early on, the book of **Hebrews** circulated with the Pauline Letters, even though it doesn't claim Pauline authorship.) Careful study of these "Pauline" letters, though, convinces most scholars that Paul didn't write all of them. Some were probably written by Paul's followers after his death, for reasons we discuss more fully below.

From the outset, it's important to clarify the starting point scholars take on the question of authorship. The widely shared assumption is this: *if a letter says Paul's its author, we accept that claim unless there's compelling evidence that leads us to question it.* In chapter 14, we'll dig deeper into that evidence and discuss methods for assessing it. For now, we'll simply introduce the three categories used to rank the likelihood that Paul wrote each Pauline letter. (See Figure 11.1.)

The Undisputed Letters

Scholars broadly agree that Paul wrote Romans, 1 and 2 Corinthians, Galatians, Philippians, 1 Thessalonians, and Philemon, known together as the **undisputed letters**. Among these letters, two stand out for different reasons: **Philemon** alone addresses an individual, rather than a Christian community, while only **Romans** was written to a group of believers Paul hasn't yet met. Besides their authenticity, the undisputed letters also share a common purpose: to interpret the gospel message about Jesus the Christ for communities living throughout the first-century CE Mediterranean world.

The Deutero-Pauline Letters

A second tier of the Pauline corpus known as the **deutero-Pauline Letters** includes 2 Thessalonians, Colossians, and Ephesians. (*Deutero* means "second" in Greek.) Most scholars question Paul's authorship of these three letters, but to varying degrees. Among them, 2 Thessalonians sounds the most authentic in terms of style and content, though fewer than half of NT scholars think Paul wrote it. A careful reading of Ephesians convinces a more sizeable majority that an unknown follower of Paul's composed the letter after his death. Colossians lies between the two.

In general, these letters fit the theology and worldview of the undisputed letters fairly well, but they also feature meaningful differences in writing style, as well as some traceable development of Pauline thought. That suggests to many an original setting that postdates Paul. Put simply, if Paul didn't write these letters, their authors do a fairly effective job of channeling what Paul might have said in a different place and time.

The Pastoral Letters

Only a small percentage of scholars think that Paul wrote the **Pastoral Letters**, a term that refers to 1 and 2 Timothy, along with Titus. Addressed to individual church leaders rather than to communities, these letters are "pastoral" in at least two respects: they offer pastoral guidance, as if from a mentor to his trainees, and they're concerned with orthodox credentials and theology among the early church's pastoral leadership.

Why is their authorship so much in doubt? As we'll see, both the language and the content of the Pastorals differ quite dramatically from the undisputed Pauline letters. Sometimes, they contradict Paul's thought outright, such as when the writer claims that women will be saved by giving birth (1 Tim 2:15)! In addition, evidence found in them points to a historical setting several decades after his death. Intriguingly, it is these least-reliably Pauline letters that mandate the clearest prohibition against women's leadership in the church.

WHY THE "FORGERY"?

You may be troubled to learn that someone other than Paul probably wrote letters in Paul's name. If Paul didn't write them, does that make these writings less authoritative—for both ancient and contemporary readers? To address these concerns, let's consider the question of **pseudepigraphy** (or "false writing") in the ancient world. How widespread was the practice? And what motivated those who wrote in someone else's name?

Ancient Jewish and Christian writers frequently attributed their writings to venerable characters from the biblical tradition. Indeed, an entire

FIGURE 11.2: A CASE OF ANCIENT FORGERY: THE ACTS OF PAUL

In the second century CE, a pseudonymous document called The Acts of Paul gained widespread popularity, partly because of Paul's reputation among believing communities. It includes a "Third Letter to the Corinthians," which addresses potential misreading of the two canonical (and authentic) letters, as well as The Acts of Paul and Thecla (see below). But a church leader named Tertullian writes that a certain presbyter ("elder") acknowledged that he'd embellished the traditions it contains "for love of Paul" and was removed from his position of leadership in the church. It's an interesting case that shows both the positive intentions behind a forgery and the negative ramifications for the person who committed it.

YOUR TURN: Do contemporary forgeries matter? Why or why not?

collection of Jewish texts are known collectively as the **Pseudepigrapha,** since they claim authorship by figures from the remote and/or mythic past such as Enoch, Abraham, Moses, Solomon, and Ezra. Among early Christian writings, we've already seen that the **Nag Hammadi** library falsely attributes gospels, apocalypses, and other texts to apostles such as Thomas, Peter, and Judas—as well as to Mary Magdalene. Even philosophical traditions such as **Plato's Dialogues** are "pseudepigraphic" in that they weren't written by Plato himself.

As commonplace as pseudepigraphy was in the ancient world, it wasn't universally accepted. A Roman writer named Galen anticipated that others would pen works in his name and offered guidelines about how to tell the authentic from the forged writings. It's not surprising, then, that at least one second-century bishop who wrote in Paul's name was demoted for doing so. (See Figure 11.2.) How did pseudepigraphy function in the Pauline corpus? Let's consider three complementary factors that likely lie behind the "ghost-writing" of several Pauline letters.

1. Authority: To name Paul as author is to claim the apostle's endorsement of the views the letter contains. His supposed authorship thus confers an authoritative "seal of approval" upon the letters' message.

2. Memorial: Letters written in Paul's name also build on the legacy of his thought established during his lifetime. Since his own missionary work was probably cut short at his death in Rome, his followers likely memorialized the apostle by extending that legacy both chronologically and geographically.

3. Application: The pseudepigraphic letters also carry forward Paul's tendency to adapt the gospel message to changing circumstance. Already in the authentic letters, the apostle reframes his views on such questions as Jewish law depending on the audience's makeup and setting. For Paul and his successors, core claims about Jesus's messiahship are flexible enough to apply in different ways to different communities.

To say that Paul probably didn't write some letters found in the Pauline corpus doesn't mean we dismiss them out of hand. After all, regardless of authorship, they belong to the canon of NT writings believers consider sacred to this day. Even the disputed letters signal that Paul's influence among earliest Christians outlasted his lifespan. But the fact that Paul didn't write all the Pauline letters *does* affect our study of the "historical Paul." As we search for clues about Paul's own career and worldview, we'll confine our inquiry to the undisputed letters, weighing them against the witness of Acts, which took shape sometime after his death. Let's turn, then, to consider several key facets of Paul's historical ministry.

Review and Reflect

- What are the three groups of letters that compose the Pauline corpus? Which letters belong to which group?

- Consider the question of authorship. How do you respond to the likelihood that Paul didn't write all the "Pauline" letters? Do the motivations seem plausible? Why or why not?

WILL THE REAL PAUL PLEASE STAND UP?

Both the book of Acts and the seven undisputed Pauline letters provide important insights about Paul's life, his worldview, and his missionary career. On some points, they agree quite closely. On others, they exhibit "irreconcilable differences." How do we know what's true and what's spin? As a starting point, let's consider the sources: When, why, and for whom did Paul and Luke write?

Written mostly in the 50s CE, Paul's letters predate Acts by about three decades. They're also "occasional" letters, meaning that they deliver Paul's message to particular groups of people, concerned with particular questions about how to live together. They're something like an internal memo between a trusted advisor and small groups of early Christians.

As we've seen, Acts probably dates to the 80s CE and addresses Theophilus—either a real person or a generic stand-in for non-Jewish "God-lovers." Most scholars see Acts as a polished account of the early decades after Jesus's death and resurrection, one that leaves out some of the messier elements of the movement's life together. Acts reads like a glossy public relations brochure that smooths over any discord or division to promote a unified, idealized report.

These differences in audience, setting, and purpose help to explain many of the disparities in details between Acts and Paul's letters. But we also find meaningful alignment among our sources. To trace the contours of the "historical Paul," we'll rely on information provided by both Luke and Paul, noting along the way where their accounts converge and diverge and how we decide which version is more reliable.

Paul's Backstory

Both Acts and Paul's letters highlight the apostle's backstory as a vigorous opponent of the earliest Christian movement. They both portray him as a "Jew among Jews" and even agree on significant details. In both, Paul appears as

- a born Jew (Acts 22:3; Phil 3:5; Rom 11:1)

- an educated Pharisee (Acts 22:3; Gal 1:14; Phil 3:5)

- a persecutor of the early church (Acts 9:1-2, 22:4-5; Gal 1:15; 1 Cor 15:9)

Other elements of his pre-Christian career that are mentioned by Acts but not Paul himself seem plausible if not certain. That he was from Tarsus in Cilicia (Acts 9:11; 21:39; 22:3) makes sense of his capacity with Greek, which is solid if not refined. His letters sometimes use rhetorical strategies that suggest a philosophical education, and when Paul quotes scripture, he refers to the Septuagint (LXX), the version Jews in the Greco-Roman diaspora would have known. We can't say for sure that he was trained by **Gamaliel** in Jerusalem (Acts 22:3), but it's clear that he was among the 15 to 20 percent of the population that was literate.

Based on both sources, Paul was a Pharisee who looked forward to the messianic age. (See Figure 11.3.) It's just that, like most Jews in his time and ever since, he had no reason to think that messianic age had begun. After all, its telltale markers included the resurrection of the dead for a day of judgment and the glorious aftermath it would usher in: the "new creation" marked by God's reign on earth and the cosmic restoration it promised. That's why, when he heard people proclaiming a crucified messiah, he found their message to be a dangerous delusion. What made no sense to him—at least before a mysterious encounter with the risen Lord—was the notion that God's Christ would

FIGURE 11.3: PAUL'S WORLDVIEW

As an apocalyptic Jew, Paul looked forward to the messianic age in which God would establish justice and righteousness on earth. Like many Jews in his day, he probably thought a messiah would lead the charge to establish this new world order in Jerusalem but inaugurating peace throughout the whole world. Here's how he likely thought this apocalyptic drama would unfold:

JEWISH APOCALYPTIC WORLDVIEW

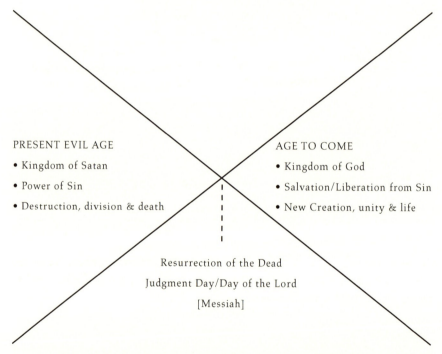

PRESENT EVIL AGE

- Kingdom of Satan
- Power of Sin
- Destruction, division & death

AGE TO COME

- Kingdom of God
- Salvation/Liberation from Sin
- New Creation, unity & life

Resurrection of the Dead

Judgment Day/Day of the Lord

[Messiah]

Paul's "revelation" of the risen Lord didn't make him abandon this worldview. Instead, he adjusted its timeframe, introducing an overlapping era in which the messianic age had begun—and was evident among believing communities—but hadn't yet prevailed on earth. In Paul's view, those who called Jesus "Lord" took his death and resurrection to be the inaugural moment of the new creation. Their calling, he thought, was to live in devotion to Christ and his sacrificial ways and, in so doing, to bear witness to God's justice and righteousness on earth. While he thought a judgment day was coming soon, Paul also encouraged believing communities to live as evidence that God's saving (or "liberating") power was already at work among them. Consider this revision of his framework:

PAUL'S POST-REVELATION WORLDVIEW

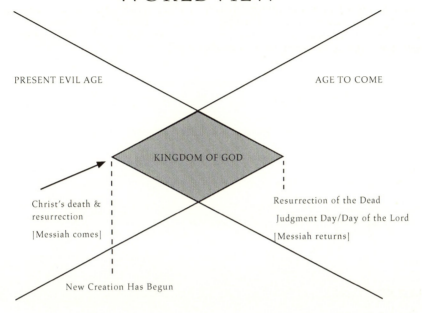

PRESENT EVIL AGE   AGE TO COME

KINGDOM OF GOD

Christ's death &
resurrection   Resurrection of the Dead

[Messiah comes]   Judgment Day/Day of the Lord

                                    [Messiah returns]

New Creation Has Begun

YOUR TURN: How might Paul's Christian apocalyptic worldview lead him to see Christian communities today? What would qualify them as faithful to the qualities of the messianic age?

die on a Roman cross, the very symbol of brute imperial strength. So he set out as an authorized agent of the "thought police" devoted to ridding Jewish communities of those spouting such offensive claims.

Paul's "Revelation"

Many speak of Paul's "conversion" to Christianity from his native Jewish tradition. But this understanding of Paul's story is anachronistic—Christianity as we know it didn't exist yet—and assumes a radical break in Paul's thinking. It's true that Paul *did* change his mind about Jesus's messianic status. But this shift brought an *adaptation* of his Jewish apocalyptic worldview rather than an abrupt *departure* from it. How and why did this shift occur?

Already, we've considered Luke's story, told in Acts, about Paul's vision on the Damascus Road. Paul's own version of this episode is much sparser.

Twice, he mentions a life-changing encounter with the risen Lord. In 1 Corinthians, he notes that only after appearing to other followers, "last of all [Jesus] appeared to me, as if I were born at the wrong time" (1 Cor 15:8). In Galatians, Paul says that God "was pleased to reveal his Son to me" (Gal 1:15-16; cf. 1 Cor 9:16). These cases confirm two important features of the Acts account: (1) Paul's experience convinced him that Jesus was dead no more; (2) Paul's experience came out of the blue, as a disruptive encounter that caused him to rethink much of what he'd taken for granted about God's Messiah. (See Figure 11.4.)

FIGURE 11.4: REVELATION IN OTHER RELIGIOUS TRADITIONS

Revelation—or a powerful sense of connection to divine truth—plays an important role in many religions' foundational stories. Consider these examples, from both Eastern and Western traditions:

- In Jewish tradition, Moses was a fugitive from the authorities when a voice called to him from a burning bush. In the exodus story, this outlaw shepherd takes up the case of an oppressed Hebrew people and leads them out of slavery and into the wilderness, where God gives the covenant in another revelation.

- In Buddhist tradition, Siddhartha Gautama leaves a comfortable life in search of meaning. After living as an ascetic, he finds "enlightenment" while sitting under a tree.

- In Muslim tradition, the prophet Mohammed was on retreat in a cave when Allah imparted the Qur'an to him. His wife Khadijah was the one who confirmed its legitimacy.

- Joseph Smith reported divine visions that directed him to buried golden tablets in New York State. He translated the contents of the tablets into the Book of Mormon.

In some cases, revelation comes in response to those who seek divine guidance. In other cases, it comes as a jarring, unexpected disruption of life as they've known it. In each case, the revelation carries with it a compelling call that shapes the course of human history.

YOUR TURN: What do you think when you hear the term *revelation*? Have you ever had an "aha" moment that makes you rethink important questions or even your life's direction? What makes revelation authentic? What makes it dangerous?

What changed, for Paul, as a result of this revelation? Simply put, he re-mapped his worldview to accommodate his new conviction that Jesus was indeed the Jewish Messiah. As a result, instead of a curse (see Deut 21:23), Jesus's death on a Roman cross became for Paul the turning point toward the salvation of the whole world. In Paul's revised understanding, Jesus's death and resurrection instituted the messianic age, even if it wasn't yet fully evident on earth.

For Paul, the human weakness displayed in Jesus's passion thus became a revelation of divine strength. The resurrection—and Paul's experience of a living Lord—confirms this. Paul grew convinced that God had decisively defeated the present evil age by absorbing its death-dealing blow and bringing new life out of it. In his death, then, Jesus bore the brunt of human sin but wasn't defeated by it. Paul calls Jesus's resurrection "the first crop of the harvest" (1 Cor 15:20)—that is, an advance notice that the dead will be raised for the coming **day of judgment** and, for the righteous, a destiny of salvation, or liberation from the present evil age.

Whatever the nature of Paul's encounter with the risen Jesus, it altered the trajectory of his own life and, since we're still reading about him, what became Christian tradition as a whole. Once convinced that the messianic age had indeed dawned in Jesus's death and resurrection, Paul devoted himself to proclaiming that "good news" far and wide, as he called others to live as witnesses to the countercultural values of God's kingdom.

Paul's Apostleship

Paul's missionary career spanned at least two decades and four major areas of the ancient Mediterranean world: Galatia, Asia Minor, Macedonia, and Achaia. (See Figure 11.6). Using both Acts and Paul's letters, scholars have pieced together a rough itinerary of his travels and his letter-writing activity (see Figure 11.7). His work as an apostle meant building and nurturing relationships with mostly non-Jewish (Gentile) believers who shared his commitment to Jesus as Lord.

How did Paul become an "apostle to the Gentiles" (see e.g., Rom 11:13; Gal 1:16; 2:7-9; Acts 14:27; 18:6)? After all, we've already noted he was steeped in Jewish thought. But Paul saw the movement's early appeal to non-Jewish followers as evidence that the messianic age had begun, since his own tradition looked forward to the day when all nations would worship the Lord God. Convinced that such expansive redemption was at hand, Paul broadly and boldly proclaimed the message about God's Messiah. (See Figure 11.5.)

Both his background as an active suppressor of Jesus's followers and his focus on Gentiles brought some degree of tension to Paul's relationship with

FIGURE 11.5: PAUL'S MISSIONARY CHURCHES

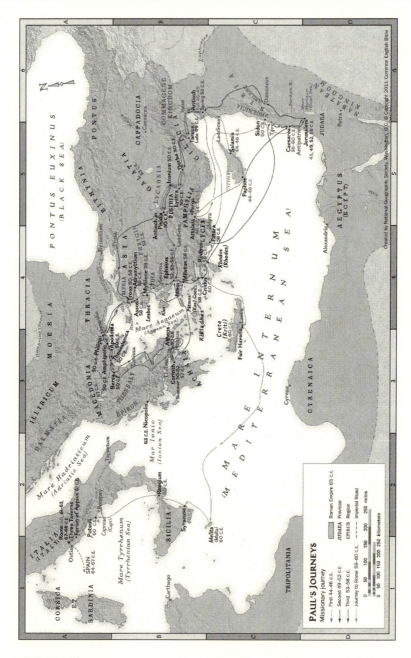

(Wikimedia Commons)

FIGURE 11.6: PAULINE CHRONOLOGY

We don't know exact dates for Paul's activities, but scholars attempt to reconstruct a chronology of his life and writings by plotting the letters' content within a framework based partly on Acts. Here's a plausible chronology of Paul's missionary career:

5–10 CE	Born in Tarsus, in the region of Cicilia
20–30 CE	Educated in both Greco-Roman philosophy and Jewish tradition, perhaps partly in Jerusalem (see Acts 22:3; Phil 3:5; 2 Cor 11:22)
Early 30s CE	Opposed Christ-followers as faithful Pharisee (Gal 1:13; Phil 3:5-6)
Mid 30s CE	Had revelation that convinced him that Jesus was Messiah
Late 30s CE	Spent three years in Arabia, returning to Damascus, Syria to promoting the movement
40s–50s CE	Traveled throughout the Mediterranean, returning several times to Jerusalem
50 CE	Wrote First Thessalonians, the earliest remaining Pauline letter (if 2 Thessalonians is authentic, it was written soon thereafter)
Mid 50s CE	Wrote Philippians and Philemon (both possibly from Ephesus); 1 and 2 Corinthians (2 Corinthians probably combines at least two separate letters); Galatians
Late 50s CE	Wrote Romans
Late 50s/early 60s CE	Wrote Colossians, if authentic
Early 60s CE	Ended career under house arrest in Rome
64–68 CE	Was executed in Rome by Emperor Nero

Jesus's original circle of apostles based in Jerusalem. It's a tension that's evident in clear differences between Acts and Paul's own writings about his relationship to Jerusalem leaders. For instance, while both sources say Paul visited Jerusalem after meeting the risen Lord, details about that visit are hard to reconcile:

1. Acts says Paul stayed in Damascus, for "some time" and escaped from there to Jerusalem (Acts 9:20-23). Paul insists he spent three years in Arabia—a detail Luke leaves out—and then stayed in Damascus before visiting Jerusalem (Gal 1:17).

2. When Paul does visit Jerusalem, Acts says the apostles are (understandably) afraid and mistrustful of Paul (Acts 9:26); Barnabas

Figure 11.7: Laws for Righteous Gentiles

In Jewish tradition, both the Tosefta and the Talmud look for the inclusion of "righteous Gentiles" in the world to come. (See e.g., *Sanhedrin* 105a.) How do non-Jews attain righteous status? Both texts affirm a "short list" of rules they think were given to Adam and/or Noah, characters in Genesis who precede Moses and the law. Here are the rules that pertain to non-Jews:

- Do not deny God.

- Do not blaspheme God.

- Do not murder.

- Do not engage in illicit sexual relations.

- Do not steal.

- Do not eat from a live animal.

- Establish courts of justice to enforce these rules.

In the 1980s, Rabbi Menachem Schneerson launched a campaign to codify and inform non-Jews about the "Noahide commandments," and Rabbi Moshe Weiner published this code as *Sefer Sheva Mitzvot HaShem* (The Book of Seven Divine Commandments) in 2008–9. Known today as the Chabad Movement, the group promoting the Noahide commandments claims worldwide authority.

YOUR TURN: How do these laws compare to legal codes in civil society today? What's missing? What's added?

intercedes on his behalf and legitimizes his conversion (Acts 9:26-27). By contrast, Paul says he only met with Cephas (Peter) and Jesus's brother James (Gal 1:18-19).

These differences probably reflect Luke's and Paul's respective concerns. To tell a harmonious story, Luke emphasizes Paul's deference to Jerusalem leaders; remember, Jerusalem plays a central role for Luke, both in Jesus's story and in the life of the early church. Paul, though, strikes an almost defiant chord toward the group, especially those who've insisted that Gentile Galatians must follow Jewish law in order to follow a Jewish Messiah. Paul writes as one who's utterly convinced he has the right answer, even if the authorities disagree.

A similar tension appears when we examine Luke's and Paul's differing accounts of the **Jerusalem Council** (see Acts 15:1-35; Gal 2:1-10). Some

FIGURE 11.8: CHANGING TEXTS TO PROTECT THE PATRIARCHY?

In several cases, the NT manuscript tradition shows just how ill at ease some scribes were with evidence that Paul valued female church leaders—and how freely they altered the texts to diminish women's status. There's the case of **Nympha**, for instance, credited in Colossians with hosting a church "in her house" (Col 4:15). In some manuscripts, her name changes to the masculine form (Nymphas), as if the scribe can't believe (or bear to convey) that a woman would have been named "head of household." Or consider **Junia**, named as an "apostle" in Romans 16:7. Some scribes change her name to a "him," while others rewrite the verse to imply she wasn't an apostle at all. And then there's the dynamic duo, **Prisca** (or Priscilla) and **Aquila**: they're named together in Acts 18, as well as in Romans 16 and 1 Corinthians 16, and in each case her name appears first. But some manuscripts reverse the order of their names, while others omit Priscilla entirely.

YOUR TURN: What do you think might motivate scribes to emend the texts in ways that downplay women's leadership roles?

scholars think they're reporting on different meetings, but the two passages address a common question considered by Paul and the Jerusalem leaders: To what extent must Gentile converts comply with Jewish law? Two striking variances arise when we compare accounts:

1. According to Acts, Paul and Barnabas initiate the conversation to show their respect for the Jerusalem leaders' authority (Acts 15:2). But Paul insists his trip to Jerusalem comes only from a divine prompting, not from a human desire for approval (Gal 2:2). What's more, he maintains that Jerusalem authorities "didn't add anything" to his message (Gal 2:6) and that they received Barnabas and him "as equals" (Gal 2:9).

2. In Acts, the diplomatic decision reached by the Jerusalem Council specifies a very short list of commandments that Gentile Christians must observe—a sort of "Torah light": they must "avoid the pollution associated with idols, sexual immorality, eating meat from strangled animals, and consuming blood" (Acts 15:20; see Figure 11.8). Paul doesn't mention these prohibitions, insisting that Jerusalem leaders only asked Gentile Christians to "remember the poor" (Gal 2:10).

In any case, Paul's backstory, his life-changing revelation, and his calling as an apostle to the Gentiles form the foundation of the "historical Paul." As a

Jew, he came to see Jesus's crucifixion and resurrection as the hinge on which salvation history swings toward redemption. In his letters, we find evidence that Paul meant both to inform non-Jewish hearers about God's saving work on the cross and to transform believers in their new life "in Christ." Let's turn, then, to the defining features of Paul's message.

WHAT ARE THE MAIN PARTS OF PAUL'S MESSAGE?

The seven authentic Pauline letters found in the NT convey a wide range of concerns. Some register a tone of approval and encouragement, while others can sound downright combative. Some seem steeped in lofty theological discussion, while others consider more mundane topics such as lawsuits, marriage, and food. Over the next two chapters, we'll explore Paul's message as it addresses concrete communities. To orient ourselves, though, we'll offer here a broad overview of three topics that dominate Paul's letters.

Paul and Jewish Tradition

Those who think of Paul as the apostle who preached a law-free gospel to the Gentiles (see e.g., Rom 8:2) sometimes fail to notice that his message is Jewish to the core, since it grows out of a thoroughly Jewish expectation for God's redemption of the world. In Acts, Paul begins most missionary visits in local synagogues, explaining how Jesus's story fulfills Jewish teaching (e.g., in Damascus: Acts 9:20; in Salamis: Acts 13:5; in Pisidian Antioch: Acts 13:14; and so on). And although his letters don't mention this pattern, Paul freely cites Jewish scripture, even when writing to non-Jews (e.g., 1 Cor 15:3-4; Rom 1:2-3).

Though he addresses mostly Gentile believers, Paul's own relationship to Judaism is more complex than we might expect. For instance, Paul never abandons a sense of priority for Jews within God's plan of salvation. As he writes in Romans, the good news comes to the "Jew first and also to the Greek" (Rom 1:16). In a similar vein, Paul insists that devotion to the risen Jesus means exclusive worship of the Jewish God (e.g., 1 Thess 1:9-10).

Scholars disagree about whether or not Paul continued to observe Jewish law. In a later letter, he calls the law "holy, righteous, and good" (Rom 7:12), affirming its validity. What Paul challenges is Torah's *function* as a means of salvation. He sees it as a useful but preliminary pointer to God's righteousness, which he thinks is fully evident in Christ's faithfulness (see Gal

3:23-25; Rom 8:3). As a result, Paul sees Torah's ethnic identity markers—circumcision, dietary laws, and the sacred calendar, for instance—as obstacles for Gentiles and thus nonessential for non-Jews.

Paul also had to square up to what was, for him, a disappointing truth: most Jews found little in Jesus's story to confirm that he was God's anointed one. More than that, Paul mentions overt opposition from Jewish leaders, including at least one lashing (2 Cor 11:24). He explains this resistance as a temporary condition that makes room for Gentiles in the people of God (Rom 11:25-26). Ultimately, Paul remains convinced that all Jews will eventually come around to embrace Jesus's messianic vision for a new world order.

Paul and the Cross

Christ's death on a Roman cross initially stoked Paul's vigorous suppression of the movement that hailed Jesus as the Messiah. But after his revelation, the cross lies at the heart of Paul's gospel message. He rarely alludes to Jesus's earthly ministry, focusing instead on Christ's saving death, and he summarizes his message this way: "I had made up my mind not to think about anything while I was with you *except Jesus Christ, and to preach him as crucified*" (1 Cor 2:2, emphasis added). For Paul, Jesus's state-sanctioned execution by Roman officials has disclosed God's righteousness; in Christ's humiliating death, Paul thinks the cosmos has tilted toward redemption (Rom 3:20-22).

As we've noted, this conviction reflected a dramatic shift in thinking for Paul. For Paul, Christ's death liberates humanity in several complementary ways:

- It redefines "strength" as vulnerable solidarity. Paul's world, like ours, measured human value in terms of physical, mental, and spiritual strength. Those who showed fortitude achieved social status and privilege; the weak and vulnerable often suffered neglect or, worse, derision. Crucifixion itself was the supreme example of this, since only the lowest members of society could be executed in this way. Paul thinks that, on the cross, Christ showed that God's "power is made perfect in weakness" (2 Cor 12:8). Christ's death redeems human weakness through his vulnerable solidarity with the weak.

- It models the supreme act of faithfulness. As we'll see, the phrase that's often translated "faith in Christ" can also be read as "Christ's faithfulness" (see e.g., Gal 2:16; Rom 3:22). Many scholars think

Paul's saying that Christ's faithfulness—not our beliefs—opens the way for our "righteousness," which becomes effective through full-fledged human trust that mimics Jesus's.

- It provides a pattern of self-sacrifice. On a practical level, Paul sees Christ's self-emptying death as the embodiment of that faithfulness. Put simply, Christ's loyalty to God means he forfeits self-concern for the sake of others—especially the weak. Paul implores his audiences to have the "same mind" that Christ Jesus had (see Phil 2:1-11): a disposition that prioritizes the well-being of others over self-interest or even self-protection. Rather than a coercive homogeneity, this way of self-sacrifice promotes a kind of pluralistic unity that recognizes difference, honors the less (conventionally) honorable, and values members on their own terms (see Rom 12:1-12; 1 Cor 12:12-26).

- It sets the world free from sin. Paul stresses the redemption that comes through Christ's death as a freely given "ransom" (Rom 3:24)—that is, a payment that liberates the world and its inhabitants from the power of sin. Paul associates "sin" with a cosmic force at work in the present evil age to destroy, degrade, or devour. In Paul's worldview, Christ's death has set the cosmos free from sin's power "once and for all" (see Rom 6:5-11). Thus the cross secures a new world order based on neither merit nor ethnicity. It's a world order that prevails wherever it's received as a free gift.

- It promises life out of death. It's striking that Paul has more to say about Jesus's death than about his resurrection. Yet God's power to bring life out of death hangs in the air throughout his letters. Paul's convinced that, as the present evil age gives way to "new creation," God's resurrection power is palpably at work—not just on Easter, but in those whose lives *reflect* the liberation Christ's saving death has secured.

In all these ways, Paul thinks of the passion as the defining moment in salvation history. Jesus's death and resurrection, he maintains, have decisively secured the destiny of the cosmos, which is liberation from evil. For Paul, the cross exemplifies the kind of full-throttle faithfulness to God that will mark those who trust that the messianic age is unfolding in their midst (see Gal 2:19; Rom 6:1-11). Rather than defending or safeguarding his strength, Paul suggests, Christ put human weakness on full display, entrusting it to a God who secures life even out of death.

Paul and "New Creation"

Paul cares deeply about how believers reflect the "new world order" that prevails in the messianic age. They belong, he says, to the "new creation" (Gal 6:15), and his letters consistently hold their audiences to ethical standards that reflect their life "in Christ." Sometimes, he praises them for their devotion to one another and to their partnership in the gospel. In other cases, he rebukes them for acting according to the standards of the present evil age, which is marked by discord, division, and death. For those "in Christ," Paul insists, "There is neither Jew nor Greek; there is neither slave nor free; nor is there male and female" (Gal 3:28). All human distinction and stratification—by religion, ethnicity, socioeconomic status, and gender—falls away for those who are united "in Christ."

On ethno-religious distinction, Paul and Acts agree that the law's separation of Jew from Gentile belongs to the old world order (see Acts 15:9; Gal 2:6; Rom 10:12). For Jews in the diaspora, Torah played a central role in safeguarding Jewish identity and social cohesion through its "boundary markers" (e.g., circumcision, dietary laws, and their sacred calendar). These practices set Jews apart from their Greco-Roman neighbors and bound them to one another as a distinctive ethnic group. Paul's vision for the "new creation" relegate such concerns to the old age that's "passing away" (see 1 Cor 7:31).

On socioeconomic distinction, Paul's vision for the "new creation" entails and also challenges the way things are. When he sends a slave named Onesimus back to his owner, Paul asks that Philemon consider him "a dearly loved brother" (Phlm 16), using familial language that subverts the stratified social order. Paul also assails the Corinthians for their meal practices that reflect culture's divide between the "haves" and the "have-nots" (see 1 Cor 11:17-34).

On gendered distinction, the question is more complex, since many associate Paul, either approvingly or not, with the prohibition against female church leadership. But as we'll see in chapter 14, the passages that restrict church office to men probably weren't written by Paul. Indeed, Acts and Paul's (authentic) letters suggest that Paul's views on gender, too, challenged cultural views about female inferiority.

Consider Paul's message in context: Greco-Roman writers generally took for granted that women's bodies were incomplete versions of the male. Many thought that gender formation had to do with arrested development in the womb—as if being a woman arises out of a fetus's "failure to thrive"! As a result, women were seen as less than fully human, a view akin to the notion that enslaved Africans in America counted as three-fifths of a person.

Contrast this view with reports in Acts and Paul's letters about the role of women in early Christian gatherings. Though Acts mostly features Paul's interaction with men, we've already heard about a female merchant named **Lydia** who leads believers in Philippi (Acts 16:11-15, 40). In fact, Paul's letter to the Philippians names two other women—**Euodia** and **Syntyche**—as his "coworkers" in spreading the gospel message (Phil 4:2-3).

Paul also greets several female leaders when he writes to the Roman church. There, he commends a woman named **Phoebe**, whom he calls a "servant"—the same word in Greek for "deacon" (*diakonos*: Rom 16:1). He also mentions **Prisca** among his "coworkers" (Rom 16:3) and **Junia**, who's "prominent among the apostles" (Rom 16:7). Scholars continue to debate the question of just how egalitarian Paul was, but the evidence indicates that he readily named women as "apostles," "deacons," and "coworkers."

Later generations would develop Pauline traditions in different directions. Within the NT, we'll see that the Pastoral Letters, written in Paul's name but not by the apostle himself, restrict women's church leadership in explicit ways and sometimes through bizarre claims. But other writings such as the Acts of Paul and Thecla spin Paul's story in a way that lends prominence to a female apostle and companion.

WHAT THEN CAN WE SAY ABOUT THE HISTORICAL PAUL?

A review of Acts and Paul's undisputed letters yields a fairly robust list of features we can associate with the "historical Paul." Here's a short list:

- He was an educated, Hellenized Pharisee who pivoted from zealous opposition of a Jewish messianic movement to ardent advocacy for it.

- The transition happened when he became convinced, through a personal "revelation," that the Jesus who was crucified by Roman authorities had been raised from the dead by the power of God.

- He traveled widely throughout the Roman Empire, convincing many Gentiles (and likely some Jews) that the messianic age had begun and that God's son would soon return to preside over a "new creation" marked by justice and righteousness.

- Together with Jerusalem-based leaders, he forged a middle-ground understanding of the role of Jewish law for non-Jewish believers. Retaining its ethical concerns, especially for the poor and marginalized, Paul thought the "boundary markers" found in Torah didn't pertain to Gentile believers.

- He wrote letters, mostly to communities he'd helped to establish (Romans is an exception). The NT contains at least seven of them.

- His thoroughly Jewish vision of the "new creation" established by Jesus the Messiah devalued identity markers linked to religion, socioeconomic status, and even gender and embraced a new pluralistic identity shared by those "in Christ."

- His message wasn't always received favorably—either by religious leaders or by Roman officials. In fact, other sources report that he shared Jesus's fate of execution at the hand of imperial authorities.

Review and Reflect

- What changed, for Paul, as a result of his "revelation" of the risen Jesus? What remained the same?

- Reflect on the various ways Paul understood the saving power of the cross. How do they make sense in light of his Jewish apocalyptic thought? How do they challenge conventional notions of strength and victory?

HOW WILL WE READ PAUL'S LETTERS?

To read Paul's letters on their own terms, as first-century messages crafted for believing communities, we'll keep several features in mind.

The Genre of Ancient Letter-Writing

Paul used—and adopted—the convention of letter-writing to interpret the gospel for the audiences he addressed. Few people hand-write letters these days, but we do use e-mail, text messaging, and various forms of social media to express our views. Perhaps without even noticing, we follow certain rules: tweets are limited to 280 characters, and "u" is an acceptable spelling for "you" in text messages but not (I remind students) in an e-mail.

Literary evidence from the first century shows that ancient letters generally followed rules of their own, including this basic structure:

1. Sender: In place of a return address or "from" line, ancient letter-writers identified themselves by name and often by social position.

2. Addressee: Next comes what we call a "salutation," which names the letter's intended recipient.

3. Greeting: Conventions in ancient letter-writing include a brief message of greeting, usually including well-wishes to the audience.

4. Thanksgiving: Often, the letter writer begins the body of the letter by conveying gratitude for the relationship or for something the recipient has done.

5. Body: This is the main, and usually longest, part of the letter and generally combines information with a request. If the writer wants to persuade someone to do something, you'll find that argument here.

6. Closing: Ancient letters close with a standard blessing, which sometimes follows personal greetings to members of the household or community.

Paul's letters follow this format quite closely. (See Figure 11.9.) But they also stand out in a couple of important ways. For one thing, most of Paul's letters *name at least one coauthor.* In 1 Corinthians, it's **Sosthenes**; in 2 Corinthians, Philippians; in Philemon, it's **Timothy**; 1 Thessalonians adds **Silvanus** to the Paul-Timothy duo; and Galatians is sent by Paul and an even more expansive group: "all the brothers and sisters [who are] with me" (Gal 1:2). In fact, among the letters we're confident Paul actually wrote, only Romans claims him as solo sender. What does this pattern of coauthorship indicate? For all Paul's bravado, he crafts his message as part of a unified front. Pay close attention, when we read the letters themselves, to just how often Paul mentions coworkers or others who join in his apostolic efforts.

Second, while ancient letters typically express gratitude, Paul *expands the thanksgiving section* of every letter except Galatians, where it's omitted. Paul uses the section to affirm God's active work among and through his audience. He writes of the fellowship he enjoys with them, the joy they bring him, and the testimony they offer the world, in both word and deed—sometimes through suffering. This pattern, too, serves a strategic rhetorical purpose. Beginning most letters with an elaborate expression of appreciation builds Paul's relational authority. Like a parent's inclination to praise first and instruct second, Paul's opening note of gratitude paves the way for specific guidance about the community's conduct.

FIGURE 11.9: ANCIENT LETTER WRITING

Sometime in the second century CE, a young man named Apion enlisted in the Roman army and later wrote his father this letter, probably through dictation to a professional writer:

> Apion to his father and Lord Epimachos: many good wishes. First of all I hope that you are in good health and that things are going well for you and my sister and her daughter and my brother. I thank the Lord Serapis for saving me right off when I was in danger at sea. When I arrived at Misenum, I received three gold pieces from the Emperor as road money, and I'm doing just fine. Please write me a line, my lord father, about your own well-being, second about that of my brother and sister, and third so that I may devotedly greet your hand, because you brought me up well and I may therefore hope for rapid promotion, the gods willing. Give my regards to Capiton and my brother and sister and Serenilla and my friends. I'm sending you my little portrait through Euktemon. My new Roman name is Antonius Maximus. All my best.
> (See https://earlychurchhistory.org/communication/letter-writing-in-the-ancient-world/)

YOUR TURN: What elements from Paul's letters do you find in this ancient letter? Imagine life without a smartphone or e-mail. What role might letters play in "distance relationships" like these?

Other People's Mail

It's obvious by now that Paul wasn't writing to us, and his letters reveal just one side of an ongoing conversation begun in person. (Romans, again, is an exception to this rule.) In many cases, Paul knows members of his audience by name, since he's sometimes spent months living and working among them.

The relational nature of the letters reminds us that they aren't statements of refined doctrine or even universal teachings. They're inherently subjective, emotionally tinged messages intended to persuade hearers about how to understand and live according to the "good news" about Jesus Christ. But the letters don't tell the whole story, nor do they provide direct access to points of view other than Paul's.

Scholars use the term **mirror reading** to describe inferences that help identify those points of view. Here's an example of how this reading strategy works. When Paul writes to the Corinthians about Christ's bodily resurrection (1 Cor 15), scholars think he's challenging those who've spiritualized both Christ's resurrection and their own. Why do we come to this conclusion? Here are a few examples from the text that inform this view:

- "So if the message that is preached says that Christ has been raised from the dead, then how can *some of you say*, 'There's no resurrection of the dead'?" (1 Cor 15:12, emphasis added). Paul seems to combat the view, held by some of the Corinthians, that denies Jewish expectation for a general and bodily "resurrection of the dead."

- "But *someone will say*, 'How are the dead raised? What kind of body will they have when they come back?'" (See 1 Cor 15:35, emphasis added.) Here, Paul addresses skeptics whose worldview is likely shaped by the science of the day.

In both cases, Paul uses a rhetorical strategy called a **diatribe**, which cites the point of view he means to recalibrate. When Paul writes this way, we catch a glimpse of the other side of the conversation, even if only through Paul's expression of it.

Since we don't have direct access to Paul's conversation partners, we have to exercise caution about taking Paul's portrait of them at face value. Haven't we all found ourselves misunderstood or misrepresented, especially by those who think we're wrong? We'll bear in mind, then, that Paul's letters offer a one-sided account of the conversation to which they belong.

"Word on Target"

Admitting there's much we *don't* know about Paul's conversation partners injects a healthy humility into our third interpretive strategy as well. Already, we've used the phrase "word on target" to highlight the contextual nature of the Gospels. But originally, it was used to remind readers that Paul's letters first addressed real people in concrete life circumstances.

Especially since the Protestant Reformation and Luther's influential reading of Paul, many have tried to synthesize Paul's thought into something like a systematic theology, sometimes reducing Paul's message to one main idea. Luther thought Paul was mostly concerned with salvation by grace through faith alone. Others have claimed that Paul was a mystic whose letters lay out what it means to be "in Christ." Still others have emphasized Paul's interest in promoting social order. Those who try to determine the essence of Paul's teachings, though, often do so by ignoring most of what the apostle has to say.

Let's be honest: Paul wasn't a monk living in a cell, writing out a coherent theological treatise untouched by the messiness of life as we know it. He also shows little interest in producing a self-consistent, rationally defensible set of teachings. Instead, he addresses communities living at the cusp of the messianic age. More than anything, he wants them to negotiate a way of living together in the world that bears witness to Jesus's messiahship. They are, as he puts it more than once, the "body of Christ" in the world (see Rom 12; 1 Cor 12).

In one of his letters to the Corinthians, Paul explains his missionary strategy this way: "I have become all things to all people, so I could save some by all possible means" (1 Cor 9:22). For Paul, the one constant lies in the gospel: that is, the "good news" that in Christ, God's renewal of the world has begun. Being "all things to all people" doesn't mean compromising the core of who he is and what he believes, but it does mean expressing his message in terms that reflect the contingent settings of different audiences. As we study the letters, we'll explore those circumstances and how they shape the content of Paul's letters.

Messianic Community

A final interpretive strategy grows out of Paul's core conviction that Jesus's death and resurrection have inaugurated the messianic age. As a result, he says that those who are "in Christ" inhabit that new epoch, even as the present evil age fades from view. For Paul, time is short: the coming end of evil looms near, as judgment will soon bring salvation to the faithful and triumph for God's life-giving power.

This schema positions those who are "in Christ" as a messianic community. In Paul's view, that means their life together should reflect the divine priorities associated with the new creation: righteousness, justice, and peace. For Paul, living in right relationship with God and others isn't mainly about going to heaven when you *die*; it's about showing the world what it means to *live* as residents of God's reign. He has a lot to say, then, about behavior, because he thinks it should reflect that reign, which is gaining a foothold among believers on earth. Pauline ethics are inherently eschatological.

This overarching concern means we'll read Paul's letters with a keen interest in their vision for a communal life that puts on display the "new creation" God has begun in Christ. Of course, the communities he wrote to had their strengths and weaknesses, and the letters are rather clear about both. But each one aims to encourage and instruct believing communities that would show the world what the new life "in Christ" looks like.

SUMMARY

This orientation to Paul and his letters has highlighted several features of his apostolic mission and its "paper trail" in today's New Testament. There's a lot we don't know about Paul, but his influence in the life of the church—from its first generation until today—is beyond question. Our overview of his authentic letters lays important groundwork for the more detailed study that will follow in the next two chapters. There, we'll pay close attention to the particular ways in which Paul navigates his pluralistic setting, interpreting the good news of a Jewish Messiah for both Gentiles and Jews living throughout the first-century Mediterranean world.

Review and Reflect

- List and explain the four strategies we'll use to study Paul's letters.

- Reflect on the task of listening in on a one-sided conversation. What can we learn by hearing only one voice?

GO DEEPER

Boyarin, Daniel. *A Radical Jew: Paul and the Politics of Identity*. Contraversions: Critical Studies in Jewish Literature, Culture, and Society. Berkeley: University of California Press, 1994.

Elliott, Neil, and Mark Reasoner. *Documents and Images for the Study of Paul*. Mineapolis: Fortress, 2012.

Harrill, Albert. *Paul the Apostle: His Life and Legacy in Their Roman Context*. Cambridge: Cambridge University Press, 2012.

Nanos, Mark D., and Magnus Zetterholm, eds. *Paul within Judaism: Restoring the First-Century Context to the Apostle*. Minneapolis: Fortress, 2015.

Pascuzzi, Maria. *Paul: Windows on His Thought and His World*. Winona, MN: Anselm Academic, 2014.

Sanders, E. P. *Paul and Palestinian Judaism*. Philadelphia: Fortress, 1977.

Chapter Twelve

What Does It Mean
to Be "in Christ"?
Paul's "Word on Target"

CONVERSATION STARTERS

- How does Paul's apocalyptic worldview shape his message to each community?

- What kind of relationships do these letters reflect? In what ways do Paul's messages grow out of those relationships?

- What elements of Paul's message stay the same across these letters?

- What does it mean to be "in Christ" in these letters?

- What's the relationship, in Paul's view, between believing communities and the wider Greco-Roman culture?

Now that we've explored Paul's life story and worldview in broad terms, it's time to get specific. What do his letters reveal about Paul's apostleship and his relationship to the communities to whom he writes? The next two chapters examine in detail Paul's ongoing conversations with those who are "in Christ" and his views on how these (mostly) Gentile believers might share in the decidedly Jewish "good news" about God's Messiah named Jesus.

This chapter will follow the chronology provided earlier as we discuss each of the following authentic Pauline letters: 1 Thessalonians, Philippians, Philemon, and 1 and 2 Corinthians. (We'll turn to Galatians and Romans in the next chapter.) In each case, we'll consider the letter's setting—within both the Roman Empire and Paul's missionary career—as a backdrop to the message it contains. Though there's plenty of overlap among the letters' content, we'll read each letter as a "word on target," deliberately crafted for its audience.

Here's a snapshot of each letter's defining message:

- 1 Thessalonians: The Eschatological Letter

- Philippians: The Joyful Letter

- Philemon: The Liberating Letter

- 1 Corinthians: The Cruciform Letter

- 2 Corinthians: The Reconciling Letter

1 THESSALONIANS: THE ESCHATOLOGICAL LETTER

Like the Gospel of Mark, 1 Thessalonians is likely the earliest in its NT family of Paul's letters. Like Mark, it conveys the most urgent sense of Jesus's coming, which seems in this letter to be just around the corner (see e.g., 1 Thess 1:29; 3:13). As Paul writes to believers at Thessalonica, he reviews the apocalyptic scheme he thinks is unfolding before their eyes and urges them to wait expectantly for the judgment day, when Jesus will "rescue [them] from the coming wrath" (1 Thess 1:10). That rescue—salvation itself—courses through this letter.

Setting

In Paul's day, Thessalonica was the capital of the region known as Macedonia, the northern part of modern-day Greece. (See Figure 12.1.) Located at an important crossroads and boasting an impressive port, the bustling city was home to a cosmopolitan population of around one hundred thousand. Both literary and archeological remains confirm Thessalonica's atmosphere of religious pluralism. There, Jewish synagogues appeared alongside temples for ancient deities such as Serapis, Isis, and Osiris.

Acts says that Paul first visited the city during his second missionary journey, probably in the late 40s CE. As Luke tells the story, Paul first shares the message about Jesus's messiahship in the Jewish community gathered at their synagogue, explaining the necessity of Jesus's suffering by citing Jewish scripture (Acts 17:2-4). Though "some were convinced and joined Paul and Silas" (Acts 17:4), Luke writes, others reported Paul to imperial officials for

FIGURE 12.1: MACEDONIA AND ACHAIA (THESSALONICA, PHILIPPI, CORINTH, EPHESUS)

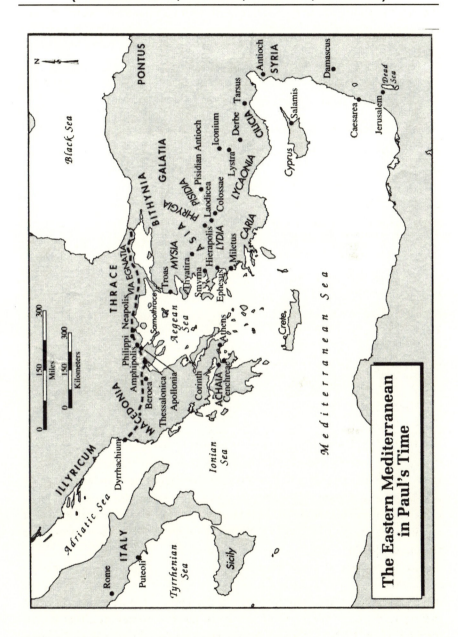

The Eastern Mediterranean in Paul's Time

the treasonous act of naming "someone else as king: Jesus" (Acts 17:7). After all, in the Roman Empire, religious pluralism had its limits: ultimate loyalty, officials insisted, belonged to Caesar.

The letter itself hints at the harassment Paul's audience faced for devotion to Jesus—not Caesar—as Lord. Paul praises the example of the Thessalonians' faithfulness to God throughout the region (1 Thess 1:7-9), a faithfulness that means, like Paul himself (1 Thess 2:2), they've suffered reprisal from neighbors (1 Thess 2:14-15). Paul doesn't specify the root cause of this opposition, but it likely arises from their failure to conform to cultural expectations of religious and political devotion.

But Paul isn't strident or combative toward popular culture in this letter. Indeed, scholars note that his moral instructions borrow freely from philosophical wisdom that's current in the first-century Mediterranean world. When he writes, "Live quietly, mind your own business, and earn your own living" (1 Thess 4:11), for instance, Paul invokes pragmatic advice from **Epicurean** and **Stoic** thought. (See Figure 12.2.) He also strikes a pluralistic tone by encouraging Thessalonian believers to behave "appropriately toward outsiders"—that is, not to rile up their neighbors deliberately. He takes the "winning friends and influencing people" approach, rather than mocking or degrading nonbelievers.

The Message: The Coming "Day of the Lord"

This letter builds on the personal relationship forged with Thessalonian believers when Paul first visited the city. It's something of a follow-up memo, meant to encourage the Thessalonians' countercultural witness to the gospel. Readers acquainted with Paul's writings are sometimes surprised to find little in this letter that *sounds* like Paul: there's no cross or grace or mention of the Jewish law. What *does* the letter contain? Paul's message has two main parts: first, the apostle makes a deliberate case for his relational authority; second, he uses this authority to instruct those "in Christ" to be "blameless in holiness" (1 Thess 3:13) as they await the "day of the Lord" (1 Thess 5:2). As a whole, the letter looks forward with bated breath to Christ's coming and the eschatological salvation it will bring.

Greeting and Thanksgiving

First Thessalonians reads, in part, like the kind of report card your parents might put on your refrigerator. This community, Paul makes clear, has shown exemplary faithfulness to the gospel. In the greeting, Paul names coauthors **Timothy** and **Silvanus** (1 Thess 1:1). He then adds an extended message of

FIGURE 12.2: PAUL AND POPULAR PHILOSOPHY

Throughout his letters, Paul seems to echo familiar teachings from broader Greco-Roman culture. When he encourages the Thessalonians to "live quietly, mind your own business, and earn your own living" (1 Thess 4:11), Paul's words resonate with philosophical writings such as these:

- "Protection from other men . . . in its purest form comes from a quiet life withdrawn from the multitude." (Epicurus, "Principal Doctrines")

- "Be for the most part silent, or speak merely what is necessary, and in few words." (Epictetus, *Handbook*)

YOUR TURN: What's the relationship between Paul's message and the popular culture of his day? What's the relationship between Paul's instructions and popular culture today?

gratitude (1 Thess 1:2-10), praising the Thessalonians' "faith, . . . love, and and hope" (1 Thess 1:3) and calling them "imitators of us and of the Lord" (1 Thess 1:6). In the face of suffering, they've become "an example to all the believers in Macedonia and Achaia" (1 Thess 1:7); their reputation for faithfulness spans modern-day Greece.

Paul ends this opening section by reminding the Thessalonians of their two-staged conversion. As Gentiles, they "turned to God from idols . . . [to serve] the living and true God" (1 Thess 1:9). The first shift has pivoted religious loyalties *away* from the diverse religious landscape of the Greco-Roman world (see chapter 2) and *toward* exclusive allegiance to the one (Jewish) God. This stage constitutes, in Paul's view, a necessary step on the way to calling a Jewish man named Jesus both Lord and Christ.

The second shift, though, is what makes the Thessalonians believers. Besides devotion to the Jewish God, they've bought in to Paul's apocalyptic framework and now await "his Son from heaven . . . the one who will rescue us from the coming wrath" (1 Thess 1:10). Paul says later that "the Lord himself will come down from heaven" (1 Thess 4:16; also 3:13; 5:2) to bring salvation to those who are "in Christ." The rest of the letter unfurls as a charter for what that life "in Christ" means for these believers.

"Like a Nursing Mother"

Throughout this letter, Paul depicts his relationship to the Thessalonians in intimate, even familial, terms. Indeed, the first two chapters conjure up memories of his earlier visit and remind them they're never far from his mind.

First, Paul fondly recalls his time in Thessalonica, saying his "visit . . . wasn't a waste of time" (1 Thess 2:1). He reminds them that neither he nor his partners in ministry cowered when they met opposition, since they meant to please God rather than humans. They were also financially independent so they wouldn't burden Thessalonian believers (1 Thess 2:9).

That independence, though, didn't signal emotional distance: quite to the contrary. Paul's gentle care for them is akin to that of a parent. He's both like a "nursing mother caring for her own children" (1 Thess 2:7) and like a father (1 Thess 2:11). Paul anchors his missionary zeal in compassionate, rather than coercive, strategies. (See Figure 12.3.)

Even while he's away, Paul says the Thessalonians remain "in our hearts" (1 Thess 2:17). Unspecified obstacles have prevented his return (he says "Satan stopped us"), but Paul has sent Timothy both "to strengthen and encourage" believers (1 Thess 3:2) and to check in on their life together "in Christ." The verdict? It's overwhelmingly positive, and Paul prays that things will continue in such a fruitful direction (1 Thess 3:12–13).

"Blameless in Holiness"

Paul's prayer for the Thessalonians' love and holiness signals what's on his mind as he pivots toward the conduct that befits their life together. His call to holiness is rooted in Jewish tradition, where Torah instructs people to "be holy" because God is holy (e.g., Lev 11:45; 19:2; 20:7). For his Gentile audience, Paul interprets holiness in terms that sound a lot like **Stoic** philosophy: "learn how to control your own body in a pure and respectable way," he writes (1 Thess 4:4). For Paul, that means not mistreating or taking advantage of others (1 Thess 4:6). Paul also praises the broad impact of the Thessalonians' "loving deeds . . . throughout Macedonia" (1 Thess 4:10), adding only that they should "do so even more" (1 Thess 4:11).

But as we noted in the last chapter, Paul's ethics—his concern for holiness and love—are rooted in his eschatology: the end is coming soon, and with it, the day of judgment. And it's this concern that dominates the rest of the letter. Apparently, some Thessalonian Christians are anxious about the eternal salvation of loved ones who've died. They've been told that the day of the Lord's coming is near, but they're worried that only those who're still alive will reap its rewards. Paul's eager to reassure them that "the dead in Christ will rise first" (1 Thess 4:16 NRSV) to stand before God's designated judge.

If you're familiar with popular notions of "rapture" in our world today, Paul's words may seem to confirm them. After all, Paul says that "we who are . . . still around will be taken up . . . in the clouds to meet with the Lord

FIGURE 12.3: PAUL AS "MOTHER"?

Despite his reputation in some circles as a misogynist, Paul uses decidedly feminine metaphors to convey his authority over the Thessalonian community. Not surprisingly, contemporary feminist scholarship has directed increased attention to this motif. (See, for instance, Beverly Roberts Gaventa, *Our Mother Saint Paul* [Louisville, KY: Westminster John Knox, 2007].)

But consider this prayer written by a medieval archbishop of Canterbury named Anselm:

O St. Paul where is he that was called
   the nurse of the faithful, caressing his sons?
Who is that affectionate mother who declares everywhere
   that she is in labor for her sons?
Sweet nurse, sweet mother,
who are the sons you are in labor with, and nurse,
but those whom by teaching the faith of Christ you bear and instruct? . . .
And if in that blessed faith we are born and nursed by other apostles also,
it is most of all by you,
for you have labored and done more than them all in this;
so if they are our mothers, you are our greatest mother.

(*The Prayers and Meditations of St. Anselm*, trans. Benedicta Ward [London: Penguin, 1973], 152)

YOUR TURN: What does Paul's use of feminine imagery suggest to you? How does Anselm develop this imagery?

in the air" (1 Thess 4:17). (See Figure 12.4.) But Paul doesn't use the word *rapture*. Nor does he say anyone will be "left behind" to suffer cataclysmic destruction of the world. He simply offers a pastoral reassurance that "those who have died" will secure salvation "at the Lord's coming" (1 Thess 4:15). It's as if he says, "Don't worry, Grandma goes first, but you'll be reunited in the end."

To this word of comfort, Paul adds a measure of caution against trying to pinpoint exactly when this day will come. Paul's last main point is that the Lord will arrive "like a thief in the night" (1 Thess 5:2)—that is, unannounced and when people have been lulled into complacency. The only warning sign he names is the catch phrase "peace and security" (1 Thess 5:3), words associated in Paul's context with the Pax Romana. (See Figure 12.5.). But it's also a timeless phrase Hebrew prophets used to critique the propaganda of unjust rulers (Jer 6:14; Ezek 13:10). Those who place their faith in such measures, he insists, find themselves ill-prepared for God's ultimate verdict.

FIGURE 12.4: WHAT'S "THE RAPTURE"? WHO'S "LEFT BEHIND"?

In the book *Left Behind* by Tim LaHaye and Jerry Jenkins, millions of people are "raptured" to heaven, leaving loved ones and chaos in their wake. Though the novel is fiction, it reflects a theological view known as dispensationalism, the view that history is marching through a series of epochs (or "dispensations") toward Christ's reign on earth. It's a complex and modern scheme that's based on certain interpretations of certain texts. First Thessalonians 4:16-17 supplies the concept of "rapture," even though the term doesn't appear there: "This is because the Lord himself will come down from heaven with the signal of a shout by the head angel and a blast on God's trumpet. First, those who are dead in Christ will rise. Then, we who are living and still around will be taken up together with them in the clouds to meet with the Lord in the air. That way we will always be with the Lord."

In the novel, believers are "taken up" from their daily lives, leaving behind the unfaithful, who have seven years to get their lives in order before final judgment. But as many scholars note, such an interpretation of Paul's writing misses its contextual meaning. In Roman imperial terms, the meeting with the Lord is like an official welcome for a foreign "head of state," who arrives to visit the host's country, not to whisk the host away to a far-off land. This reading also fits with Paul's apocalyptic eschatology, which looks forward to the renewal of creation, not its violent destruction.

YOUR TURN: Read N.T. Wright's blog post "Farewell to the Rapture": ntwrightpage.com/2016/07/12/farewell-to-the-rapture. Choose and respond to one of the questions he poses at the end.

Conclusion

In closing, Paul issues a final appeal to a community that awaits "Christ's coming" (1 Thess 5:23). The themes of holiness and love show up again here, as does a rare allusion to Jesus's earthly teaching: "Make sure no one repays a wrong with a wrong, but always pursue the good for each other and everyone else" (1 Thess 5:15). A concluding reference to the gathered community and the "holy kiss" (1 Thess 5:26; cf. Rom 16:16; 1 Cor 16:20; 2 Cor 13:12) provides a snapshot of the Thessalonians' life together.

Review and Reflect

- How does Paul's interest in the Lord's coming affect his message to the Thessalonians? Give two examples.

- Reflect on Paul's conversation with the Thessalonians' pluralistic setting. How does he both engage different traditions and clarify his own worldview?

FIGURE 12.5: "PEACE AND SECURITY" THEN AND NOW

Scholars have noted that Paul subtly challenges Roman ideology when he says that promises of "peace and security" are signs of coming judgment. One ancient historian expresses the founding of the Roman Empire this way: "On that day [that is, when the empire was established] there sprang up once more in parents the assurance of safety for their children, in husbands for the sanctity of marriage, in owners for the safety of their property, and in all men the assurance of safety, order, peace, and tranquility" (Velleius Paterculus, *Compendium of Roman History*, II. 103.5).

But Rome's "peace and security" came at a great cost to those whose lands were subjected to military conquest and occupation. Notably, Thessalonica had gained "free colony" status because the city participated in the destruction of Philippi. Paul thus suggests that the "peace and security" they've gained isn't consistent with life "in Christ," whose peace entails human well-being, not human subjugation.

YOUR TURN: Reflect on the phrase "peace and security" in our world today. How and where can you see the promise of "peace and security" legitimizing state-sanctioned violence? What might Paul say to our world?

PHILIPPIANS: THE JOYFUL LETTER

Just as 1 Thessalonians stands out for its focus on the Lord's coming, Philippians registers a distinctively joyful tone. Words such as *joy* and *rejoice* appear sixteen times in four brief chapters. Paul and his coauthor Timothy delight in many things: the Philippians' partnership in the gospel (Phil 1:5-7), their concern for him (Phil 4:10), and even his own suffering (Phil 1:12-18). Indeed, some readers are surprised to learn that this most joyful letter could also be called "the prison letter," since it (like Philemon) was composed from a jail cell (Phil 1:7, 13-14, 17). As we'll see, that combination of joy and suffering isn't a coincidence. Paul's joy erupts not despite his suffering but because of it. (See Figure 12.6.)

Setting

Philippians addresses the first believing community Paul founded in Macedonia, according to Acts 16:11-40. The city itself lay on the **Via Egnatia** and featured a strong Roman presence. Archeological evidence confirms that the imperial cult was alive and well, and ancient writers name Philippi as a favorite retirement spot for Roman soldiers. The Gentile community to whom Paul writes likely included at least some well-connected members, as Paul sends greetings from "Caesar's household" (Phil 4:22).

FIGURE 12.6: PRISON LETTERS

Like Paul, other people of faith have been imprisoned because their witness to the new life "in Christ" brought them into conflict with the prevailing powers-that-be. Like Paul, they view suffering not as something to be avoided but as a channel through which God's power breaks through. Here are two excerpts from contemporary prison letters:

> We have to learn that personal suffering is a more effective key, a more rewarding principle for exploring the world in thought and action than personal good fortune. (Dietrich Bonhoeffer, *Letters and Papers from Prison—Reader's Edition* [Minneapolis: Fortress, 2015])

> The early Christians rejoiced when they were deemed worthy to suffer for what they believed. (Martin Luther King Jr., "Letter from Birmingham Jail" [1963])

YOUR TURN: Learn a bit more about the context of one of these prisoners. What connections can you find between their circumstance and Christian faith, and Paul's?

This cosmopolitan, imperial setting serves as backdrop to Paul's calculated use of cultural discourse to convey his decidedly countercultural gospel message. His instruction about "what really matters" coins a phrase that's a twist on Stoic thought (Phil 1:10). He uses language of "citizenship" to locate believers within God's rule, not Rome's (Phil 1:27; 3:20). He even applies a military term to his description of the congregation (Phil 1:27-28). In each case, Paul's conversation with popular culture reframes well-known concepts to convey his message about Jesus the Jewish Christ.

Though Paul says he's writing from prison, he doesn't say where. In fact, none of his letters mention where he's "done time" (cf. 2 Cor 11:23). Some think Paul wrote Philippians from Rome (the traditional view), while others consider Caesarea (in Palestine) or Ephesus more likely locations. But more than the "where," Paul's concerned about the "why." He offers two answers: in terms of cause (the *sociopolitical* level), he's been arrested for an allegiance to God that likely seemed seditious to imperial officials (Phil 1:13); in terms of purpose (the *theological* level), he's in jail so that the gospel gains a wider hearing (Phil 1:12).

The Message: "Complete My Joy"

Many people recommend Philippians as a fairly easy "way in" to Paul's letters. Not only does it exude joy and heap praise on its readers, but it's also pretty straightforward: you don't have to do much detective work to get at what Paul's saying. But don't let this simplicity fool you. Philippians deftly weaves together joy and suffering, praise and criticism, hope and concern— all in ways intended to strengthen a community devoted to Christ as the un-imperial Lord whose reign will soon arrive in full measure.

Greeting and Thanksgiving

Though Paul names **Timothy** as coauthor (Phil 1:1), he quickly switches to first-person singular in his greeting. The letter's opening section is particularly effusive, as Paul gushes with gratitude for the Philippian community's partnership "in the ministry of the gospel" (Phil 1:5). They've prayed for him, they've paid his expenses, they've offered their love, and they've even suffered for the gospel. As in 1 Thessalonians, Paul looks forward to the "day of Christ Jesus" (Phil 1:6; cf. 1:10), when God will declare decisive victory on earth and deliverance for those found to be "sincere and blameless" (Phil 1:10).

Close readers will detect, though, subtle hints that things aren't all sweetness and light in Philippi. If God has begun a "good work" there, it won't be completed until the "day of Christ Jesus" (Phil 1:6). Paul thinks it's his job to advance this cause: he prays (and instructs them) "so that [they] will be able to decide what really matters" (Phil 1:10). Here, Paul apparently coins a term (*ta diapheronta*) based on Stoic teachings about "what doesn't matter" (Greek: *ta adiaphora*). Paul then spells out the things that do.

"Suffering for Christ's Sake"

The letter's body opens with Paul's interpretation of his imprisonment. On one level, Paul's circumstance falls in the "doesn't matter" category: he contemplates dying in jail and can't decide whether he prefers life or death (Phil 1:21). While his language echoes philosophical treatises on suicide, scholars generally don't think he contemplates ending his own life.

At a deeper level, Paul detects in his imprisonment something that *does* matter, in that his suffering has "advanced the gospel" (Phil 1:12). For one thing, Paul notes that his time with the Praetorian Guard has given his message about the Lord a hearing. What's more, other evangelists have increased their impact in his absence. Their motives may be questionable, he muses, but he rejoices simply that "Christ is proclaimed in every possible way" (Phil 1:18).

Besides his own suffering, Paul cites the Philippians' suffering as evidence that they're living "in a manner worthy of Christ's gospel" (Phil 1:27). Paul's language here redefines their citizenship as residents of an alternative world order shaped by their loyalty to a crucified Lord. For Paul, their identity as believers has less to do with dogma or doctrine than with steadfast devotion to God. Since this kind of citizenship can make them a target of imperial power, Paul sees their suffering as a litmus test for faith that belongs to the things that do matter after all. And apparently, they're passing that test.

"Being United"

Paul's discussion of faithful suffering paves the way for what's really on his mind: community cohesiveness. He tackles this concern from three different angles, perhaps in hopes that at least one will register for his audience. (Alternatively, the letter might combine separate appeals made at different times.) Let's consider each rhetorical tool Paul deploys.

1. Scholars think that Paul quotes an earlier tradition in the **Christ Hymn** that anchors this section (Phil 2:5-11). These poetic verses celebrate Christ's example of self-emptying sacrifice, as well as his exaltation and the universal praise he wins as risen Lord. But if Paul inserts rather than writes this lofty piece, he does so strategically. In the passage that precedes it, he urges the Philippians to be united in mind, heart, and spirit, and he warns against self-interested action (Phil 2:1-4). He presents the hymn, then, as a pattern for their own behavior; they should "adopt the attitude that was in Christ Jesus" (Phil 2:5). What kind of "attitude" does the Christ Hymn illustrate? Christ gave up equality with God to take the form of an obedient slave (cf. Phil 1:1); Christ was also honored in a way that glorified God. Paul uses the Christ Hymn to promote Jesus's example for the community. Like him, they are called to humility; like him, they will "shine like stars in the world" (Phil 2:15).

2. The next chapter gets more specific about an issue that threatens the Philippians' unity. In Paul's abrupt change of tone, some scholars detect a literary seam that shows the "stitching together" of two separate letters into one. Here, the apostle warns the Philippians to "watch out for the 'dogs'" (Phil 3:2). Though he's alluded to opposition vaguely before (e.g., Phil 1:28), he now targets those who insist that non-Jewish believers be circumcised. Perhaps ironically, Paul applies this epithet—commonly used by Jews to describe Gentiles (see e.g., Mark 7:27)—to Jewish

believers. In any case, he thinks their teachings forge division rather than build unity among Jewish and Gentile believers.

Paul addresses this threat by listing his own credentials as a righteous Jew. As Jesus has forfeited his privileged place with God, Paul has forfeited his blameless status under the law and has "lost everything" for Christ (Phil 3:8). As Jesus has been exalted, Paul, too, looks forward to attaining "the resurrection of the dead" (Phil 3:11). His example, then, offers the Philippians a pattern that will lead to their unity (Phil 3:15 NRSV).

3. The third glimpse of Paul's interest in unity appears in a brief passage in which he urges **Euodia** and **Syntyche** to have the "same mind in the Lord" (Phil 4:2 NRSV). Notably, these women have "struggled together" with Paul and, along with **Clement**, belong to a group known as his "coworkers" (Phil 4:3). Even the mention of that struggle may offer a subtle reminder that suffering should build unity, not division.

Conclusion

Paul ends this letter with words of practical encouragement, as well as a "thank-you note" for the tangible support the Philippians have sent his way. He tells them to "rejoice in the Lord always" (Phil 4:4) and to replace worry with prayer; he also encourages them to think about things that are true, honorable, just, and excellent (Phil 4:8; see Figure 12.2). For Paul, their habits of mind and heart go beyond mere philosophy for living. His reminder that "the Lord is near" (Phil 4:5) drives home the eternal import of their conduct.

Finally, Paul walks a thin line between expressing gratitude for the Philippians' financial support on the one hand and insisting that he doesn't need it on the other. When Paul calls their gift "an acceptable sacrifice that pleases God" (Phil 4:18), he prioritizes their disposition of generosity rather than his gain. It's a fitting end to a letter that conveys the palpable joy that comes from trusting God's "good news" wholeheartedly, regardless of the cost.

Review and Reflect

- What's the relationship between suffering and joy in Philippians? Give two examples to explain your answer.

- How does Paul both use and redefine elements of popular culture to convey his message?

FIGURE 12.7: MANUMISSION IN THE ROMAN EMPIRE

The possibility that Paul wants Philemon to release Onesimus from slavery is plausible in its ancient setting. *Manumission*, the act of freeing slaves, was relatively common and happened so often that the Emperor Augustus limited its practice. Slaves who had enough resources could buy their free status as *libertus*, but owners also freed slaves for other reasons such as loyalty or on the death of the slaveholder. Former slaves were known as *libertini* and gained a limited form of Roman citizenship; they could vote and prosper economically, but they couldn't run for office. Children of freed slaves, though, enjoyed full citizenship status.

YOUR TURN: Learn a bit more about Roman slavery. How did it differ from the American practice of enslaving African people?

PHILEMON: THE SLAVERY LETTER

Paul's letter to a slaveholder named **Philemon** is the shortest among the authentic Pauline epistles and the only one directed to an individual. In some ways, it's fairly straightforward. Paul is sending a slave named **Onesimus** back to his owner (Phlm 12). But Paul's message in this letter proves hard to decipher, and interpreters disagree over whether or not Paul expects Philemon to set Onesimus free upon his return. (See Figure 12.7.)

Setting

As with Philippians, Paul writes the letter to Philemon from prison (Phlm 1, 9, 10, 23). Some manuscripts say that Paul is in Rome, but historians find this claim problematic for two reasons. First, Paul's desire to visit Philemon (Phlm 22) doesn't fit his intended itinerary stated elsewhere (Rom 15:22-24). Second, the distance between Rome and Colossae, where Philemon lives, puts Onesimus farther away than is plausible. In any case, Paul sends this appeal to Philemon on behalf of Onesimus, who's served Paul during his imprisonment (Phlm 10).

The Message: "More Than a Slave"

Greeting and Thanksgiving

Though Paul calls Philemon a "dearly beloved coworker" (Phlm 1), he adds others to his list of addressees: a woman named **Apphia** (perhaps Philemon's wife), a "fellow soldier" named **Archippus** (possibly their son), and "the church that meets in your house." Clearly, Paul will make his appeal to Philemon as head of household. But drawing others into the conversation, even only informally, may involve his use of social pressure to convince Philemon to "do the right thing" (Phlm 8).

That said, Paul focuses his message of thanksgiving on Philemon, as the letter shifts to the singular pronoun "you" in Philemon 4. Paul expresses his gratitude to Philemon in familiar language, hailing his coworker's "love and faithfulness" (Phlm 5; see also 7) as well as his "partnership" (Phlm 6). The section's conclusion signals Philemon's leadership position among the faithful in Colossae.

"Welcome Onesimus"

When Paul turns to the question of the slave Onesimus, his language grows notably indirect. As is often true in his letters, Paul bases his request on relational authority. He refuses to command Philemon, saying he'd "rather appeal to you through love" (Phlm 9). He also writes eloquently of his "child Onesimus" (Phlm 10) who's both "useful" (Phlm 11: a play on words, since this is the meaning of Onesimus's name) and a "dearly loved brother" (Phlm 16). Though Paul has pondered keeping Onesimus in his service, he's returning this slave to his owner.

The terms of the return are hard to nail down. Paul wants Philemon to have Onesimus "back forever—no longer as a slave but more than a slave—that is, as a dearly loved brother" (Phlm 15-16). Does Paul intend a change of status for Onesimus, from slave to free man? Or does he just want Philemon to treat this slave with a dignity that conveys his love and faithfulness? We can't know for sure. Elsewhere, Paul discounts distinction among different social groups (Gal 3:27), and the tone of Philemon suggests his implicit request goes beyond "playing nice." Yet, the apostle may be bending over backward in his appeal because Onesimus has robbed Philemon in some way and deserves punishment (see Phlm 18). Regardless, Paul promises a follow-up visit to reaffirm the friendship he hopes this letter will not weaken (Phlm 22).

Review and Reflect

- What evidence from the letter supports the view that Paul wants Philemon to release Onesimus from slavery? What evidence leaves that question open?

- Reflect on what we don't know about this letter. Is it significant? Why or why not?

THE CORINTHIAN CORRESPONDENCE: AN UNFOLDING CONVERSATION

Together, 1 and 2 Corinthians preserve remnants of an on-going dialogue between Paul and the Corinthian believers. Scholars think these two books combine parts of at least three letters, but both letters refer to other exchanges—letters, reports, and visits—that we don't have access to (e.g., 1 Cor 1:11; 5:9; 2 Cor 2:1, 4). Our discussion will follow the twists and turns of this conversation, noting key ways in which Paul interprets Jesus's status as Christ and Lord for this mostly Gentile community.

Setting

First-century **Corinth** was the capital of the Roman province of Achaia (modern-day Greece) and was a thriving melting pot of cultures, religious views, and commercial ventures. Strategically located on a strip of land linking the Achaian peninsula to the mainland (see Figure 12.1), Corinth boasted two ports that made it a regional economic hub. Roman forces had destroyed the ancient Greek city located at Corinth in 146 BCE. In Paul's day, the city rebuilt in its place was only about a hundred years old. As a result, ancient writers note Corinth's reputation for social and economic mobility. That made it hospitable to immigrants, including freed slaves eager to start life afresh.

Hints about Corinth's dominant cultural values appear throughout Paul's correspondence with the community there. As in other cities we've considered, religious and philosophical pluralism was the order of the day. Corinth was home to a small Jewish community that Paul likely visited (see Acts 18:1-18), but Corinthians also worshipped **Isis** (a popular Egyptian goddess), the emperor, and other gods from the Greek pantheon. Add to these diverse religious options the strong influence of Greek philosophies (Stoics, Epicureans, and so on), and you catch a glimpse of the city's diverse array of worldviews.

Besides Corinth's freeform spirituality, ancient writers note that it was a capital for loose living. Scholars question whether or not Corinth was less moral than other Greco-Roman cities, but it is true that ancient writers used the city's name when they coined language relating to commercialized sex. "What happens in Corinth stays in Corinth" may well have been its marketing tagline. (See Figure 12.8.) Besides this licentious standing, Corinth was also known for celebrating sports, arts, and culture in the **Isthmian games** that took place there every two years. In Corinthian society, strength had a lot to do with physique, artistic ability, and socioeconomic status.

FIGURE 12.8: SEX AND MONEY: CORINTH'S REPUTATION

Here are a few examples of the link Athenian authors forged between Corinth and the sex trade:

- Comedian Aristophanes used the term *korinthiazesthai* to communicate the verb "to fornicate" (Fr. 354).

- Playwrights Phileteaerus and Poliochus each titled a work *Korinthiastes* (*The Whoremonger*) (Athenaeus 313c, 559a).

- When the philosopher Plato meant "prostitute," he used the term *korinthia kore*, "a Corinthian girl" (Rest. 404d).

YOUR TURN: Reflect on the relationship between sex and commerce. In light of Paul's views about the messianic age, how might those who are "in Christ" distinguish themselves from wider social practices?

These entrenched values meant that Paul had his work cut out for him. After all, there was little about the city's cultural milieu that fit easily with his apocalyptic notions of a Jewish Messiah who had been executed by Roman officials. Perhaps that's why Paul stayed so long during his first visit to Corinth (eighteen months, according to Acts) in the late 40s CE. He also remained in close contact with the community there, exchanging letters, visiting in person, and sending his coworkers such as **Timothy** and **Titus** to touch base with the Corinthians. Together, the two letters the NT preserves from that protracted exchange show just how complex, and sometimes testy, the relationship could be. Let's listen in.

1 Corinthians: The Cruciform Letter

This epistle reads like a rapid-fire laundry list of concerns ranging from lawsuits (1 Cor 6:1-11) to head coverings (1 Cor 11:2-16) to "speaking in tongues" (1 Cor 14:6-25) to the question of bodily resurrection (1 Cor 15:12-58). Though the topics may seem only loosely related, Paul's "message of the cross" (1 Cor 1:18) is the thematic glue that holds his message together. Both directly and indirectly, Paul explains that Christ's crucifixion is *the* defining event for the Corinthians' life together. Because they're "in Christ," they're called to "follow [Paul's] example" (1 Cor 11:1), just as Paul follows Christ's. That's why we call this Paul's cruciform (or cross-shaped) letter, since the cross emerges as a consistent pattern for believers' conduct across an array of particular practices. As those "on whom the ends of the ages have come" (1 Cor 10:11 NRSV), their "meantime" life together embodies the saving power of the cross for the world to see.

Greeting and Thanksgiving (1 Cor 1:1-9)

Paul strikes a familiar tone as this letter begins, conveying gratitude and praise to the Corinthians. But embedded in this opening section is the subtle challenge to live as "those who have been made holy" and are "called to be God's people" (1 Cor 1:2; literally, "holy ones")—that is, those who are "in Christ" must distinguish themselves from wider culture. In a world that values *economic status*, Paul calls the Corinthians "rich through him in everything"; in a world that prizes erudite *wisdom*, he hints that their "wealth" encompasses a different kind of "knowledge" (1 Cor 1:5); in a world that honors *spiritual gifts*, he relegates their importance to what really matters: the Corinthians' readiness for the coming "day of our Lord Jesus Christ" (1 Cor 1:8). As we shall see, each of these themes plays out elsewhere in the letter.

The thanksgiving culminates with the letter's thesis: Paul appeals for the Corinthians to "agree with each other" and not "be divided into rival groups" (1 Cor 1:10). Already, we've seen in Philippians that Paul think division works at cross-purposes with the gospel; in this letter, he goes into greater detail about the Corinthians' discord and its remedy in the gospel of the crucified Messiah. Our discussion will highlight both the problems in Corinth and the solution Paul prescribes. (Notice that it takes Paul fourteen chapters before he even mentions the resurrection, which is the topic of 1 Corinthians 15.)

"Agree with Each Other" (1 Cor 1:10–4:21)

Paul turns first to the problem of divisions or "cliques" within the believing community. Paul mentions a report from **Chloe's people** that the Corinthians are lining up behind preferred figure heads—among them, Paul, **Apollos**, **Cephas** (Peter), and even Christ (1 Cor 1:11-12). Apparently, the "cult of the personality" is alive and well in Corinth! But rather than vying among competitors, Paul rejects the contest completely, insisting that only Christ is worthy of such devotion and calling both himself and the other apostles God's servants and coworkers (1 Cor 3:5-9).

Interpreters think Apollos may have been more impressive than Paul in terms of public speaking abilities, looks, or charisma. After all, Paul sounds like he's on the defensive. He states rather emphatically that he *didn't* present himself as "an expert in speech or wisdom" (1 Cor 2:1). He also explains he *didn't* intend for faith to "depend on the wisdom of people but on the power of God" (1 Cor 2:5) and even calls the world's wisdom "foolishness to God" (1 Cor 3:19). It's even possible that, in Paul's absence, Apollos has won over some Corinthians to his corner.

Whatever the reality on the ground, Paul combats the emerging pattern of division with what he calls the "message of the cross" (1 Cor 1:18). He reminds the Corinthians that, when he was with them, the cross was all he talked about (see 1 Cor 2:2). Why was this the case? And how does this cruciform message mend the schisms that have appeared among the Corinthians? These chapters flesh out some of the meaning Paul sees in Jesus's horrific death:

- **Rethinking "Wisdom"**

  Paul says the cross shows that "God chose what the world considers foolish to shame the wise . . . [and] what the world considers weak to shame the strong" (1 Cor 1:27). This turns on end conventional notions of wisdom and foolishness, weakness and strength, so that boasting—a chief contributor to the "cult of the personality," in Paul's view—loses its power.

- **Rethinking "Power"**

  As long as people depend on their own ingenuity, they exert leadership that is "worldly wise" and separates the "haves" from the "have-nots." The cross shows what it's like, instead, to depend not on human power but "on the power of God" (1 Cor 2:5). It frames Corinthian leaders as servants, since they "belong to Christ, and Christ belongs to God" (1 Cor 3:23).

- **Rethinking "Judgment"**

  Jesus's execution on a Roman cross reminds believers that the end of the present evil age has not yet come. Paul advises against arrogant judgment—against him or anyone else—since God's ways remain hidden (1 Cor 4:1-6). Only at the "right time" will the Lord "bring things that are hidden in the dark to light" (1 Cor 4:5). Meanwhile, both Paul and his competitors are "managers of God's secrets" (1 Cor 4:1).

Paul concludes this section with a fatherly warning that he's coming soon to see if the arrogance that's been reported to him has subsided (1 Cor 4:14-21). Once again, his authority rests on relationship. His stern message here ends with hope for "a gentle spirit" (1 Cor 4:21).

"Honor God with Your Body" (1 Cor 5:1–14:40)

After the opening concerns about factionalism, Paul turns to a list of issues related to the "body"—in both the individual and collective sense. Here's
a short list of the items on Paul's mind:

- Immoral conduct (mostly, sex)

- Lawsuits (within the community)

- Marriage (and married sex, of course)

- Food (what to eat and how to share it)

- Hairstyles and coverings (varying according to gender)

- Church gatherings (how the spirit shows up)

While some of Paul's guidance is clear, some remains obscure. What does
Paul mean when he tells the Corinthians to "hand this man over to Satan to
destroy his human weakness" (1 Cor 5:5)? Or that "a woman should have
authority over her head, because of the angels" (1 Cor 11:10)? These verses
remind us that we don't have full access to the mind of Paul, even if he does
claim to have the "mind of Christ" (1 Cor 2:16). Still, we can point out several recurrent themes that help us understand Paul's cruciform response to the
Corinthians' troubles. Here are some of the most important ones:

1. **Body Matters**

   Paul wants the Corinthians to know their faith in Christ isn't
   just a spiritual matter; it has grave implications for their *bodily
   conduct*. Throughout this section, Paul frames various appetites—
   from sex and marriage to food and shared meals—in relation to
   the Corinthians' life "in Christ." By way of mirror reading, scholars infer that Paul's conversation partners subscribed to a kind of
   spiritual libertinism: since they were "free in Christ," they might
   have reasoned, how they lived mattered little.

   But Paul doesn't mince words on this point. He rebukes the community for boasting that they tolerate sexual immorality (1 Cor
   5:1-8), but he also warns against rigorous sexual asceticism (1 Cor
   7:1-40). He has a lot to say about meals with unbelieving neighbors
   as well as within the believing community. After all, eating together
   was (and for many, still is) a practice that sealed social bonds and

built community. To honor the "Lord's body and blood" (1 Cor 11:27), for Paul, is to recognize that Christ's life and death infuse believers' bodies with the weighty significance that comes from being "parts of Christ" (1 Cor 6:15).

2. **Freedom for Others**

Another theme that emerges in this chapter has to do with the freedom that comes from being "in Christ." Apparently, some believers interpreted Paul's message in libertarian terms—as in, "you can't tell me what to do!" But Paul carefully recalibrates freedom from restraint as freedom for others. Just because something's permitted, he insists, doesn't mean it's beneficial (1 Cor 10:23). Thus Paul distinguishes between rights and true freedom in Christ.

When it comes to what believers can eat, what they share with others, and even how they participate in worship, Paul suggests that freedom "in Christ" is the freedom to advance others' well-being rather than to insist on one's own entitlement. Paul wants the Corinthians to follow his—and Christ's—examples by shifting their focus from self to others (see 1 Cor 10:33–11:1). Though it may appear as the ultimate human constraint, Christ's death on a Roman cross, for Paul, embodies just this kind of freedom.

3. **Mutual Concern**

As part of the wider Greco-Roman world, Corinthian society deliberately separated the "haves" from the "have-nots" and assigned value accordingly. Paul sees such stratified status and resource-allocation as antithetical to the life "in Christ" believers are called to embody. Some have more food than others, but Paul insists that a "Lord-like supper" (1 Cor 11:20, author's translation) leaves no room for one person to go "hungry while another is drunk" (1 Cor 11:21).

Likewise, his discussion of the church as body of Christ promotes an ethos of mutual concern—especially for those members with "less honor" (see 1 Cor 12:25-26). And rather than exalting those with impressive spiritual gifts, Paul's concern lies squarely with how those gifts affect others, even outsiders. Again, the cross as reconciling act turns on end conventional notions of importance and embodies the solidarity with weakness Paul calls the Corinthians to display.

4. **Eschatological Ethics**

For Paul, Christ's death has brought the beginning of the end of the present world order and its coercive, degrading, and destructive ways. For Paul, the "day of the Lord"—when the scales of justice are set to the right—lies not far from view. As we noted in the last chapter, this eschatological vision anchors Paul's ethics: the Corinthians' bodily conduct, their impact on others, and their concern for the weak all constitute evidence of their fitness for coming judgment. They are those on whom the "ends of the ages have come" (1 Cor 10:11 NRSV). Throughout this section, Paul reminds them of their status as those who've been "made right with God" (1 Cor 6:11) and so are called to reflect that condition even when tested.

Though Paul doesn't explicitly mention the cross in each instance, Jesus's saving death is never far from view. For Paul, Jesus's execution as the Jewish Messiah has already subverted much conventional protocol, and it's up to the church to display the new world order he's established in living color. It's no wonder that Paul works his way, case by case, through these questions, urging the faithful Corinthians to take their cues from the "message about the cross" rather than from wider society.

The "Resurrection of the Dead" (1 Cor 15:1-58)

Only as this cruciform letter draws to a close does Paul turn to the rest of the story: the claim that death has met its match in resurrection. Apparently, some believers have wondered openly about both Christ's resurrection and the general resurrection Paul's taught them will soon follow (see 1 Cor 1:12). Paul tackles this skepticism directly but carefully, laying out his position in several rhetorical moves:

1. Paul summarizes for the Corinthians the "good news" he's proclaimed to them (1 Cor 15:1-11). Notably, he begins not with Jesus's teachings or earthly career but with Christ's death "for our sins in line with the scriptures" (1 Cor 15:3). But he also goes beyond burial to relate Jesus's post-crucifixion appearances—first to the twelve in his closest circle, then to "more than five hundred

brothers and sisters at once" (1 Cor 15:6), then to "James, then to all the apostles" (1 Cor 15:7), and finally to Paul himself (1 Cor 15:8). For Paul, these bona fide reports of the risen Lord substantiate the core claim that Christ did indeed rise from the dead.

2. As with his self-sacrifice, Christ's resurrection is decisive but not exclusive to him. Paul says Christ is the "first crop of the harvest" who rules "until he puts all enemies under his feet" (1 Cor 15:12-34). That is, Christ's own resurrection means that one day soon, all of creation will be released from death-dealing forces. In Paul's view, Christ's resurrection constitutes a turning point, in that his life-out-of-death pattern will soon prevail throughout the cosmos. Jesus's resurrection is simply the "first crop." Soon, those who "belong to Christ" will be raised "at his coming"; and ultimately, death will lose its sting so that "God may be all in all" (1 Cor 15:28).

3. Finally, Paul deals in particulars, tackling a question about the kind of body that will be raised to new life (1 Cor 15:35). His instructions about bodily resurrection flesh out a concept that avoids the problem of decayed, diseased, or dilapidated corpses. (Take heart, he says: no wrinkles or sags will remain at the Lord's coming.) He calls the resurrected form a "spiritual body" and likens it to the difference between a seed and the plant it generates. Both share physicality and DNA, but they look nothing like each other. (See Figure 12.9.)

Paul's discussion of bodily resurrection relies on Jewish scripture more heavily than any other section of the Corinthian correspondence. For one thing, Paul likens Christ to Adam since his resurrection ushers in a new human condition—this time, one marked by life rather than death (1 Cor 15:21-22, 45). Paul also speaks of the fulfillment of Hebrew prophets such as Isaiah (1 Cor 15:54), who dares to promise God's victory even over death.

Why cite Jewish tradition for a Gentile audience? Paul may think the Corinthians have taken the message about Jesus's resurrection as a metaphor for their own spiritual and physical freedom. In response, Paul anchors the gospel message in a tradition that says God works in the course of human history. Thus he elevates the *bodily* resurrection so that it's on par with *bodily* crucifixion. That's good news, he thinks, because it shows that God is still at work in the flesh-and-blood bodies of those who "belong to Christ" (1 Cor 15:23). Thus this concluding chapter lends an exclamation point to the rest of the letter's message that the body matters.

FIGURE 12.9: REINCARNATION IN HINDUISM

Ancient Hindu texts also take up the question of the afterlife but answer it differently. The Bhagavad Gita—arguably the central Hindu sacred tradition—features the revelation of the god Krishna to a warrior named Arjuna. Krishna describes reincarnation this way: "Just as a man discards worn out clothes and puts on new clothes, the soul discards worn out bodies and wears new ones" (2.22).

In Hindu thought, the goal of life is union with the divine Brahman. The way of reunion is known as dharma, and the effects of human choices are called karma. But Hindus take the "long view" when it comes to attaining the liberation (or "moksha") this union entails. That's where reincarnation comes into play. As humans progress toward this union, they're reborn over the span of countless life cycles. It's a way of ensuring consequences—both positive and negative—in the afterlife while holding out hope that every soul might eventually find salvation.

YOUR TURN: Reread 1 Corinthians 15. Reflect on one similarity or one difference between Paul's thought and Hindu reincarnation.

Conclusion

The letter's last chapter draws us into the particular contingencies of the moment, as Paul situates the conversation within his unfolding plans. He mentions the collection he'll take to the Jerusalem church once he passes through town (1 Cor 16:1-3). He notes tentative plans for an extended visit with them (1 Cor 16:5-9). And he encourages a warm reception for other apostles whose work he endorses (1 Cor 16:10-18). Paul signs off with the Aramaic phrase "**marana tha**," which means either "Our Lord, come" or "Our Lord has come."

Review and Reflect

- Identify two problems that Paul diagnoses among the Corinthians, and explain how he addresses those problems.

- Why might Paul place so much more emphasis on the cross than on the resurrection in this letter? Reflect on what you've learned about Corinth and its believing community.

2 Corinthians: The Reconciling Letter

As confident as Paul sounds at the end of 1 Corinthians, the letter that follows it in today's Bible strikes a more tentative tone in his conversation with the same church. Much of 2 Corinthians sounds like a public relations campaign devoted to mending Paul's reputation and relationships there. This rhetorical shift reminds us that Paul's standing among believers could be just as shaky in his own day as it can be in ours.

Let's begin by tracing, as best we can, the ins and outs of this tortuous relationship. In the wake of 1 Corinthians, Paul's dealings with the church at Corinth may have unfolded in this way:

- Paul sent Timothy to Corinth (1 Cor 16:10-11) and received a disturbing report from him while still in Ephesus.

- As a result, Paul decided to visit Corinth, not just after his stay in Macedonia (1 Cor 16:5), but both before and after (2 Cor 1:15-16). This "painful visit" (2 Cor 2:1 NRSV) didn't go well and probably included at least one major confrontation.

- After leaving Corinth, Paul followed up—from either Macedonia or Ephesus—with a letter marked by sadness (2 Cor 1:23–2:4; 7:5-11). Some scholars think 2 Corinthians 10–13 preserves this letter, often called the "letter of tears" (see 2 Cor 2:4).

- Perhaps still reeling from his second visit, Paul changed plans again, sending Titus in his place in order to avoid further relational damage. To Paul's delight, Titus reported that the harsh letter had brought repentance, rather than hardening, to the community (2 Cor 7:6-7).

- Paul then wrote 2 Corinthians (at least chapters 1–9) as a prelude to further reconciliation with the community.

- Possibly, 2 Corinthians 10–13 comprises a later letter that's been tacked on to the first nine chapters. If so, this letter reflects relational backsliding, since Paul sounds as defensive as ever about his apostolic credentials.

- Second Corinthians 6:14–7:1 may preserve a separate exchange as well, since neither the style nor content of this passage fits the rest of the letter.

Put simply, the messiness of the letter's literary composition is matched only by the messiness of Paul's ongoing conversation with the Corinthians. But it also provides a helpful window into Paul's relationship management strategy. Paul relentlessly prioritizes smoothing things over with the Corinthians; he refuses to cut and run. Perhaps that comes from his personal stubbornness. But it's also probably evidence that reconciliation is more than a personal matter for Paul; it's also a theological matter. Paul believes those who are "in Christ" have been given a "ministry of reconciliation" (2 Cor 5:18), and this letter bears witness to that ministry, from his side of the relationship. As we'll see, Paul's rhetorical strategy strikes a delicate balance: he ardently *defends* his own integrity even as he freely *affirms* his audience and the value of the relationship they share. It's a strategy that apparently yields results, at least from time to time.

Greeting and Thanksgiving (2 Cor 1:1-11)

Paul names **Timothy** as this letter's coauthor, a detail that makes sense in light of the sequence of events discussed above. Instead of conventional thanksgiving, Paul begins his message with a prayer to bring the Corinthians comfort (2 Cor 1:3-11). This opening move connects Paul's own troubles and the comfort he's received from God with the Corinthians' circumstance: "if we have trouble," he says, "it is to bring you comfort and salvation" (2 Cor 1:6). Paul's opening lines lay a foundation for the work of mending fences that follows throughout the letter.

"By God's Mercy": Apostolic Defense, Part One (2 Cor 2:12–6:13)

One prong of Paul's strategy of rapprochement has to do with defending his authority, integrity, and conduct as an apostle. He insists that "God is the one who establishes us" and has "sealed us" (2 Cor 1:21–22) in every facet of ministry. Several examples illustrate this part of his rhetorical approach.

First, Paul defends his *change in plans*. Originally, he'd intended to visit Corinth twice—on the way both to and from Macedonia (2 Cor 1:16). He insists that the decision to forego the second visit grew out of his "godly sincerity and pure motives" (2 Cor 1:12) rather than dissemblance. Since the first visit was so disastrous, he says, it made sense to take a time out and compose his message in writing instead of bringing it in person. Paul adds that he meant the (earlier) "letter of tears" both to show his love and to test the Corinthians' obedience (2 Cor 2:4, 9).

Second, Paul defends his *qualifications for ministry*, even when he's not winning any popularity contests. He says God has infused him with the aroma of Christ—a scent that repels some and gives life to others (2 Cor 2:15-16). He's not like those who "hustle the word of God" for a profit (2 Cor 2:17), Paul says. His competence derives not from himself but from God (2 Cor 3:5).

He also defends his (and Timothy's) afflictions as *evidence of authentic ministry*. The more their bodies break down in the face of persecution and trial, the more they're "transformed into . . . [the Lord's] image from one degree of glory to the next" (2 Cor 3:18). Paul uses images of clay jars and earthly tents to stress that their current dwelling in the world isn't their permanent one. Meanwhile these "ministers of God" (2 Cor 6:4) have faced a long list of physical, emotional, and political abuses but have "served with the Holy Spirit, genuine love, telling the truth, and God's power" (2 Cor 6:6-7). In all these ways, Paul aims to convince the Corinthians of the authenticity of his apostleship.

Finally, Paul defends the *reconciling nature of his ministry*. At the heart of this letter lies a passage that provides the theological foundation for his restored relationship to the Corinthians. Here, he states emphatically that those who are "in Christ" belong to God's "new creation" (2 Cor 5:17). And if God has reconciled believers through Christ, they also have a part to play in Christ's ministry of reconciliation. In Paul's apocalyptic worldview, the "new creation" is a realm marked by harmony and joy.

"Prove the Authenticity of Your Love": Apostolic Appeal (2 Cor 6:14–9:15)

If Paul bases his reconciling appeal mostly on his own legitimacy, he also calls on the Corinthians to "open [their] hearts wide too" (2 Cor 6:13). That is, he affirms their partnership with him in the ministry of reconciliation and asks that they, too, display their earnestness. For one thing, he describes the visceral joy with which he received Titus's favorable report about their repentance. He praises the "godly sadness" that led to important changes in "hearts and lives" (2 Cor 7:5-15). This response, in turn, inspires his confidence in them.

Paul also invites the Corinthians to go beyond mere words in their ministry of reconciliation. He devotes two chapters to a financial appeal, making the case for their contributions to an offering for the saints in Jerusalem (2 Cor 8–9). Partly, Paul leverages the competitive zeal of Corinthian culture when he notes the Macedonian churches' generous participation (2 Cor 8:1-6). He also insists the Corinthians' offering will not just benefit the Jerusalem church but will also enrich them "in every way" (2 Cor 9:11). Once again, Paul takes the cultural value of wealth and redefines it as a matter of giving, not getting. And Paul's convinced the Corinthians will pass this test of their commitment to the ministry of reconciliation.

FIGURE 12.10: WHO WERE THE "SUPER-APOSTLES"?

Twice in 2 Corinthians (11:5; 12:11), Paul calls his evangelistic competitors "super-apostles." Who were they, and why does he use the term? Of course, we know these teachers only through Paul's account of them. Given his emphasis on his own weakness and humility, Paul uses the term ironically. They were "super" in their estimation of their own abilities, in their brashness, and in their fan base. In Paul's account, they come across as everything that he's not: glossy, good-looking, smooth-tongued public speakers whose messages drew lots of "likes." They were also profiting handsomely from that popularity.

Notably, we don't learn much about how their teachings differed from Paul's, since he stressed instead their apparent success in contrast with his failure and weakness. His defense lies in his own conduct as a servant-like missionary and his refusal to seek wealth as a reward for the gospel.

YOUR TURN: Reread 2 Corinthians 10–13. What do you learn about the super-apostles? Whom do they remind you of? Why? What's Paul's main concern about them?

"Take Me for a Fool": Apostolic Defense, Part Two (2 Cor 10:1–12:13)

Paul's defensive rhetoric escalates in the letter's three concluding chapters. The pointed rhetoric, along with a sharp focus on detractors called "**super-apostles**" (2 Cor 11:5; 12:11), lead many scholars to think 2 Corinthians 10–13 originally was a different letter. (See Figure 12.10.) As we read it today, though, this concluding apology conveys Paul's clearest expression of how the "power of God" works to legitimize his calling. Here are some ways he defends himself against others' attempts to discredit him:

1. Then as now, Paul had earned a reputation for his literary skills, but some found his physical appearance and speech-making abilities lackluster (2 Cor 10:10). In response, Paul draws attention to the consistent *content* that links his letters with the message he'd delivered in person. He concedes he's "uneducated in public speaking" (2 Cor 11:6); his amateur rank, though, confirms rather than undermines his legitimacy.

2. Paul uses a literary convention called a "**fool's speech**" (see Figure 12.11) to mock the charges against him. Taking on the dramatic persona of fool, Paul freely boasts in character, but about his own weakness rather than his strength. His extensive struggles only showcase that weakness, and through it, the power of God

FIGURE 12.11: THE FOOL'S SPEECH AS RHETORICAL DEVICE (AND STEPHEN COLBERT?)

In the ancient world, the "fool's speech" was a literary device featured in comedic works intended to parody—or poke fun at—others' views. Typically, the fool was depicted as an uneducated, lower-class character whose speeches contained, ironically, more wisdom than the educated elite. Stephen Colbert's *The Colbert Report* features a contemporary example of a "fool" who parodies views he takes to be wrong or dangerous. Notably, Colbert is a committed Catholic whose religious views inform his politics. He has embraced the role of "fool" in ways that connect him to Paul's use of this approach.

YOUR TURN: Watch any clip from *The Colbert Report*, and connect one detail of Stephen Colbert's performance to Paul's own self-representation as a "fool" in 2 Corinthians 10–13.

(2 Cor 10:9). Human foes have beaten and imprisoned him; natural forces have endangered him; and relational stress has demoralized him. All of this, he says, leads him to brag "about my weaknesses" (2 Cor 11:30).

3. Paul says his "visions and revelations from the Lord" (2 Cor 12:1) confirm his access to divine power. He's probably talking about himself when he describes an ecstatic, out-of-body experience that a "man in Christ" had (2 Cor 12:2-5). In any case, he mentions a **thorn in my body** (2 Cor 12:7) that keeps him from being conceited on the basis of spiritual elitism. He doesn't say more about the nature of this thorn, but he does say the struggle it caused brought this message: "My grace is enough for you, because power is made perfect in weakness" (2 Cor 12:9). He concludes his defense by reminding the Corinthians that they have seen the signs of an apostle with their own eyes: "signs, wonders, and miracles" (2 Cor 12:12).

Conclusion (2 Cor 12:14–13:13)

As it appears in the NT today, this letter ends without a clear outcome in view. Paul's not at all sure his attempt to build bridges with this fractured and fractious community will be successful. Even if 2 Corinthians combines two or more letters, this closing message fits the tentative nature of Paul's unfolding conversation with the Corinthian church. Things remained fragile, even in the wake of his best efforts to reconcile. In any case, Paul asks the Corinthians to "put things in order" and "live in peace" (2 Cor 13:11) as they await his next visit (2 Cor 13:1).

SUMMARY

In this chapter, we've considered an array of conversations about what life "in Christ" looks like for believing communities Paul's established. In each case, those churches (and their members) inhabit the meantime reality that Paul has laid out for them. In Christ's death and resurrection, Paul says God established a decisive foothold for the divine reign that will renew all of creation. Therein lies believers' hope. For now, though, they make up the "body of Christ" in a world still subject to conventional values and powers. That's the challenge Paul issues: to order their life together according to different values, and trusting in a different kind of ultimate power. More than just belief in Jesus, Paul engenders an alternative allegiance to a God whose strength appears in weakness, whose glory comes through sacrifice, who affirms the basic dignity of all.

Review and Reflect

- How does Paul work to reconcile his relationship to the community in 2 Corinthians? Give two examples.

- Reread 2 Corinthians 10–13. What makes Paul sound foolish? Why does he embrace the role? Does his strategy work in your view? Why or why not?

GO DEEPER

Callahan, Allen Dwight. *Embassy of Onesimus: The Letter of Paul to Philemon*. The New Testament in Context. Harrisburg, PA: Trinity Press International, 1997.

Crocker, Cornelia Cyss. *Reading 1 Corinthians in the Twenty-First Century*. Harrisburg, PA: T&T Clark, 2004.

Marchal, Joseph. *Philippians: An Introduction and Study Guide; Historical Problems, Hierarchical Visions, Hysterical Anxieties*. T&T Clark's Study Guides to the New Testament. Edited by Benny Liew Harrisburg, New York: T&T Clark, 2017.

McNeel, Jennifer Houston. *Paul as Infant and Nursing Mother: Metaphor, Rhetoric, and Identity in 1 Thessalonians 2:5-8.* Early Christianity and Its Literature 12. Atlanta: SBL Press, 2014.

Wan, Sze-Kar. *Power in Weakness: The Second Letter of Paul to the Corinthians.* The New Testament in Context. Harrisburg, PA: Trinity Press International, 2000.

Chapter Thirteen

How Are Jews and Gentiles Related? Galatians and Romans

CONVERSATION STARTERS

- Why does Paul take such an angry tone in Galatians?

- Who are "the Teachers"? What did they teach? How does Paul respond?

- How does Romans differ from other Pauline letters?

- Who are Paul's conversation partners in Romans?

- How does Paul explain the role of nonbelieving Jews in God's plan of salvation?

To this point, we've considered letters Paul wrote to mostly non-Jewish audiences about what it means to be "in Christ"—that is, to cast allegiance with Jesus the Jewish Messiah. For this "apostle to the Gentiles," the new world order established in Christ's death and resurrection affects every aspect of believers' lives: their conduct as individuals, their common life as the body of Christ (1 Cor 12:27), and their relationship to the wider world. But though Paul's own worldview is decidedly Jewish, the letters we've studied have only hinted at questions about the early Christian movement's relationship to Jewish thought and practice.

In Galatians and Romans, though, those questions play a more central role in Paul's message. Though the audiences of both letters remain mostly Gentile, both engage questions such as how Jewish must Gentile believers be, who counts among the "children of Abraham and Sarah," and how Christ's story relates to Jewish scripture. They're natural questions for a fledgling movement with deep Jewish roots and an expansive evangelizing reach.

Paul's answers to these questions are far from simple. To understand his perspective, we must go beyond quoting a verse here or a passage there. Instead, we'll follow the twists and turns in Paul's unfolding conversations with Jewish tradition, with other Jewish believers in Jesus, and with the (mostly Gentile) communities united around their loyalty to Jesus, the Jewish Messiah.

Partly, the complex responses we'll trace have to do with what's going on in the Galatian and Roman churches. As we'll see, the relational dynamics that lie behind these letters are quite different. In Galatians, Paul counters a group of Jewish Christian evangelists who insist Gentile believers go "all in" as Jews. By contrast, the letter to the Romans asserts the primacy of Jews in God's plan of salvation, perhaps because Jewish believers were being marginalized by Gentiles in the church there. Only by keeping the dialogical nature of these letters in view can we begin to appreciate the ways they tackle questions that continue to inform Jewish-Christian conversations today.

GALATIANS: THE POLEMICAL LETTER

In many ways, Galatians reads like an e-mail dashed off in the heat of the moment, when tempers have flared and the writer should have paused before pressing "send." Paul calls people names ("You irrational Galatians!" Gal 3:1) and wishes his opponents would "castrate themselves" (Gal 5:12). His polemic has two targets. On the one hand, he stares down the apostolic competition, evangelists making the rounds in Galatia while Paul's away. We'll use a contemporary scholar's terminology by calling them the **Teachers**. On the other hand, Paul faults Galatian believers themselves for so easily caving to the Teachers' message. This letter, then, proceeds point by point both to discredit the Teachers and to win back the hearts and minds of those Paul thinks they've duped. As one voice in this three-way conversation, Paul's letter is anything but civil and reminds us that internal disputes (in a community, a family, or a faith tradition) can often be the most brutal in tone. Before we turn to Paul's pointed message, let's situate this letter in its own place and time.

Setting

Paul addresses "the churches in **Galatia**" (Gal 1:2; notice the plural). But scholars aren't sure where these churches were located in the Roman province of that name (see Figure 12.1). Acts recounts Paul's missionary efforts both in the northern region near Ancyra (present-day Ankara)—a region associated with the Galatian ethnic group (see Acts 16:6; 18:23)—and in the south, where such cities as Iconium, Lystra, and Derbe were located (see Acts 14:1-23). In either case, Paul takes for granted that his audience knows him personally and has welcomed him in the past.

Dating the letter is impossible to do with certainty. Some scholars (a minority) think that the Jerusalem visit Paul mentions in Galatians 2:1-10 is separate from and predates the so-called **Jerusalem Council** of Acts 15. This may be the easiest way to explain disparities between Paul's and Luke's versions of the story, but it's more likely that both authors are relating the same event to serve different aims. For Luke, it's important to portray a unified front shared by Paul and Jerusalem's leaders, while Paul uses the episode to illustrate that his gospel's (mostly) law-free message has the support of Jerusalem leaders.

This leads most scholars to think that Paul probably wrote Galatians a bit later in his career, perhaps in the mid-50s CE. Other internal clues also point in this direction. For one thing, Galatians lacks the urgent eschatological feel of 1 Thessalonians, where the "coming of the Lord" seems to lie just around the corner. This letter also refers to other encounters such as the **Antioch Incident** (Gal 2:11-21), which may indicate Paul's career is gaining some longevity. Finally, the concerns mentioned in Galatians fit more closely with later letters such as 2 Corinthians and Romans. Like the Corinthians, the Galatian Christians have welcomed apostles who think Gentiles should keep Jewish law. As in Romans, Paul reflects in some detail about the connection between Jewish tradition and God's universal redemption of the world. All of this evidence suggests that Galatians stands between these two letters, both conceptually and chronologically. Let's turn, now, to this heated letter.

The Message: "Another Gospel"

Greeting and (Non-)Thanksgiving (Gal 1:1-11)

The opening lines of Galatians point to what's on Paul's mind and how he will counter his opponents and gain the Galatians' ear. The greeting itself signals his two-pronged approach. First, Paul notes that his *authority* comes from "Jesus Christ and God the Father," not from "human agency" (Gal 1:1).

Second, he sets an apocalyptic tone when he says that the *freedom* from being in Christ liberates believers from "this present evil age" (Gal 1:3).

Galatians is the only Pauline letter that omits a conventional thanksgiving. In its place, Paul launches a verbal shock and awe campaign. "I'm amazed," he says, "that you are so quickly deserting the one who called you by the grace of Christ to follow another gospel" (Gal 1:6). In what follows, Paul attempts to reengage the Galatian "deserters" even as he challenges his competitors' claims.

"Through a Revelation from Jesus Christ" (Gal 1:11–2:10)

As in other letters, Paul establishes his authority early on. But this time, he takes a different approach. Elsewhere, we've noticed Paul's relational appeals that call on mutual bonds of affection or fond memories of time spent together. Here, Paul recounts the story of his own "revelation" to show that God is at work through him. Unlike Luke's version of the event in Acts, Paul doesn't mention a location or any details about what he's seen. Paul also reports his post-revelation visit to Jerusalem quite differently, claiming to have only met Cephas (Peter) and "James, the brother of the Lord" (Gal 1:19) as opposed to making the rounds among disciples (see Acts 9:27).

As we've noted, these differences fit Paul's rhetorical aims in Galatians. Later, we learn that Paul's opponents (the Teachers) are Jewish Christians whose authority comes from the Jerusalem mother church. Paul goes them one better: his authority isn't from Jerusalem; it's from God. He even insists the Jerusalem leaders were "glorifying God because of me" (Gal 1:24)!

This insistence on his own, God-given authority affects how Paul recounts events around the Jerusalem Council. Here, Paul says he went to the holy city "because of a revelation" (Gal 2:2)—not because he operated under any human authority. The outcome? "Influential" leaders treated Barnabas and him "as equals" (Gal 2:9), he says, and confirmed their mission to Gentiles, asking only that they "remember the poor" (Gal 2:10). Thus Paul stresses that both his initial revelation about Christ and his role as apostle to the Gentiles came from God, not humans, and that Jerusalem leaders recognized both.

"Free for Freedom" (Gal 2:11–6:10)

The rest of Galatians sketches a stark contrast between the Teachers' message and Paul's. In his view, it's nothing less than the difference between slavery and freedom. Paul winds his way through Jewish tradition to undercut

FIGURE 13.1: TORAH-OBSERVANT CHRISTIANITY

The question of how Jewish Jesus's followers must be has been around for a long time. In chapter 5, we met the **Ebionite** Christians, Jewish believers whose views we learn about from ancient Christian writers. They followed Jewish law and especially valued the Gospel of the Hebrews, a text that is lost to us today. (This may have been our Gospel of Matthew, a different version of Matthew, or an entirely different law-friendly Gospel.)

Even today, those who identify as "**Messianic Jews**" affirm both Jesus's messianic status and the validity of observing Torah's instructions about sacred food, sacred time, and circumcision. The current form of messianic Judaism originated in the 1960s. It's a small group with about five hundred houses of worship in the US and almost a half million adherents worldwide. The "Jews for Jesus" website announces: "We are Jewish people who believe in Jesus and we want to tell everybody about Jesus the Messiah." (See www.jewsforjesus.org.)

> **YOUR TURN:** Make your best case either for or against this statement: followers of a Jewish Messiah must become Jewish by following Torah.

what he's called "another gospel"—that is, the Teachers' message about what it means for Gentiles to follow the Jewish Messiah. To listen in on this rather combative attack, we'll summarize the Teachers' views and then lay out Paul's response to them.

"Another Gospel": The Teachers

Since Galatians mostly responds to the Teachers' message, we'll begin there. Remember, all we know about their "gospel" comes from their ardent critic; we have no way to take them on their own terms. We can reconstruct, through the strategy we've called mirror reading, what were likely its core elements:

1. **Jewish law:**

   Apparently, the Teachers told the Galatians that, as believers in a Jewish Messiah, they had to follow Jewish religious practices known together as the "**works of the Law**" (see e.g., Gal 2:16). This term probably signals specific parts of the Torah that provide ethnic boundary markers: circumcision, dietary laws, and the sacred calendar. These practices took on central importance during the Babylonian exile in the sixth century BCE, since they helped the dislocated Jewish people preserve ethnic identity outside Judea. The Teachers apparently thought these practices were vital to emerging Christian identity as well. (See Figure 13.1.)

FIGURE 13.2: BIBLE AND CULTURE: RELIGIOUS AND CIVIL LAW

What's the relationship between religious and civil law? People answer this question in different ways in our world today. You've probably heard about ISIS and its vision for a caliphate governed by a traditionalist version of **Shari'ah**, Islamic law based on the Qur'an and its interpretation. The term itself means "way" and functions historically much as **Torah** does in Judaism. At issue in both religions is the degree to which ancient precepts apply to contemporary settings. (Both legal codes call for stoning and capital punishment for a wide range of offenses—practices that contemporary societies reject as archaic.)

In the US, the role of the Ten Commandments in the public sphere—such as on the courtroom walls—has been a matter of public debate. In 2005, the Supreme Court banned such a display in court buildings because it's a religious code that privileges Judaism and Christianity. The Torah also contains provisions, even within the Ten Commandments, that aren't part of US civil law, such as the observance of the Sabbath and the prohibition against coveting.

One group of Middle Eastern Christians has written a document entitled "From the Nile to the Euphrates: A Call to Faith and Citizenship," which considers the role of religious law in pluralistic society. It states, "In our Arab societies, there is a thin and dubious line between divine laws and human legislation. Religions, after all, can best serve as value resources for constitutions, whereas a legislative authority that is constituted by free and fair elections must frame conventional laws that are to be upheld by an independent judiciary" (see "From the Nile to the Euphrates: The Call of Faith and Citizenship; A Statement of the Christian Academic Forum for Citizenship in the Arab World," a PDF published by cafcaw.org [Bethlehem: Diya Publisher, 2014]).

YOUR TURN: What role, if any, should religious law play in civil society? Why? What's at stake?

2. **Jewish story:**
   Adhering to the "works of the law," the Teachers taught, qualified Gentile believers as "**children of Abraham**"—that is, members of the Jewish family established in the early chapters of the biblical story. Thus, they took their place within a chosen people who lived in covenant relationship with God.

3. **Jewish Christ:**
   The Teachers thought that, as God's "anointed one," Jesus held special status because he inaugurated a messianic age in which the Torah would gain universal validity. (See Figure 13.2.) In other words, the Torah provided the constitution, in their view, for the kingdom of God on earth.

301

FIGURE 13.3: SUBMISSION IN ISLAM

In contemporary Western thought, many people see **"submission"** as an oppressive notion, and Paul certainly thinks those who "want to be under the Law" (Gal 4:21) are taking on an unnecessary burden. The Qur'an takes an interesting and complex position in relation to religious law and submission. On the issue of Jewish dietary law, for instance, Mohammed's revelation claims that additional restrictions have been added to God's original teachings: "Except for what Israel made unlawful for himself, all food was lawful to the Children of Israel before the Torah was revealed" (3:93). On the issue of submission, though, the Qur'an states, "Any who direct [or "submit"] themselves wholly to God and do good will have their reward with their Lord: no fear for them, nor will they grieve" (2:112). In other words, submission to God uplifts the human spirit rather than oppressing it.

YOUR TURN: Can you think of a way in which "submission" to rules or practices can bring a sense of freedom? What's the difference between a "submission" that liberates and one that stifles people?

In short, the Teachers' views may not have been as rational as Paul claims. It made good sense to expect non-Jewish believers in a Jewish Christ to become thoroughly Jewish and to reimagine their status not as Gentiles but as members of God's covenant people. It's not entirely surprising that Paul says at least some Galatians "want to be under the Law" (Gal 4:21) as part of their new identity in Christ. (See Figure 13.3.)

Paul says, "Not so fast!" He thinks the stakes are high on this question about how Jewish Jesus's followers must be, and he crafts Galatians as a counter-claim that leaves little room for compromise. The problem, he thinks, is not that the Teachers have gone *too far* by drawing Gentiles into the Jewish people; it's that they haven't gone *far enough* in embracing the radically different world order that Jesus the Messiah has established. Now that we have a better handle on the Teachers' position, let's dive into Paul's message—both its rhetorical rebuttal and the positive alternative he offers.

"The Faithfulness of Jesus Christ": Paul's Response

Among the "works of the law" the Teachers require, **circumcision** seems the most problematic for Paul. And understandably so. It's one thing to remove an infant male's foreskin; it's quite another to ask adult males to undergo such a painful, permanent, and—for some—strange procedure. As a result, the requirement of adult circumcision may well have created an obstacle for men who otherwise found the Christian message compelling.

Paul counters this insistence in several places. Already, he's mentioned his association with a Gentile apostle named **Titus**, who remained uncircumcised

(Gal 2:3). He's also confirmed his calling to proclaim the gospel to "the people who aren't circumcised" (Gal 2:7). Later, his response grows more emphatic: "Look, I, Paul, am telling you that if you have yourselves circumcised, having Christ won't help you" (Gal 5:2). He goes on to explain that those who submit to circumcision effectively choose the "way of the law" over than the "way of the cross" (see Gal 5:2–12). He even concludes by wishing the Teachers would "castrate themselves" (Gal 5:12).

Likewise, Paul registers concern about the obstacle that **dietary laws** create. He recalls a time when Peter reversed his view on whether or not to share a meal with Gentiles who hadn't adopted kosher laws. Known as the **Antioch Incident** (Gal 2:11–14), this story shows that adherence to Torah can lead to isolation and factionalism, which Paul thinks violates the gospel. After all, Peter had separated himself from Gentiles at mealtime "because he was afraid of the people [from James] who promoted circumcision" (Gal 2:12).

Finally, Paul takes issue with Galatians who observe the Jewish **sacred calendar** (see Gal 4:10). He doesn't explain why, but it's likely that this fits the Teachers' aim of assigning Gentile Christians a distinctly Jewish identity. Together with circumcision and dietary restrictions, observing the Jewish Sabbath and other holidays established a clear social and ethnic boundary around the Jewish people.

In response to the Teachers' message, Paul both maintains the validity of Jewish law and qualifies its function for believers. For one thing, Paul positively appraises Torah's *role throughout history*, extolling the guidelines it's provided for understanding human sin (see Gal 3:22). The Greek term Paul assigns to Torah is *paidagogos*, a term we might liken to a "nanny" or "childcare worker" (Gal 3:24). In Paul's view, Torah has protected God's children from harm—dietary laws and regulations against incest come to mind—and trained them in valuable habits, such as taking a day of rest and setting limits of retribution against offenders. (See Figure 13.4.)

But it's the Teachers' insistence that the "works of the law" remain valid *entrance requirements* for non-Jewish believers in the messianic age that raises Paul's strong objections. In Christ, he thinks the terms of humanity's relationship to God have shifted, and shifted radically. In the new world order, Paul says, "a person isn't made righteous by the works of the Law but rather through the faithfulness of Jesus Christ" (Gal 2:16). He then works rhetorically to drive home the point that it's faith, not the "works of the Law," that brings liberation. (See Figure 13.5.) Thus, he isolates what was probably the Teachers' first step toward faith—conformity with the entire Jewish law—from a second step of faith in Jesus as the Christ. For Paul, the second step is all that matters.

Figure 13.4: Zen Buddhist Bankei and Rules

Seventeenth-century Japanese **Zen Buddhist** master Bankei became disillusioned with the basic duties of Buddhist practice that he encountered in Japan and had this to say about religious rules:

"Originally, what people call the precepts were all for wicked monks who broke the rules; for the one who abides in the Unborn Buddha Mind, there's no need for precepts. The precepts were taught to help sentient beings—they weren't taught to help buddhas!"

(*Bankei Zen: Translations from the Record of Bankei*, trans. Peter Haskel [New York: Grove Press, 1984], 7)

YOUR TURN: Connect Bankei's view of these "precepts" with Paul's view of Jewish law in Galatians. What similarities or differences do you detect?

Figure 13.5: Faith in/of Jesus Christ

In Galatians 2:16, Paul writes, "We know that a person isn't made righteous by the works of the Law but rather through the *faithfulness of Jesus Christ*" (italics added). The Greek form of the italicized phrase is *pistis iēsou christou*, a grammatical construction that suggests that the "faith" (= *pistis*) belongs to "Jesus Christ" (= *iēsou christou*). Though one of the earliest English translations (KJV) preserved this reading, Martin Luther's German Bible introduced a different nuance to the phrase, as he rendered it as the German equivalent of "faith in Jesus Christ." Luther associated the Teachers' insistence on believers' adherence to the "works of the law" with the Catholic Church's indulgence system. Luther's emphasis on "salvation by faith through grace" emphasized Christian faith in opposition to religious duties. In Reformed Christianity, having faith in Jesus is the one and only way to salvation.

Contemporary scholarship has reopened the question of Paul's language here. Many think Paul views Christ's faith, not believers' faith, as paramount in salvation. In this view, human belief has less to do with doctrine or ideas and more to do with trusting in Christ's witness of faithfulness. Indeed, the rest of Galatians 2:16 captures this sense, as Paul writes, "We ourselves believed [or trusted] in Christ Jesus so that we could be made righteous by the faithfulness of Christ and not by the works of the Law."

YOUR TURN: Reflect on the difference in meaning between the "faithfulness of Jesus Christ" and "faith in Jesus Christ," in light of Paul's letter to the Galatian churches. What's at stake?

FIGURE 13.6: CHRISTOLOGICAL EXEGESIS

Paul's strategy for reading Jesus "backward" into Jewish scriptures persists among early Christian interpreters. Here's what one second-century Christian writer has to say about this kind of "christological exegesis": "If anyone, therefore, reads the Scriptures [meaning the Christian Old Testament] with attention, he will find in them an account of Christ, and a foreshadowing of the new calling. For Christ is the treasure which was hid in the field, that is, in this world (for 'the field is this world'); but the treasure hid in the Scriptures is Christ, since He was pointed out by means of types and parables" (Irenaeus of Lyons, *Adv. Haer.* 4.26.1). Many modern scholars take issue with this interpretive strategy, since it can imply that Jewish sacred traditions have little or no meaning on their own terms, apart from a christological reading.

> **YOUR TURN:** What do you think about this strategy? What is its value for believers? Its potential danger for believers or people of other traditions and worldviews?

"Children of Abraham"

Paul agrees with the Teachers that non-Jewish believers are "children of Abraham." But he offers his own extended interpretation of the biblical story that, once again, separates this narrative identity from Torah and its covenantal requirements. His strategy is twofold:

1. Paul notes that, in the biblical story, God's covenant with Abraham predates the covenant with Moses by more than four hundred years (see Gal 3:17). In his view, the covenant with Abraham is all about promise, not restriction; after all, even Abraham's own circumcision comes *after* he shows his faith in God. Paul also uses a reading strategy called ***christological interpretation*** to detect Christ's presence in the Jewish story long before Jesus walked the earth. (See Figure 13.6.) In this case, he thinks God's promise to Abraham's offspring is a promise "to one person, who is Christ" (Gal 3:16 NRSV). For Paul, the line from Abraham to Gentile believers doesn't run through Jewish law; it runs through faith.

2. Paul introduces a bold interpretive twist in his reading of scripture when he calls Galatian believers children of **Sarah** (see Gal 4:21–5:1). In the biblical story, Abraham's wife, Sarah, gives birth to **Isaac**, father of the people of Israel, while Sarah's slave, **Hagar**, bears **Ishmael**, the traditional patriarch of a non-Jewish people. But Paul reads scripture **allegorically**, playing with the contrast between slavery and freedom to redraw lines of ancestry. He insists that those

who remain under Torah's sway are children of the slave woman, while those who claim freedom in Christ are children of Sarah. Such interpretive freedom turns the literal meaning of scripture on its head and probably caused great offense among the Teachers.

In both ways, Paul reapplies motifs embedded in the biblical story—motifs of promise, faith, and freedom—to those not originally included in its narrative design. Quite apart from compliance with Jewish law, Paul insists, the Galatian Christians are children of Abraham and Sarah because they're heirs to God's promise, Abraham's faith, and the freedom that comes from that faith.

"The Law of Christ"

Paul reminds the Galatians of his own Jewish identity early in this letter, describing his "previous life in Judaism" (Gal 1:13). As we've noted, many scholars think Paul still saw himself as Jewish, even after his "revelation from Jesus Christ" (Gal 1:12). We've seen, too, that his hopes for the messianic age are rooted in Jewish apocalyptic thought, even if he accommodates its scheme to open up a temporal meantime between Jesus's death and resurrection and the full establishment of God's reign on earth.

Against the Teachers, Paul emphatically denies that Torah constitutes the law of the land in the messianic age and that believers must follow its code in order to live as inhabitants of God's kingdom. His view of the new world order is decidedly more radical. Rather than a kind of tribalism that's gaining cosmic power, God's coming reign will encompass all of creation not by a legal code but by new life in Christ, marked by faith.

Paul's concept of faith is complex and nuanced. It goes way beyond contemporary notions about believing ideas about God or Jesus. For Paul, believers' faith takes its cues from Christ's faith—that is, his unwavering allegiance to God, which led to his death and resurrection. Paul puts it this way: "Scripture locked up all things under sin, so that the promise based on the faithfulness of Jesus Christ might be given to those who have faith" (Gal 3:22). Christ's faith has flung open the prison doors of sin and brought liberation to the cosmos. But, at least in the short term, not everyone walks through those doors. Only those who trust in God's freedom exhibit the faith necessary to embrace it.

That leads to a second facet of this new regime: its lack of distinction among members. As "God's children," those who have been "baptized into Christ"—that is, into the messianic community his faith establishes—are "one in Christ" (Gal 3:27-28). That means that status assigned based on

FIGURE 13.7: SIKHISM ON RELIGIOUS DIFFERENCE

A religious tradition known as Sikhism emerged in the Punjab region of Northern India—at the intersection of Muslim and Hindu cultures—in the late fifteenth century CE. Two centuries later, seventeenth-century a Sikh guru (teacher) named Gobind Singh addressed the question of religious difference, which had led to violence against Sikhs:

Let no one mistake of thinking there is a difference.

There is not one God for Hindus and another for Muslims.

Worship the one God who is the divine Preceptor for all, the One Form whose Light suffuses all.

Temples and mosques are the same.

Hindu worship and Muslim prayer are the same.

All people are the same. (Akal Ustat, Swayyas)

YOUR TURN: Research Sikh teaching on religious difference, and compare it to Paul's teaching (see especially Galatians 3:27).

religion, ethnicity, gender, or social status gives way to mutual status as God's children and heirs. (See Figure 13.7.)

Ultimately, Paul warns the Galatians not to use their freedom as an "opportunity to indulge . . . selfish impulses, but serve each other through love" (Gal 5:13). It's a radical kind of freedom—one that introduces voluntary servitude to the mutual care for one another. In yet another twist, he says they should "carry each other's burdens" so that they "fulfill the law of Christ" (Gal 6:2). This "christological law," then, carries forward Torah's core values (see Gal 5:14) but not its religious code demarcating socioethnic boundaries.

Conclusion (Gal 6:11-18)

Paul ends Galatians by returning to his vigorous attack on the "circumcision faction." Indeed, the concluding verses shed important light on the Teachers' motivations, at least as Paul portrays them. Their insistence that Gentile believers be circumcised fits too cozily, he says, with the stratified social order of the day (see Gal 6:12). This may be a pragmatic way to avoid persecution, Paul says, but it's at odds with the radical nature of the gospel. In the new world order Jesus the Jewish Messiah has instituted, "being circumcised or not being circumcised doesn't mean anything." (Gal 6:15). What does count, in Paul's book? It's the "new creation" inhabited by those who cast their allegiance with Christ and the law of freedom he brings. It's a rebranding of the "Israel of God"—defined not by the tribalism or ethnicity or geography or religious practice, but by that faith.

Review and Reflect

- Name and explain three differences between the Teachers' views and Paul's.

- What does "faith" mean in Galatians? How does that relate to "faith" in popular culture today?

ROMANS: THE DIPLOMATIC LETTER

In the chronology of Paul's authentic letters, Romans was probably his last. As he writes, Paul says he has completed his time in Macedonia and Achaia and intends to visit Rome en route to Spain (Rom 15:23-24). But first, he's headed to Judea to deliver a gift from his Gentile churches for "the poor among God's people in Jerusalem" (Rom 15:26). Acts says it was on this trip to Jerusalem that Paul was arrested, tried by Roman and Jewish officials, and extradited to Rome (see Acts 21:17–25:12). Though Paul's plans are thwarted—he probably died a political prisoner—the impact of this letter has far surpassed that of any stopover visit he might have made.

In the order of the Pauline corpus, Romans comes not last but first. It's both the longest and the most refined of Paul's letters. Some have called Romans a summary of Paul's thought, but it's more accurate to see it as a sophisticated reflection on the Jew-Gentile issue. Like Galatians, Romans addresses the role of Jewish law within emerging Christianity, but it also broadens the question to consider the relationship between believing non-Jews and non-believing Jews within God's plan of redemption. As a result, many scholars see Romans as a sustained defense of God's righteous plan to renew creation. Within that plan, Paul urges Roman believers to live together as those animated by that life-giving power.

The conversation found in Romans differs from the conversations in Paul's other letters, where he engages people he knows personally. Paul didn't

---

FIGURE 13.8: CLAUDIUS AND JEWISH EXPULSION FROM ROME

Ancient sources disagree when it comes to the question of Emperor Claudius's expulsion of Jews living in Rome during his rule (41–54 CE). Acts says it happened around 49 CE and brought Priscilla (or Prisca) and Aquila to Corinth, where Paul got to know them (see Acts 18:2). The historian **Suetonius** briefly describes an expulsion in these terms: "Since the Jews constantly made disturbances at the instigation of Chrestus, he [the Emperor Claudius] expelled them from Rome" (*Divus Claudius* 25.4). Though some historians think "**Chrestus**" refers to Christ and thus to a Jewish-Christian dispute, others think the term refers to someone who bears the popular name *Chrestus*, which means "useful" and was common among slaves. Finally, **Cassius Dio** denies the expulsion explicitly: "As for the Jews, who had again increased so greatly that by reason of their multitude it would have been hard without raising a tumult to bar them from the city [Rome], he [Claudius] did not drive them out, but ordered them, while continuing their traditional mode of life, not to hold meetings" (*Roman History*, 60.6.6-7, trans. Earnest Cary; for full text see: https://lexundria.com/dio/60.6/cy).

Some reconcile these disparities by saying Cassius Dio's statement refers to an earlier, softer suppression of the Jewish community. In any case, we do know of two prior expulsions of Jews, one dating from the previous century and a second by Tiberius in 19 CE—both on the grounds that Jews were evangelizing too aggressively.

YOUR TURN: Reflect on the dynamics between Jewish and Gentile believers within the Roman church. How might Roman Christianity have evolved without the presence of Jewish believers? What might their return to Rome have meant for the community?

bring the gospel message to Rome. He did know some Roman Christians (the letter's last chapter is full of name dropping), probably from time they spent elsewhere by choice or because they'd been expelled by the Roman emperor Claudius. (See Figure 13.8.) But he hadn't lived and worked among them. That difference makes the letter's tone more formal and distant than the other letters we've studied.

Rather than interpersonal conversation, Romans presents Paul's masterful engagement with both Jewish and Greco-Roman thought. More than any other letter, Paul weaves Jewish scripture into his unfolding argument, marking the Christ event as the culmination of God's revelation to the Jewish people. But Romans also makes full use of a rhetorical strategy called ***diatribe***. This style of argument involves anticipating and answering questions from an imagined conversation partner. In both ways, Paul crafts a dialogue with Roman believers in their native cultural language.

Setting

This rhetorical strategy fits the religiously mixed backgrounds of the Roman community. Scholars think it's likely that banished Jewish believers who returned to Rome after Claudius's death in 54 CE to find a Gentile Christian community tied only loosely to the movement's Jewish roots. From the letter's opening verses, Paul insists on the gospel's scriptural foundation and the Jews' priority in God's plan of salvation (see e.g., Rom 1:16). Thus, Paul again sides with those on the weaker side of the community's power structure, lifting up the "inferior" Jewish believers.

We should note, too, that this letter originally addressed those living at the heart of Roman imperial power. Paul's message isn't overtly seditious and even encourages submission to Roman authorities (see Rom 13:1-7). He doesn't foment insurgency or challenge the present world order, at least not explicitly. Yet Paul's apocalyptic hope courses through the letter in subtle ways. He reaffirms his calling to "bring all the nations to submission to faith" (Rom 1:5, author's translation), rather than submission to Roman power. He frames present suffering as "labor pains" that will give way to redemption from the present world order (Rom 8:22-23). And he encourages the faithful not to be "conformed to the patterns of this world" (Rom 12:2) but to return evil with good. In all these ways, Paul signals that the "way things are" will not last; God's renewal of all things—including earthly power structures—is at hand. Let's turn, now, to that message.

The Message: "God's Righteousness Is Being Revealed"

Greeting and Thanksgiving (Rom 1:1-17)

Paul begins this letter with an extended introduction of himself and the "good news" he proclaims (Rom 1:1). Not only was the gospel promised "ahead of time through [God's] prophets in the holy scriptures," but God's Son Jesus was also "descended from David" (Rom 1:2-3). In other words, Paul anchors his message in scripture, even if its reach extends far beyond the Jewish people. Indeed, Paul notes his own calling to bring "the nations" (or "Gentiles": *ethnē*) to "obedience" marked by faith (Rom 1:5). In these opening verses, Paul highlights the ethnoreligious origins of Jesus's messiahship as well as its universal scope.

Paul give thanks for the Roman community because their reputation for faithfulness has spread "throughout the whole world" (Rom 1:8). He understands the significance of their sociopolitical location; Rome was, for Paul, ground zero for the "whole world." So he conveys his eagerness to visit in person and share mutually in their faith.

The opening section concludes with the letter's thesis statement: "I'm not ashamed of the gospel: it is God's own power for salvation to all who have faith in God, to the Jew first and also to the Greek. God's righteousness is being revealed in the gospel, from faithfulness for faith, as it is written, *The righteous person will live by faith*" (Rom 1:16-17).

In two short verses, Paul spells out key concerns that will appear throughout this letter: power, salvation, faith, Jewish priority, Gentile inclusion, and righteousness. In a nutshell, the rest of Romans explores the ways in which *Christ's faith has liberated the cosmos from the power of sin, revealing God's righteousness and inspiring faith in God for Jew and non-Jew alike.*

"A Sweeping Victory" (Rom 1:18–8:39)

At the heart of Paul's message to the Romans lies this claim: no matter what forces may threaten or destroy, "in all these things we win a sweeping victory through the one who loved us" (Rom 8:37). What kind of victory does Paul have in mind, and how does he think that God's love, expressed in the human Jesus Christ, secures that victory? These are the questions that dominate the first eight chapters of Romans.

Paul's discussion of these questions unfolds in this way:

1. **Diagnosing the Problem** (power of sin): Rom 1:18–3:20

2. **Naming the Solution** (Christ's faith): Rom 3:21–4:25

3. **Claiming the Outcome** (peace with God): Rom 5:1–8:39

Let's consider each step in the sequence.

1. Diagnosing the Problem (Rom 1:18–3:20): Paul opens his argument with a doom loop. He surveys the human condition and finds much to lament, from Gentile ungodliness to Jewish unrighteousness. Thus he diagnoses widespread patterns of sin and its corollary, divine wrath. Gentiles, he argues, should know better, since creation itself makes God's ways and power an open book. This view, known as **"natural theology,"** leads Paul to condemn Gentile sin in vivid detail. "Ungodliness" shows up when Gentiles worship both images and themselves instead of God. (See Figure 13.9.) But Paul doesn't stop there: he uses a stock rhetorical form called a **vice list** to name a wide range of destructive behaviors—from envy to murder, from insolence to arrogance (see Rom 1:29-31).

FIGURE 13.9: BIBLE AND CULTURE: HOMOSEXUALITY

For many, Romans 1:26-27 is the touchstone biblical verdict on both male and female homosexual relations (see also 1 Cor 6:9-10 and 1 Tim 1:9-10). Here's what Paul says in these verses:

> That's why God abandoned them [that is, idol worshippers] to degrading lust. Their females traded natural sexual relations for unnatural sexual relations. Also, in the same way, the males traded natural sexual relations with females, and burned with lust for each other. Males performed shameful actions with males, and they were paid back with the penalty they deserved for their mistake in their own bodies.

However, the interpretation of these verses is far from settled. Besides the standard view of Paul's weighing in against homosexual practice here, consider these differing voices in the conversation:

- Most ancient interpreters, including Augustine, disputed the view that Paul had female homosexuality in mind.

- Some interpreters argue that Paul's using diatribe in a way that cites others' views in order to condemn them (see Rom 2:1 for the condemnation).

- Others note that he's making a point from the perspective of natural theology, which says God's ways are evident in the created order. In this view, only same-sex relations with those born without homosexual orientation are shameful acts.

- Still others think Paul *is* condemning homosexuality but that his teachings are limited by social constructs of his day. (These interpreters would also set aside the authority of passages that sanction slavery, for instance.)

- Finally, some stress the wider context, which concerns idolatry, and think Paul has in mind those sexual practices that are part of ancient cultic worship that's sexual in nature.

In other words, interpreters recognize different aspects of Paul's conversation with his wider world and with our world across place and time.

YOUR TURN: Read Romans 1:18–3:20. How do these verses fit in the broad argument Paul is making here? Does the context shape your view of these passages? Why? Why not?

It's not just Gentiles who become objects of Paul's withering critique. In a deft move, Paul turns the tables, in two ways, on any who might cheer on his attack. First, he uses the rhetorical form of **diatribe** to anticipate and counter the human tendency to judge others. Judgment, he says, belongs to God alone (see Rom 2:1-16). Second, he pivots to any Jews in his audience who think their status as God's people exempts them from accusation (see Rom 2:13). Compared with Galatians, Paul tones down his warning against circumcision, insisting that such practices find their value as a spiritual, not a physical, condition (Rom 3:29). He concedes advantage to the Jew but registers a ringing condemnation of Jewish unfaithfulness. This leaves "both Jews and Greeks . . . all under the power of sin" (Rom 3:9). An array of biblical texts from the Psalms, Ecclesiastes, and Isaiah drives home Paul's point (Rom 3:10-18). In sum, Paul finds that neither nature's witness nor the law's guidelines have been able to establish God's righteous ways on earth.

2. Naming the Solution (Rom 3:21–4:25): In Paul's view, the power of sin is both pervasive and destructive. What then is its remedy? How might its stranglehold on creation be broken? With two small words—"but now"—Paul turns again, this time to name sin's solution. Here, Paul elaborates on his claim in Galatians that salvation comes through Christ's faith and amplifies his discussion of Abraham as primogenitor of that faith. As we've seen elsewhere (e.g., Phil 2:5-11), Christ's faith displays the kind of full-fledged allegiance to God that led both to his death and, ultimately, to his resurrection as well.

But how does that kind of faithfulness solve the problem of human sin? Let's consider several facets of Christ's faith as the hinge on which the doors swing toward redemption:

- Christ's faith *isn't* a novelty; it stands in continuity with Jewish tradition.

  This strategy for breaking sin's vice grip on the world may operate "apart from the Law," but it is "confirmed by the Law and the Prophets" (Rom 3:21). Paul notes that Abraham's faith in God established his own righteousness *before* circumcision and that the promise of Abraham's inheritance rested on his *faith*, not his performance of the law. What did Abraham's faith entail? Abraham trusted that "God was able to do what he promised" (Gal 4:21)—namely, to bring life through his own "good as dead" body, and Sarah's as well (Rom 4:19). Thus Christ carries forward, and reiterates, Abraham's faith in God's life-giving power when the forces of death seem to prevail.

- Christ's faith *is* game-changing; it reveals divine righteousness with unprecedented effect.

    Once again, Paul uses apocalyptic language to assert the disruptive and decisive significance of Christ's death and resurrection. As long as sin held universal sway, God's righteousness was hidden from view. With Christ's death, Paul insists, "God displayed Jesus as the place of sacrifice where mercy is found" (Rom 3:25). God's righteousness thus jumps the balance sheet, declaring the "sins that happened before" null and void (Rom 3:25). The problem is solved not on conventional terms but through a revolutionary approach.

- Christ's faith doesn't play favorites; it levels the playing field between Jew and Gentile.

    Paul has an expansive view of the impact of Christ's faithfulness. After all, since "God is one" (Rom 3:30), why would God differentiate between groups when it comes to releasing them from the power of sin? Even Abraham, Paul says, is the "father of all of us" (Rom 4:16).

- Christ's faith offers the gift of redemption.

    It turns out, Paul says, that the solution to the human condition doesn't have anything to do with trying harder or being smarter or more successful. It's about trusting, like Abraham and Jesus, that God is at work to defeat forces of sin and death. It's about having "faith in the hope" (Rom 4:18) that, in Christ's faithfulness, God has indeed reprogrammed the code that opens the doors from death to life.

Sure, Paul thinks humans participate in this new world order through a faith of their own. But that faith is less a matter of what people believe and more a matter of entrusting their lives to God's priorities and to God's power.

3. Claiming the Outcome (Rom 5:1–8:39): Indeed, the next four chapters capture Paul's musings on what that way of faith looks like for the Roman Christians and other believers. Here, he grapples with the meantime reality in which sin lurks around every corner, both personally and cosmically. What difference does this change in status make if the rest of the world remains unredeemed? Paul explains several ways in which the new world order Christ established already marks those who follow in his way of faith:

- A new starting point: "peace with God" (Rom 5:1)

  One fundamental that's changed, in the aftermath of Christ's faith, is humanity's starting point in relation to God. Since Adam, Paul thinks the old world order has operated according to a binary opposition between ungodly humans—all of us, he thinks—and God (see Rom 5:12-21). Humans were enemy combatants, serving under the "rule" (or kingdom) of sin. Christ's faith has changed all of that, he thinks. Through the free gift of Christ's righteousness, the terms of the relationship have been restored and renewed from the start. We are, he thinks, no longer a problem to be solved.

- A new rule of law: "slaves to God" (Rom 6:22)

  Paul talks a lot about "rule" in Romans. He uses political language—imperial language, really—to convey the terms by which God's power operates. If he's writing about spiritual matters, they're not *just* spiritual to him, since power relations impact daily affairs at the most pragmatic level (see Rom 12–15 for more elaboration on this). In any case, Paul insists that Christ's faith has inaugurated a new era in which the "law of the Spirit of life" has set the cosmos free from the "law of sin and death" (Rom 8:2). He notes, more carefully than in Galatians, the Torah's rightful place in bringing the sinful condition to light. He even calls the law "holy, righteous, and good" (Rom 7:12). But since Christ came, Torah's relevance and authority have given way to a new "law" that gives life.

- A new identity: "children of God" (Rom 8:14 NRSV)

  Those who shift their allegiance from the old regime to the new, Paul says, undergo another change of relational status as well—from slaves to children, and "fellow heirs with Christ" (Rom 8:17). Paul thus deploys household imagery to convey the intimacy with God that comes as a by-product of those who are "conformed to the image of his Son . . . [who is] the first of many brothers and sisters" (Rom 8:29).

- A new perspective: "a sweeping victory" (Rom 8:37)

> Ultimately, Christ's faith secures the hope that present suffering is an inevitable part of the apocalyptic drama that will soon culminate with God's final defeat of sin and death (see Rom 5:3-5; 8:18-25, 35-36). Paul locates himself squarely in the meantime, poised between the end of sin's rule and the dawn of the world's redemption. Thus he's caught, like the Romans, amid creation's "labor pains" (Rom 8:22) that precede the full liberation of the cosmos. Already, believers are united in Christ's death: "the person we used to be was crucified with him" and has escaped the bondage of sin (Rom 6:5-6). The "down payment" of God's life-giving spirit (Rom 8:11) ensures the glory that will soon be revealed, the "sweeping victory" that will bring nothing less that the renewal of all creation.

The first eight chapters of Romans contain staggering claims about the import and impact of Christ's faith. Paul maintains that God's righteousness is alive and well and on full display for all to see it. It undoes the effects of Adam's sin, carries forward the promise to Abraham, and establishes a fundamentally new world order in which people—all people—can be heirs to God's glory. It's against this backdrop that Paul turns to what is, for him, a question filled with personal angst: Why are most Jews so resistant to this "good news"?

"All Israel Will Be Saved" (Rom 9:1–11:36)

Nowhere else in Paul's writings does he consider the question of "Israel's" unbelief in such a sustained and deliberate way. Some scholars see Romans 9–11 as a dramatic aside that's unrelated to the rest of Paul's message. But it's an issue that's both personal for Paul, a faithful Jew himself, and inherently connected to the letter's broader concerns. He cares deeply about his flesh-and-blood relatives in the faith, and his tone vacillates between frustration and judgment, on the one hand, and compassion and awe, on the other. In this section, Paul works out a complex and nuanced explanation of Jewish unbelief that ultimately gives way to the mystery of God's plan.

We may safely assume that this question wasn't just relevant for Paul. Already, we've noted that the Roman church probably counted many Jews among its members, and Paul writes in part to confirm their central, even leading, place among those who are "in Christ." They, too, may well have been troubled by rejection by friends and family members' unbelief. They,

too, may have wondered, as personally as Paul does, about the role of unbelieving Jews in God's rule on earth.

What does Paul have to say on the matter? First, he affirms the heritage
of the "Israelites" (the biblical term for the ancient people entrusted with Torah). Not only were they adopted as God's children (cf. Rom 8:15), but "the
glory, the covenants, the giving of the Law, the worship, and the promises
belong to them" (Rom 9:4). What's more, "the Christ descended from [their]
ancestors" (Rom 9:5).

How then to account for their (almost universal) rejection of Jesus as
the Jewish Christ? Paul offers various explanations. For one thing, he notes
a pattern of Israel's recalcitrance throughout scripture. He cites a wide array of sacred texts—from the Law (especially Deuteronomy) to the Prophets
(especially Isaiah and Hosea) to the Writings (especially Psalms)—as evidence
that God's people have often strayed in their relationship with their Lord.
Paul credits the Jewish people for being "enthusiastic about God" (Rom 10:2)
but says their zeal is uninformed. He claims that Israel's striving for a "Law
of righteousness" failed because they thought they could attain righteousness
by "doing something" (Rom 9:31-32). Though they've been privy to "Christ's
message" (Rom 10:17), they've shown themselves once again to be a "disobe-
dient and contrary people" (Rom 10:21).

For Paul, though, God's purposes operate at a deeper level than human
agency (Rom 9:16). This leads him to two important claims. First, God's
righteousness doesn't depend on human compliance. In diatribe style, Paul
asks, "Has God rejected his people?" and answers emphatically: "Absolutely
not!" (Rom 11:1). For one thing, there's a "remaining group"—including
Paul—who are already heirs to salvation (Rom 9:27; 11:5). Thus God's rejection of Israel is out of the question. But Paul's defense of God's righteous
plan also explains Jewish rejection of Jesus as an interim condition that makes
room for non-Jews in the family tree. If temporary exclusion of nonbelieving Jews allows Gentiles to be "grafted in among the other branches" (Rom
11:17), Paul thinks the "natural branches [i.e., the Jews]" will be "grafted
back onto their own olive tree" (Rom 11:24).

Indeed, Paul's lengthy reflection on the subject culminates with this categorical claim: "all Israel will be saved" (Rom 11:26). He simply can't conceive
of any other outcome. After all, "God's gifts and calling can't be taken back"
(Rom 11:29). By its nature, divine mercy ultimately outlasts and overrides divine judgment. How and why is this the case? At last, Paul's best efforts at rea-
sonable discourse and rhetorical flourish give way to mystery, awe, and praise:
"God's riches, wisdom, and knowledge are so deep! They are as mysterious as
his judgments, and they are as hard to track as his paths!" (Rom 11:33). Who

knows how and why? No one, really. All Paul knows is this: "all things are from him and through him and for him" (Rom 11:36). It's a rare—and for some, refreshing—outburst of humility on Paul's part.

"Be Transformed" (Rom 12:1–15:13)

In a pattern we've seen before, Paul's message moves toward practical matters as the letter nears completion. Paul encourages the Roman believers in their conduct toward one another and the world around them, alluding both to Jesus's teachings and, more vaguely, to specific Jew-Gentile issues plaguing their community.

Paul's exhortation opens with an appeal for Roman believers to present their "bodies as a living sacrifice that is holy and pleasing to God" (Rom 12:1). He thus reminds them that their bodily conduct—and not just their spiritual or emotional mind-set—matters to God. He warns against conformity to the "patterns of this world" (Rom 12:2)—patterns that reflect the forces of the present evil age still operative in social, economic, and political systems. In other words, he urges Roman Christians to calibrate their views about what is "good and pleasing and mature" (Rom 12:2) according to divine, rather than human, standards.

Most of this section concerns the community's moral and ethical bearings toward both insiders and outsiders. Paul returns briefly to the metaphor of the "one body" of believers discussed in 1 Corinthians 12 (see Rom 12:4-8) and highlights the distinctive gifts of members as the basis for humility. He also echoes Jesus's Sermon on the Mount (see Matt 5–7) when he writes, "Bless people who harass you—bless and don't curse them" (Rom 12:14; cf. Matt 5:44). Paul takes matters a step further, urging his audience not to seek revenge and quoting Proverbs 25:21-22 as a basis for treating even enemies with generosity. He even says such conduct heaps "burning coals of fire upon [the enemy's] head" (Rom 12:20).

Paul elaborates on this implicit caution against judging others and cedes such authority to God alone (see Rom 14:1-12). Here, Paul's apocalyptic hope for the coming end frames the current reality. "Our salvation," he says, "is nearer than when we first had faith" (Rom 13:11). Such an imminent sense of God's judgment makes human judgment folly, in his view.

This section also highlights some division, within the Roman Christian community, between the "weak" and the "powerful." This time, it's *dietary restrictions* and the *sacred calendar* that mark the dividing lines. Paul never says so explicitly, but he hints that Jewish Christians (the "weak") observe kosher and Sabbath restrictions while Gentile believers (the "powerful") do not.

Paul's tone is less strident than in Galatians, probably since no one is insisting that Gentile Christians follow Torah as a condition of their faith. Indeed, Paul leaves a wide berth for disagreement on these matters: "it's between you and God," he says (Rom 14:22).

What Paul *does* care about, in light of these differences, is believers' ability to function as "one body" (Rom 12:5) rather than separate—and competing—coalitions. To attain that unity, he calls the Romans to a spirit of "welcome" (see Rom 14:1; 15:7). He shuns dispute and commends patient, selfless concern for the weaker members: "Each of us should please our neighbors for their good in order to build them up" (Rom 15:2).

The body of the letter ends with a resounding appeal for mutual welcome. Paul quotes a series of Jewish sacred texts that affirm the place of the Gentiles in God's ultimate plan of salvation. To Jewish members of the Roman community, he demonstrates that the Gentile believers confirm God's work among them. To the Gentile Christians, Paul recalls the Jewish roots of the messianic movement. Their ability to "welcome each other" (Rom 15:7) confirms that God's reconciling power is at work in the world.

Conclusion (Rom 15:14–16:27)

Before signing off, Paul reiterates his own calling as apostle to the Gentiles (Rom 15:14-21), affirms his plans to visit Rome (Rom 15:22-33), and conveys particular greetings to a long list of Roman believers (Rom 16:1-16). In these ways, Paul strengthens his authority and standing among the audience—most of whom he's probably never met.

The list of those he greets by name offers an intriguing window into the leadership of the early Christian movement. The list includes several women, including a "servant" (or deacon) named **Phoebe** (Rom 16:1) a "coworker" named **Prisca** (probably married to **Aquila**; see Rom 16:3; cf. Acts 18; 1 Cor 16:19), a **Mary** who's "worked very hard for you" (Rom 16:6), and even an "apostle" named **Junia** (Rom 16:7). Clearly, such a prominent group of female leaders troubled the scribes who preserved Romans, as well as translators across the ages. Through revisions great and small, they have played down the apparently progressive role Paul presumes among female partners in the gospel. After all, over time, church leadership became limited to gendered males (see e.g., 1 Tim 2:8-15). Did Paul change his mind on the topic? That's a question we'll consider in the next chapter. For now, we simply note that Paul went to great lengths to drop names when it came to showing the Roman Christian community he was well connected to their members—male and female—even if he didn't establish the church.

As far as we know, the only time Paul spent in Rome was as a prisoner. Acts reports that, upon his arrival in Palestine, he was arrested, tried, and extradited to Rome, where he remained under house arrest for months, or even years. Scholars think he died there at the hands of Roman officials, just like his own Lord had about thirty years earlier. The evidence is circumstantial and depends on piecing together a few biased accounts of his career. But chances are, Paul died for much the same reason Jesus did: he made too public a pronouncement of a new world order, challenging settled cultural values along the way. Despite diplomatic attempts to appease imperial officials, Paul's message vaunted weakness, not strength, and promoted devotion to a crucified criminal. That likely made him an enemy of the empire.

Still, like his Lord's, Paul's legacy lived on, first in letters probably written in his name, and ultimately, through the inclusion of the Pauline corpus in the NT canon. To this, Paul might well marvel that this afterlife, too, is as "hard to track as [God's] paths" (Rom 11:33).

Romans winds its way through a delicately balanced conversation about the priority of Jews in God's redemptive work, the inclusive scope of the spirit's work among all creation, the faithfulness of Christ as the game-changing episode of salvation history, and the inexorable promise that God's righteous ways will prevail. Paul takes deliberate care to engage both scripture and conventional rhetoric to translate the story of God's power over sin for a community located at the nexus of imperial power. If creation is still "groaning together and suffering labor pains up until now" (Rom 8:22), Paul is convinced of this: "nothing can separate us from God's love in Christ Jesus our Lord: not death or life, not angels or rulers, not present things or future things, not powers or height or depth, or any other thing that is created" (Rom 8:38-39). As Paul's final letter, Romans may also be Paul's most deeply hopeful.

Review and Reflect

- Identify key similarities and differences between Galatians and Romans—their messages, themes, audience, and tone.

- How does Paul's apocalyptic worldview continue to influence his message? Give three examples of its impact on his letter to the Romans.

GO DEEPER

Bird, Michael F., and Preston M. Sprinkle, eds. *The Faith of Jesus Christ: Exegetical, Biblical, and Theological Studies.* Peabody, MA: Hendrickson, 2009.

Elliott, Neil. *The Arrogance of Nations: Reading Romans in the Shadow of Empire.* Paul in Critical Contexts. Minneapolis: Fortress, 2008.

Lopez, Davina C. *Apostle to the Conquered: Reimagining Paul's Mission.* Paul in Critical Contexts. Minneapolis: Fortress, 2008.

Martyn, J. Louis. *Galatians.* Anchor Bible Series. New York: Doubleday, 1997.

Sumney, Jerry L., ed. *Reading Paul's Letter to the Romans.* Resources for Biblical Studies. Atlanta: Society of Biblical Literature Press, 2012.

Chapter Fourteen

How Does the Pauline Conversation Continue? Pauline Traditions

CONVERSATION STARTERS

- Why do scholars think Paul didn't write at least some letters attributed to him?

- What's changed in Thessalonica since Paul's first letter?

- How does Colossians both echo and revise Paul's earlier teaching?

- What's the relationship between Ephesians and Colossians?

- What makes the Pastoral Letters "pastoral"?

- What features of the Pastoral Letters seem strikingly out of synch with Paul's undisputed letters?

Have you ever left a class or a party or a dinner table carrying the conversation on in your head? Perhaps it's what you said that you'd like to retract, or what you didn't say that you'd like another chance to express. On really important matters, you might even circle back to the conversation much later, after some time has passed. You think about what you said, what you meant, and how it relates to changing circumstance.

In many ways, part of the Pauline corpus does just that: it carries the Pauline conversation forward, channeling Paul's voice as new questions arise. By now, you're familiar with the scholarly consensus that some letters that claim to be written by Paul probably weren't. In this chapter, we'll consider the evidence that leads to this conclusion and invite you into the conversation.

Over the past few chapters, you've grown acquainted with Paul's worldview as we've probed the breadth, depth, and nuance of his thinking on such matters as Christ's faith, the coming "day of the Lord," and the cross as a pattern of selfless concern. We've also seen his take on the Jewish law change, at least in tone and emphasis, depending on the audience for whom he writes. Hopefully, you've gained a feel for Paul along the way—both his writing style and the content of his message. Let's review the main features of Paul's thought:

- Jesus was the Jewish Messiah whose faithfulness to God culminated in his death and resurrection.

- That death and resurrection brought a decisive turning point that instituted the "new creation" and brought "peace with God" for those who reside in it.

- A coming day of judgment, or "day of the Lord," looms near. This will be the moment of resurrection and reckoning, when God will liberate (or "save") the cosmos—and the faithful among it—from the present evil age.

- This "salvation" awaits those who trust in God and God's unconventional power, a power evident in weakness and activated by self-emptying concern for others.

- Meanwhile, believers gather as Christ's "body" in the world, bearing witness to that power through the way they live.

Paul's letters address believers who *already* belong to God's new world order but await the ultimate glory that's *not yet* fully in view. Mostly, he encourages specific churches throughout the Mediterranean to represent the "body of Christ," even when their countercultural allegiance to Christ brings suffering.

Against this backdrop, we turn to the two tiers of "Pauline" letters whose authorship remains a point of scholarly conversation: the **deutero-Pauline** (2 Thessalonians, Colossians, Ephesians) and **Pastoral** (1, 2 Timothy, Titus) **letters**. In what follows, we'll weigh the style and content of each letter as we engage the question of authenticity in terms of internal and external criteria. Here are some of the questions we'll explore:

- Does the *writing style* sound like Paul?

  Based on our study of the undisputed letters, we're familiar with the apostle's syntax, tone, and vocabulary (much as
  your professor may be familiar with yours!). We'll note those
  places where these disputed letters use words and other literary features that make scholars question Paul's authorship.
  (This question is akin to noting the difference in musical style
  between hip-hop and country.)

- Does the *message* sound like Paul?

  Of course, Paul's allowed to change his mind about things. But
  it's unlikely he'd introduce a completely new topic or spin without a clear explanation of why. (Think of hearing your favorite
  politician endorse the views of her most ardent opponent.)

- Does the *historical setting* fit Paul's?

  This question has to do with anachronism. In some cases, the
  "Pauline" letters clearly address a place and time that's far removed from Paul's historical career. This is especially true for the
  Pastoral Letters, as we'll see. (Imagine a supposedly eighteenth-
  century letter that mentions George Washington on his iPhone,
  and you've got the gist of this criterion.)

None of these lines of inquiry works on its own to undermine a letter's
authenticity. After all, like good scientists and jurors, scholars require a pre-
ponderance of evidence to shift them from the default view that, if a letter
claims to be written by Paul, it was. Think of the scales of justice tipping
toward or away from authenticity. Let's see how the evidence stacks up.

THE DEUTERO-PAULINE LETTERS

As a group, 2 Thessalonians, Colossians, and Ephesians are closer to the
undisputed Pauline letters than the Pastoral Letters are in terms of both style
and content. Among them, scholars think 2 Thessalonians shows the most af-
finity with Paul, while Ephesians has least in common with the first seven letters
we've studied. Though the question remains a matter of meaningful debate,
most scholars think someone else wrote all three in Paul's name. (For this conversation, we'll refer to "the writer" or "the author," leaving open the question
of whether or not each letter was written by Paul.)

2 Thessalonians

It doesn't take long to read 2 Thessalonians, since it spans only three chapters. But for those well-acquainted with 1 Thessalonians and the rest of Paul's undisputed letters, this brief letter toggles between the familiar and unfamiliar. In some cases, 2 Thessalonians sounds very much like the sequel it claims to be. But elsewhere, its vocabulary, concepts, and even tone depart in jarring ways from what we've read in the undisputed letters.

Pauline Echoes

Let's begin with the familiar. Second Thessalonians opens with a recognizable Pauline flourish. Both the greeting and the thanksgiving use terms we've come to associate with the apostle's writings: "grace and peace" (2 Thess 1:2); "your faithfulness" (2 Thess 1:3); "bragging about you" (2 Thess 1:4); the list goes on. Similar overlap with the undisputed Pauline letters appears elsewhere as well. The writer mentions the audience's "harassments and trouble" (2 Thess 1:4), for instance. And later, we find the affirmation that God "chose you from the beginning to be the first crop of the harvest" (2 Thess 2:13). The writer encourages imitation of Paul's conduct (2 Thess 3:7, 9), especially his self-sufficiency—a theme found in both 1 Thessalonians and 1 Corinthians. Finally, the letter concludes with a commonplace Pauline blessing of peace and grace (2 Thess 3:16-18). From start to finish, we can say that 2 Thessalonians often sounds like Paul in terms of word choice and writing style.

In a similar vein, 2 Thessalonians engages questions we've encountered before—and mostly from a similar worldview. For instance, the Lord's coming and the judgment it will bring are pressing concerns here. The writer says believers' persecution makes them "worthy of God's kingdom" (2 Thess 1:5) and hopes that the "name of our Lord Jesus will be honored by you" (2 Thess 1:12). So far, so good.

Evidence Against Authenticity

Under careful scrutiny, though, the scales begin to tip toward pseudepigraphy, for two main reasons. The first has to do with language and tenor. Paul's authentic letters may *imply* that the day of judgment will involve "fire and brimstone" (cf. 1 Cor 3:13), but 2 Thessalonians strikes a sharply vengeful tone: Jesus will "give justice with blazing fire" (2 Thess 1:8) to the unfaithful, who will "pay the penalty of eternal destruction" (2 Thess 1:9). Elsewhere we find an unprecedented (for Paul) *ad hominem* attack on "inappropriate and evil people" (2 Thess 3:2) who're persecuting the Thessalonians. The provocative edge of 2 Thessalonians simply fits better with the landscape of Revelation than with the body of undisputed Pauline writings.

The evidence continues to mount against Pauline authorship when we plot the letter's message in relation to 1 Thessalonians. There, Paul encourages believers to live as if waiting on tiptoes for the Lord's coming (see 1 Thess 4:13–5:11); it's clear Paul thinks the day of judgment is at hand. But 2 Thessalonians works in the other direction, emphasizing life in a protracted meantime. One presenting problem the writer diagnoses among the Thessalonians is that some think "the day of the Lord is already here" (2 Thess 2:2). Wait, what?! It's hard to fathom that this kind of **realized eschatology** would gain traction so quickly on the heels of Paul's first (authentic) letter. (Scholars think that, if authentic, 2 Thessalonians was written soon after 1 Thessalonians.)

Even more suspiciously, the writer lays out in detail the events that will precede Christ's coming (2 Thess 2:1-12) and mentions a figure called the "**person of lawlessness**"—probably an allusion to Jewish tradition (see esp. Dan 11:21-45). (See Figure 14.1.) In all his talk about the coming end, Paul never mentions this person elsewhere. But here, the "person of lawlessness" appears as both antitype and precursor to Christ's decisive rule. For now, the author says, Satan's power operates through this figure's rebellious, covert maneuvers. But he'll be "revealed when his time comes" (2 Thess 2:6), when "the Lord Jesus will destroy [the person who is lawless] with the breath from his mouth" (2 Thess 2:8).

How might we account for these changes? Both the passing of time and Paul's developing thought could explain these modifications to his message about the Lord's coming. He could also simply have grown embattled and embittered with age. But two points strain the possibility of this scenario: (1) The timeframe required for these developments simply doesn't fit the widely accepted Pauline chronology we've considered above. (2) Conceptually, we have no data points to plot a trajectory that veers in the direction of a more vengeful and specific scenario for the coming end. In some places if not in its entirety, 2 Thessalonians departs radically from the Paul we've come to know.

There's one more piece of indirect evidence against Pauline authorship of 2 Thessalonians. Many scholars think the writer protests too much that the letter *is* authentic (see 2 Thess 3:17; cf. 2:2). True, Paul often signs off himself, perhaps because he's dictated his message to a scribe and wants to add a personal greeting at the end (see 1 Cor 16:21; Gal 6:1; Phlm 19). But this letter ends with a suspiciously vigorous insistence that it's coming from Paul, really, it is!

FIGURE 14.1: "PERSON OF LAWLESSNESS": FROM ANCIENT TIMES TO TODAY

Most ancient manuscripts call this figure the "person of sin," though text critics think "person of lawlessness" is the original reading. Interpreters across time and place have associated this person with the "antichrist," who appears in 1 and 2 John as one who "denies the Father and the Son" (1 John 2:22). But who is this "person of lawlessness"? The answers, as you might expect, are many and varied, in both Christian tradition and other religious texts. Let's review some proposed identities:

- Many ancient interpreters linked this "person of lawlessness" with ruling emperors such as Caligula or Nero. Protestant Reformers thought the "person of lawlessness" was the pope. Some dispensationalist Christians today think the "person of lawlessness" will broker a (temporary) peace deal in the Middle East, which will bring cataclysmic violence and then Christ's rule.

- Outside Christianity, other traditions assign a role to similar figures. In Islam, the "Deceiving Messiah" (*Al-Masih ad-Dajjal*) will cross the globe, entering every city except Mecca, Medina, Jerusalem, and Mount Sinai, before Christ returns at the day of resurrection.

- The Bahai faith takes a different approach and includes this explanation in its sacred text: "Christ was a divine Center of unity and love. Whenever discord prevails instead of unity, wherever hatred and antagonism take the place of love and spiritual fellowship, Antichrist reigns instead of Christ." (*The Promulgation of Universal Peace: Discourses by Abdul Baha Abbas* [Chicago: Executive Board of Bahai Temple Unity, 1921–22], 1:4)

YOUR TURN: Reread 2 Thessalonians 2 and reflect on the writer's concerns. What do you think about the character? Why do readers come to so many different conclusions?

Summary

In sum, 2 Thessalonians is the most "Pauline" deutero-Pauline letter. In places, it sounds unquestionably authentic. But a (relatively slim) majority of scholars find the case for pseudepigraphy more convincing. They explain the seemingly authentic elements as the writer's effective efforts to represent Paul's views, while the material that's more alien to Paul's worldview strikes a discordant tone they attribute to the passing of time and, with it, changes in the Thessalonians' cultural landscape.

Review and Reflect

- Name the two strongest pieces of evidence both for and against the view that Paul wrote 2 Thessalonians.

- Consider the view that "the day of the Lord is already here." Why might some have endorsed this view, and why might the writer challenge it?

Colossians

The writer sends this letter to believers in Colossae, a town located in a region of Asia that never appears on Paul's itinerary. Unusually for the Pauline corpus, Colossians doesn't imply any personal relationship between author and audience. Instead, Paul's coworker **Epaphras** has proclaimed the gospel in this community (Col 1:7; 4:12-13; cf. Phlm 23), perhaps on Paul's behalf. Based on his reports about the Colossian church, Paul writes from prison (Col 4:3, 10, 18) in an undisclosed location. In places, Colossians sounds true to Pauline thought as we've come to understand it. The writer praises the audience's faith, mentions suffering on their behalf, combats religious regulations, and reminds them of "Christ living in you" (Col 1:27; cf. Rom 8:10; 2 Cor 13:5; Gal 2:20). Other details from the letter, though, strike a chord that's somewhat out of key.

"Into the Kingdom of the Son He Loves" (Col 1:1-14)

Colossians begins on a familiar note of thanksgiving and prayers offered on the hearers' behalf. They've responded to the "good news" (Col 1:5) through "faith and love" (Col 1:4-5), so that the message is "bearing fruit and growing among" them (Col 1:6). The writer prays that they'll be "filled with the knowledge of God's will" (Col 1:9) and for their strength, endurance, and patience (Col 1:11). True, the syntax in this section is more rambling than Paul's staccato style. (Col 1:3-8 is one sentence in Greek!) But many of the words and their meaning fit well with Paul's other letters.

The opening section culminates, though, with a central affirmation that reframes two key Pauline concepts. First, the writer claims that God has "transferred us into the kingdom of the Son" (Col 1:13). This hint of **realized eschatology** will grow clearer as the letter progresses, but already it stands in tension with the undisputed letters, where believers are still "waiting for [God's] Son

FIGURE 14.2: GOD'S CO-CREATOR IN HELLENISTIC JUDAISM

Several Jewish writings in circulation during the first century CE indicate that God had a partner in the creative process. The book of Proverbs, for instance, features a personified figure named "Wisdom" who claims, "The LORD created me at the beginning of his way, before his deeds long in the past" (Prov 8:22) and who was "beside him as a master of crafts" (Prov 8:30) during creation itself. Later writers, such as **Philo of Alexandria**, assign an active role in creation to God's "Word": "But the shadow of God is his word [*logos*], which he used like an instrument when he was making the world" (*Alleg. Interp.* 3.31). The writer of Colossians both adopts these existing views of God's co-creator and interprets them messianically. That is, Colossians equates both "wisdom" and "word" with the Christ.

> **YOUR TURN:** Why might it have been important to the author of Colossians to borrow and reinterpret existing religious views? What's gained through this approach? What's lost?

from heaven" who will deliver them from the "coming wrath" (1 Thess 1:10). Second, the writer says that God "forgave our sins" (Col 1:14). This view of "sins" as personal misdeeds is unprecedented in the undisputed letters, where Paul writes of sin as a cosmic spiritual force (see Rom 5:12; Gal 3:22).

"First Place in Everything" (Col 1:15-23)

The body of Colossians begins with a hymn that provides a conceptual anchor for the letter (Col 1:15-20). Like Colossians as a whole, this hymn remixes Pauline ideas into a strikingly cosmic Christology. Elsewhere among letters, Paul's written about Christ as *God's image* (Col 1:15; cf. 2 Cor 3:18), the *church as Christ's body* (Col 1:18; cf. Rom 12:5; 1 Cor 12:12), and the resurrection of evidence that Christ is the "*firstborn from among the dead*" (Col 1:18, italics added; cf. 1 Cor 15:20, 23). But this hymn elevates and amplifies both Christ's cosmic role and the church's cosmic nature as well.

For one thing, Christ's temporal existence goes back to the very beginning of things, when he was "firstborn of all creation" (Col 1:15 NRSV; cf. John 1:1-3) and even God's partner in the act of creation (Col 1:16; cf. Heb 1:2). (See Figure 14.2.) He's also the cohesive force through which "all things are held together" (Col 1:17) and the "head of the body, the church" (Col 1:18). While the authentic Pauline letters use the term *church* to refer to specific believing communities, this writer speaks of the church in universal terms, as the body of all believers everywhere. The writer highlights Christ's divine nature as well, saying that the "fullness of God was pleased to live in him" (Col 1:19; cf. Col 2:9; Eph 1:23; 4:10). In all these ways, Colossians extends Pauline claims to emphasize Christ's cosmic identity and mission.

"What Is Missing from Christ's Sufferings" (Col 1:24–2:3)

As Paul does in Philippians, Colossians' author rejoices in suffering on believers' behalf (as well as on behalf of their neighbors, the **Laodiceans**; see Col 2:1). We learn later that the writer has been detained (see Col 4:10, 18), but the suffering in view here seems more closely tied to the struggle associated with promoting the gospel (Col 1:29). Notably, this apostolic suffering completes "what is missing from Christ's sufferings" (Col 1:24), an insufficiency that appears nowhere else in Pauline writings. Also distinctive in this section is the writer's use of the term *mystery* (or *secret plan*) to convey the content of the gospel (see Col 1:26, 27; 2:2). The "mystery" that's now been revealed is "Christ living in you" (Col 1:27), and it is this life in Christ that the rest of the letter explicates.

"Convincing Arguments" (Col 2:4-23)

In what follows, the author works rhetorically to dismantle alternative teachings that might lure the Colossians through "convincing arguments" (Col 2:4). On one level, the content of these arguments brings a sense of déjà vu. Haven't we read in Galatians about the "slavery" (Col 2:8) that comes from religious regulations related to food and the sacred calendar (Col 2:16)? Circumcision may be in play here as well, though it's not an explicit part of the opposition's teachings (see Col 2:11-13). And hasn't Paul there attributed such practices to the "elemental spirits" (Greek: *stoicheia*; Col 2:8, 20 NRSV; cf. Gal 4:3, 9)?

But Colossians also features terms and claims that diverge from Paul's authentic writings. The writer uses Platonic language to contrast the "shadow" of false teachings with the "substance" of Christ (Col 2:17; cf. Heb 8:5; 10:1). The worship of angels (Col 2:16, 18) is part of the problem, while Paul elsewhere assigns angels a positive role in his cosmology (see 1 Cor 11:10; 13:1). Likewise, Colossians views visions with suspicion (Col 2:18), while Paul mentions his own visions as part of his list of apostolic credentials (1 Cor 15:3-11; 2 Cor 12:1-5).

In contrast to the "philosophy and foolish decepti
moted by others, Colossians reminds believers of the
in Christ—quite apart from religious regulations (Col
author says believers have been "buried with [Christ] through ᵤₐᵣ
2:12; cf. Col 3:1; Rom 6:3-5). But this writer adds that they've been "raⁱᵤᵥ
with him through faith in the power of God" (Col 2:12). The undisputed
letters look forward to believers' resurrection—emphatically so in 1 Corinthians 15—but nowhere does Paul say that resurrection has *already* happened.
Likewise, Colossians insists that Christ has *already* "disarmed the rulers and
authorities" (Col 2:15), while Paul anticipates the time "when all things have
been brought under [Christ's] control" (1 Cor 15:28). Clearly, the time frame
has shifted, affirming the power Christ wields as a reality that's accessible in
the here and now to believers.

"Put on the New Nature" (Col 3:1–4:6)

As in Paul's undisputed letters, Colossians presses toward moral exhortation. Here, though, it grows out of their status of being "raised with Christ"
(Col 3:1). For now, believers' life may be "hidden with Christ in God" (Col
3:2), but when Christ is revealed that life will be "revealed with him in glory"
(Col 3:4). Meanwhile, the writer encourages the audience to "put to death the
parts of your life that belong to the earth" (Col 3:5)—that is, vices from immorality and greed to anger and obscene language (Col 3:5, 8). Instead, they
should "put on" such qualities as compassion, patience, and "love, which is
the perfect bond of unity" (Col 3:14). Throughout this section, we find Pauline concepts conveyed in language that's sometimes distinctly un-Pauline.

The writer's concern with conduct leads to rather conventional instructions about the domestic sphere (Col 3:18–4:1). (See Figure 14.3.) Paul has
shown little interest in either supporting or undermining social order, since
he thought "the world in its present form [was] passing away" (1 Cor 7:31).
But this **"household code"** conforms to imperial hierarchy: wives should
"submit" to their husbands and children and slaves should "obey" their parents and masters. In a subtle shift, the author tempers the message by addressing those in power as well. Husbands must "love" their wives and not
"be harsh with them" (Col 3:19); fathers must not "provoke" their children
(Col 3:21); and masters must be "just and fair" toward slaves, since they, too,
have a "master in heaven" (Col 4:1). Colossians works to adopt the kind of
social hierarchy that sustains the Roman Empire even as the writer adapts it
to address those in power as well. (See Figure 14.4.)

FIGURE 14:3: HOUSEHOLD CODES

The household codes found in Colossians 3:18–4:1 and Ephesians 5:21–6:4 join in conversation with their Greco-Roman world. Consider these passages from Aristotle's *Politics* that address similar questions of domestic order:

> Of household management we have seen that there are three parts—one is the rule of a master over slaves . . . another of a father, and the third of a husband. A husband and father rules over wife and children, both free, but the rule differs, the rule over his children being a royal, over his wife a constitutional rule. For although there may be exceptions to the order of nature, the male is by nature fitter for command than the female, just as the older and full-grown is superior to the younger and more immature. (*Pol.* 1.7)

> The freeman rules over the slave after another manner from that in which the male rules over the female, or the man over the child; although the parts of the soul are present in all of them, they are present in different degrees. For the slave has no deliberative faculty at all; the woman has, but it is without authority, and the child has, but it is immature. (See Jowett translation, available for download here: http://classics.mit.edu/Aristotle/politics.1.one.html.)

YOUR TURN: Reread the NT household codes and reflect on both similarities and differences. In what ways do the NT passages reflect wider culture? In what ways, if at all, do they reframe or challenge cultural views found in Aristotle?

"Say Hello" (Col 4:7-18)

Colossians ends on a typically Pauline note, with a series of greetings to and from his partners in ministry. Among those named, there's a striking correlation with Paul's letter to Philemon, which also mentions Onesimus, Epaphras, Mark, and Demas. This is not surprising, since Philemon and his slave Onesimus belonged to the Colossian community (Phlm 10). Still, the closing includes language that's out of step with the undisputed letters, as in Epaphras's prayer that the Colossians will "be fully mature and complete in the entire will of God" (Col 4:12).

Summary

In Colossians, we find a vocabulary that sometimes sounds very much like Paul. Yet the letter also develops Paul's core claims in ways that fit better in the decades following Paul's death. Diminished hopes for an eschatological

FIGURE 14.4: FILIAL PIETY IN CONFUCIANISM

"Filial piety" is a core virtue in the Chinese way of life promoted by Confucius and his followers. Confucius thought that rampant corruption in ancient Chinese culture came from lax morals and social disorder. He thought the antidote lay in cultivating key virtues such as justice, kindness, propriety, integrity, and knowledge. **Filial piety** entails proper respect for elders and for other social hierarchies based on gender, age, and authority. Confucius's disciple Youzi puts it this way: "A man who respects his parents and elders is not likely to question the authority of his superiors. Such a man will never provoke disorder. . . . Respect for parents and elders constitutes the essence of goodness" (*Analects*, Book I, Chapter II).

> **YOUR TURN:** How do family relationships affect society? Do you agree or disagree with Confucius about the importance of "filial piety"? Why?

day of the Lord, greater interest in the divine and cosmic nature of Christ, the church's status as a cosmic body of Christ, and increasing conformity to surrounding culture all suggest that time has passed and that the church is in it for the long haul. It seems most plausible that the author of Colossians was a strong student of Paul's who wrote to keep the apostle's views in contemporary conversation with a changing world.

> ### Review and Reflect
>
> - Name two significant similarities and two significant differences between Colossians and the undisputed Pauline letters.
>
> - Consider the writer's connection between Christ's and the church's elevated, cosmic status and identity. What's surprising? Significant? Challenging? Disturbing?

Ephesians

In the most reliable manuscripts, the final deutero-Pauline letter doesn't even name its audience. Today, we call it "Ephesians" since scribes added this designation early on. But since Paul had an extensive career in Ephesus (see Acts 18–20; 1 Cor 16:8), it's striking that Ephesians is highly impersonal. This mismatch leads scholars to doubt that the letter originally addressed the church at Ephesus.

Compared to 2 Thessalonians and Colossians, Ephesians' language and content make it the least likely candidate for authenticity in this subgroup.

Since it has most in common—among its Pauline counterparts—with Colossians, many scholars think Ephesians' author used Colossians as a template and expanded on its message in greater detail. In particular, Ephesians' eloquent vision for the church as witness to God's reconciling power in heaven and on earth has made it a favorite among interpreters across time.

Besides lacking an addressee in its earlier versions, Ephesians departs in other ways from the conventions of ancient letter-writing found throughout the Pauline corpus. In place of the extended thanksgiving we've come to expect from Paul, the letter begins with a blessing that uses language of Jewish prayer (Eph 1:3). A word of thanks does follow (see Eph 1:16), but it's embedded in a reflection on God's power at work among believers. There's no clear thematic marker of the letter's main concern, and the closing section lacks the typical "sign off" found across the undisputed epistles.

The absence of concrete concerns—false teachings to be corrected (2 Corinthians, Galatians, and Colossians), reports about division in a specific community (Romans, 1 Corinthians, and Philippians), or pastoral issues (1 and 2 Thessalonians)—further illustrates how different Ephesians is from the other Pauline letters we've considered. Many views found here imply that time has passed since Paul's missionary ventures. Most scholars attribute Ephesians to a circle of Paul's followers who wrote for broad circulation among Gentile communities in the last third of the first century CE.

"Destined by the Plan of God" (Eph 1:1–2:10)

Ephesians' opening section celebrates the initiative God has taken to secure redemption through Christ. The writer places a heavy emphasis on God's "goodwill and plan" (Eph 1:5, 9, 10, 11), which has reached its "climax of all times: to bring all things together in Christ, the things in heaven along with the things on earth" (Eph 1:10). This divine plan casts a lofty vision of cosmic unity that makes personal salvation a subsidiary point. (See Figure 14.5.)

For their part, believers are called to recognize "God's power that is working among us" (Eph 1:19). It's the same power, the writer says, that God deployed to raise Christ from the dead, to "put everything under Christ's feet" (Eph 1:22), and to make him "head of everything in the church, which is his body" (Eph 1:22-23). In turn, the church is the "fullness of Christ, who fills everything in every way" (Eph 1:23). As in Colossians—only more so—Christ's cosmic power extends to the church.

The writer continues to stress God's mercy, love, and grace as the operative factors that lie behind believers' salvation. God's relentless plan "for these good things" has brought not just their redemption but their glory and power

FIGURE 14.5: DOES GOD HAVE A "PLAN" FOR YOUR LIFE?

Has anyone ever told you that "God has a plan for your life"? Or perhaps that "everything happens for a reason"? For some Christians, Ephesians supplies biblical support for these popular claims. Consider these examples from the letter:

> God destined us to be his adopted children through Jesus Christ because of his love. This was according to his goodwill and plan. (Eph 1:5)

> We were destined by the plan of God, who accomplishes everything according to his design. (Eph 1:11)

> Instead, we are God's accomplishment, created in Christ Jesus to do good things. God planned for these good things to be the way that we live our lives. (Eph 2:10)

In these and other passages, Ephesians makes bold claims about God's sovereign plan—that is, the notion that all of creation and all of history lies within God's authority and care.

But careful attention to Ephesians also leads us to exercise caution in applying this "plan" language to personal fortune—good or bad. The author isn't talking about winning the lottery, finding a parking place, choosing a career, finding a life partner, or receiving a cancer diagnosis. In context, the "plan" Ephesians affirms is God's plan "to bring all things together in Christ, the things in heaven along with the things on earth" (Eph 1:10). That's an expansive vision for unity and reconciliation throughout all creation, rather than a life script that's somehow divinely crafted.

> **YOUR TURN:** What's the difference between saying that "God has a plan for your life" and saying that "God has a plan for the universe"? Do you believe either statement? Why or why not?

as well. As the writer puts it, "God raised us up and seated us in the heavens with Christ Jesus" (Eph 2:6). Paul's future-oriented, temporal eschatology is almost entirely absent in Ephesians (though cf. Eph 1:22; 3:13; 5:16). In its place is a strong sense that God has accomplished what God set out to do in Christ: to establish through grace God's power over all.

"The Barrier of Hatred That Divided Us" (Eph 2:11–3:21)

That Ephesians addresses Gentile believers grows increasingly clear as we make our way through the letter. The writer reminds hearers of their former life as the "uncircumcised" (Eph 2:11) and as "aliens" and "strangers to the covenants of God's promise" (Eph 2:12). But Christ has changed their status before God; they are now "fellow citizens with God's people" (Eph 2:19).

Again, the writer uses terminology that's prominent in Colossians to say this is all part of God's "secret plan" (Greek: *mysterion*; e.g., Eph 3:4). Here, though, that plan relates specifically to the inclusion of Gentiles as coheirs who "share with the Jews in the promises of God" (Eph 3:6). Indeed, Christ has "made both Jews and Gentiles into one group . . . [and broken] down the barrier of hatred that divided" (Eph 2:14). All tension and nuance around Torah-observance has faded from view, as God has rendered the "detailed rules of the Law" null and void (Eph 2:15).

In effect, this decisive shift collapses Jewish tradition into the early Christian movement. From the writer's perspective, God has secured peace and unity by discrediting Judaism on its own terms and folding it into the "secret plan" of Christ. As we've seen, other Jewish believers—not to mention most Jews, who remained unconvinced that the Messiah had come—disagreed with the view that the Law's provisions no longer held sway. (Remember the Ebionite Christians, for example.)

For its Gentile audience, though, Ephesians assigns the church a leading role in showing "the rulers and powers in the heavens the many different varieties of [God's] wisdom" (Eph 3:10). It's this diversity—the inclusion of "every ethnic group in heaven or on earth" in God's plan (Eph 3:15)—that shows forth "love's width and length, height and depth" and manifests the "fullness of God" in the church (Eph 3:18-19).

"Grow in Every Way into Christ" (Eph 4:1–6:9)

The last main section of Ephesians encourages the audience to "live as people worthy of the call" they've received from God (Eph 4:1). The writer places special emphasis on their unity, promoting "the peace that ties you together" (Eph 4:3). Such harmonious relations proceed organically: they are one body, have one spirit, are called in one hope, and share "one Lord, one faith, one baptism, and one God and Father of all, who is over all, through all, and in all" (see Eph 4:4-6; cf. Gal 3:20). As members of God's household, their conduct will bear witness to the unity that holds all things together. (See Figure 14.6.)

Ephesians develops even further Colossians' claim that Christ is the head of the body, the church. The writer calls people to use their diverse gifts in "building up the body of Christ" (see Eph 4:12). Their maturation proceeds from Christ as their head, since "the whole body grows from him . . . [and] builds itself up with love as each one does its part" (Eph 4:16). In contrast to their "former [Gentile] way of life" (Eph 4:22), the believers should don the garb of the "new person created according to God's image" (Eph 4:24) and

FIGURE 14.6: THE QUR'AN ON UNITY

The revelation recorded in the Qur'an (Muslim scripture) affirms the oneness of God as a basis for human unity: "God bears witness that there is no god but Him" (Sura 3:18), and this God has revealed truth in traditions "given to Moses, Jesus, and the prophets from their Lord" (Sura 3:84). Indeed, the Qur'an teaches, humanity was a "single community, then God sent prophets to bring good news and warning, and with them He sent the Scripture with the Truth, to judge between people in their disagreements" (Sura 2:213). The Qur'an includes this appeal: "Hold fast to God's rope all together; do not split into factions. Remember God's favour to you: you were enemies and then He brought your hearts together and you became brothers by His grace" (Sura 3:103).

YOUR TURN: In what ways do these teachings echo Ephesians? What stands out to you as distinctive?

"[follow] the example of Christ" (Eph 5:2; cf. 1 Cor 11:1). They are to live as "children of light" (Eph 5:8).

Embedded within the series of moral exhortations is a revised and expanded version of the household code found in Colossians. Ephesians applies the metaphor of Christ as head of the church to the household structure, likening husbands' "headship" to Christ's (Eph 5:23; cf. 1 Cor 11:3). Similarly, husbands should love their wives "just like Christ loved the church and gave himself for her" (Eph 5:25). What is more, this sacrifice renders both church and wife "holy and blameless" (Eph 5:27). Once again, the writer has gone beyond teachings found in the undisputed Pauline letters, and even in Colossians, to imply that husbands are responsible for their wives' salvation.

"Stand Your Ground" (Eph 6:10-17)

The letter culminates with another metaphor that conveys the power God confers on believers in the context of an ongoing spiritual battle. Emboldened by God's "powerful strength" (Eph 6:10), believers should "put on God's armor" to "make a stand against the tricks of the devil" (Eph 6:11). These enemies are no mere mortals. They're "forces of cosmic darkness" that animate the present evil age (Eph 6:12). Notably this call to arms commends an "armor of God" that features unconventional weaponry: a belt made of truth; a breastplate fashioned out of justice; boots that mobilize a message of peace; a shield of impenetrable faith; a helmet forged out of salvation; and a sword that penetrates with the Spirit, which is God's word (see Eph 6:14-17).

FIGURE 14.7: GOD AND GUNS?

Ephesians may recommend things like faith, salvation, and truth as weapons in the battle against evil, but people today sometimes cite the letter's "armor of God" passage as biblical basis for arming citizens in our own context. NRA (National Rifle Association) spokesperson Dana Loesch wears a tattoo of Ephesians 6:12-13 on her forearm, and white evangelical Christians are more likely than other religious groups to carry guns, to feel safer with guns around, and to prefer minimal restrictions around gun ownership.

Other Christians challenge the alliance between evangelicals and guns, from a variety of perspectives. Some point to ancient interpreters, such as Athanasius of Alexandria, who claims that "Christians, instead of arming themselves with swords, extend their hands in prayer." Others who consider themselves "pro-life" on abortion think that stance requires them to support more aggressive gun control legislation. Still others see the gun culture as inconsistent with Jesus's nonviolent resistance of evil.

YOUR TURN: What's your view on "God and guns"? How does Ephesians' view of the "armor of God" relate to the aims of an armed citizenry?

This equipment, rather than the standard-issue, battle-ready apparel, equips believers for a "stand your ground" agenda that's as strikingly countercultural today as it was in the first century. (See Figure 14.7.)

Closing (Eph 6:21-22)

We've already noted that Ephesians closes abruptly, with little sign of a conventional closing to a letter. It does mention **Tychicus**, the purported emissary who'll deliver the letter, calling him a "loved brother and faithful servant" (Eph 6:21). Otherwise, the ending combines familiar wishes for "peace" and "grace" with turns of phrase unprecedented among Paul's authentic letters (esp. "love with the faith," Eph 6:23).

Summary

For reasons both stylistic and substantive, most scholars agree that Paul didn't write Ephesians. The letter does develop the apostle's teachings in recognizable ways, advancing the Pauline conversation long after heat-of-the-moment disputes about Jew and Gentile have subsided, at least in some communities. In the writer's view, the Gentiles have been seamlessly enfolded into God's covenant people. They're empowered by God's Spirit to display the peace and unity that break down division—not just on earth but in the heavenly realm as well. They're to imitate Christ as they live as "children of the light" as they "submit to each other" (Eph 5:21). Even if Paul didn't write it, Ephesians casts a vision for maturing in Christian faith and life that readers have found inspiring ever since.

Review and Reflect

- Explain two striking features of Ephesians that show either Paul's influence or the likelihood that someone wrote this letter in Paul's name.

- Identify two passages that seem countercultural—in either the first or the twenty-first century, or both.

THE PASTORAL LETTERS

For the last two hundred years, scholars have treated 1 and 2 Timothy, together with Titus, as a subgroup called the "**Pastoral letters**," or just the "Pastorals." The term comes from the fact that they're written to individual church leaders—or "pastors"—rather than communities. (Among the authentic Pauline letters, only Philemon addresses an individual.) But they're also "pastoral" because they have a lot to say about the qualifications required for church leaders. As we'll see, these letters encourage pastors to safeguard doctrines against ideologies that would compromise their "sound teaching."

If you've immersed yourself in Paul's undisputed letters, even a quick read through of the Pastorals raises suspicion about their authorship. A basic word count makes this point: 306 out of the 848 words found in these three books don't appear in the undisputed letters. Terms such as "conscience," "sound teaching," "bulwark of the truth," and "mystery of our religion" signal to careful readers that we're in a conceptual and linguistic landscape that's far from Paul's. What's more, these letters include a heavy dose of *ad hominem* attack—that is, assault on opponents' *character* more than their *views*. For these and other reasons, it's safe to say that someone wrote the Pastorals in an effort to channel the apostle's authority, more than his teaching, for those leading churches decades after his death. (For the record, a small number of scholars believe Paul did write the Pastorals, mostly because the letters say so. Most trained specialists, including many Christian scholars, find the evidence simply doesn't support the letters' claim that Paul wrote them.)

FIGURE 14.8: PLAIN DRESS AND MODESTY

A number of Protestant groups promote what's called "plain dress," based in part on 1 Timothy 2:9. These include Anabaptists such as the Amish and Mennonites, as well as some Quakers, Methodists, Mormons, and Seventh-day Adventists. Provisions that limit nonessential decoration and reflect simple designs apply both to men and to women, though cultural attention focuses mainly on women's modesty.

In her article, "Modesty: I Don't Think It Means What You Think It Means," Rachel Held Evans notes that the word translated as "modest" applies elsewhere to men (1 Tim 3:2) and has more to do with the economic dimension of clothing than with some kind of protection of sexual purity. She writes, "Ironically, I've heard dozens of sermons about keeping my legs and my cleavage out of sight, but not one about ensuring my jewelry was not acquired through unjust or exploitive trade practices—which would be much more in keeping with biblical teachings on modesty" (see Q Ideas: qideas.org/articles/modesty-i-dont-think-it-means-what-you-think-it-means/. [2015]).

YOUR TURN: Reflect on 1 Timothy 2:9. Why might its author care about the "modesty" of both women and men (see 1 Tim 3:2)? What's your take?

If the Pastorals' authorship is pseudonymous, so, too, are the individuals they purportedly address. **Timothy** was indeed one of Paul's closest coworkers (see Acts 16–19) and interacted with both the Thessalonian and Corinthian communities (1 Thess 3:1-6; 2 Cor 1:19). Likewise, **Titus** joined Paul at the Jerusalem Council (Gal 2:1-10) and helped collect money for the mother church (2 Cor 8:6, 16-24). But the letters' time frame rules out the possibility they were actually written to these historical figures.

Why do scholars count the Pastorals among the latest NT writings? Three factors locate these letters in the late first or early second century CE: the Pastorals' *language*, the *views* they oppose, and the *church structure* they assume. All three are anachronistic in Paul's lifetime but fit well within developing thought and practice of the Christian movement around the turn of the second century CE.

Today, Christians vary widely on their approach to the Pastoral Letters. Some churches adopt their teachings—especially the ban on women leaders (1 Tim 2:12) and a statement on the inspiration of scripture (2 Tim 3:16)— as a center of gravity for faith and practice. A few even adopt the dress code promoted in 1 Timothy 2:9. (See Figure 14.8.) Other churches mostly ignore these letters, assigning them only marginal authority, especially when they diverge from Jesus's own interaction with women and Paul's endorsement of female church leaders. Whether you find these letters inspiring or backward, they lend an important voice to the NT's animated internal conversation. Their presence in the canon also reminds us of the human tendency to take sides in that conversation when it gets pointed.

Among the three letters, 1 Timothy and Titus most resemble each other. In fact, most of Titus recapitulates its longer companion. Second Timothy is most Pauline in language and content—an observation that leads some scholars to think it is authentic. We'll begin by highlighting the Pastorals' shared concerns and features. Before concluding, we'll point to some elements of 2 Timothy that better fit the undisputed Pauline letters.

Unlike the deutero-Pauline Letters, the Pastorals show very little contact with the Pauline worldview. When familiar words such as *faith, law,* and *righteousness* do appear, they take on new meaning. Faith, for instance, becomes a belief system rather than the kind of trust Jesus displayed toward God (see e.g., 1 Tim 4:6). The writer merges the law's guidelines, more or less, with the "sound teaching" and the "glorious gospel" (see 1 Tim 1:8-11) and skirts detailed discussion of Torah. Righteousness appears as a goal to be pursued or achieved (see 1 Tim 6:11; 2 Tim 2:22; 4:8), rather than a gift that comes from Christ's reconciling faith.

As a whole, the Pastorals show keen interest in several concerns we haven't encountered in Paul's undisputed letters. Here's a brief summary of some main issues in question:

Sound (Literally, "Healthy") Teaching

This term appears nowhere in the undisputed Pauline letters but repeatedly in the Pastorals (1 Tim 1:10; 4:6; 6:3; 2 Tim 1:13; 4:3; Titus 1:9, 13; 2:1-2). This writer has little to say about Paul's core gospel message and the saving power of Christ's death. Instead, the rhetorical focus lies with highlighting what's amiss with the "wrong teaching" promoted by others (see 1 Tim 1:3). Scholars detect some evidence that the doctrinal errors concern Jewish law (see 1 Tim 1:6-11; Titus 1:14), though it's hard to say exactly what's being taught. The critique of "myths and endless genealogies" (1 Tim 1:4), along with warnings against "so-called 'knowledge'" (1 Tim 6:20; cf. 2 Tim 3:7), may point to an early whiff of **Gnosticism** in the air. The writer's condemnation of those who "prohibit marriage and eating foods that God created" (1 Tim 4:3) also fits that alternative form of Christianity. (See Figure 14.9.) The Pastorals thus weigh in heavily against conversation partners who promote esoteric views and practices that locate them outside mainstream society. Think of the Pastorals, then, as products of "thought police" who care a lot about doctrinal limits.

FIGURE 14.9: SETHIAN GNOSTICISM

As gnostic Christianity took root in the second century CE, one popular version viewed Jesus as the incarnation of the divine being named Seth, who was Adam and Even's third son in the Genesis creation story. This brand of **"Sethian" Gnosticism** appears in early Christian writings such as the Apocryphon of John, Thunder Perfect Mind, and the Gospel of Judas, which feature complex myths about creation intended as a prologue to the biblical account. Here are some key elements of **Sethian Gnosticism**:

- The original god, known as the Invisible Spirit, spawned a "fullness" (Greek: *pleroma*) of demigods (or "aeons").

- One of those aeons, "Sophia" (or "wisdom"), had a son named Sakla (or Ialdabaoth), a pretentious and ignorant god responsible for creating the world and all that's in it. (He's often associated with the creator God of the Hebrew Bible.)

- Though the material world is a disaster, humans carry with them a spark of the divine—or at least some of them do—inherited from Sophia's line.

- The divine aeon associated with Seth came to earth in the form of Jesus to show the way for humans to escape their evil bodies and return to the divine realm.

- That salvation comes through three channels: knowledge (*gnosis*) about our origins; a special form of baptism; and an ascetic lifestyle that denies bodily pleasure.

YOUR TURN: Read at least one Sethian gnostic text (or a lengthy passage from it), and create a conversation between a Sethian gnostic and the author of the Pastoral Letters.

Moral Propriety

In some ways, the "sound teaching" that does appear in the Pastorals takes the form of moral instruction for daily life. Notably, the teachings here have more in common with Greco-Roman moral philosophers than they do with the undisputed Pauline letters. Their interest in "godliness" (1 Tim 2:2; 3:16; 6:3, 5-6; Titus 1:1), as well as attributes such as "a pure heart, a good conscience, and a sincere faith" (1 Tim 1:5), establish conventional decorum as the standard for proper living. Notably, the writer wants believers to live a "quiet and peaceful life in complete godliness and dignity" (1 Tim 2:2; cf. Titus 3:1)—a far cry from the rabble-rousing apostle who kept landing in jail! There's little in the Pastorals that distinguishes "Christian" morality from behaviors promoted by Greco-Roman writers.

Church Leadership

Propriety permeates the Pastorals' instructions about church leaders as well. Directives to Timothy range from the sublime ("Train yourself for a holy life!"; 1 Tim 4:7) to the medicinal ("Don't drink water anymore, but use a little wine because of your stomach problems and your frequent illnesses"; 1 Tim 5:23). The writer also targets different groups of church leaders, such as "supervisors" (or "bishops," 1 Tim 3:1; Titus 1:7), "servants" (or "deacons," 1 Tim 3:8), "elders" (1 Tim 4:14; 5:17; Titus 1:5), and perhaps a designated office of "widows" (1 Tim 5:9-10). Scholars think these specific offices appeared late in the first century CE, as the church grew more institutionalized—and long after the Apostle Paul died. In any case, the criteria for church authorities fits nicely within Greco-Roman standards for civic leaders.

Women

The Pastorals' views on women merit careful consideration for two reasons: these letters depart quite radically from Paul's thought and practice, and they've played a key role in limiting female church leadership for almost two millennia. Remember that women appeared alongside men as Paul's missionary counterparts. He calls them "coworkers" (Rom 16:3; Phil 4:2-3), "apostles" (Rom 16:7), and "servants" (Rom 16:1) and implies that they lead prayers in worship (1 Cor 11:5). The Pastorals curtail that role dramatically, explicitly prohibiting women from teaching men (1 Tim 2:12) and implicitly leaving them out of consideration for offices of bishop, deacon, and elder—all of whom are male. The Greek uses the same word for *women* and *wives*, leading some interpreters to limit prohibitions to married women. (See e.g., 1 Tim 2:12 and 3:11.) But the wider context is so male-centered that gender, rather than marital status, is probably the governing category. The writer of 1 Timothy even says that women "will be saved through childbearing" (1 Tim 2:15 NRSV).

Widows

In the ancient world, widows constituted a protected class (see Exod 22:22; Deut 24:17-22), since women's economic well-being depended mostly on their husbands. Fittingly, then, the Pastorals promote familial care for widows (1 Tim 5:4, 8, 16). But the writer also expresses concern about their proper conduct (1 Tim 5:5-7, 13). A widows' "list" may have constituted a "separate but [not] equal" group of church leaders characterized by exclusive commitment to Christ (see 1 Tim 5:11-12). Some think it was deviant widows who promoted the "godless myths" (1 Tim 4:7) the Pastorals try to supplant.

It's helpful to recall that the conversations captured in the Pastorals leave us with more questions than answers. But the language and content of their message belongs to a setting far removed from the early decades after Christ's death, when Paul and his cadre roamed the Mediterranean telling people about God's crucified Son and the coming day of the Lord. Instead of "people, get ready," the Pastorals chime in with something like this: "people, settle in, dress appropriately, don't drink too much, obey authorities—basically, don't call attention to yourselves."

As we've signaled, though, these statements don't quite apply to 2 Timothy. While this letter shares some concerns and language with its Pastoral counterparts, 2 Timothy stands out from them for two rather Pauline-sounding reasons. First, it presents suffering as a constituent part of faithful living (e.g., 2 Tim 1:8-12; 2:3; cf. 1 Cor 4:9-13; 2 Cor 4:7-12; Phil 1:27-30). Second, it combats realized eschatology that claims "the resurrection has already happened" (2 Tim 2:18) by stressing the future dimension of "salvation" (2 Tim 2:10) and life (2 Tim 1:1; 2:11). If the letter includes enough details to associate it with the (much later) Pastorals, we should note that its writer channels Paul in ways that differ from them.

Summary

The Pastoral Letters (especially 1 Timothy and Titus) belong to a world that's far removed from Paul in both setting and message. In some ways, these letters' pseudonymous appeal to Paul's legacy reads like a power play intended to shore up the author's views on the church's relationship to broader society. That relationship is more settled than we've seen before. What's more, the vocabulary, presumed church structure, and emerging doctrines better fit the late first or early second century CE. That the Pastorals authorize certain views by invoking Paul's name should not keep us from seeing how un-Pauline they often sound.

Review and Reflect

- Explain the four main issues addressed in the Pastoral Letters.

- Consider the ways the Pastoral Letters accommodate values from wider culture. Why might it have been important for Christians to blend in? In what ways does this approach differ from Paul's?

GO DEEPER

Bassler, Jouette M. *1 & 2 Timothy and Titus*. Abingdon New Testament Commentaries. Nashville: Abingdon Press, 1996.

Beker, J. Christiaan. *The Heirs of Paul: Paul's Legacy in the New Testament and in the Church Today*. Philadelphia: Fortress, 1991.

Ehrman, Bart D. *Forged: Writing in the Name of God—Why the Bible's Authors Are Not Who We Think They Are*. San Francisco: HarperOne, 2012.

Lincoln, Andrew, and A. J. Wedderburn. *The Theology of the Later Pauline Letters*. New Testament Theology. Cambridge: Cambridge University Press, 1993.

Talbert, Charles H. *Ephesians and Colossians*. Paideia Commentaries on the New Testament. Grand Rapids, MI: Baker Academic, 2007.

Thurston, Bonnie Bowman. *All the Fullness of God: The Christ of Colossians*. Eugene, OR: Cascade Books, 2017.

Chapter Fifteen

What Do the Other Voices Have to Say? Hebrews and the General Letters

CONVERSATION STARTERS

- What main points does Hebrews make? What's the connection between Christ and "the Hebrews"?

- What's the relationship between faith and works in James?

- What makes suffering worthwhile, according to 1 Peter?

- What views do 2 Peter and Jude promote and oppose?

- How do the Johannine letters remix John's Gospel? How does their message relate to what's happening in their community?

For many Christians, the Gospels and Pauline Letters make up the most revered parts of the NT. And it's true that the catchall collection known as the "general" letters, along with the book of Hebrews, include some of the last writings to be officially included in the canon. Historically speaking, they're further removed from both Jesus's and Paul's careers. But that doesn't mean they're an insignificant part of the NT. Far from it. Consider these verses:

> We don't have a high priest who can't sympathize with our weaknesses but instead one who was tempted in every way that we are, except without sin. (Heb 4:15)

> But how can I see your faith apart from your actions? Instead, I'll show you my faith by putting it into practice in faithful action. (Jas 2:18)

> You yourselves are being built like living stones into a spiritual temple. You are being made into a holy priesthood to offer up spiritual sacrifices that are acceptable to God through Jesus Christ. (1 Pet 2:5)

> Dear friends, let's love each other, because love is from God, and everyone who loves is born from God and knows God. The person who doesn't love does not know God, because God is love. (1 John 4:7-8)

In these later traditions, we find writers who continue to reflect quite eloquently on Christ's significance for those who've come to claim him as Lord, Messiah, and Savior.

This chapter explores these canonical conversation partners as they stake out a place in the world for believers still awaiting Christ's coming but trying to live faithfully in the meantime. Sometimes, they consider the movement's relationship to—and growing distinction from—its Jewish roots (see esp. Hebrews and James). Sometimes, these writings negotiate their hearers' setting in the wider Greco-Roman world (see esp. 1 Peter). Other voices seem more internally focused, weighing in on competing claims about Jesus's divine nature (see esp. 1, 2, and 3 John) or translating a Jewish message for a non-Jewish audience (see esp. 2 Peter). In every case, the authors contend rhetorically with the fact that the hoped-for end, the final victory of Christ, has not yet arrived. Its delay hovers over these texts as they settle in, sometimes awkwardly, for the duration.

HEBREWS

Most manuscripts call this text the "Letter to the Hebrews," but it neither follows the conventional epistolary form nor explicitly addresses the "Hebrews." Only its closing greetings (Heb 13:19-25) sound letter-like, but Hebrews doesn't name sender or intended audience or point to any underlying relationship between them. Early on, Hebrews circulated with the Pauline corpus, though even the second-century church leader **Origen** could tell by reading Hebrews that Paul didn't write it. As for the "Hebrews" designation, this scribal addition probably reflects a best guess, based on the writer's extensive use of Jewish scripture to support claims about Christ. One clue embedded in the closing greeting—a reference to the "group from Italy" (Heb 13:24)—points to Rome as a possible destination for Hebrews. The fact that **First Clement** (95 CE) cites Hebrews supports this view, since Clement was a Roman bishop.

If not a letter, what is Hebrews? Most scholars today think of this book as an extended sermon. After all, the writer bases this "message of encouragement" (Heb 13:22; cf. Acts 13:15) on Jewish scripture. Hebrews may have been accompanied by a separate short letter mentioned in the same verse—perhaps as a cover letter that's been lost.

A careful reading of Hebrews yields important if indirect evidence about its first hearers. They're second-generation believers, since they've embraced "those who heard" the Lord (Heb 2:3). They're also somewhat beleaguered, perhaps weary of waiting for the coming end (see Heb 3:14; 6:11). And they've faced various forms of harassment—from verbal abuse to detainment to confiscation of property—all for the threat their way of life has posed to civic officials (see Heb 10:32-35). These contingencies leave them vulnerable, in the writer's eyes, to a kind of spiritual lethargy (see Heb 5:11; 6:12), or worse, apostasy (see Heb 2:1-3; 3:12-14; 4:1; 10:25, 35-36).

Hebrews is among the most sophisticated NT writings, in terms of literary polish. Its syntax is elaborate and complex, and its unfolding conversation weaves religion and culture together in nuanced ways. Its writer uses Jewish tradition exhaustively, citing the Torah, Prophets, and Writings such as Psalms, while alluding to nonbiblical traditions about **Melchizedek**. Hebrews also employs motifs from everyday life, including athletics (Heb 5:14; 12:1-3), farming (Heb 6:7-8), and education (Heb 5:12-14; 12:7-11), to illustrate key concepts.

Despite admirable artistry and eloquent claims about Christ, Hebrews has sometimes played a sinister role in Christian history. Like the Gospel of John, its message to believers on the bottom side of power emboldens them by way of (negative) comparison to the Judaism. Over time, Hebrews' nuanced affirmation of Moses has often lost out to its stark claims about Christ's supremacy. (See Figure 15.1.) With this in mind, we'll attempt to recover the animated conversation as a word of hope for those at the margins of the socioreligious order.

Hebrews brings believers a threefold word of exhortation. First, the writer stresses the *supreme revelation* of God in Christ, comparing his witness and mission favorably with Moses and other figures in Jewish tradition. Second, *Christ's humanity* enables direct access to God. Third, Christ's intercession and example can bolster believers, renewing their faith and fervor as they *await the coming end*. We'll consider each of these claims in turn.

"So Much Greater"

The book of Hebrews uses a thoroughly Jewish framework to make its case for Christ. Every single chapter highlights both Jesus's *continuity* with

FIGURE 15.1: CHRISTIAN ANTI-SEMITISM

Already, we've seen how some Gospel texts—especially from Matthew and John—have been lifted from their original context of "family squabbles" and used to vilify and even justify violent acts against Jews. Hebrews, too, has played a role in the long and sordid history of Christian anti-Semitism. But if this book's emphasis on Jesus's supremacy laid a foundation for such anti-Jewish thought, other early Christian writings that aren't in the NT only intensified it. Consider these excerpts from the *Epistle of Barnabas* and Melito of Sardis.

The *Epistle of Barnabas* was written in the late first or early second century CE, probably in Alexandria, Egypt, where allegorical interpretation of Jewish scripture was the order of the day. In general, it portrays Christians as a "new people" who have inherited God's covenant in place of Jews. Consider this example: "Now let us see whether this people or the first people has the inheritance, and whether the covenant had reference to us or to them" (*Barn.* 13:1). Notice the sharp us/them distinction. In essence, the writer empties Jewish scripture of all meaning apart from its anticipation of Christ and the "new law of our Lord Jesus Christ" (*Barn.* 2:6).

About a century later, a bishop named Melito from Sardis (in Asia Minor) blamed the Jewish people for God's murder. Hear his own words:

This one was murdered. And where was he murdered? In the very center of Jerusalem! (chap. 72)

Why, O Israel, did you do this strange injustice? You dishonored the one who had honored you. You held in contempt the one who held you in esteem. You denied the one who publicly acknowledged you. . . . Why did you do this, O Israel? (chap. 73)

The one who hung the earth in space is himself hanged; the one who fixed the heavens in place, is himself impaled; the one who firmly fixed all things, is himself firmly fixed to the tree. The Lord is insulted, God has been murdered, the king of Israel has been destroyed, by the hand of Israel. (chaps. 95–96)

See earlychristianwritings.com/text/melito.html.

YOUR TURN: Why do you think some Christians increasingly saw themselves as God's chosen people and blamed Jews for Jesus's death? What are some of the implications of this shift?

God's revelation to the Hebrew people and his *superior disclosure* of "God's being" (Heb 1:3). This framework is what convinces most scholars that the writer addresses Jewish Christians, whose faith may be flagging due to the delayed "day of the Lord." If they're drawn back to their native landscape of Judaism, this writer insists at every turn that Christ both fulfills and exceeds the faithful ways disclosed in that sacred tradition.

The book begins with just such a balancing act. The writer affirms God's voice through the words of the prophets "in the past" (Heb 1:1) but announces that "in these final days . . . [God] spoke to us through a Son" (Heb 1:2) whose credentials are unprecedented: he's the "light of God's glory and the imprint of God's being" (Heb 1:3). After "cleansing . . . the people from their sins," he "sat down at the right side of the highest majesty" (Heb 1:3). In all these ways Christ has become "so much greater than the other messengers" (Heb 1:4). Indeed, this supremacy serves as a governing motif for the entire book.

The writer compares Jesus to a long list of Jewish figures, highlighting in each case the ways he surpasses them. He's better than "angels" (or "messengers") because he's God's Son who's both participated in creation and now rules at God's right hand (see Heb 1:5-14). Likewise, Christ's status as Son puts him ahead of Moses, who was "faithful in God's house," but as servant, not son (Heb 3:1-6). Joshua may have led the wandering Hebrews into the promised land, but it is Christ who offers true "Sabbath rest" (Heb 4:1-11).

Christ's role as "great high priest" (Heb 4:14) means he outshines the priestly orders of both Aaron and Levi, whose standing in Jewish tradition was unassailable. Hebrews assigns Christ to the order of **Melchizedek** (Heb 5:6; 6:20; 7:1-17) an obscure figure whose appearance in Jewish scripture long predates the priesthood as religious institution. Melchizedek appears briefly in Genesis 14 as a Canaanite king-priest who confers the blessing of his god upon Abram. In exchange, the patriarch presents a tenth of his possessions as an offering. Hebrews claims that this gift itself, along with Melchizedek's blessing of Abraham, establishes this "order" based on the "power of a life . . . rather than a legal requirement about physical descent" (Heb 7:16). It is to this permanent office of priest that Jesus belongs.

Christ's superiority to Jewish tradition also means he's "arranged a better covenant . . . with better promises" (Heb 8:6) than the mountaintop covenant given to Moses. Yet even this "new covenant" confirms scripture: the writer cites Jeremiah 31:31-34 as a framework for the kind of laws implanted "in their minds" and "on their hearts" (Heb 8:10) that Christ has brought to fruition. Ultimately, Christ's role as high priest merges with his role as sacrifice to preempt the perennial offerings mandated in Jewish tradition. Christ's "one sacrifice for sins for all time" (Heb 10:12) put an end to the yearly practice of atoning for sin (Heb 10:18).

In all these ways, Hebrews presents Christ as both fulfilling and exceeding Jewish tradition. Rather than nullifying the law, the writer says Jesus completes it so as to render its conventional practice ineffectual. For Hebrews' first hearers, the message about Christ's supremacy shores up his distinctive, and glaring, witness to God's ways.

FIGURE 15.2: JESUS'S SUFFERING IN CONVERSATION

Not all early believers were convinced that Jesus suffered on the cross. And there's a logic to their views. After all, if he was really God, would the creator of the universe and the Lord of Lords willingly be subject to such degrading, violent force? Among those who disputed Jesus's suffering were the **Adoptionists**, so named because they thought God "adopted" Jesus at the baptism. They also thought God's spirit left Christ's human body before his death. We can see evidence of this perspective in the noncanonical Gospel of Peter. Though its passion story follows much of what we find in the canonical Gospels, it takes a more Adoptionist tack with respect to Jesus's death. For one thing, the writer describes Jesus hanging on the cross this way: "he was silent, as if having no pain" (v. 10). When he utters his last breath, Jesus says, "My power O power, you have forsaken me" (v. 18)—a subtle revision of the "cry of dereliction" that suggests God's very presence has departed from his body.

The other two Abrahamic traditions deal with Jesus's suffering destiny quite differently. Judaism affirms Jesus as a wise sage, rabbi, and even prophet and views his death as consistent with the suffering of the faithful in sacred tradition. For Jews, Jesus isn't God; he's a teacher who was executed by the powers that be. Islam shares Judaism's nondivine view of Jesus. Like Moses before him and Mohammed after him, Jesus was a prophet who came to point the way to Allah. But unlike Judaism, Islam bristles at the notion that God's anointed prophet would succumb to imperial strength. Thus, Islamic tradition takes a position akin to early Christian Adoptionists: Jesus, in this view, didn't really die on the cross; it was an illusion. Here's what the Qur'an teaches about Jesus's death:

Those who say, "We have killed the Messiah, Jesus, son of Mary, the Messenger of God." They did not kill him, nor did they crucify him, though it was made to appear like that to them; . . . they certainly did not kill him—God raised him up to Himself. God is almighty and wise. (Sura 4:157-58)

YOUR TURN: What's at stake in the question of Jesus's suffering on the cross? Why does it matter whether or not he suffered? And from what perspectives might his suffering carry meaning?

"Like His Brothers and Sisters in Every Way"

As lofty a portrait of Christ as Hebrews presents, this message also reaffirms his utter humanity. In particular, Jesus's bona fide suffering paves the way for the direct access he provides to God. Through his suffering, he "learned obedience" and so became the "source of eternal salvation for everyone who obeys him" (Heb 5:8-9). (See Figure 15.2.)

The emphasis on Christ's humanity fosters a close connection with the faithful throughout this book. Not only does Jesus call believers "brothers and sisters" (Heb 2:11-12; cf. 2:17), but this human kinship also enables him to "become a merciful and faithful high priest" (Heb 2:17). As a human being, Jesus, too, was tempted, and so he is "able to help those who are being tempted" (Heb 2:18). Indeed, he was "tempted in every way that we are" (Heb 4:15). Even at the point of dire suffering, "Christ offered prayers and requests with loud cries and tears as his sacrifices" (Heb 5:7). By fully inhabiting human suffering—in full expression of human anguish—Christ has bridged the gap between the human condition and God's ways.

Ultimately, Jesus appears as "faith's pioneer and perfecter" (Heb 12:2). That he "endured such opposition from sinners" (Heb 12:3) offers a source of encouragement to the faithful who likewise suffer for their loyalty to God. Like him, Hebrews' audience can look forward to joy, trusting Christ has opened access to the "holy of holies, . . . through a new and living way that he opened up for us through the curtain, which is his body" (Heb 10:19-20).

"Let's Hold On"

Hebrews' sermon-like reflection on both Christ's supremacy and his human plight pauses frequently to encourage the audience to remain steadfast in their allegiance to Christ as Lord. These interludes read as public service announcements and come along just when the lofty prose might find its hearers nodding off. (The writer signals as much; see Heb 5:11.) Sometimes, these exhortations take the "carrot" approach, appealing to the audience's better selves. In other places, a harsh, edgy word of warning that sounds like a "big stick." Let's consider some elements of these intermingled words of exhortation.

As we've indicated, one stark reality frames Hebrews' message: the end has not yet come. Hebrews hasn't abandoned the notion that Christ will come back to complete his messianic task. Indeed, the writer puts it bluntly, insisting Christ "will appear a second time, not to take away sin but to save those who are eagerly waiting for him" (Heb 9:28). This promise hangs over every appeal for the audience's perseverance in the faith (see e.g., Heb 3:14; 6:11; 10:25).

Partly, the writer bases this appeal for their resilience on past performance. Like Christ himself, they've endured suffering in the form of "insults and abuse in public" (Heb 10:33) as well as the "confiscation of . . . possessions" (Heb 10:34). But they've also joined in solidarity with those on the receiving end of persecution (Heb 10:33). This reminder anchors the promise that "the one who is coming will come and won't delay" (Heb 10:37). They need only hold on "a little while longer" before they receive the reward. Like

Christ's, the audience's hardship brings occasion for growth and maturity. Not only does Hebrews encourage the audience to "press on to maturity" (Heb 6:1), but the writer also invites them to bear their suffering "for the sake of discipline" (Heb 12:7). If it "seems painful at the time," it also leads to their sharing in God's holiness (Heb 12:10).

At times, the tone of Hebrews grows less invitational and more biting. The writer says some harsh things, for instance, about those "who turn away once they have seen the light" (Heb 6:4; cf. 12:16-17). (Hint: They're a lost cause.) There's even a bit of name-calling: some are "lazy and . . . haven't been listening" (Heb 5:11). And scary things await those who persist in sin when they know better (see Heb 10:26-31).

Together, these positive and negative words promote endurance among its hearers. They've "seen the light" (Heb 6:4; 10:32). Now they need only hang on until the end. They can trust that their sins are forgiven, since Christ has both presided over and performed the ultimate sacrifice. They can trust that they're now his brothers and sisters whose own suffering leads them toward the glory that he's disclosed.

Review and Reflect

- What are the three main points of Hebrews? Illustrate each with a verse or a passage.

- Consider the writer's claims about Jesus in relation to Jewish tradition. In what ways does Hebrews honor Jesus's heritage? In what ways does it diminish Judaism?

JAMES

Like Hebrews, the book of James bears little resemblance to the epistolary form we found in Paul's letters. Though it names a sender and its recipients, this text lacks any relational basis for the communication, and it ends without any personal greetings. James belongs to the NT collection known as the "catholic" or "general" letters since it has a broad audience in view, but scholars today think of James as a literary hybrid that combines Jewish wisdom with Greco-Roman diatribe.

Traditionally, readers have associated the purported author with James, Jesus's brother, who emerged as a leader in the Jerusalem church after the Apostle James died (see Acts 12:17; 15:19-29; 21:18, 23; Gal 1:19; 2:6, 9).

Called "the Just" in early Christian tradition, James apparently anchored the emerging Christian movement in Jewish tradition, though Luke says he presided over the **Jerusalem Council** decision that limited Torah's commands for non-Jewish believers. Josephus reports that James and others were executed by the high priest Ananus II in 62 CE, a move that gave great offense to many residents of Jerusalem, as well as to Roman officials, who demoted him.

Many scholars doubt the claim that Jesus's brother wrote James. They concede that much of the book's instruction fits early Jewish Christianity. After all, it's strong on Jewish tradition, citing scripture and naming figures such as Abraham, Rahab, Job, and Elijah. James also alludes to many of Jesus's teachings on topics such as prayer, temptation, possessions, judgment, and oaths. Why then the suspicion? James is simply more sophisticated in its use of both scripture and Greco-Roman rhetorical style than we'd expect from a man from Nazareth, a small Galilean village whose residents normally didn't pursue formal education. This book uses eloquent syntax and refined vocabulary—with many words taken from broader society—in ways that convey impressive literary skill. Scholars who doubt James wrote James think that, like the deutero-Pauline and Pastoral authors, someone attached James's esteemed reputation to a set of instructions he might well have endorsed.

Notably, James only names Jesus twice (Jas 1:1; 2:1). In contrast to Hebrews, James minimizes theological and christological discussion, devoting almost all its attention to believers' conduct in the wider world. This book works as a conversation at both the literary and conceptual level. It uses the rhetorical form of **diatribe** to engage its audience in lively exchange through direct address, invitational language, and the use of rhetorical questions. But scholars also think James converses with other Christian claims on such topics as faith, temptation, and the question of repentant sinners (see Figure 15.3). We'll plot that conversation by listening in, quite briefly, on a number of topics that concern this author.

"Patient Resolve"

Like most other NT books, James speaks to those who've passed through hardships described here as "tests" (sometimes translated as "trials" or "temptations"). The writer doesn't describe this testing in great detail, but we can infer it has to do with both external pressure and internal desire (see Jas 1:14). In both cases, believers build endurance through their "patient resolve and steadfastness" (Jas 5:10). And as we've seen so often before, the end is clearly in view: "the coming of the Lord is near" (Jas 5:8).

FIGURE 15.3: JAMES IN THE NT CONVERSATION

James is a great example of one NT voice that's sometimes out of synch with its canonical conversation partners. Here are a few points on which James and other voices disagree:

> First Peter instructs its audience not to "be surprised about the fiery trials that have come among you to test you" (1 Pet 4:12), while James challenges the notion that God tests people: "No one who is tested should say, 'God is tempting me!' This is because God is not tempted by any form of evil, nor does he tempt anyone" (Jas 1:13).

> Hebrews says, "It's impossible to restore people to changed hearts and lives who turn away once they have seen the light. . . . They are crucifying God's Son all over again and exposing him to public shame" (Heb 6:4-6). But James writes, "If any of you wander from the truth and someone turns back the wanderer, recognize that whoever brings a sinner back from the wrong path will save them from death and will bring about the forgiveness of many sins" (Jas 5:19-20).

> Paul insists that "a person is treated as righteous by faith, apart from what is accomplished under the Law" (Rom 3:28). By contrast, James stresses "that a person is shown to be righteous through faithful actions and not through faith alone" (Jas 2:24).

> **YOUR TURN:** What's the role of disagreement or tension within the NT canon? What interpretive strategy might people use to make sense of such differing claims?

"Poor As Heirs of the Kingdom"

James views economic abundance, and the status it affords, with deep suspicion. Instructions about wealth and poverty sound very much like Jewish wisdom. In some cases, James points out common-sense truths about the fleeting nature of material possessions, as well as the use of wealth to coerce and oppress others. The wealthy will "waste away" (Jas 1:11); it is the rich who "make life difficult for you" and "drag you into court" (Jas 2:6). In other cases, the writer warns the rich directly: "Pay attention, you wealthy people! Weep and moan over the miseries coming upon you" (Jas 5:1). What miseries does James have in mind? It's the travails that come when the cries of oppressed people have reached the "ears of the Lord of heavenly forces" (Jas 5:4; cf. Exod 2:27-28). The author then implies that the "self-satisfying life . . . of luxury" will bring, for the wealthy, "the day of slaughter" (Jas 5:5), rather than the day of salvation.

"One Lawgiver and Judge"

James ties judging closely to Jewish law, in two respects. First, to judge according to the law is to submit to a similarly exacting kind of judgment (see Jas 2:1-13). In other words, "there will be no mercy in judgment for anyone who hasn't shown mercy" (Jas 2:13; cf. Matt 7:1-2). Second, the writer reminds the audience that there's "only one lawgiver and judge" (Jas 4:12)—namely, God and not the believer. Like Paul, James assigns the judging task to the only one deemed worthy (see Rom 2:1; 12:19): "Look! The judge is standing at the door!" (Jas 5:9; cf. Matt 24:33).

"Tame the Tongue"

Spoken words matter to James. Perhaps this is because it was God's word that has activated life in believers in the first place, so that "the word planted deep inside you" (Jas 1:21) should give rise to language that befits this "wisdom from above" (Jas 3:17). But James also recognizes the latent power in this "small part of the body" (Jas 3:5). What does James have to say about what believers have to say? For one thing, James promotes what our family calls a "KYMS" strategy: Keep Your Mouth Shut! (Jas 1:19). It's a matter of taming the tongue, which the writer says is harder than taming all kinds of animals (Jas 3:8). Put simply, the tongue has the capacity to operate as a "world of evil at work in us" (Jas 3:6) because it's able to "bless the Lord" and "curse human beings made in God's likeness" (Jas 3:9) at the very same time. Grumbling against one another (Jas 5:9), arrogant boasting (Jas 3:14; 5:16), speaking untruth (Jas 3:14), and swearing by oaths (Jas 5:12) all constitute language that feeds disorder and evil (Jas 3:15).

"Ask God"

What kind of language does James sanction? Prayer offers a means of petitioning God that arises from faith. Not surprisingly, the writer commends believers' earnest prayers for wisdom (Jas 1:5) rather than requests that come from human cravings that arise from "friendship with the world" (Jas 4:1-4). (Prayers for a winning lottery ticket just *might* fall in this category.) James goes so far as to say these latter prayers will remain unanswered, since they come from "evil intentions" (Jas 4:3), while "prayer that comes from faith will

FIGURE 15.4: FAITH HEALING THEN AND NOW

People in every time and place have summoned divine power to heal human ailments. From Shiva in Hinduism to Asclepius and Isis in the mystery religions of the Mediterranean world, a long list of deities promises well-being to those devoted to their worship. In native sacred traditions, healers called shamans mediate nature's life force to restore bodily or mental wholeness by offerings and prayers to ancestors and the use of herbal potions, among other approaches.

Modern Western medicine has generally seen "faith healing" as an inadequate and ineffective response to human disease. Yet even in the Western context, movements such as the Christian Science Church have offered a countercultural way of health. Published in 1875, Mary Baker Eddy's *Science and Health* posits that illness is spiritually and psychologically rooted, not physical, and that healing comes only through prayer. Though Christian Scientist believers don't avoid all kinds of medical care, they do believe that prayer is most effective for healing the mistaken mind-set that's at the heart of physical disease.

YOUR TURN: Why do people turn to supernatural forces for healing? What's your view on "faith healing"?

heal the sick, for the Lord will restore them to health" (Jas 5:15). This verse lies at the heart of some "faith healing" ministries, as well as the Christian Science movement. (See Figure 15.4.) But the Greek text is more at home in the NT's apocalyptic worldview than in the era of modern science. Now that you know a bit about that worldview, consider this alternative translation: "Prayer of faith will save the sick, for the Lord will raise them up." It may be that James is more concerned with end-time salvation than with physical healing in the here and now.

"Faithful Action"

Have you ever heard anyone say, "Your actions speak so loudly I can't hear a thing you say"? It's not a quotation from James, but it's a fair summary of the writer's view on faith and works. Scholars think James issues a direct and emphatic counterpoint to Paul's view that it's faith, not works, that make people right with God (see Gal 2:16; Rom 3:28). Indeed, James asks rather pointedly, "Can faith save you?" (Jas 2:14 NRSV). Paul might say, why yes, it can! James isn't convinced and declares instead, "I'll show you my faith by putting it into practice in faithful action" (Jas 2:18). For this writer, words are cheap; it's how believers live that really matters.

Besides the kind of speech discussed above, that faithful action takes many forms. It can look like caring for "orphans and widows in their difficulties"

FIGURE 15.5: "IF THE LORD WILLS" AND *IN SHA ALLAH*

James seems to echo Jesus's instruction about not worrying (see Matt 6:34) when mocking those who make plans without knowing "about tomorrow" (Jas 4:14). But this writer takes matters a step further, suggesting that believers preface any plans with the phrase, "If the Lord wills" (Jas 4:15). It's a way of reminding them that they're not in ultimate control of their lives. Islam captures a very similar notion through the commonplace Arabic phrase, *in sha Allah*, which means "if God wills." It's a term that acknowledges, as James puts it, that we don't really know about tomorrow.

YOUR TURN: What's the difference between saying "I'll see you tomorrow" and "If the Lord wills, I'll see you tomorrow"?

(Jas 1:27)—that is, the vulnerable members of society. It means honoring the poor at least as much as the wealthy (Jas 2:1-7). It forfeits selfish ambition in favor of a "humble lifestyle" (Jas 3:13). It's evident among those who "sow the seeds of justice by their peaceful acts" (Jas 3:18). In all these ways, believers humble themselves before God rather than playing God themselves (Jas 4:10, 13-16). (See Figure 15.5.)

Review and Reflect

•   Choose two themes that strike you as most significant in James, and relate them to other NT readings. How are they similar or different?

•   The writer says "friends of the world" are automatically "enemies of God." In what ways does this claim ring true or false to you?

1 PETER

The two NT letters attributed to Jesus's disciple Peter have little in common—except their reputed ties to the apostle. But in both cases, scholars have reason to doubt that Peter actually wrote these letters. It's more likely that whoever did write them wanted to secure a seal of approval for their messages. That impulse worked, since the claim that Peter wrote them was likely what led to their inclusion in the NT canon.

Why do scholars doubt Peter's authorship of 1 Peter? Besides the question of Peter's literacy (see our discussion about James above), this letter slips in one historical marker that makes Peter's authorship anachronistic: the use

FIGURE 15.6: PETER'S CRUCIFIXION

Why do scholars think Peter, like Jesus, was crucified? Several ancient writers mention Peter's death in varying degrees of detail. Here are a few examples:

> Pope Clement I's *Letter to the Corinthians* says that, "Through jealousy and envy the greatest and most just pillars of the Church were persecuted, and came even unto death. . . . Peter, through unjust envy, endured not one or two but many labors, and at last, having delivered his testimony, departed unto the place of glory due to him."

> Tertullian's (second century CE) *Scorpiace* 15 mentions that "the budding faith Nero first made bloody in Rome. There Peter was girded by another, since he was bound to the cross."

> Origen's *Commentary on the Book of Genesis III* (quoted in Eusebius's *Ecclesiastical History* III, 1) maintains that "Peter was crucified at Rome with his head downwards, as he himself had desired to suffer."

YOUR TURN: Consider the likelihood that Peter, like Jesus, died on a Roman cross. From our earlier discussions of crucifixion, what does this say about Peter and his reputation among Roman officials?

---

of the term **Babylon** as code name for Rome (1 Pet 5:13). Ancient sources say Peter was crucified by Roman officials, probably in the 60s. (See Figure 15.6.) But Babylon became a reference to Rome only *after* the Jewish War brought Jerusalem's destruction in 70 CE. (Like the Babylonians six centuries earlier, the Romans not only devastated the city but also deported some of its population, making them exiles.)

First Peter addresses "God's chosen strangers in the world of the diaspora" (1 Pet 1:1) located geographically in five Roman provinces of Asia Minor (modern-day Turkey). The letter itself indicates they're former Gentiles (1 Pet 1:14, 18) who have taken on a new identity as "God's people" (1 Pet 2:9-10; cf. Hos 1:9). Thus the author reads these non-Jewish believers into the Jewish story. Like the exiled Judeans before them, these Gentile Christians face challenges associated with their religious minority status and their exclusive allegiance to their Lord.

This letter balances a call to "be holy in every aspect of your lives" (1 Pet 1:15) with a command to "live honorably among the unbelievers" (1 Pet 2:12) harassing them for their devotion to Christ. Ultimately, when they "suffer because of righteousness" (1 Pet 3:14), they follow Christ's example (1 Pet 2:21) while awaiting salvation (1 Pet 1:5). Let's briefly consider these key facets of the letter's message.

"A Holy Nation"

The writer makes it clear that Christians in Asia Minor have earned quite a reputation by casting their allegiance with Christ. It's not so much their *beliefs* that have garnered (negative) attention from their peers. Remember, the ancient world generally tolerated a wide variety of religious and philosophical views. Instead, it's their conduct. They've said "no thanks" to all kinds of fun going on around them: heavy drinking, lavish meals, and wild parties—along with idol worship (1 Pet 4:3). They have distanced themselves from their desire-driven host culture and branded themselves "immigrants and strangers in the world" (1 Pet 2:11). The letter's call to "be holy . . . just as the one who called you is holy" (1 Pet 1:15) thus echoes Torah's mandate (see Lev 19:2) for God's exiled people not to become too at home in the wider world.

"Live Honorably"

That doesn't mean, though, that believers should be morally smug or dishonor their dissolute neighbors. Instead, the writer encourages their "honorable deeds" (1 Pet 2:12) that will, in the long run, bear effective witness to nonbelievers. This letter commends respect toward authorities (see 1 Pet 2:13-15) and cautions believers not to return harassment in kind (1 Pet 2:16). Like Colossians and Ephesians, 1 Peter endorses a household code that reflects the prevailing social order (see 1 Pet 2:18–3:7). Thus Paul's (and Jesus's) more socially disruptive teachings give way to cultural accommodation, perhaps as a defensive move in a setting where "new age" religions were viewed with suspicion.

"Suffering Unjustly"

Stories about Peter's martyrdom make this apostle a fitting so-called author for this letter. Though the believers addressed here don't seem to be dying for their faith, the theme of righteous suffering appears from beginning to end. They're "distressed . . . by various trials" (1 Pet 1:6); they "suffer because of righteousness" (1 Pet 3:14); they've met "fiery trials" (1 Pet 4:12); and they're sharing in the suffering that believers "throughout the world" (1 Pet 5:9) currently face. To be clear, the writer doesn't sanction *all* suffering as the plight of believers; nor does the letter encourage them to seek out martyrdom.

Rather, 1 Peter suggests their suffering comes from their calling Christ "Lord" (see 1 Pet 3:15) and distancing themselves from broad social practice, which the writer calls "unrestrained wickedness" (see 1 Pet 4:4).

That they find themselves at odds with, and even rejected by, friends and neighbors only fits the Christian script. After all, Christ's example—both his suffering and his noncombative response—charts the course for followers as well. Just as Christ was the rejected cornerstone, they, too, are "living stones" whose spiritual edifice now reflects God's "amazing light" (see 1 Pet 2:1-10). All of this unfolds, not surprisingly, in the context of eschatological hope; for this writer too, "the end of all things is at hand" (1 Pet 4:7, author's translation).

Review and Reflect

- Why is it fitting that this letter's been attributed to Peter, and why are scholars confident he didn't write it?

- Consider the tension between "standing out" (holiness) and "fitting in" (honor) in this letter. How does 1 Peter position the believers in relation to the wider world?

---

2 PETER AND JUDE

As the NT canon took shape, 2 Peter, Jude, and 3 John remained "on the bubble" for quite a while. We'll treat the first two of these together, since scholars think 2 Peter was composed with Jude as a template. Let's start with Jude, the earlier and briefer of the two.

Tucked away near the end of the NT, Jude is a short letter that claims Jesus's (and James's) brother as author (see Mark 6:3). Paul names Jude as a key figure among Jewish Christians (see 1 Cor 9:5), and this letter shows familiarity with Jewish tradition—including texts such as *1 Enoch* and (possibly) the *Testament of Moses* that aren't part of Jewish scripture. Some scholars think Jude is an early, authentic vestige of the conversations that animated the early Christian movement.

What is Jude's main concern? It's "godless people" who have "slipped in among you" with a way of life Jude describes as "unrestrained immorality" (Jude 4). The writer likens them to those in Jewish tradition who "didn't maintain their faith" (Jude 5)—from the people of Sodom and Gomorrah to Cain to Balaam to the uprising of Korah. Guided by "ungodly desires" rather than the "Spirit" (Jude 18-19), they're "irrational animals" (Jude 10) in Jude's view. And their vices are deep and wide: they're "faultfinding grumblers," they "speak arrogant words," and "they show partiality" when there's something they can gain (Jude 16). The writer thus calls hearers to "fight for the faith" (Jude 3) as they "build each other up . . . [and] keep each other in the love of God" (Jude 20—21).

Second Peter builds on Jude's message and likewise mentions fallen angels, Sodom and Gomorrah, and Balaam as precursors to the "false teachers" who've appeared among believers (see esp. 2 Pet 2:1-18). In terms of genre, this letter reads like one of the many testaments attributed to such biblical figures as Abraham, Moses, and Elijah that circulated in the late first century CE. What's unique to 2 Peter—and helps scholars to date it in the late first century—is the way it links false teachers' immorality to their denial of the coming day of the Lord.

Second Peter begins with a summary of Peter's teaching presented as the apostle approaches death (see 2 Pet 1:12-15). This testament describes the life of faith as sharing "the divine nature" and escaping "the world's immorality" (2 Pet 1:4). Its language belongs mostly to the lexicon of Greco-Roman moral philosophers, using words such as *godliness*, *goodness*, *self-control*, *affection*, and the like. Once again, the writer uses terms from popular culture to convey instruction about the Christian life.

If this letter uses Jude, 2 Peter expands and refines its denunciation of false teachers. As in Jude, these teachers exhibit "unrestrained immorality" (2 Pet 2:2, 18) and act like "irrational animals" (2 Pet 2:12). They're greedy (2 Pet 2:3, 14), deceptive (2 Pet 2:3), and lustful (2 Pet 2:14). What's more, they scoff at the notion that the Lord will return (see 2 Pet 3:4). In response, the writer explains that "with the Lord a single day is like a thousand years and a thousand years are like a single day" (2 Pet 3:8; cf. Ps 90:4). In other words, history unfolds according to God's timing, not ours. As with Paul, this writer's ethics are eschatological (see 2 Pet 3:8-13). Together, then, Jude and 2 Peter register a sharp rebuke toward those whose views and behavior don't fit their understanding of the Christian faith.

THE JOHANNINE LETTERS

Traditionally, interpreters thought the same "John" who wrote the Gospel by that name also wrote three letters found near the end of the NT. And for good reason. They repeat a number of images and concepts found there. Here's an abbreviated list of some of that overlap:

- Contrasts such as light and darkness, love and hate, God and the devil, truth and lies

- God as "the Father"

- "Remaining" in Christ and God

- A "new commandment"

- "Conquering" the evil one

- Opposition from "the world"

- The promise of "eternal life"

To read these letters is to find yourself in the "thought world" of the Fourth Gospel.

Today, though, scholars generally doubt that Jesus's disciple John wrote these letters—or, as we've seen, the Gospel itself. Careful attention to the letters' content leads most scholars to think they address the same community as the Fourth Gospel (possibly Ephesian believers?), but at a later date, after the Gospel has become a core part of their teaching. As we'll see, these letters carry on a conversation about Jesus's meaning on two levels. At the literary level, they elaborate and refine many of the Gospel's claims about Christ and the life of faith. At the historical level, they seem to engage, and sometimes dispute, those who have interpreted the Gospel in a certain way.

Though we call them "letters," only 2 and 3 John follow the epistolary format we've described above. First John reads like Hebrews and James— as more of a sermon than a letter. The two bona fide letters in this group claim authorship by "the elder" (2 John 1:1; 3 John 1:1), a term that helps scholars date them to a late first- or early second-century CE setting, when such offices became part of the institutional church. They also both name recipients. Second John addresses "the chosen gentlewoman and her children" (2 John 1). Since the writer clearly addresses a group of believers and refers in closing to another "chosen sister" (2 John 13), scholars think this is an image for the church. Third John starts out by naming **Gaius** as its recipient but then shifts to the plural form of "you," so it likely was written for a community rather than an individual. That means that none of these "general letters" circulated to a general audience, at least at first, and one of them isn't a letter at all. Still, as part of the NT conversation, they open a window into one community's deliberations about who Jesus was, really, and what his legacy entails.

"God Is Love"

If you're looking for scripture that underscores the central role of love in the Christian life, look no further than the Johannine letters (especially 1 and 2 John). Together, they read as almost a "cover" of the Farewell Discourse from John's Gospel (John 13–17). There, Jesus gives his disciples a "new commandment" that they "love one another" in the manner that he's loved them: selflessly, even laying down lives for one another (see John 15:12-13). He also tells them to "remain in" him, even when the world "hates" them. It is this abiding presence, he says, that secures their "eternal life."

First and 2 John take up all of these themes and amplify them. For this writer, the litmus test of faith has less to do with either works (as in James) or correct belief and morality (as in Jude and 2 Peter). Instead, believers' love for one another distinguishes their Christian identity: "This is the message that you heard from the beginning: love each other" (1 John 3:11). Love is *the* qualifying trait of God's children (see 1 John 4:7-21). In this way, the author reduces (or expands, depending on your perspective) the Gospel's message to one fine point: if you claim to love God, you must love each other.

"Come as a Human"

If these letters mostly repeat the Fourth Gospel's message in miniature, they do so at least partly by countering believers who have left the church (see 1 John 2:19; 2 John 7). On what grounds? The writer names these points of theological difference: they deny both that "Jesus is the Christ" (1 John 2:22) and that he "has come as a human" (1 John 4:2; 2 John 7). Scholars think the view under attack here fits a form of Gnosticism called **docetism**. This term comes from the Greek verb "to seem" and designates those who fully accepted Jesus's divine nature but insisted that he only "seemed" human. (See Figure 15.7.)

To be fair, it's easy to see how readers of the Fourth Gospel might have inferred as much. After all, we've noted John's keen interest in Jesus's divine origins, his intimate ties to the Father, and his divine destiny. And if some in John's community were inclined to affirm Jesus's divinity at the expense of his humanity, they have good company among readers of the Fourth Gospel today.

In some ways, the Johannine letters are less about winning this schismatic group back into the fold and more about forging durable ties between the human Jesus and his sacrificial act of divine love on the one hand, and the community's enduring witness to that love in their life together on the other. For this writer, it's a package deal; the call to radical love can't be severed from

FIGURE 15.7: DOCETISM

The term ***docetism*** refers to a version of early Christian Gnosticism that denied the bodily incarnation—and especially death—of Jesus as the Christ. The word itself derives from the expression "to seem to be"—as in, the Christ only *seemed to be* human. The Johannine letters may preserve a lively conversation with those in John's community who had interpreted the Gospel in a docetic light. In response, the author of the letters insists with vigor that Jesus did indeed come in the flesh.

But these members of the Johannine community weren't the only ones who downplayed Jesus's humanity. We've already noted features of the Gospel of Peter that dehumanize Jesus, especially his suffering destiny. In addition, noncanonical voices such as the Gospel of Judas, Philip, and Basilides all hint at underlying doceticism. Here are a few sayings that illustrate this stream of thought:

> Gospel of Philip: "Jesus took them all by stealth, for he did not appear as he was, but in the manner in which they would be able to see him. He appeared to them all. He appeared to the great as great. He appeared to the small as small. He appeared to the angels as an angel, and to men as a man." (See http://www.earlychristianwritings. com/text/gospelphilip.html.)

> Gospel of Basilides (as cited in Irenaeus, *Haer.*, I:24:4): "But the father without birth and without name, perceiving that they would be destroyed, sent his own first-begotten Nous (he it is who is called Christ) to bestow deliverance on them that believe in him, from the power of those who made the world. He appeared, then, on earth as a man, to the nations of these powers, and wrought miracles. . . . For since he was an incorporeal power, and the Nous (mind) of the unborn father, he transfigured himself as he pleased, and thus ascended to him who had sent him, deriding them, inasmuch as he could not be laid hold of, and was invisible to all."

YOUR TURN: Reflect on the Fourth Gospel and its portrait of Jesus. What details lend themselves to a docetic reading? Why might the author of the Johannine letters have felt compelled to "correct" this view?

the decidedly human career of God's Son, come in the flesh. Only through the human Jesus, the writer insists, can we see divine love fully disclosed.

"We Are from God"

As a whole, the Johannine letters harshly criticize the sectarian group that has taken a bogus message from the Gospel on the road. They're "**antichrists**" (1 John 2:18, 22; 4:3; 2 John 7), meaning their views cut against the grain of the gospel; they're "from the world" and speak from a "spirit of error" (1 John 4:5-6). The writer's response? Cut them off. As in, when they stop by your house, don't invite them in (2 John 10-11).

But this approach draws a clear line in the sand that demarcates insiders from outsiders, making the community itself more sectarian by definition. In the Gospel, that line is still permeable. There, Jesus sends his followers into the world that hates them, so that they become part of God's saving plan for the cosmos. But the Johannine letters come from a later phase in the community's life, when it's time to circle the wagons, strengthen their own social cohesion, and await Christ's coming (1 John 2:18, 28; 3:17). Though the Johannine letters offer a message of love that many find exquisite and compelling, it's a message originally crafted for insiders or like-minded believers, not for the world at large.

Review and Reflect

- Describe the concerns of the Johannine community and the writer's response to them.

- Consider the sectarian roots of the message to love one another. What's the difference between love for those who share your views and for those who don't?

SUMMARY

The NT writings considered in this chapter span a range of historical and theological perspectives. Together, though, they provide a window into the currents of conversation emerging as the early Christian movement made its way in the Mediterranean world. In some books, the relationship to Jewish tradition stands out as a dominant topic, even if the NT writers don't agree on that relationship. Other writings considered in this chapter concern the movement's relationship to the Greco-Roman culture to which they belong. Still others address points of theological distinction among the communities' members, or former members. In each case, these writers stake out their place in the world in conversation with both insiders and outsiders. Together, they base ultimate hope in the coming "day of the Lord" and with it, the messianic age of justice and righteousness Christ's return will secure once and for all.

GO DEEPER

Batten, Alicia J. *What Are They Saying about the Letter of James?* New York: Paulist Press, 2009.

Beker, Adam, and Annette Yoshiko Reed. *The Ways That Never Parted: Jews and Christians in Late Antiquity and the Early Middle Ages*. Minneapolis: Fortress Press, 2007.

Donelson, Lewis R. *From Hebrews to Revelation: A Theological Introduction*. Louisville, KY: Westminster John Knox, 2001.

Isaacs, Marie E. *Reading Hebrews and James: A Literary and Theological Commentary*. Reading the New Testament Series. Macon, GA: Smyth and Helwys, 2002.

Moss, Candida R. *The Myth of Persecution: How Early Christians Invented a Story of Martyrdom*. San Francisco: HarperOne, 2013.

Is This the End?
Revelation

CONVERSATION STARTERS

- What's an "apocalypse," and what setting do apocalypses typically address?

- What can we know about the author and audience of Revelation?

- What are the main claims of this book?

- How do the images and symbols work in Revelation?

- How do different readers understand Revelation today?

For many readers, Revelation is the most daunting—and possibly frightening—book in the New Testament. If you're even vaguely acquainted with this text, you may have heard about its infamous beast, marked with the number 666, who opposes God and God's people with mighty force. You may be familiar, too, with Revelation's predictions of cosmic disaster: plagues, earthquakes, and oceans of blood. And you may have the impression that the heavy-handed, judging, war-mongering Jesus of Revelation bears only faint resemblance to the Jesus found elsewhere in the Christian Bible.

To some degree, this popular take on Revelation is not far off base. Revelation *does* herald cosmic disaster; it *does* pit God against Satan, sometimes embodied in a beast; and Jesus *does* appear as a warrior on a white horse who secures victory for God by annihilating the opposition. A simple, start-to-finish reading of Revelation leaves us mostly with a grim picture of things to come and only a final flourish of hope.

In some ways, it's an odd finish to a collection of writings mostly geared toward describing Jesus's mission on earth and its lasting implications for believers after the resurrection. As different as the other NT books can be, they hold in common quite a this-worldly perspective. Jesus himself lives and dies in a particular Palestinian Jewish context. Communities of believers grapple with his messiahship in conversation with both Judaism and their Greco-Roman world. And then there's Revelation, which seems more interested in other-worldly realities, such as the heavenly throne room and an earth filled with dragons and beasts and other odd creatures.

For these and other reasons, Revelation is in "last place" in the NT canon on many levels. In terms of order, it concludes Christian scripture. It's also preoccupied with "what must take place after this" (Rev 4:1)—that is, with a future that brings the end of the world as we know it. But Revelation was also among the last books to secure canonical status. Many church leaders found it terrorizing and susceptible to dangerous misinterpretation. Eastern Christianity hesitated for centuries to count Revelation as scripture.

Almost two millennia later, many Christians still aren't sure what to do with Revelation. Some dismiss this book as a sort of drug-induced horror film that sanctifies violence and denigrates women. Even if it remains in the Bible, these readers insist, it's not a center of gravity for understanding Christian faith. However, some find in Revelation a blueprint for reading the sociopolitical landscape of our time. This "historicizing" approach treats Revelation as code to be cracked, as if its vision were written for our twenty-first-century setting. (Of course, contemporary readers who take this approach aren't the first ones to think Revelation addresses their own place and time.)

This chapter differs from both responses. As we have with the other NT writings, we'll explore Revelation in conversation with its own world. By considering both its conversational style (literary form) and its conversation partners (historical context), we come closer to reading Revelation on its own terms. In this way, we begin to detect both the present meaning and the future hope its message brings to those suffering for their loyalty to that alternative world order we've been calling the "kingdom of God."

THE GENRE OF APOCALYPSE

Throughout our study, we've noted the pulse of Jewish apocalyptic thought coursing through the NT. From the Gospels to Acts and the Pauline corpus to the Catholic letters, we've encountered the view that Jesus's

FIGURE 16.1: APOCALYPSE OF PETER

Found among the Nag Hammadi library, the Apocalypse of Peter features a first-hand account of Peter's encounter with the risen Jesus and was even included in some early collections of Christian scripture. Here is a brief passage from this apocalypse:

> And the Lord showed me a very great country outside of this world, exceeding bright with light, and the air there lighted with the rays of the sun, and the earth itself blooming with unfading flowers and full of spices and plants, fair-flowering and incorruptible and bearing blessed fruit. . . . And the dwellers in that place were clad in the raiment of shining angels and their raiment was like unto their country; and angels hovered about them there. And . . . with one voice they sang praises alternately to the Lord God, rejoicing in that place. . . . And over against that place I saw another, squalid, and it was the place of punishment; and those who were punished there and the punishing angels had their raiment dark like the air of the place. And there were certain there hanging by the tongue: and these were the blasphemers of the way of righteousness; and under them lay fire, burning and punishing them. And there was a great lake, full of flaming mire, in which were certain men that pervert righteousness, and tormenting angels afflicted them. (*Apoc. Pet.*, 15-22; see http://www.earlychristianwritings.com/text/apocalypsepeter-roberts.html)

YOUR TURN: What details from this excerpt fit the genre of *apocalypse*?

life, death, and resurrection brought the dawning of God's kingdom on the earth—a kingdom of justice and righteousness and peace. We've connected that view to the historical Jesus himself, and we've noted the ways in which NT writers both adopt and adapt Jewish apocalyptic thought to make sense of their meantime reality. If they believed the "new creation" had dawned in Jesus, they had to contend with the fact that it wasn't yet fully in view. In different ways, each book grapples with the delay of Jesus's "coming" (***parousia***) that will establish God's reign in palpable ways.

As we turn to Revelation, we find ourselves in familiar territory, at least to some degree. It, too, is shot through with the promise that God's kingdom will soon arrive on earth. What's different about Revelation is its literary form, or genre: it is the only full-length NT **apocalypse**. (Its name in Greek, *apocalypsis*, makes this identification crystal clear.) Yet as an apocalypse, Revelation fits well among both Jewish and Christian apocalypses of its day. (See Figure 16.1.) We begin, then, by noting the features that make Revelation an apocalypse in the technical sense. Within this genre, Revelation sounds less like a bizarre aberration and more like a recognizable literary type that reinterprets earthly existence in light of heavenly visions. Like its NT conversation

FIGURE 16.2: WHO (OR WHAT) IS "666"?

In the middle of John's vision about the two beasts, we find these words: "This calls for wisdom. Let the one who understands calculate the beast's number, for it's a human being's number. Its number is six hundred sixty-six" (Rev 13:18). John wants us to understand he's using code language to equate the mythical beast with a real-live human being. But whom does the number designate?

To answer the question, we have to understand the ancient practice of **gematria**, which uses the numeric value of letters (think Roman numerals) as a sort of secret code. Many interpreters think the beast's number denotes "Nero Caesar," since the letters of this name add up to 666. Those who adopt a historicizing view of Revelation have linked this number to a wide range of figures—from popes, to dictators, to transnational organizations. Others think the "understanding" John promotes is more symbolic and view the number as utter imperfection (as opposed to "777," which would be a "perfect number").

YOUR TURN: What kind of "wisdom" do you think John intended here? Why?

partners, Revelation, too, views present circumstance through the lens of Jewish apocalyptic thought.

Literary Form

What literary features do apocalypses share? For one thing, they typically relate a narrator's *journey into the heavenly realm*, where God sits on a throne. In most Jewish apocalypses, that narrator is a legendary figure such as Enoch, Daniel, or Ezra, who is escorted by an interpreting angel into celestial territory, usually through a "door" (see Rev 4:1-2; cf. Isa 6:1; Dan 7:1; 2 Cor 12:1-10). The word *apocalypse* conveys pulling back the curtain of the heavens to "reveal" a world that's usually hidden from human sight.

A second literary trademark of this genre has to do with what the visionary sees: a stunning barrage of *graphic images and symbols*. On one level, these images attempt to convey the ineffable—or what defies human language—such as God's glory and the evil impulse of earthly rulers' beastly nature. Often, both real and imagined animals designate heavenly and earthly characters. For instance, John sees "four living creatures" (lion, ox, eagle, and human) who worship around God's throne (Rev 4:6; cf. Ezek 1:10). Later, two beasts represent earthly rulers (Rev 12–13; cf. Ezek 29:3; Dan 7:3-7). On another level, apocalypses sometimes use symbols and images to encode meaning that's too dangerous to convey in plain speech. One convention called **gematria** uses numbers to allude cryptically to historical figures (see Figure 16.2).

A third and related literary trait found in apocalypses is *cosmic dualism*. We've seen this binary worldview in play elsewhere in the NT—especially in the Johannine literature. But Revelation epitomizes the notion that opposing forces are at odds with each other at every level: personal, sociopolitical, environmental, and cosmic. Dichotomies show up at every turn, marking sharp distinctions in terms of time (present versus future), spiritual powers (good versus evil), and human morality (righteous versus unrighteous). In other words, apocalypses leave little room for discussion or what we call "gray areas."

Social, Political, and Religious Function

These literary traits fit well with the social, political, and religious function that apocalypses share. As many scholars have noted, the genre itself is closely related to the Hebrew Bible's prophetic tradition. Indeed, the earliest apocalypses are part of larger prophetic books, such as Isaiah (Isa 24–27) and Ezekiel (Ezek 40–48). Like conventional prophecy, these apocalypses address the gap between the way things are and the way they could or should be—in ways that extend beyond personal concerns to encompass wider society. Like the prophets, apocalypses suggest that those who hold earthly power are subverting God's covenant values of justice and righteousness, and both prophetic and apocalyptic texts call for allegiance to those values.

But if the prophets challenge their hearers to "straighten up and fly right" through fairly direct messaging, apocalypses take a different tack. Rather than outright oracles, they include the audience on the visionary's heavenly journey and expose hearers to an alternative kind of power. Apocalypses afford us a chance to peek in to God's "command and control" room and come away more convinced than ever that God's reign will ultimately prevail. They also spy God's justice at work in heaven as a preamble to the divine justice that will soon arrive on earth.

Why the shift from prophecy to apocalypse? The historical contexts in which apocalypses grew popular help us grasp the impetus that lies behind this literary genre. From the writers' perspective, things have gone from bad to worse, and those who trust in God's ways seem to be on the losing side of history. Another rant about righteousness, they think, will only get them in trouble.

Some apocalypses appeared, for instance, during the oppressive regime of Antiochus IV Epiphanes, the Syrian ruler who occupied Palestine in the second century BCE. Besides a heavy-handed military occupation, the Syrians also tried to erase distinctive Jewish practices, such as dietary laws and circumcision, and native culture. While the Maccabeans responded with an armed uprising, the book of Daniel includes an apocalypse that sends a different message: hang on; God's power in heaven will soon make its way to earth. Other apocalypses—including parts of *1 Enoch*—address the Roman occupation of Palestine under which Jesus lived and died. Together, apocalypses stand as a creative form of literary resistance whose greatest weapon was the imagination. Peering into God's throne room allows their audiences to claim anew their conviction that the "arc of the universe bends toward justice," even when that justice seems far from view. (See Figure 16.3.)

As a result, this genre locates the audience's present crisis within a wider framework of time and space. Their suffering is temporary, in that it will give way to God's triumph. It's also only part of the story, since God remains in charge of the cosmos. In short, apocalypses bring both meaning and hope to those who experience oppression at the hands of earthly forces. They reimagine power, reinterpret suffering, and reaffirm that history is moving inexorably toward God's decisive defeat of evil.

Review and Reflect

- What three literary features do apocalypses share?

- Reflect on apocalypses as "creative resistance." How might they function in this way?

THE AUTHOR AND AUDIENCE OF REVELATION

Now that we have situated Revelation within the genre of apocalypse, we turn to the specifics of this work's setting and message. Like all NT texts, Revelation offers a window into a first-century conversation between a writer and an audience. And as with the rest of the NT's contents, we'll offer some observations about these conversation partners without answering all questions about them in detail.

Revelation stands out from other apocalypses because it names its author as a contemporary figure rather than a venerated character from the biblical tradition. But who was this John? Early church traditions identify him with the apostle, John of Zebedee, with the writer of the Fourth Gospel and Johannine letters, or with both. But like many ancient claims about authorship, these connections find little support in the evidence at hand.

Several observations undermine either possibility. For one thing, John's first vision takes him to heaven where he sees "twenty-four elders" praising

FIGURE 16.3: CREATIVE RESISTANCE

Resistance movements in a variety of settings use creative strategies to imagine the end of human subjugation. Because systemic oppression works to dehumanize those whom its violence targets, the arts are a particularly effective way of responding not with more violence but with an affirmation of the human spirit.

Stories from the Holocaust consistently point to the role of the arts in resisting Nazi strategies designed to dehumanize Jews and other targeted groups. One example comes from the Terezín concentration camp, where pianist Gideon Klein both played and taught others to do likewise as what one author has called "a revolt against the regime" (Ruth Elias, *Triumph of Hope* [Hoboken, NJ: Wiley, 1999]). In the autobiography *Night*, Elie Wiesel recalls a prisoner named Juliek playing the violin: "It was pitch dark. I could hear only the violin, and it was as though Juliek's soul were the bow. He was playing his life" (New York: Bantam, 1960).

In a similar manner, the artist Banksy has painted a number of murals on the wall that separates Palestinians from their wider landscape. Like Revelation, the one below "pulls back the veil" of reality to envision a world marked by freedom and life.

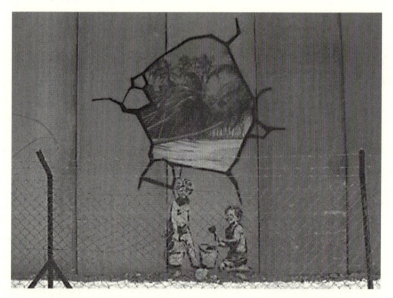

A Banksy graffiti mural at the Israeli West Bank barrier wall bordering Palestinian communities. Bethlehem (Wikimedia Commons)

YOUR TURN: What makes "creative resistance" both "creative" and an effective means of "resistance"?

FIGURE 16.4: THE ISLAND OF PATMOS

Patmos is a small island in Greece, believed to be the location of the vision given to the disciple John and where he wrote the New Testament book of Revelation.

God (see Rev 4:4, 10). The number probably designates two traditional "twelves"—the mythical tribes of Israel and the apostles. Since the vision presumes the apostles have died, this John can't be the John of Zebedee who would be counted among them. Clear differences between Revelation and the Fourth Gospel also make it unlikely this evangelist is the same as the visionary. The Gospel's writing style, for example, is much more fluid than Revelation's, which may be deliberately written in nonstandard Greek. The content differs as well. Both the Fourth Gospel and the Johannine letters assign central importance to love, a concept that's strikingly absent from Revelation's series of apocalyptic visions. For all these reasons, it's likely that we don't have access to any other writings by this John.

Whoever he was—and the name *John* was as common in the ancient world as it is today—this John writes from an island called **Patmos** (see Figure 16.4), where he has been exiled "because of the word of God and my testimony about Jesus" (Rev 1:9). Apparently, John's devotion to Jesus, the Jewish Messiah, put him on a watch list as a potential threat to imperial peace and security. We also know he is steeped in Jewish thought, since his visions borrow freely from a wide array of biblical and noncanonical Jewish writings. Here's what we can say about John: he was probably a Jewish believer with enough stature in the church to draw the attention of Roman officials.

For whom does John write? Revelation says John sends this dictated message to "the seven churches that are in Asia" (Rev 1:4; see Figure 16.5). This detail suggests that, like Paul and his churches, John had some kind of relationship with believers in this region, which he may have called home. From other sources, including some Pauline letters, we know believing communities had popped up in the towns named here. Together, they distinguished themselves by their allegiance to God and God's Messiah Jesus, whom they called Lord. As a result, Revelation suggests that many believers experienced various kinds of persecution for such faith.

It's hard to pinpoint the precise date and setting of this work. Some interpreters think Revelation 13:18 links the "number of the beast"—the infamous **666**—with **Nero Caesar**, who blamed Christians for a devastating fire in Rome, in the 60s CE. But even if this connection is accurate, Revelation as we read it today postdates Nero's rule, since it uses the code name "**Babylon**" for Rome (see Rev 14:8; 17:5; 18:2). In the late second century CE, Irenaeus links Revelation's message to the reign of **Emperor Domitian** (81–96 CE), but evidence for any widespread targeting of Christians during this time is sparse. Most scholars think Revelation was written in the late first or early second century CE.

If we can't specify a date, we can offer general observations about the religious and political climate of the Roman Empire that made Christians vulnerable to persecution. As we've discussed, believers' loyalty to God and to the Christ precluded participation in local or imperial religion. For this reason alone, many outsiders viewed them with suspicion. That loyalty probably entailed social and economic practices that were countercultural as well. For these and other reasons, John's intended audience stood out for their faith in God and their conviction that God's alternative world order would soon prevail.

THE BOOK OF REVELATION

Revelation conveys a message from a mystical prophet named John to those who find themselves in the crosshairs of imperial power. The text's spectacular account of John's voyage into the heavens frames lived reality within the wider canvas of God's sovereign reign. As a result, Revelation imbues their suffering with meaning—as part of God's unfolding plan—while insisting that it leads inexorably to vindication and glory. Let's follow the contours of this conversation and its imaginative, disorienting visions. (See Figure 16.6.)

FIGURE 16.5: MAP OF ASIA MINOR AND THE SEVEN CHURCHES

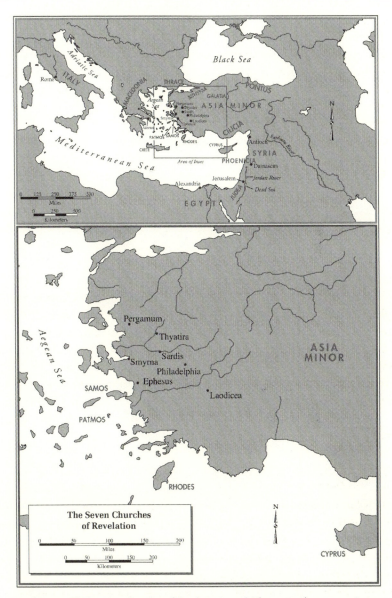

Asia Minor with the seven churches of Revelation noted. These were the seven major churches of early Christianity as mentioned in the book of Revelation. The proximity of the Greek Island of Patmos is also noted.

FIGURE 16.6: AN OUTLINE OF REVELATION

Introduction (1:1-20)

Letters to Seven Churches (2:1–3:22)

Apocalyptic Visions (4:1–22:7)

> Heavenly Court (4:1–5:14) + Seven Seals and Trumpets (6:1–11:19)
>
> Dragon, Beasts, Lamb (12:1–14:20) + Seven Plagues and Bowls (15:1–16:21)
>
> Judgment of Babylon (17:1–19:10) + Cosmic Victory and New Creation (19:11–22:7)

Conclusion (22:8-21)

Introduction (Rev 1:1-20)

Revelation's opening chapter serves as a reader's guide to the rest of the book. For one thing, John calls his message prophecy, a term that sets Revelation apart in the NT (Rev 1:3). For while other writers relay prophetic concerns, no other text claims that it's prophecy from start to finish. What does John mean by "prophecy"? Though Revelation includes future prediction, it is more than a script for the unfurling of historical events. As with the Hebrew prophets, John's main interest lies in reinterpreting present circumstance through the lens of God's sovereign ways, which will soon prevail.

That prophetic bent leads to a second feature of these verses: John's attention to both perceived and real power. From the outset, the prophet calls Jesus "the ruler of the kings of the earth" (Rev 1:5), a bold, almost defiant, insistence that the risen Lord is already sovereign over human rulers. Pressing the point further, John says the faithful on earth constitute a(-n alternative) "kingdom" (Rev 1:6, 9). More than just a heavenly triumph, Jesus has secured divine victory on earth, in and through the faithful community.

John's vision of the Human One serves as a transition to both the series of letters and the ensuing revelation. John identifies this living one as the dead-and-raised Jesus, from whose mouth comes a "sharp, two-edged sword" (Rev 1:16). God's word becomes the weapon that sets the righteous apart from the unrighteous. This encounter is reminiscent of other visits to the heavenly realm found, for instance, in Isaiah 6 and Daniel 7. From the outset, this work shows itself to be divinely imparted and faithfully recorded by John for the benefit of the seven churches.

Letters to the Seven Churches (Rev 2:1–3:22)

Before John's journey into heaven, he transcribes a series of seven letters delivered to him while he was "in a Spirit-inspired trance on the Lord's day" (Rev 1:10). In terms of structure and content, these passages resemble ancient imperial mandates more than any standard epistolary form. A "messenger" (Greek: *angelos*) delivers seven context-specific decrees to seven believing communities: Ephesus, Smyrna, Pergamum, Thyatira, Sardis, Philadelphia, and Laodicea. Each one reads like a report card assessing the fitness of the churches' witness to Jesus's Lordship.

Often, the risen Lord applauds hearers' "patient endurance" and faithfulness under fire (e.g., Rev 2:2, 19). The persecution they face ranges from slander to bodily harm, and even to death (Rev 2:9-10, 13). The prophet also praises their good works of "love and faithfulness, . . . service and endurance" (Rev 2:19). Since they "hold fast" to Jesus's teachings, they are those are those who "conquer" (Rev 2:26; 3:12, 21) and will sit "with me on my throne, just as I emerged victorious and sat down with my Father on his throne" (Rev 3:21).

But these letters single out other communities for indictment, offering a scathing critique of those who submit to "false teachings," some of which John mentions specifically. For instance, John alludes to but does not explain the corrupting views of the **Nicolaitans**, rejected by the Ephesians (Rev 2:6) but tolerated by some at Pergamum (Rev 2:15). Other practices rebuked here include eating food sacrificed to idols and fornication (Rev 2:14, 20). These examples point to a broader concern: to call Jesus "Lord" is to cast exclusive loyalty to the God of Israel and so to adhere to a Jewish moral code rather than a Greco-Roman one. In John's binary worldview, there is no room for a Christian witness that is "neither cold nor hot" (Rev 3:15); full-throttle allegiance to God's kingdom is the only acceptable way.

Taken together, these letters clearly assess faithfulness with an eye to what is "about to unfold after this" (Rev 1:19). Those who endure patiently, John promises, will gain a share in the divine authority (Rev 3:11; cf. 3:21). Even those who miss the mark hear an invitation to repent (Rev 2:16; 3:3; 3:19). Time is short, but the opportunity to make amends still remains.

Apocalyptic Vision (Rev 4:1–22:5)

The messages to the churches serve as something of a warm-up for the full-fledged apocalypse that follows. (Notice that John's "Revelation" is singular; the vision may feature manifold images, but it appears in this book as one, comprehensive apocalypse.) Without warning, John spies a door open to the heavens and hears a voice beckoning him (Rev 4:1). The rest of Revelation finds him in the company of a messenger, shuttling back and forth between heaven and the created world, watching an apocalyptic drama unfold.

These chapters bombard us with graphic images that give Revelation a 3-D, surround sound effect. Emeralds and rainbows, colored horses and earthquakes, dragons and martyrs dripping in blood all take their place in the vivid landscape that John describes. For some, that is Revelation's appeal; others hesitate even to read such a disturbing text. In what follows, we will try both to appreciate Revelation for what it is—an impressionistic portrait of the "last things"—and to understand its urgent message.

One challenge Revelation presents is its complex sense of time. Without even thinking about it, readers assume that time in Revelation unfolds in a linear, conventionally historical manner—that is, with one episode following another in sequence. After all, the visions begin with this invitation from a heavenly voice: "Come up here, and I will show you what must take place after this" (Rev 4:1). The visions themselves come packaged as a series of series: seven seals are broken, seven trumpets blown, and seven plagues announced.

But a careful reading of Revelation exposes problems with such a linear view. After the sixth seal is opened, for instance, stars fall from the sky, which itself vanishes, and both mountains and islands disappear (Rev 6:13-14). How is it, then, that the stars are back in place two chapters later (Rev 8:12), only to have their "light darkened" once again (a third of them, anyway)? Though the cosmic events described in these visions would bring life on earth to an abrupt halt, we meet people who are alive and well in the very next chapter (Rev 9:4-5).

From a "big picture" perspective, Revelation does progress relentlessly toward evil's decisive defeat. Along the way, though, the events that lead to that defeat play out in a spiral effect. That makes reading Revelation as a predictor of future, historically noteworthy events challenging indeed. It's also probably why interpreters keep missing the mark in their predictions of a coming end. In what follows, we'll take a different approach, noting the vision's progression. Growing more acquainted with the content of John's Revelation will position us to explore some of its meaning in John's setting.

Setting the Stage (Rev 4:1–5:14)

The visions begin, rather importantly, in a heavenly throne room, where John observes the active worship of God (Rev 4:2; see also Isa 6:1-12; Dan 7:9). God is not the only one seated on a throne, though; twenty-four elders dressed in white and wearing gold crowns (Rev 4:4) appear as chief worshippers rather than equals. (The number is significant, probably combining traditions about the twelve tribes of Israel with the twelve apostles.) In a revision of Ezekiel 1:5-25, "four living creatures" (Rev 4:6) also surround God's throne.

Focus turns next to the scroll in God's right hand, sealed and waiting for someone worthy enough to open it. Who might that be? An elder has the answer: "the Lion of the tribe of Judah," who soon appears as "a Lamb, standing as if it had been slain" (Rev 5:5-6). This is, of course, the crucified and risen Jesus, who appears as a sacrificed lamb some twenty-eight times in Revelation. Jesus plays many roles in Revelation: he receives angels' praise (Rev 5:12-13); he serves as John's personal guide; he sits in judgment (Rev 14:14); he fights the final battle (Rev 19:11-16); and his parting words to John reiterate Revelation's opening claim that he's the "Alpha and the Omega" (Rev 21:6; 22:13; cf. 1:8). Revelation thus has a thoroughly christological framework from start to finish.

Seven Seals and the 144,000 (Rev 6:1–7:17)

Revelation's series of series begins as the lamb opens seven seals. The first four unleash the "four horses of the apocalypse" widely known in Western culture. (See Figure 16.7.) Together, they symbolize evils John's audience would well have recognized: warfare, violence, hunger, and death. The opening of the fifth seal reveals the souls of those "slaughtered on account of the word of God" (Rev 6:9)—presumably the victims of the horses' devastation. The sixth seal releases cosmic destruction that sends everyone, regardless of station in life, running for cover (Rev 6:15). And understandably so: the blackened sun and falling stars are enough to bring the world as we know it to an end.

In a dramatic pause between the sixth and seventh seals, John spies four angels gathering a faithful remnant of 144,000. They come from every scattered "tribe of the Israelites" (Rev 7:4) and are marked "with a seal on [their] foreheads" (Rev 7:3) that exempts them from coming destruction. As a spiritual and symbolic designation, the "twelve tribes of Israel" are foundational to the coming new creation, but not exclusively so. Soon, we read, they're joined by "a

FIGURE 16.7:
FOUR HORSEMEN OF THE APOCALYPSE

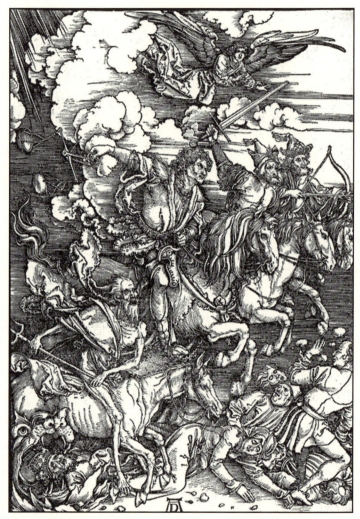

The Four Horsemen of the Apocalypse, Albrecht Dürer, 1498, woodcut
(Wikimedia Commons)

FIGURE 16.8: COSMIC DISASTER IN BUDDHISM

Some Buddhist traditions predict a coming "end of the world" that shares specific features such as a series of "seven" and a devastating fire with Revelation's visions. In the following passage, the coming cosmic disaster confirms a core teaching of Buddhist thought, which is the impermanent nature of existence:

> Now there comes, O monks, a season when, after . . . many hundreds and thousands and hundreds of thousands of years, it does not rain; and while it rains not, all seedlings and vegetation, all plants, grasses, and trees dry up, wither away and cease to be. [A second through sixth sun each appears, leaving the earth drier and drier.] After a last vast interval, a seventh sun appears, and then, monks, this great earth, and Sineru, the monarch of mountains, flare and blaze, and become one mass of flame. . . . Therefore, monks, do those who deliberate and believe say this: "This earth and Sineru, the monarch of mountains, will be burnt and perish and exist no more," excepting those who have seen the path [of enlightenment that recognizes impermanence]. (Aṅguttara-Nikāya, VII, 6.2 Pali Canon: The Sermon of the Seven Suns)

YOUR TURN: What similarities or differences do you detect between this Buddhist instruction and John's Revelation?

great crowd . . . from every nation, tribe, people, and language" (Rev 7:9) who have, John learns, "come out of the great ordeal [Greek: *thlipsis*]" (Rev 7:14).

Seven Trumpets, a Little Scroll, and Two Witnesses (Rev 8:1–11:19)

When the Lamb opens the seventh seal, a half hour of silence precedes a second series—this time, of seven angels blaring trumpets (Rev 8:1-2). With each blast, more cosmic destruction ensues. The images in this series bear a close resemblance to the plagues found in the exodus story (see Rev 9:18, 20), including bouts of blood, hail, and locusts. The first four trumpets unleash calamity that disrupts the natural order, while the fifth and sixth lead to violence carried out against humans.

Two brief episodes that confirm John's prophetic calling fill an interlude between the sixth and seventh trumpets. First, an angel gives him a "little scroll" to eat, in the manner of the Hebrew prophet Ezekiel (Rev 10:9-20; cf. Ezek 2:8–3:3). Next, while he measures out God's temple (Rev 11:1-3; cf. Ezek 40:3–42:20), John encounters "two witnesses" (Rev 11:3), whose shared career lasts 1,260 days. As with Moses and Elijah, supernatural powers confirm their testimony (Rev 11:6), which leads to their death at the hands of the beast. After the "breath of God" resuscitates them, they ascend to the heavenly realm.

With the sound of the seventh trumpet, a heavenly choir sings, "The kingdom of the world has become the kingdom of our Lord and of his Christ" (Rev 11:15). The chorus suggests a resounding finish to our drama, complete with a reprise from the twenty-four elders we met earlier on. But God's victory has only happened in heaven. As we'll see, the conflict with sinister forces rages on.

A Woman and Child Meet a Dragon and Beasts (Rev 12:1–13:18)

Before a final series of seven, John recounts a sign that interprets the audience's suffering as part of the unfolding apocalyptic drama. In it, "a woman clothed with the sun" (Rev 12:1) gives birth to a "male child who is to rule all the nations with an iron rod" (Rev 12:5; cf. Ps 2:8-9). But since a "great fiery red dragon" (Rev 12:3) means to devour the newborn, he's snatched away to God just in the nick of time. A battle in heaven follows. The archangel **Michael**'s army (Rev 12:7; see Dan 10:13; 12:1) roundly defeats the dragon. The outcome is a familiar one, as the dragon—also called the "old snake," the devil, and Satan—is flung from heaven to the joyful cries of those who hail his demise (Rev 12:10-12).

But apparently the dragon doesn't give up easily. He pursues the woman, who probably represents the church in John's day, with relentless tenacity. To do so, two beasts appear as the dragon's authorized agents of evil. First comes the beast "coming up out of the sea" (Rev 13:1), imagery that likens him to the mythic sea monster **Leviathan** (see e.g., Ezek 29:3). But the beast's "death-blow" to the head (Rev 13:3 NRSV) probably also links this beast with the historical emperor Nero, who committed suicide in 68 CE. A second beast rises "from the earth" (Rev 13:11) and actively promotes the first beast's authority. This beast compels worship of the first beast, as well as the production of images that honor the first beast—probably in the form of statues and coinage. The two beasts work in tandem and may both be identified by the number "**666**."

144,000 (Again), Judgment, and Seven Bowls of Anger (Rev 14:1–16:21)

Leaving behind the beasts and their coercive force, John's vision returns to the faithful remnant of 144,000 before reporting angelic messages about

Figure 16.9: Seventh-day Adventist Eschatology

Based on one historicist reading of Revelation by Ellen G. White, Seventh-day Adventists understand their mission as one that delivers the messages of the three angels during a time they call "Investigative Judgment." The Seventh-day Adventist movement White established describes its mission, which includes door-to-door evangelizing, in terms of Revelation 14:

> The mission of the Seventh-day Adventist Church is to proclaim to all peoples the everlasting gospel of God's love in the context of the three angels' messages of Revelation 14:6-12, and as revealed in the life, death, resurrection, and high priestly ministry of Jesus Christ, leading them to accept Jesus as personal Saviour and Lord and to unite with His remnant church; and to nurture believers as disciples in preparation for His soon return. (From the "Mission Statement of the Seventh-day Adventist Church," 1993; rev. 2004)

YOUR TURN: Learn a bit more about the Seventh-day Adventist church, and connect its reading of Revelation to what you've learned about John's first-century CE setting.

coming judgment. One angel bears good news for "every nation, tribe, language, and people" that the "hour of [God's] judgment has come" (Rev 14:6). (See Figure 16.9.) A second angel hails the fall of Babylon (Rev 14:12). The third warns against worshipping the beast and calls people to keep both "God's commandments" and "faith with Jesus" (Rev 14:12).

Judgment itself spans the next several chapters. Seven angels pour out seven bowls of God's anger (Rev 16:1-21). Each one drenches one aspect of the cosmos: earth, sea, springs of water, sun, earthly power (the "beast's throne," Rev 16:10), the river Euphrates, and the air. Many of the plagues inflicted by these bowlsful of wrath repeat images we've seen before, such as blood, fire, thunder, and a tumultuous earthquake.

Of special note is the sixth bowl, poured on the Euphrates—an admittedly odd item in the list of targets mentioned here. For John, the Euphrates had both mythic significance because of its ties to Babylon and strategic importance as a natural border between Rome's authority and the Parthians to the east. It's fitting, then, that this sixth bowl is the one that finds opposing armies, stirred by "demonic spirits," assembled for battle at **Harmagedon** (Rev 16:14, 16; cf. Judg 5:19; 2 Kings 23:29-30; see Figure 16.10). Ultimately, a "wine cup of [God's] furious anger" finds Babylon itself (Rev 16:19).

FIGURE 16.10: ARMAGEDDON

The term *Armageddon* (or *Har magedon*) refers geographically to a strategic, hilltop site located on the trade road from Egypt to Syria, in modern-day Israel. Only in the book of Revelation is this location associated with an end-time battle, though it is mentioned among stories about ancient Israelites in Jewish scripture. In recent decades, US President Ronald Reagan may have been the first national leader to subscribe openly to "Armageddon theology." Convinced that the end of the world was near and would culminate with a battle in the Middle East, Reagan promoted foreign and domestic—especially environmental—policies in light of the view that the world was spinning toward its violent end.

Modern Megiddo in Israel. "Mount" Tel Megiddo is not actually a mountain, but a tell, a hill created by many generations of people living and rebuilding on the same location. (Wikimedia Commons)

YOUR TURN: Spend a few minutes researching online the impact of "Armageddon theology" on foreign or domestic policy, from the Reagan administration to the present day. How might the belief that a cosmic showdown will soon take place in modern day Israel shape a person's approach to such topics as nuclear war, the Middle East, the environment, and other issues?

Babylon's (Rome's) Final Defeat (Rev 17:1–20:15)

The drumbeat of judgment crescendos toward a defining event: the "judgment upon the great prostitute" (Rev 17:1; cf. 17:5)—that is, Babylon herself. (See Figure 16.11.) In John's setting, of course, "Babylon" designates the Roman Empire and its "rulers of the earth." On what grounds does God's judgment fall on Babylon? Simply put, an illicit union with gods of money and violence—especially violence against the "saints" and "Jesus's witnesses" (Rev 17:6). John's vision once again borrows imagery from Jewish prophets such as Hosea, who likens God's people to a "prostitute" because they've sold themselves to other gods (see Hos 1:2).

After condemning Babylon for her opulent, death-dealing ways, John hears another, by-now-familiar heavenly refrain: "Hallelujah! The salvation and glory and power of our God!" (Rev 19:1). Soon, a warrior on a white horse arrives, joined by heavenly armies in force (Rev 19:11-21). This rider, though, differs from other warriors we've seen. He's named "Faithful and True" as well as the "Word of God" (Rev 19:11, 13). We learn of only one weapon: a sharp sword that comes from his mouth (Rev 19:15). By now, the audience recognizes this warrior as the risen Jesus.

Notably, it's not the rider on the white horse who makes war but the "beast and the kings of the earth and their armies" (Rev 19:19) who oppose him. They quickly end up, along with the false prophet, in a fiery lake, and their armies die by the sword that comes from the rider's mouth (Rev 19:20-21). But if the beast dies, the "dragon, the old snake, who is the devil and Satan" lives on, bound and locked in a pit for a thousand years (Rev 20:2). During this millennium, Christ shares judging authority with faithful martyrs, who've been given new life in the first resurrection. Afterward, Satan will be set free only to meet a fiery destiny. Everyone else will be raised to stand in judgment based on "what they had done" (Rev 20:13). (See Figure 16.12.)

New Creation (Rev 21:1–22:5)

With evil defeated, John's vision gives way to "a new heaven and a new earth" (Rev 21:1). Its crowning jewel, the **new Jerusalem**, arrives from heaven "as a bride beautifully dressed for her husband" (Rev 21:2). Built on the foundation of the twelve apostles, this new creation finds God's throne on the earth, as God makes a home among mortals (Rev 21:3). From this throne, a river flows out through the tree of life, whose "leaves are for the healing of the nations" (Rev 22:2; cf. Gen 2:9; Ezek 47:7-12). With gates never to be shut,

FIGURE 16.11: JEZEBEL AND THE SUN WOMAN: A FEMINIST AND WOMANIST CONVERSATION

What are we to make of the women in John's Revelation? It's a complicated question that leads interpreters to differing conclusions. One feminist scholar, Tina Pippin, approaches it this way:

> Reading for gender in the Apocalypse reveals the ideological commitments of the text. The female figures in the text are marginalized, scapegoated, and silenced. The central scene of this erotic fantasy is in the death of the Whore (the evil city) and the transformation of the Bride into the heavenly city. The pure and faithful males are called to come out of the Whore and enter into the Bride. The themes of death and desire are strong in the Apocalypse; although both men and women die, the social construction of the female body is central. This body is both adored and destroyed. The Apocalypse is a misogynist male fantasy of the end of time. ("Eros and the End: Reading for Gender in the Apocalypse of John," *Semeia* 59 [1992]: 193)

While womanist scholar Love Sechrest doesn't deny Revelation's misogynistic stereotyping, she explores the agency of Jezebel and the Sun Woman through the experience of women leading the Civil Rights and #blacklivesmatter movements, claiming that

> the Civil Rights mothers and the #Blacklivesmatter daughters exercise agency in real, though different ways while they are also being marginalized through a combination of cultural stereotyping and political critique. Like the antetypical Sun Woman, the Civil Rights mothers had to be resourceful in using all of the resources in the environment to survive and to participate in their own rescue. . . .

> Somewhat like "Jezebel," the #Blacklivesmatter daughters are openly exercising agency in the public square and are on the receiving end of hostility for their troubles. Just as John rebuked "Jezebel" from within the Christian movement for countenancing compromise with trade guilds and the imperial cult, so too are the #Blacklivesmatter daughters being rebuked by their allies on the US political left who scold them for their forceful, public, and disruptive resistance to ongoing violence and injustice. . . . In Revelation "Jezebel" is threatened with violence on a scale that exceeds that which is directed towards other compromisers in the seven churches in a way that seems analogous to the over-militarized state sanctioned violence that the #Blacklivesmatter daughters face today. . . .

> If the ideologies of revelation are deemed oppressively misogynistic, then it can help to read the text through the analogous experiences of contemporary marginalized women of color who *are* agents and who take up the work of saving their sons, daughters, and themselves using the God-given resources available to them through the public demonstration of the power of their intellect, the strength of their resistance, and the moral force of their choices. ("Antitypes, Stereotypes, and Antetypes: Jezebel, the Sun Woman, and Contemporary Black Women," in *Womanist Interpretations of the Bible: Expanding the Discourse*, eds. Gay L. Byron and Vanessa Lovelace [Atlanta: SBL Press, 2016], 135)

YOUR TURN: How do Pippin's and Sechrest's readings make you think differently about Revelation and its women?

FIGURE 16.12: ISA (JESUS) AND ESCHATOLOGICAL JUDGMENT

In both the Qur'an and the Hadith (a secondary collection of Muslim teachings), the coming day of judgment plays an even more central role than it does in the New Testament. Consider this detailed example: "The Trumpet shall be blown, and all that is in the heavens and the earth shall swoon except those whom Allah will please to exempt. Then the Trumpet will be blown for the second time and behold! They shall all stand up, looking around" (Qur'an 39:68).

One teaching describes Jesus's role this way: "The Hour will not be established until the son of Mary [i.e. Jesus] descends amongst you as a just ruler, he will break the cross, kill the pigs, and abolish the Jizya tax. Money will be in abundance so that nobody will accept it [as charitable gifts]" (Sahih al-Bukhari, Volume 3, Book 43: Kitab-ul-`Ilm, Hâdith Number 656).

YOUR TURN: What connections do you see between these passages from Muslim scripture and Revelation? How does the day of judgment appear as a hopeful promise in both?

the holy city reestablishes Edenic qualities in a creation that brings wholeness, not destruction.

Conclusion (Revelation 22:6-21)

Revelation ends with a resounding appeal by the risen Jesus to take this revelation with utter seriousness. He calls the words "trustworthy and true" pointers to "what must soon take place" (Rev 22:6). He also reiterates that John's message is both authoritative and inviolable—under threat of eternal banishment from "the holy city" (Rev 22:19). But this last section isn't all dire warning. It's also full of hope—specifically hope for the arrival of the risen Jesus, who will sit in judgment as God's reign gains a foothold on earth.

It's fitting for Revelation to wind down on such a hopeful note. After all, despite their different voices, all NT writers agree that what makes Jesus the Christ is the notion that he will usher in God's kingdom. The final chapter—of both Revelation and the Christian canon—leaves no wiggle room: Jesus promises not once but three times, "I'm coming soon" (Rev 22:7, 12, 20). He tells John, too, that the "time is near" (Rev 22:10). Thus Revelation's last word issues an abiding promise that Jesus the Messiah will preside over God's rule on earth.

As one of the later NT texts, John's Revelation doubles down on its apocalyptic hope, rather than diluting it. After all, over time, believers—even NT texts such as the Fourth Gospel—have downplayed the notion that Jesus will really return. But not John. This exiled visionary doesn't flinch from the claim that the way things are—with evil still palpably at work in the world—is not the way things will soon be. In the meantime, suffering and death constitute part of a divine game plan to bring oppressive forces to their knees and refashion the cosmos as a place of life and beauty and peace.

Review and Reflect

- Explain the "spiral effect" of Revelation's sense of time. Give two examples to illustrate.

- Consider the charges against Babylon. What makes its power so evil, in the view of Revelation?

REVELATION'S MESSAGE

It's a long and winding road from John's first glimpse into the heavenly throne room to new Jerusalem's shimmering streets of gold. Along the way, the revelation can be hard to follow and even harder to understand. But just as Monet's water lilies grow clearer when we stand at a distance, it's important not to get so focused on Revelation's bizarre details that we miss the impression of John's message. We'll consider that message as a conversation about three main topics: God's sovereign power; coming judgment; and human faithfulness. Together, these interlocking pieces of John's Revelation speak a word of meaning and hope to those suffering for their loyalty to Jesus as Christ and Lord.

God's Sovereign Power

The first and last word of John's Revelation is this: God reigns. As we noted early on, these words are important because they signal John's deep interest in the power structures of the world and their effects on human beings. For those who felt they were on the wrong side of (Roman) power, John sees through present reality to affirm that a regime change is at hand.

This apocalypse reveals God's sovereign power in many ways. There's the havoc unleashed in the cosmos, of course, as stars and rulers fall from their lofty places. But John's vision also keeps circling back through the heavenly throne room, where voices rise to praise God's power and authority (Rev 11:15-18; 12:10-12; 15:3-4; 19:1-8).

Rather than mere religious escapism, as if the heavenly realm were all that mattered, John's message follows the impulse of Jewish apocalypse to insist that God's sovereign power will take root on earth—and very soon. This is not some Homeric God who sometimes dabbles in earthly affairs but prefers the safe distance of heaven. This is a Genesis God, deeply invested in "walking alongside" human beings in their earthly home (see Gen 2:8). In this two-storied universe, God's sovereignty over the whole cosmos necessarily means that God will soon secure an uncontested home "with humankind" (Rev 21:3).

And in a sense, for John, God already has. A human being named Jesus lived on the earth, as God's word in human flesh; on this point, Revelation and the Fourth Gospel agree. If he was executed for his witness to that divine word, he revealed in the process that God's power engenders life, not death; abundance, not dearth; joy, not anguish. Like John, some from traditional "Israel" and from the "multitude of nations" have cast wholesale allegiance with this kind of power and so find themselves to be vanguards of God's coming reign.

Yet these early loyalists to God's kingdom know firsthand that their allegiance to a different world order bring suffering in the short term. In Revelation, John locates them within what he calls the "great hardship" (Rev 7:14) that is standard fare in the cosmic conflict of apocalypse. As the forces of evil rise up to resist God's incursion into the world, those who stand with God find themselves battered and bloodied and sometimes killed as a result. In Revelation, not only does a sovereign God know about this anguish, but this God also allows it.

Ultimately, though, to affirm God's sovereign power is to trust that God, not Satan, will prevail. That makes the suffering of those on God's side temporary and provisional. It also promises their eternal vindication, as they join in the chorus that worships God and the Lamb. But for John, this is about more than just going to heaven when you die. His vision of the new creation involves the faithful in the impending regime change: as a "kingdom and priests to our God, . . . they will rule on earth" (Rev 5:10; see Dan 7:27-28). God's sovereign power, it turns out, is inherently shared power.

Coming Judgment

For those who live relatively comfortable lives, the phrase "coming judgment" is hard to hear in hopeful terms. But in Revelation, this promise is part and parcel of the buoyant message John delivers, since it means God's justice system will soon replace the earthly power structures that degrade and devour the weak. If John's audience was experiencing the throes of imperial power, word of coming judgment was good news indeed.

What kind of systems does John see crumbling under this judgment? We don't have to look far afield for clues about the strategies those systems deploy. For one thing, John's vision of the beasts' conduct makes it clear that corrupt, earthly power depends on *state-sanctioned violence* (Rev 13:7). In the Roman imperial context, we know that violence operated through both military and judicial means. Roman authorities used both armed forces and courts to promote "peace and security" among its conquered peoples. As we've seen, Jesus himself was crushed by this system.

Both John and his audience probably suffered Roman reprisal for their devotion to God's reign. After all, John notes that Rome has grown "drunk on the blood of the saints and the blood of Jesus' witnesses" (Rev 17:6). It's an intoxication induced by power exerted by force. Somewhat paradoxically, Rome's violence sets the terms of its own demise. God's judgment brings destruction for those who "destroy the earth" (Rev 11:18).

As we've seen, God's indictment against "Babylon" extends to its *economy* as well. The prophet says that "the merchants of the earth became rich from the power of her loose and extravagant ways" (Rev 18:3). In an ancient rendition of open market capitalism, those at the top of the socioeconomic order profit heavily from colonization, at the expense of those living in Rome's occupied territories. On this count, divine justice arrives in like measure: "To the extent that she glorified herself and indulged her loose and extravagant ways, give her pain and grief" (Rev 18:7).

Finally, Revelation brings an indictment against *state-sanctioned religion.* During the short-lived dominion of the first beast, John notes that "the whole earth . . . worshipped the beast and said, 'Who is like the beast, and who can fight against it?'" (Rev 13:3-4). In other words, the beast took on godlike status. Indeed, the second beast made that status official and the worship of the first beast compulsory (Rev 13:12). In the end, John proclaims that there will be "no rest day or night for those who worship the beast" (Rev 14:11). For them, judgment comes in the form of endless torment.

But there is another side to coming judgment in Revelation. For the faithful, judgment brings exoneration, vindication, and restoration. Those who honor God—whose deeds fit God's priorities, not Rome's—find that judgment brings eternal bliss. Already John's Revelation insists faithful martyrs have been marked for such a destiny. In the end, those who refuse to worship the beast, too, will find their just reward. Together, they'll inhabit the new Jerusalem Christ's coming will bring. The vision of Revelation 21 is poignant. It promises the end of personal suffering: hunger, thirst, and even emotional distress. The Lamb will "wipe away every tear from [the] eyes" (Rev 7:17; 21:4). Death, mourning, and crying belong, the voice says, to the "first things" that give way to the "new heaven and the new earth" established at the culmination of time.

Exhortation to Faithfulness

Together, Revelation's affirmation of God's power and its promise of coming judgment give rise to its urgent exhortation to faithfulness. John's dualistic worldview makes that faithfulness an all-or-nothing matter. Either his audience will live out their allegiance to God's in-coming reign, he suggests, or they'll be seduced into worshipping imperial power and its violent, opulent ways. Remember, John conveys this revelation less as a sales pitch for outsiders than as an internal memo for those who have cast their loyalty with God and God's Messiah.

To be clear, John's exhortation does not promote suffering for its own sake, as if human travail is life's main goal. Instead, the distress he signals comes as a result of explicit, countercultural allegiance to another kingdom. The faithful suffer, John says, because they "keep God's commandments and hold firmly to the witness of Jesus" (Rev 12:17). Their faith in God and commitment to God's priorities set them on an inevitable collision course with the dragon and its minions.

Note that John discourages actively resisting such opposition, at least by conventional means: "If any are to be taken captive, then into captivity they will go. If any are to be killed by the sword, then by the sword they will be killed" (Rev 13:10). This verse echoes prophetic accounts of Israel's submission to the exile imposed by the first "Babylon" (see Isa 52:13–53:12), which leads in turn to redemption. But it also harkens back to Jesus's warning that those "who use the sword will die by the sword" (Matt 26:52).

Instead, this extended vision encourages John's audience by means of an alternative form of resistance: the human imagination. John invites hearers to see through their trauma into another realm, where both personal and cosmic calamities give way to God's redemptive power. At the personal level, John's apocalypse pronounces those who've died for their faith "alive on arrival." From the "twenty-four elders" (Rev 4:4, 10; 5:8; 11:16; 19:4), to the 144,000 sealed as God's faithful servants (Rev 7:3-4; 14:1-3), to those who have come out of the "great hardship" (Rev 7:14), the faithful live on to play a part in the new creation. In a more grandiose sense, Revelation promises that soon, all human suffering will disappear from the cosmos. With the Lamb on the throne, God will "wipe away every tear from their eyes" (Rev 7:17; 21:4).

Death, mourning, crying, and pain all belong to the realm of "first things" (Rev 21:4) that pass away in the rehabilitated cosmos.

This promise provides the backdrop for the call to endurance and faithfulness (Rev 13:10; cf. 14:12). For John's audience, the apocalypse brings less doom and more hope than we might expect. If they have stood against the ways of the world, they've likely faced some reprisal for it. Thus John's vision speaks a word of hope, as the "one seated on the throne" utters these words: "Look! I'm making all things new" (Rev 21:5).

SUMMARY

Revelation is an outlier in the NT on many counts. As the only full-fledged apocalypse, its graphic images can be jarring and disconcerting to those drawn to the kinder, gentler Jesus of the Gospels. And its interest in the heavenly realm seems far removed from Paul's pragmatic counsel about living together as Christ's "body" in the world.

Church leaders who challenged the wisdom of considering Revelation "scripture" anticipated, quite rightly, that readers might misconstrue its message. Rather than a word of hope for first- or early second-century CE believers suffering for their faith, Revelation sounds to many like a dire, doomful prediction of the end of the world. But when we read Revelation *as an apocalypse*—a specific genre of literature that creatively reframes human travail in the context of divine power—we can reclaim its meaning for its first audience. In this light, cracking its code has little to do with identifying the beast or setting dates for Christ's millennial rule in historical terms. Reading Revelation on its own terms means understanding its critique against an empire that rules by force, that devalues human life, and that promotes its own worship. It means listening to this promise that God and God's life-giving ways are stronger than the forces of death that seem to be in charge.

That makes Revelation a fitting conclusion for the NT after all. Like the Gospels and other writings, Revelation addresses those living in a world that's not always hospitable to those who opt out of the values and practices that mark mainstream society. Like many other NT books, John writes for some who've been directly targeted for their countercultural faith. And like the rest of the NT, Revelation hangs on this hope: a man named Jesus, himself a martyr for his resolute faith in God's sovereign power, has defeated death and so is "making all things new" (Rev 21:5). It's this hope that's been the gift of Revelation, and the entire NT, to believers across place and time.

- Describe three main claims that Revelation offers its audience. Give examples from the text.

- Reflect on Revelation's place in the NT conversation. What does this book add? How does it complicate or clarify or amplify points made by other conversation partners in the canon?

GO DEEPER

Blount, Brian K. *Revelation: A Commentary*. NTL. Louisville, KY: Westminster John Knox, 2009.

Collins, Adela Yarbro. *Crisis and Catharsis: The Power of the Apocalypse*. Philadelphia: Westminster, 1984.

Gorman, Michael J. *Reading Revelation Responsibly: Uncivil Worship and Witness; Following the Lamb into the New Creation*. Eugene, OR: Cascade Books, 2011.

Kiel, Micah D. *Apocalyptic Ecology: The Book of Revelation, the Earth, and the Future*. Collegeville, MN: Liturgical Press, 2017.

Kirsch, Jonathan. *A History of the End of the World: How the Most Controversial Book in the Bible Changed the Course of Western Civilization*. New York: Harper-Collins, 2006.

Levine, Amy-Jill, ed. *A Feminist Companion to the Apocalypse of John*. FCNTECW 13. London: Bloomsbury Publishing, 2010.

Scripture Index

Apocrypha

Bhagavad Gita

Qu'ran

Subject Index

413

Made in the USA
Columbia, SC
31 August 2019